CANTONESE:
A COMPREHENSIVE GRAMMAR

CANTONESE:
A COMPREHENSIVE
GRAMMAR

Stephen Matthews and Virginia Yip

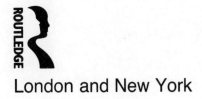

London and New York

First published 1994
by Routledge
11 New Fetter Lane, London EC4P 4EE

Simultaneously published in the USA and Canada
by Routledge
29 West 35th Street, New York, NY 10001

Routledge is an International Thomson Publishing company

Reprinted with corrections 1996

Typeset in Times by
Florencetype Ltd, Stoodleigh, Devon

Printed and bound in Great Britain by
TJ Press (Padstow) Ltd, Cornwall

British Library Cataloguing in Publication Data
A catalogue record for this book is available from the British Library

Library of Congress Cataloguing in Publication Data
Matthews, Stephen, 1963–
    Cantonese: a comprehensive grammar / Stephen Matthews and
Virginia Yip.
        p.   cm.
    Includes bibliographical references and index
    1. Cantonese dialects – Grammar.   I. Yip, Virginia, 1962–
II. Title.
    PL1733.M38   1994   93–36173
495.1'7–dc20

ISBN 0–415–08945–X

CONTENTS

LIST OF TABLES

ACKNOWLEDGEMENTS

Research for this grammar was supported by a grant from the Hongkong Research Grants Council (project HKU238/92H). We are grateful to Helen Kwok, a pioneer in the study of Cantonese grammar, for acting as consultant to the project; to Mimi Chan, head of the Department of English at the University of Hongkong, for supporting the project; and to our research assistants, Betty Hung and Cream Lee, for their assistance, native intuitions and experience in teaching Cantonese. We thank Moira Yip whose encouragement and work on Cantonese have been a lasting influence, as has Bernard Comrie's exemplary work in comparative grammar.

We are deeply indebted to Thomas Lee for reading the manuscript and painstakingly providing detailed comments on each chapter. His superb standards of scholarship combining the best of East and West have inspired our work immensely. Discussions with Thomas have proved to be most stimulating. We thank Cheung Kwan-Hin and Eric Zee for their expertise and valuable comments on phonology. Cream Lee, Thomas Lee, Caesar Lun and Tang Sze-Wing have been generous with their time in the final preparation of the manuscript. Needless to say, none of the above bears any responsibility for the remaining errors and shortcomings in this grammar. We are also grateful to numerous colleagues who have discussed Cantonese grammar with us, especially Bob Bauer, Gu Yang, Gregory James, Tom Lai, Sam Leung, Leung Chung-Sum, Kitty Li, K.K. Luke, Owen Nancarrow, Keith Tong and Q.S. Tong. We have also benefited from interaction with some fine graduate students, notably Brian Chan, Alice Cheung, Patricia Man, Kitty Szeto, Raymond Tang, Tang Sze-Wing and Cathy Wong. The Linguistic Society of Hongkong has provided a valuable forum for discussion.

Thanks are also due to a number of patient informants, notably Patrick and Dan Yip and Linda Lee, and students too numerous to mention but whose help with idiomatic Cantonese has been no less valuable. We hope that their puzzlement at some of our questions will be allayed by the finished product.

We are grateful to Simon Bell, Jenny Potts and the editorial teams at Routledge for supporting the project and bringing it to completion. Finally, we thank our son Timothy, whose imminent arrival provided further incentives to complete the book, and our families for their encouragement.

ABBREVIATIONS

ADJ	adjectival marker
ADV	adverbial marker
CL	noun classifier
CONT	continuous aspect
DEG	degree expression
DEL	delimitative aspect
EXP	experiential aspect
HAB	habitual aspect
LP	linking particle
NEG	negation marker
PFV	perfective aspect
PL	plural
POSS	possessive marker
PROG	progressive aspect
PRT	particle
V-PRT	verbal particle

INTRODUCTION

While a number of excellent grammars of Mandarin Chinese are available, no substantial reference grammar of Cantonese has yet appeared in English. Chao Yuen-Ren's *Cantonese Primer* (originally written in 1947) devotes only a brief, though valuable, chapter to grammar, while Samuel Cheung Hung-Nin's (1972) grammar has unfortunately not been translated. The more thorough language courses such as Parker Huang and Gerald Kok's *Speak Cantonese* deal with grammar only in a sporadic fashion, and were written in the 1960s; works on Cantonese have often used these courses for reference purposes, for lack of more appropriate materials. Subsequent developments in the language, as well as in the linguistic description of Chinese, make a reference grammar all the more necessary. The present work is intended to fill this long-standing gap.

The lack of a grammar of Cantonese is remarkable in view of the role of Hongkong and the overseas Cantonese in business and commerce in particular. While many Hongkong people can communicate in English, there have always been some Westerners in Hongkong and abroad who have attempted to learn some Cantonese. The language has acquired the reputation of being difficult for second language learners: indeed the subtly differentiated tones and consonants which seem initially awkward, in addition to the unfamiliar sentence structures, present daunting challenges. This impression is unfortunate, however, since in certain other respects the language is relatively simple: there are no case forms or verb conjugations as in European languages, for example, and a minimum of inflectional forms to be learnt. It is the word order and syntactic structures that constitute the major grammatical difficulties. The lack of a reference grammar exacerbates the task facing learners of the language.

One reason why grammars of Cantonese are not available in English is that Cantonese is essentially a spoken language.[1] Grammars – as opposed to phrase-books – traditionally take the written form of a language as the standard to be described. To the extent that Cantonese is written down at all, it is heavily affected by standard written Chinese, which is based on Mandarin; as a result, there is no clear distinction between what is 'Cantonese' and what is 'Mandarin' (see below on the relationship between written and spoken Cantonese), rendering a grammar of written Cantonese impracticable. In the descriptive approach to linguistics on which this book is based, the spoken form of any language is taken to be primary, the written form derivative;[2] we thus reject any notion of the superiority of written language and the devaluation of spoken Cantonese which all too often results from such attitudes. In addition, there is a pedagogical consideration: to learn or teach both spoken and written Chinese simultaneously is doubly taxing, in that the burden of learning an entirely unfamiliar language is multiplied by the characters, which relate at best indirectly to the pronunciation. To learn the spoken language alone, using a romanized orthography, is a much more practicable option; successful students can then tackle the written language if they wish or need to do so. For all these reasons, we largely ignore the written language and use the Yale romanization system as an alphabetic representation of the spoken language.

The present grammar is intended to be primarily a learner–user's grammar meeting the needs of the following kinds of readers:

(a) learners using the grammar in conjunction with a language course;
(b) those who use some Cantonese socially and professionally but are looking to improve their grammatical knowledge and the accuracy of their language;
(c) those with some knowledge of Mandarin who are interested in Cantonese for comparative or practical reasons;
(d) linguists working on aspects of Cantonese or looking for a detailed description of a variety of Chinese other than Mandarin;
(e) Cantonese speakers, such as teachers of English and speech therapists, who wish to develop their metalinguistic awareness of the language;
(f) teachers of English to Cantonese speakers who want to learn more about their students' first language;
(g) teachers and students of translation/interpretation to and from Cantonese.

THE LANGUAGE AND ITS SPEAKERS

Cantonese is the most widely known and influential variety of Chinese other than Mandarin. It belongs to the **Yue** group of dialects (Cantonese *Yuhtyúh*, as in *Yuhtyúh pín* 'Cantonese film' and *Yuhtkehk* 'Cantonese opera'). Yue dialects are spoken primarily in the southern Chinese provinces of Guangdong and Guangxi, and in the neighbouring territories of Hongkong and Macau.[3] Cantonese as spoken in Hongkong is generally known as *Gwóngdūng Wá* after the province of Guangdong. Varieties of Cantonese are also used in Chinese communities in Singapore, Malaysia, North America, Australia and elsewhere as a result of emigration from the Guangdong area and from Hongkong itself.

Within China, the role of Cantonese is increasing. Far from being replaced by Mandarin, it enjoys growing prestige as a result of the rapid economic development of the southern coastal districts led by Guangdong province. Students in major cities all over China are learning Cantonese in order to do business with Hongkong and Guangdong: Cantonese is said to be 'heading north' (*bāk séuhng*: Zhan 1993).

The usage described in this grammar is that of Hongkong Cantonese. Traditionally, the speech of Guangzhou (Canton) is the standard of comparison, hence the terms *Cantonese* and *Gwóngjāu Wá*; however, the majority of Western users of the language will have more contact with Hongkong Cantonese. In Singapore, Malaysia and the overseas Chinese communities, there are distinctive varieties; yet the influence of Hongkong Cantonese is strong, due in part to films, television programmes and pop songs – 'Canto-pop'. The impact and popularity of Hongkong Cantonese in all these different forms naturally contribute to its growing prestige.

Compared to other Chinese dialects, Cantonese has a substantial literature, both oral and written, although relatively little of this has been translated. The written literature includes poetry such as the nineteenth-century love songs edited and translated by Morris (1992). Oral literature includes children's songs, of which a selection are transcribed with commentary in Chan & Kwok (1990). Recently, written literature in more or less colloquial Cantonese has begun to appear, including popular novels such as the series *Síu làahmyán jāu-gei* 'Diary of a yuppie', which attempts to represent Cantonese exactly as it is spoken. These texts include many Cantonese words which are not normally considered acceptable in standard written Chinese (see the section on spoken and written Cantonese). They are also marked by the use of English words to represent code-mixing and even to represent some Cantonese words, for example the letter *D* to represent the comparative *dī* as in *pèhng dī* 'cheaper'. Due to the low status of written Cantonese this new literature is frowned upon in traditional Chinese cultural circles but, like the use of Cantonese in pop songs, it appears to be generally accepted by speakers of the younger generation. This vernacular style is also increasingly found in Hongkong newspapers.[4]

APPROACH: DESCRIPTION AND EXPLANATION

In keeping with the goals of the Reference Grammars series, this volume aims at comprehensive coverage, providing reference for the student and scholar of the language while foregrounding the more essential aspects of sentence structure for the benefit of the learner-user.

As a grammar of the spoken language, the book is intended to reflect current usage. Several features of Cantonese described in earlier works are omitted because they are not representative of the Cantonese currently spoken in Hongkong. For example, the high level and high falling tones are considered to be non-distinctive (see below on the romanization system); as a result, the tone sandhi rule changing a high falling tone to high level as described by Chao (1947) is no longer operative. In cases of doubt, the usage followed reflects that of the second author, a native Cantonese speaker born and raised in Hongkong.

The grammar adopts the descriptive approach which is the basis of modern linguistics: it aims to *describe* how the language is actually spoken, rather than to tell the reader how it *should* be spoken. For example, the pronunciation *léih* is adopted in place of the traditional *néih* 'you'. Under this approach, there is no issue of 'correct', 'good' or 'bad' Cantonese (except perhaps in reference to a non-native speaker's use of the language, where 'good' means 'approximating to a native speaker's usage'). Instead, our focus is on **grammaticality** – i.e. what sentences are possible in spoken Cantonese – and on what kind of language is **appropriate** to which kinds of context, leading to an emphasis, within the descriptive approach, on distinctions of register: styles of speech appropriate for particular kinds of context and associated with different levels of formality. In most areas of grammar there are alternative possibilities which belong primarily to one register rather than another: a construction or idiom used in polite conversation might be out of place in the street-market, and vice versa. Cantonese lacks a strong prescriptive grammatical tradition prescribing or stigmatizing certain grammatical constructions;[5] such prescriptive ideas as there are tend to reflect the prestige of Mandarin usage, with the result that structural patterns based on Mandarin may be preferred to those indigenous to Cantonese. Such structures are included with reference to their Mandarin origin and stylistic status.

While informed by linguistic thinking and research, the grammar aims to avoid unnecessary terminology, sticking where possible to established and widely understood terms such as *subject* and *object*. Nevertheless, some unfamiliar terms such as *serial verb* and *topicalization* are introduced where there are no equivalents in traditional English grammar: serious learners of the language will need to come to terms with these concepts, which are fundamental to the grammar of Cantonese.

The format of the grammar follows the established order of parts of speech familiar to Western readers. However, this does not imply that these categories are always appropriate for Cantonese. Some discussion is devoted to the problems of applying traditional Western grammatical categories to Chinese (see in particular ch. 3).

CANTONESE AND MANDARIN

Some excellent grammars of Mandarin inevitably influence the way one describes Cantonese grammar. Chao (1968) and Li and Thompson (1981) in particular have set up a framework of categories which are widely adopted – if only as a point of departure – in discussions of Chinese grammar. The present grammar is intended to be compatible with this framework, although numerous open questions remain regarding the categories and analyses assumed. Similarly, terminology which is not part of the Western grammatical tradition is generally drawn from descriptions of Mandarin grammar such as those mentioned above. Occasionally, terms are adopted from language typology and comparative grammar, such as the term *indirect passive* (see 8.4.1 and the examples below).

For the benefit of readers with some knowledge of Mandarin, reference is made to salient similarities and contrasts. Some prior knowledge of Mandarin is an invaluable asset in the study of Cantonese. Although the two languages are not mutually intelligible, their grammatical structure is similar in most major respects. Their relationship is comparable to that between languages within the Indo-European language families: thus Cantonese differs from Mandarin to much the same extent as French differs from Spanish, or Swedish from German. While no one would suggest that French and Spanish share the same grammar, this is often assumed in the case of Mandarin and Cantonese. Chao's comment that 'one can say that there is practically one universal Chinese grammar' (1968: 13) has sometimes been taken too literally, and the perception that varieties of Chinese share the same grammar is a further reason why a Cantonese reference grammar has not been attempted thus far. Because phonology and vocabulary present the most striking contrasts, the differences in grammar, often relatively subtle, tend to be overlooked. For example, Cantonese and Mandarin appear to have very similar passive constructions. Both allow the indirect passive construction in which the passive verb retains an object:

Mandarin
Wǒ   bèi   (rén)   tōu   le   chēzi.
I   by   (person) steal- PFV   car
'I've had my car stolen.'

Cantonese
Ngóh   béi   yàhn   tāu-jó   ga   chē.
I   by   person steal-PFV   CL   car
'I've had my car stolen.'

However, in Cantonese the noun representing the agent of the action (*yàhn* if its identity is unknown) must be present, while in Mandarin (as in English) the agent can be omitted. It is just these subtle grammatical differences which are of interest to the linguist and important to the language learner; particular attention is therefore paid to these distinctive features of Cantonese grammar.

SPOKEN AND WRITTEN CANTONESE

Traditionally, Cantonese has been regarded as one of the many Chinese dialects. It does not have a standardized written form on a par with standard written Chinese.[6] No form of written Cantonese is taught in schools or used in academic settings in any Cantonese-speaking community. When it comes to the written form, it is standard written Chinese that is taught and learnt. For educated Cantonese speakers, standard written Chinese is the written form they use in most contexts. However, in colloquial genres such as novels, popular magazines, newspaper gossip columns, informal personal communications, written Cantonese may be used. When the written Cantonese contains too many exclusively Cantonese words and expressions, non-Cantonese speakers may find it totally unintelligible. Another characteristic of written Cantonese is the inclusion of English words and code-switching between Cantonese and English as seen in magazines and books for middle-class yuppies (see Bauer 1988).

If written Cantonese is represented by conventional written symbols such as characters, the situation is complicated by additional problems. Many colloquial Cantonese words lack a standard written form (see L-Y. Cheung 1983 for a list of examples). For example, the verb *sèuh* 'slide' as in *sèuh waahttāi* 'slide a slide' does not have a corresponding character nor does a cognate exist in standard written Chinese. Some characters corresponding to certain Cantonese words, especially colloquial ones may be available and used sporadically but it is not clear to what extent these have been accepted for uses of written Cantonese. Still other Cantonese words are replaced in writing by the corresponding characters in standard written Chinese. What is known as written Cantonese inevitably uses a greater or lesser number of standard written Chinese characters; if a Cantonese speaker reads such a text aloud, the result is neither Mandarin nor Cantonese but a hybrid variety. Naturally, this influence also extends to the grammar, with the result that many features of spoken Cantonese are not found in writing; indeed the grammar used is essentially that of Mandarin. The relationship between spoken and written forms of Cantonese is thus extremely complex. For these reasons, no attempt is made in this book to deal with written forms of the language. Reference is, however, made to the literary nature of certain grammatical features which are found in formal registers of speech as well as in writing. For example, in news broadcasting the passive may be used without an agent:

Yáuh sei mìhng tāu-douh-jé **beih hín fáan** loih-deih.
have four CL steal-cross-ists be sent back main-land
'Four illegal immigrants were repatriated to mainland (China).'

As illustrated above, this is a feature of Mandarin rather than Cantonese syntax (see 8.4).

ROMANIZATION

Unfortunately, a wide range of romanization systems are in use for Cantonese; no standard comparable to the Pinyin used for Mandarin has emerged, and new systems continue to appear.[7] (See Appendix for the conversion table listing the symbols used in the Yale, the International Phonetic Alphabet (IPA) and the system adopted by the Linguistic Society of Hongkong). Representing Cantonese in alphabetic form is an intrinsically challenging problem, and none of the current systems is ideal.

In this book, the Yale system developed by Parker Huang and Gerald Kok is adopted, with certain modifications. This is the system used in Huang and Kok's *Speak Cantonese* courses and other materials produced at Yale University, and in Tong and James' *Colloquial Cantonese* (1994). In Hongkong, it is used at the University of Hongkong and by the New Asia–Yale-in-China Chinese Language Centre of the Chinese University in its courses and for its new Cantonese–English and English–Cantonese dictionaries, which will complement this book.

The Yale transcription has several advantages in addition to being the most widely used system. Firstly, many of its conventions resemble the International Phonetic Alphabet and the Pinyin romanization used for Mandarin, and this will facilitate adaptation from Mandarin to Cantonese. Secondly, its notation of tones is relatively economical and iconic: rising and falling tones are shown by rising and falling accents, which are easier to follow and remember than the somewhat arbitrary numbers as used in the Sidney Lau system:[8]

lám vs. lam^2 'think'

The Yale system uses no tonal indication for the mid level (3) tone, which is appropriate since this is the most neutral of the tones:

sei vs. sei^3 'four'

The one arbitrary feature of tonal marking in the Yale system is the 'h' inserted after the vowel/diphthong for low-register tones, i.e. low rising, low level and low falling tones:

máh 'horse' (low rising)
màh 'linen' (low falling)
mah 'scold' (low level)

This is an economizing device, meaning that only five lexical tones need be indicated by diacritics, the mid and low level tones being unmarked. There is relatively little danger of the 'h' after vowels being pronounced [h], and as the only arbitrary feature of the system, it does not present the kind of burden on the learner that the numerical systems (used by Sidney Lau and some linguists) do.

The seven basic tones are represented in the standard Yale system as follows:

Cantonese Tones in the Yale System

	Rising	Level	Falling
High	á	ā	(à)
Mid		a	
Low	áh	ah	àh

The standard Yale system entails making a distinction between the high level and high falling tones (the high falling tone is shown in parentheses in the table). However, since these two tones are no longer distinctive for many Hongkong Cantonese speakers (see below), both are represented as high level in this book. Thus in our system, Cantonese has only six basic tones. But note that the distinction is retained in current dictionaries using the Yale system.

The long vowels and diphthongs are represented, as in most systems, by double letters: *aa* (long a) vs. *a* (short a), *aai* vs. *ai*, e.g. *gāai* 'street' vs. *gāi* 'chicken'.

MODIFICATIONS TO THE YALE SYSTEM

This grammar introduces certain modifications to alleviate some difficulties and deficiencies in the Yale system as used in previous works. These modifications are designed primarily to make the system easier to use, and should not be difficult for users of the Yale system to get used to.

(a) The high level and high falling tones, being no longer distinctive (see 1.4), are both written as high level: for example, standard Yale *bòng* 'help' is written as *bōng*, *tìn* 'sky' as *tīn*. The sentence particles *tìm* and *sìn* are exceptions, as they are pronounced with a clear falling tone.

(b) Hyphenation is used to show divisions within words: for reduplicated structures, including A-not-A questions (*Heui-m̀h-heui?* 'Go or not?'); compounds such as verb–object compounds (*cheung-gō* 'sing-song'); and complex numbers (*sāamsahp-luhk* 'thirty-six').

(c) The negative marker *m̀h* as in *Ngóh m̀h heui* 'I'm not going' is distinguished from the prefix *m-* as in *msyūfuhk* 'uncomfortable, unwell' (see 2.1.1, 13.1).

(d) Words are written separately unless there is strong reason to regard them as compounds. For example, classifiers and verbal particles are written separately from the noun and verb respectively because they may occur separately:

sāam ga chē	(cf. **Ga chē** hóu yáuh-yìhng.
three CL car	CL car very have-style
'three cars'	'The car is very stylish.')

bōng m̀h dóu	(cf. Ngóh **bōng** léih m̀h **dóu**.
help not succeed	I help you not succeed
'cannot help'	'I can't help you.')

(e) Apostrophes are introduced to represent reduced forms, such as *m'yéh* or *mī'eh* (a common abbreviated form of *mātyéh?* 'what?') and *sei'ah-yih*, a contraction of *seisahp-yih* 'forty-two').

Note that the romanizations used by the Hongkong government for street names, place names and personal names as found in telephone directories, birth certificates, etc. do not match the Yale system, in particular with regard to the initial consonants. For example, the surname written *Chiu* is *Jiuh* in the Yale system. This discrepancy is due to the lack of a standardized romanization system, as may be seen from the alternative spellings of the same surname: *Tse* or *Cheah* for the name romanized as *Jeh*.

Place names and personal names

Place names		Personal names	
Government romanization	*Yale romanization*	*Government romanization*	*Yale romanization*
Kowloon	Gáulùhng	Tang	Dahng
Tsimshatsui	Jīmsājéui	Tsui	Chèuih
Canton (province)	Gwóngdūng	Chiu	Jiuh
Sheung Wan	Seuhng Wàahn	Kwok	Gwok/Gok
Shatin	Sātìhn	Tse	Jeh

EXAMPLES

Grammatical points are exemplified in the following format:

Romanization: Ngóh hóu làahn wán dóu (go hóu gūngyàhn).
Gloss: I very hard find succeed (CL good maid)
Translation: 'I have difficulty finding (a good maid).'

Elements in parentheses are optional, i.e. may be omitted given a suitable context.

The literal gloss is intended to facilitate parsing of the Cantonese sentence, and to enable the translation to be idiomatic English. The translations are based on British English as spoken by the first author, but are intended to be compatible with American usage where possible. For teachers of English to Cantonese-speaking students, the glosses may also reveal the source of 'Chinglish' or typical errors: the gloss in the above example shows the source of the error type *I am difficult to find* meaning 'it is difficult for me to find (something)' which is very common in Chinese students' English.[9]

Many points which relate to discourse beyond the sentence level are illustrated with a miniature dialogue, usually shown as an exchange between A and B. For example, to illustrate the appropriate reply to a negative question:

A: Léih gāmyaht msái   fāan   gūng ge   mē?
   you today   no-need return work PRT PRT
   'Don't you need to go to work today?'

B: Haih a.
   yes PRT
   'No, I don't.'

The Cantonese *haih* shows agreement with the premise of the question ('you're right') while English uses a negative reply (see 17.1.9).

Where possible, example sentences and dialogues are taken from samples of Cantonese spoken in Hongkong. These examples are followed by an indication of the source type, as follows:

(conv.) conversation	(tel.) telephone conversation
(film) film	(TV) television broadcast
(radio) radio broadcast	(ad.) advertisement

More detailed indications of context are given where appropriate, in particular where they illustrate aspects of Cantonese culture in addition to points of grammar and usage. Example sentences not attributed to any of these sources have been constructed in consultation with other native speakers, or are recorded examples which have been modified for the purpose of exposition.

English words, although widely used by many speakers, are not generally used in the examples for practical reasons: as the pronunciation of English words varies on a continuum from pure English to pure Cantonese, it is not clear how to represent them in romanization. Moreover, it is difficult to draw the line between speaking Cantonese with English words and code-mixing or code-switching between the two languages. On these topics, see Gibbons (1979, 1987), Chan and Kwok (1984), Kwok and Chan (1985).

Idioms are separated from the text in boxed format. One reason for this format is that, although typically related to a certain grammatical structure or function word, they are idiosyncratic in some respect and call for separate treatment. A second purpose of this format is to highlight the idioms, many of which are very common and hence important to colloquial use of Cantonese. The dividing line between an idiom and an ordinary grammatical construction is not always clear; in general, however, idioms are distinguished by the following features:

(a) unlike grammatical rules and constructions which are typically applicable to all members of a syntactic category or subcategory, idioms are tightly restricted in terms of the items which may occur in them;

(b) idioms are irregular or unpredictable in some respect, especially in their meaning or function. If the meaning of the whole phrase is not the sum of the meanings of its parts, it is said to be **non-compositional**.

For example, the modal construction [verb – *dāk* – particle] expressing ability or potential is not an idiom, because it applies to any combination of verb + verbal particle (i.e. it is fully **productive**) and the meaning of the resulting expression is predictable from the meaning of its parts (see 12.3.1):

máaih dāk dóu	'can buy'
fan dāk dóu	'can fall asleep'

However, [verb – *dāk* – *gwo*] is treated as an idiom because its meaning 'safe/reliable to [verb]' is not predictable from the general meaning of the particle *gwo* 'over':

máaih dāk gwo	'safe to buy'
seun dāk gwo	'trustworthy'

LINGUISTIC LITERATURE ON CANTONESE

A number of useful studies of aspects of Cantonese grammar have been published in English, though few of these are widely available. Major studies in English are Kao (1971) on syllable structure and Hashimoto (1972) on phonology (also with some discussion of grammar); Kwok (1972, 1984) on verb phrases and sentence-final particles; Killingley (1982a, 1982b, 1983) on various aspects of Malaysian Cantonese grammar; and Luke (1990) on sentence-final particles. In Chinese, H-N.S. Cheung (1972) on the grammar of Hongkong Cantonese and Gao (1980) on that of Guangzhou Cantonese are available. A number of theses and dissertations, such as Chui (1988) and Chan (1992), have also made valuable contributions. Relevant studies are referred to in the notes to each chapter, together with an indication of their claims and findings.

DICTIONARIES

Two dictionaries which will complement the grammar have been published by the New Asia–Yale-in-China Chinese Language Centre at the Chinese

University of Hongkong. The English–Cantonese volume (Kwan et al. 1991) provides romanized forms only, while the Chinese–English volume (Chik and Ng-Lam 1989) also provides characters. Sidney Lau's Cantonese–English dictionary (1977) remains useful, especially for the large number of compound words and collocations listed, and has the advantage of being arranged alphabetically. Huang (1970) is a two-way dictionary, currently out of print.

LEARNING CANTONESE

Several courses are available which could be used in conjunction with the grammar. *Colloquial Cantonese* by Keith Tong and Gregory James, in the Routledge Colloquial series, is at the time of writing the most up-to-date such course, designed for self-taught learners. A relatively up-to-date and colloquial elementary course is *Everyday Cantonese* (1980), produced by the Extra-Mural Studies department of the Chinese University of Hongkong. This course comprises cassette tapes and a book using the Yale romanization, as does the older *Cantonese in 100 Hours*, produced by the University of Hongkong Extra-Mural Studies Department.

Of earlier materials, the Hongkong government course by Sidney Lau is particularly thorough, consisting of six volumes plus glossaries and a dictionary; however, much of the dialogue already sounds stilted, dating from the late 1950s and 1960s. Also thorough, though barely more up-to-date, is Parker Huang and Gerald Kok's *Speak Cantonese* in three volumes (Yale University Press); containing substantial texts, it is particularly useful for learners without ready access to spoken Cantonese. The US Foreign Service Institute course (Boyle 1970) is relatively thorough and accurate in its treatment of grammatical points.

1 PHONOLOGY: THE CANTONESE SOUND SYSTEM

The sound system of Cantonese is unfamiliar to speakers of European languages in several respects. Cantonese is a **tone language** in which the pitch or pitch pattern with which a syllable is pronounced is crucial to the identity of the word or syllable (1.4). The system of tones, with a minimum of six distinctive pitch patterns, is also more complex than that of Mandarin. As in Mandarin, however, the possible combinations of sounds into syllables in Cantonese are restricted by comparison with European languages (1.3).

This chapter is intended to provide sufficient background information for the grammar to be used effectively, rather than to provide a phonological analysis of the Cantonese sound system. For a fuller description, see Y-R. Chao (1947) and K-H. Cheung (1986). Some theoretical analysis of the Cantonese tone system is provided in M. Yip (1990).

1.1 CONSONANTS

1.1.1 INITIAL CONSONANTS

There are sixteen initial consonants, i.e. those which may occur at the beginning of a word. These are shown in Table 1.1, according to their phonetic features.

Table 1.1 Initial consonants

	Unaspirated	Aspirated	Fricative	Nasal/liquid
Bilabial	b	p	f	m
Dental/alveolar	d	t	s	n/l
Velar/glottal	g	k	h	ng
Labiovelar	gw	kw		
Affricates	j	ch		

The Cantonese stops pose considerable difficulty for the English speaker, because their **distinctive features** are different from those of English. Whereas English stops such as *p* and *b* are distinguished by the contrast in voicing, *p* being voiceless and *b* voiced, no Cantonese stops are distinctively voiced. Rather, the contrast is one of aspiration – whether or not a burst of air is emitted immediately after oral release in the process of articulation. In English, this feature is also present in that initial *p* is normally aspirated and *b* not; however, this contrast is not a distinctive one. The result is that Cantonese *b* as in *béi* 'give' may be perceived by an English speaker either as *p* (because of the lack of voicing) or as *b* (because of the lack of aspiration). This combination of features – voiceless and unaspirated – in initial position is unknown in English, making the Cantonese series *b/d/g* difficult to recognize. Many romanization systems add to the difficulty by representing them as *p/t/k* respectively; this includes the romanization applied to place names, so that *Kowloon*, for example, is pronounced by English speakers with an aspirated *k* [kʰ].[1] In the Yale system it would be *Gáulùhng*. The labiovelar consonants *gw* and *kw* are **coarticulated** stops, i.e. the velar sound *g* or *k* is articulated simultaneously with the bilabial *w* in *gwa* 'hang' and *kwàhn* 'skirt'. However, there is a tendency to simplify *gw* and *kw* to *g* and *k* respectively where they are followed by *o* or *u*, e.g. *gwok* 'country' is pronounced *gok*, sounding identical to *gok* 'feel'. Similarly:

Gwóngjāu → Góngjāu 'Canton'
gwú → gú 'guess'
kwòhng → kòhng 'crazy'
jeuhng-gān-kwū → jeuhng-gān-kū 'rubber band'

The simplified forms are used especially by younger speakers and in less formal speech (see 1.5). Note that the difference in pronunciation between *kwu* and *ku*, *gwu* and *gu* is a very slight one, as the lips are rounded similarly for the sounds *w* and *u*.

The alveolar affricates *j* and *ch* pose particular problems for learners and for romanization systems. Phonetically, *j* is [ts] which sounds similar to the final consonants at the end of the English word *ads* (i.e. *advertisements*) but like the Cantonese stop *d*, it is pronounced *without* voicing. Its aspirated counterpart is *ch* [tsʰ], with strong aspiration, as in *chàh* 'tea'. Both *j* and *ch* are pronounced with lips spread, rather than rounded as in English. The pronunciation of initial *j*, *ch* and *s* may be affected by the following vowel. In particular, for some speakers, the high front rounded vowel *yu* [y] tends to cause palatalization of *j* and *ch* to [tʃ] and [tʃʰ] respectively:

jyuh 'live' → [tʃyː] (compare *jaahn* 'earn': [tsaːn])
chyùhn 'whole' → [tʃʰyn] (compare *chàh* 'tea': [tsʰaː])

A similar palatalization affects *s*, which may become ʃ before *yu*:

syū 'book' → [ʃyː] (compare *si* 'try': [siː])

The mid rounded vowel *eu* may also cause partial palatalization of these consonants, as in *cheung* 'sing', *jeui* 'most', *séung* 'want'.[2] The sounds resulting from this palatalization sound similar to the corresponding

English affricates, as in *church* and *judge*. This pronunciation should not be used for *j* and *ch* throughout, however, as the palatalized variants will be very un-native-like if used before other vowels, as in *jouh* 'do' or *chàh* 'tea'; such mispronunciations are in fact characteristic of English-speaking learners of Cantonese. Note also that the retroflex sounds characteristic of Mandarin *ch*, *zh* and *sh* are unknown in Cantonese.

There are two **semivowels** which occur as initials:

> *y* as in *yàhn* 'person'
> *w* as in *wái* 'place, position'

y should be distinguished from *yu* as in *syut* 'snow' which represents the high rounded vowel. Initial *w* is also distinct from the [w] sound which is part of the labiovelar consonants *gw* and *kw*: as noted above, these are coarticulated stops, in which the *g/k* and *w* sounds are formed simultaneously.

1.1.2 UNRELEASED CONSONANTS

In final position, i.e. at the end of a syllable, stops are **unreleased**. For example, in *faat* 'law', the *-t* is formed by the tongue touching the alveolar ridge behind the teeth, but without air being released. In *ngaap* 'duck', the lips are closed as for *p* but not opened again. This neutralizes the contrast between aspirated and unaspirated consonants, since unreleased consonants cannot be aspirated. Also, the labiovelars *kw* and *gw* are not found in final position. Consequently, there are only three such unreleased stops: *-p*, *-t* and *-k*. These can be difficult to distinguish, all three tending to sound like a glottal stop to an English speaker. They are nevertheless distinctive, as in the following set:

> sāp 'wet'   sāt 'lost'   sāk 'jammed'

Some speakers do not distinguish between unreleased *-t* or *-k* in the following words:[3]

baat	baak
eight	hundred
bāk	bāt
north	pen

These word pairs are often pronounced with the same final unreleased consonants, usually both as *-t*. The change from *-k* to *-t* has been noted to be a parallel phenomenon to the change from *-ng* to *-n* (1.1.3): both cases involve the realization of a velar as an alveolar consonant (see K-H. Cheung 1986). Hence *sāk chē* 'jam car = traffic jam' would sound the same as *sāt chē* 'lost car' if the final is pronounced or perceived as an unreleased

-t. This phenomenon seems to be prevalent among speakers of the younger generation.

1.1.3   NASAL AND LIQUID CONSONANTS

The three nasals, *m*, *n* and *ng* are straightforward to pronounce; it is their distribution which raises problems. Variation and ongoing change also complicate the picture.

Initial *ng* presents some difficulty for English speakers: although the sound is essentially that in English *sing*, pronouncing it in word-initial position as in *ngóh* 'I' takes practice. Moreover, there is variation between *ng* and zero initial: *ngàuh/àuh* 'cow', *ngāam/āam* 'correct', *ngaap/aap* 'duck', etc. Currently, many Cantonese speakers of the younger generation do not pronounce *ng* in casual speech, using instead a glottal stop as in *óh* for *ngóh* 'I/me', etc; conversely, those conscious of the 'correctness' of initial *ng* in words such as *ngóh* use hypercorrect forms such as *ngōn-chyùhn* for *ōnchyùhn* 'safe' (see 1.5).[4]

The initial *n* is pronounced as a *l* by younger speakers, and by older speakers in less formal speech registers. Thus *néih* 'you' is pronounced as *léih*, *nìhn* 'year' as *lìhn*. This change to *l* is still corrected as an 'error' by some older language teachers. The *n* pronunciation is still used in highly formal registers and in some traditional forms of singing (contemporary Canto-pop, however, often uses *l*). Initial *n-* is preserved in the demonstrative form *nī* 'this' for many speakers, but also variously pronounced by other speakers as *yī*, *lī* or *lēi*:

nī go 'this' → lī go, lēi go, yī go
nī dī 'these' → lī dī, lēi dī, yī dī
nīdouh 'here' → līdouh, lēidouh, yīdouh

All three nasals are found in final position. However, the distinction between *n* and *ng* is merged in certain contexts for some speakers, e.g. *sāan* 'mountain' vs. *sāang* 'alive, produce' are both pronounced as [sāːn] (see 1.5). For some speakers, this occurs only before front consonants as in *sāan(g) jái* 'give birth', while for others it is independent of the context, e.g. *hohksāan(g)* 'student'.

1.1.4   SYLLABIC NASALS

A few syllables consist of a nasal consonant alone, *m* or *ng*. These are known as *syllabic nasals*. The main examples are the negative marker *m̀h* 'not', the numeral *ńgh* 'five', the surnames *Ǹgh* and *Ńgh*, and the verb/noun *ngh-wuih* 'misunderstand(ing)'.

The syllable *ńgh* is widely pronounced as bilabial *m̀h*, especially by those speakers who do not use initial *ng* (see above and 1.5). The surname *Ǹgh*, with a low falling tone, then sounds the same as the negative marker *m̀h*, while the numeral *m̄h* 'five' is distinguished by its low rising tone.

1.2 VOWELS

Table 1.2 shows the eight vowels used in the Yale system, including both long and short *a* (see 1.2.2). Note the following: (i) the table, following the Yale system, does not distinguish between the variants of *i*, *u* and *eu* which are distinguished in IPA and some romanization systems; (ii) all these vowels have a consistent quality throughout, rather than being diphthongized as their equivalents often are in English. For Cantonese diphthongs, see 1.2.3.

Table 1.2 Vowels

	Front Unrounded	Front Rounded	Central	Back
High	i	yu		u
Mid	e	eu		o
Low			a	aa

The vowel systems of Hongkong and Guangzhou Cantonese are compared in Lee (1983).

1.2.1 VOWEL QUALITY

i as in *sin* 'string', *yiht* 'hot' is similar to English [i] in *seen*, but the tongue position is slightly higher. Before the velar consonants *k* and *ng* as in *lihk* 'strength', *līng* 'carry', it is more like the vowel sound in English *late* but is shorter.

e is a mid front vowel, more open than *i*, as in *leng* 'pretty, nice' and *lēk* 'clever'.

yu is a high rounded vowel [y], similar to French *u* or German *ü* but pronounced further forward in the mouth, as in *syū* 'book', *dyūn* 'thin'. In British English the closest sound is *u* after *t*, as in *tube*.

eu is a mid rounded vowel, with two pronunciations according to the following consonants:

(a) before the velar consonants *k* and *ng*, the sound is [œ] as in *jeuk* 'wear' and *cheung* 'sing'. [œ] is also used in the few words ending in *-eu*, such as the noun *hēu* 'boot', the verb *sèuh* 'slide' and the classifier *déu* (*yāt déu fā* 'a flower').

(b) before *t* and *n*, as in *seun* 'believe', and in the diphthong *eui*, as in *séui* 'water', the sound is similar to French *eu*, or not unlike the vowel in British English *her* but with rounded lips.

o is similar to the vowel in British English *hot*, pronounced with slightly rounded lips, as in *chóh* 'sit', *lohk* 'go down'.

u resembles the vowel of English *food*, as in *gú* 'ancient'. It is also pronounced with slightly rounded lips. Before the velar consonants *k* and *ng* it is lower, as in *suhk* 'familiar', and can be difficult to distinguish from the still lower *o*, e.g. *duhk* 'study' vs. *dohk* 'measure', *hūng* 'empty' vs. *hōng* 'healthy'.

a is a low central vowel, as in *sān* 'new'. It resembles the vowel of English *sun* or German *hat*. *aa* is longer as in *sāan* 'hill' (see 1.2.2 below) and more open than *a*. It resembles the long *a* in British English *father*.

1.2.2 VOWEL LENGTH

Long and short *a* are distinctive in closed syllables, e.g. *sān* 'new' vs. *sāan* 'hill'. The distinction applies equally to diphthongs containing *a* sounds: thus, *gāi* 'chicken' with a short diphthong contrasts with *gāai* 'street' with a long diphthong (and the same tone). The actual difference in length depends on the syllable: in a closed syllable such as *haak* 'client', the long vowel in Cantonese may be no longer than a short one in English. The two vowels also differ in quality: short *a* is similar to the vowel of English *cut*, while long *aa* is more open, like that in *father*. But note that the difference in vowel quality is not found in diphthongs as in *gāi* 'chicken' and *gāai* 'street'.

Note that romanizations generally do not distinguish between *a* and *aa* at the end of a syllable, e.g. the classifier *bá* and particles such as *lā* are pronounced with a long vowel, but written with *a* as the length difference is not distinctive in this position.[5]

The length of other vowels varies according to the environment, but the difference is not distinctive:

Long	Short
sī 'poem'	sīk 'know'
dō 'much'	dohk 'measure'
fū 'master'	fūk 'blessing'

1.2.3 DIPHTHONGS

The following diphthongs (sounds consisting of a combination of two vowel sounds) occur:

ai	sāi	'west'	*ei*	sei	'four'
aai	sāai	'waste'	*eui*	séui	'water'
au	gau	'enough'	*iu*	tiu	'jump'
aau	gaau	'teach'	*ou*	hóu	'good'
			oi	choi	'vegetable'
			ui	guih	'tired'

Note that the long diphthongs *aai* and *aau* are distinct from *ai* and *au*, just as *aa* is distinct from *a* (1.2.2). There are no triphthongs: note that *eu* as in *seun* 'letter' is a simple vowel, and *eui* as in *chēui* 'blow' is therefore a diphthong.

1.3 SYLLABLE STRUCTURE

Like Mandarin, Cantonese has a relatively simple syllable structure: the possible combinations of sounds are severely restricted. No consonant clusters (consecutive consonants) occur,[6] hence syllables typically have the form (C)V(V)(C): (consonant) – vowel – (vowel) – (consonant). Moreover, only two sets of consonants can appear at the end of a syllable:

(a) nasals: -m, -n, -ng
(b) unreleased consonants: -p, -t, -k

1.3.1 INITIALS AND FINALS

Traditional descriptions of Chinese divide the syllable not into individual sounds (phonemes) but into combinations which occur at the beginning and end of syllables: **initials** and **finals**. The initials are the consonants discussed in 1.1, the finals are the combinations of vowel + consonant which may occur at the end of a syllable.

The significance of this classification is that only a certain number of the logically possible combinations actually occur in established **morphemes**. For example, *-ip* and *-ap* occur regularly as finals but **-eup* does not.

Table 1.3 Cantonese finals

Vowel	i	e	yu	eu	(a)	aa	o	u
V+i		ei		eui	ai	aai	oi	ui
V+u	iu				au	aau	ou	
V+m	im				am	aam		
V+n	in		yun	eun	an	aan	on	un
V+ng	ing	eng		eung	ang	aang	ong	ung
V+p	ip				ap	aap		
V+t	it		yut	eut	at	aat	ot	ut
V+k	ik	ek		euk	ak	aak	ok	uk

Out of a possible sixty-four combinations of vowels and final consonants/ vowels, only fifty-four occur, and some of these, such as -*ot*, are very rare. These gaps, and the possible combinations, appear in the Table 1.3. Note that all the simple vowels (*i, e, yu* etc.) occur as finals, with the exception that *a* does not contrast with *aa* in final position (see 1.2.2 above). Although this represents the conventional picture for standard morphemes (essentially those for which established characters exist), additional finals occur in colloquial speech:

(a) in onomatopaeic sounds, e.g. -*em* and -*up*:

lém-lém-leih | bùhp-búp tiu
lick-lick-tongue | bop-bop jump
'lick one's lips' | 'beat bop-bop' (heart)

(b) in loan-words, e.g. -*et*, -*en* and -*um*:

heui **wēt** (verb) 'go out and have fun'
hóu **fēn** (adj.) 'friends with'
būm (noun) 'pump'

These are not included in Table 1.3 as they arguably do not form part of the sound system. Nevertheless, they show that the range of possible syllables is extendable, as argued by Bauer (1985).

Additional restrictions apply to which tones can occur on which finals. For example, the finals ending in unreleased consonants all have level basic tones:

yāt 'one' (high level)   yaht 'day' (low level)

Syllables ending in unreleased consonants do not generally have rising or falling basic tones (e.g. there are no words such as **yàht*), but a rising tone may occur as a result of tone change (see 1.4.2), as in *hóu-yát* 'good-day = lucky day'; *yàhn-yát* 'person-day = seventh day of the Chinese New Year (also known as everybody's birthday)'; *jaahk-yát* 'pick-day = pick a lucky day'. Some of these changed tone forms have become the usual spoken forms of words, e.g. *wùh-díp* 'butterfly'.

1.4 TONE

The tonal system of Cantonese is considerably more complex than that of Mandarin, which uncontroversially has four distinct tones. Exactly how many tones there are in Cantonese depends on how the system is analysed. According to the traditional classification, Cantonese has nine distinct tones whereby the checked syllables are considered as belonging to categories to be contrasted with other tonal categories. However, the distinct tones before unreleased consonants are now widely seen as abbreviated counterparts of the three level tones which occur in other contexts. Only six tones are clearly distinctive in Hongkong Cantonese; an example in which the whole range of tones is distinguished is the syllable *yau*:

High level:	yāu 'worry'; 'rest' (in compounds)
High rising:	yáu 'paint' (noun);
Mid level:	yau 'thin'
Low falling:	yàuh 'oil'; 'swim' (verb)
Low rising:	yáuh 'have'; 'friend'
Low level:	yauh 'again'; 'right (hand)'

Note that in many cases, two or more words (**homophones**) exist with the same tone. These are distinguished by (a) the different parts of speech to which they belong, and (b) compound expressions in which they occur.

The system of six tones given above assumes that the high level and high falling tones are not distinctive, a point which is agreed by most recent authors (see K-H.Cheung 1986). There is currently considerable variation in the realization of these tones. Many speakers use them interchangeably, as in *sān* or *sàn* 'new', *hūnghei* or *hùnghei* 'air.' These words are most commonly pronounced with a high level tone, especially by younger speakers in Hongkong.[7] Consequently, both tones are normally shown in this book with a high level tone, whereas dictionaries using the Yale system show some with high level and others with high falling tones. A high falling tone is, however, distinctively heard on certain sentence-final particles such as *sìn* and *tìm*, and sometimes also in contracted forms such as *sà'a-yih* 'thirty-two'; these are the only words shown with high falling tones in the text (see chs 18, 21).

1.4.1 THE BASIC TONES

Linguists generally distinguish the **basic** or **lexical** tones, heard when the word is pronounced in isolation, from the **changed** or **sandhi** tones which occur only when a word occurs in particular phonological and morphological contexts (1.4.2). The Cantonese tone system involves three pitch levels: high, mid and low. These three tones exist individually as level tones, which are relatively easy to pronounce and serve as points of reference for the other three tones which fall or rise from one level to another. This gives a system of six tones, discounting as a variant the high falling tone (shown in parentheses) as described in 1.4 above:

Tones

High:	—
	/ (\)
Mid:	—
	\ /
Low:	—

Although the system shown here is essentially symmetrical, the actual pitch contours of each tone are not. In Chinese linguistics it is customary to divide the pitch range into five levels and characterize tones in terms of their starting and ending pitch levels:[8]

High level:	55	High rising:	35/25
Mid level:	33	Low rising:	23/13
Low level:	22	Low falling:	21/11

Note that some tones have alternative representations in different systems, e.g. the high rising tone is sometimes represented as 35 and sometimes 25. Similarly, 23 and 13 are both used for the low rising tone and 21 and 11 for the low falling tone.

Two particular asymmetries in the tonal system should be noted:

(a)   The high rising and low rising tones in fact begin at around the same pitch level,[9] and are distinguished by the pitch level to which they rise: the high rising tone is marked by a very steep pitch gradient, and hence easily recognized, while the low rising tone rises only to the pitch of the mid level tone.[10] The name 'high rising tone' is therefore misleading in that it rises to the high level, rather than beginning high and rising further; some linguists prefer the term 'mid rising tone'.

(b)   The low falling tone is not simply the reverse of the low rising tone, but starts at the pitch of the low level tone and drops further, sometimes ending with a 'creaky' voice quality, especially for male speakers, as the bottom of the speaker's pitch range is reached. The relatively slight fall in pitch makes this tone difficult to distinguish from the low level tone for the foreign learner. Furthermore, the low falling tone is sometimes pronounced at an even pitch: 11, below that of the low level tone. As with the two rising tones, therefore, it is the ending rather than the starting pitch which is distinctive.

Note that the **neutral tone** assigned to many grammatical words in Mandarin does not exist as such in Cantonese: although many grammatical words have the mid level tone (a distinct tone), such as the possessive/ linking particle ge and the experiential aspect marker gwo, others have high-register tones, such as the adverbial dāk and the progressive aspect marker gán.

Traditional descriptions further distinguish the **entering** tones (high, level and low) which occur before the unreleased consonants -p, -t, -k. As pointed out by Chao (1947), these are phonetically equivalent to short instantiations of the high, mid and low level tones, i.e. siht 'lose (money)' and sih 'matter' share the same low level tone, differing only in length. Some transcription systems continue to distinguish these tones, unnecessarily complicating the system with a total of nine or ten numbered tones.

1.4.2 TONE CHANGE

In many varieties of Chinese, the basic tones change in particular environments. **Tone sandhi** is the change in the tone brought about regularly by the effects of adjacent tones, as the Mandarin third (dipping) tone becomes a rising tone when it is followed by another third tone. In Cantonese, tone change is restricted to one main process which is *not* regular in this sense, but occurs due to a number of morphological and semantic factors. For these reasons, the Cantonese case is generally referred to as **tone change** rather than tone sandhi. The functions of this tone change are highly complex.

The main tonal change occurs in compounds and reduplicated expressions, in which a mid/high rising tone results. It occurs primarily where the second syllable of a compound or reduplicated word has a low-register tone:

jó   yauh → jó-yáu   sòh → sòh-só-déi
left right   silly
'about, approximately'   'rather silly'

Whereas the lexical tone of *yauh* 'right' is low level, it changes to a rising tone in such compound expressions. Similarly, the adjective *sòh* has a low falling tone, but when reduplicated the second syllable takes the changed tone. For most speakers, the resulting rising tone is the same as the high rising tone; for others, it is rather lower, being centred on the pitch of the mid level tone but rising perceptibly as the vowel is pronounced. In the Yale system it is conventionally represented by the high rising tone.

The regular tone-change phenomenon appears in various types of reduplication (see 2.2). In reduplicated adjectives with the [AAB] pattern the tone of the second element often undergoes the tone change:

kàhm-kàhm-chēng → kàhm-kám-chēng 'in a mad rush'
lahp-lahp-lyuhn → lahp-láp-lyuhn 'messy, disorganized'

In reduplicated adjectives and verbs with the suffix *-déi* and in onomatopoeic reduplication, the second syllable regularly takes the changed tone:

fèih-fèih-déi → fèih-féi-déi 'rather fat, chubby'
hàhn-hàhn-déi → hàhn-hán-déi 'rather itchy'
mìhng-mìhng-déi → mìhng-míng-déi 'understand roughly'
sàh-sàh-sēng → sàh-sá-sēng 'sloshing sound' (as in raining)
dihk-dihk-sēng → dihk-dík-sēng 'ticking sound' (of clock, watch)

In tentative or diminutive verb reduplication, exceptionally, it is the *first* verb which takes the changed tone, due to contraction of *yāt* (see 2.2, 11.2.6):

si yāt si → sí-si   bohng yāt bohng → bóng-bohng
try one try   weigh one weigh
'have a try'   'weigh'

tàih yāt tàih → tái-tàih	mahn yāt mahn → mán-mahn
mention one mention	ask one ask
'mention a bit'	'ask'

This phenomenon also occurs where the adjective is reduplicated in [adjective] *yāt* [adjective] (see 2.2):

pèhng   yāt   pèhng → péng-pèhng
cheap   one   cheap
'very cheap'

Nī   dī   sāam   péng-pèhng dōu móuh yàhn máaih ge   la.
these CL clothes cheap-cheap still no   one   buy   PRT PRT
'Nobody will buy these clothes, however cheap they are.'

tìhm yāt tìhm → tím-tìhm 'very sweet'

Kéuih siu   dou tím-tìhm   gám, hóu hó-ngoi a.
s/he   smile till   sweet-sweet so   very lovely   PRT
'He's smiling so sweetly. Really lovely.'

Tone change involving contraction of *yāt* 'one' also occurs in enumerative constructions where [*yāt* classifier] is reduplicated (see Whitaker 1956): when the second *yāt* 'one' is contracted, tone change occurs in the preceding classifier resulting in a high rising tone:

yāt geui yāt geui → yāt géui geui
one sentence one sentence

yāt dihp yāt dihp → yāt díp dihp
one dish one dish

yāt gauh yāt gauh → yāt gáu gauh
one lump one lump

In both cases of tone change with contraction of *yāt* 'one', the affected syllable is lengthened. Note that while most speakers change tone regularly in these cases, the process is not necessarily obligatory for all speakers. The change of tone often adds a touch of colour and liveliness to the utterance. Some words may occur with either a basic or a changed tone, whether or not they are reduplicated or part of a compound. In these cases, the changed tone forms tend to be more colloquial, as in *gauh-jahn-sìh/gauh-jahn-sí* 'in the old days'.

In cases where the noun is used as a container classifier (6.2.2), the original tone is retained:

yāt hahp jyūgūlīk 'a box of chocolates' *but* nī go háp 'this box'
yāt dihp choi 'a dish of vegetables' *but* gó jek díp 'that dish'

Furthermore, many instances of changed tone are associated with familiarity or intimacy. Chao (1947) notes that tone change has 'a morphological meaning, namely, "that familiar thing (or person, less frequently action) one often speaks of" '. For example, it applies to reduplicated kinship terms:

bā-bā → bàh-bā	mā-mā → màh-mā
'father'	'mother'
gō-gō → gòh-gō	jé-jé → jèh-jē
'elder brother'	'elder sister'
daih-daih → dàih-dái	muih-muih → mùih-múi
'younger brother'	'younger sister'
jái-jái → jàih-jái/jāi	léui-léui → lèuih-léui/lēui
'little boy'	'little girl'
taai-taai → taai-táai	jat → ját 'nephew'
'wife'	'nephew or niece'

Note that the first syllable typically changes to low falling tone and the second to high rising or high level or remains unchanged if it is a high tone already. These terms of address obligatorily take on the changed tones in daily spoken Cantonese but remain unchanged when they appear in written texts to be read aloud with Cantonese pronunciation.

Tone change also applies to surnames given the familiar prefix a- or the epithet lóuh 'old' (20.2) and titles of familar people:

Chàhn → A-Chán, lóuh-Chán;
Jeh → A-Jé, lóuh-Jé
sih-tàuh → sih-táu
matter-head
'boss'

When English names are referred to in spoken Cantonese, they typically end in high rising tone:

Fanny → Fēnní   Nellie → Nēlí

Many loan-words also acquire the high level or high rising tone, e.g. insurance → yinsō; order → ōdá.

Even names of familiar objects in people's daily lives take on the changed tone (see Y-S. Cheung (1969) for more examples):

chìhn/hauh mùhn → chìhn/hauh mún
front/back door   front/back door
'front/back door'

tīn   tòih → tīn tói
sky   balcony
'balcony on rooftop'

ngáahn-geng → ngáahn-géng
eye-glasses
'glasses'

yàuh tìuh → yàuh tíu
oil CL
'Chinese doughnut'

hàahm-yùh → hàahm-yú
salt-fish
'salted fish' (also slang, 'dead body')

Another phenomenon involving tone change, found in certain dialects of Guangdong province but rarely in Hongkong Cantonese, results from contraction of the aspect marker -jó:

Sihk-jó-faahn meih a? → **Sík**-faahn meih a?
eat-PFV-rice not-have PRT   eat-PFV-rice not-have PRT
'Have you eaten?'

The resulting verb with high rising tone incorporates the meaning of -jó.

As can be seen, tone change involves alternations between a mid- or low-register tone and the high rising tone. Below are some examples of tone change which are not as regular and predictable as the ones shown above:

Mid level: **seung**-pín 'photograph' ⟷ yíng-**séung** 'take photos'
Low rising: pàhng-**yáuh** 'friend' ⟷ faat-sīu-**yáu** 'fanatic'
Low level: **wuih**-yíh 'meet-discuss = conference' ⟷ hōi-**wúi** 'hold/
      attend a meeting'
Low falling: sūkmáih-**yàuh** 'corn oil' ⟷ gā-**yáu** 'fill up with fuel'

An important function of this tone change is to indicate a compound: the changed tone indicates that the word forms a compound expression with the preceding word. This alternation may be compared to the difference in stress between *bláck bírd* and *bláckbird* in English, the single stress on *blackbird* indicating that the combination is a single compound noun. For example:

yàhn 'person' → léuihyán 'woman'

Similarly, in verb–object compounds (2.3.3) the original tone of the object noun may change:

jouh yaht → jouh-yát   jouh yeh → jouh-yé
work day   work night
'work day shifts'   'work night shifts'

(Contrast the idiom *yaht jouh yeh jouh* 'work day and night' with low level tones.)

Note that the tone change is not automatic; it is a sign that the combination is **lexicalized**, i.e. a fixed combination, often with a specialized meaning which cannot be predicted from that of the two parts:

jáu 'walk, run' + louh 'road' → jáu-louh 'walk'
but jáu-lóu 'run away'

Some cases appear quite unpredictable:

góng daaih **wah** 'tell lies' *but* góng siu **wá** 'tell jokes' (Wong 1982)
ngàhn-**hòhng** 'bank' *but* kàhm-**hóng** 'piano shop'

Another contrast is that between the adverb *gam* meaning 'as, so' (9.1.3) and the form *gám* with the demonstrative meaning 'like this/that' (10.1.2). Bearing different tones, they serve different grammatical functions.

1.4.3 TONE AND INTONATION

The actual realization of tones varies according to their phonetic environment.

One relevant factor is the tone of the following syllable. There is a natural tendency to anticipate the next tone, affecting the actual pitch contour of the first. For example, in *sī-sī-màhn-màhn* 'gentlemanly' the first two syllables both have high tones but the second *sī* may differ from the first *sī* in that it will tend to drop off during the vowel in anticipation of low falling tone of *màhn* immediately following it. A second factor is **declination**: the natural tendency for the pitch level of a syllable to decline during an utterance. Given a number of consecutive syllables containing a high tone, the actual pitch level will not be identical, but will be pronounced slightly lower each time (see Wu 1989). For example:

gūngsī	gīngléih	ge	gūngyàhn
company	manager	LP	maid
'the company manager's maid'			

Although having the same high tones, *gūng* in *gūngyàhn* will be pronounced at a lower pitch than *gūng* in *gūngsī* due to declination. This does not affect the recognition of the tones, which is **relative** to the surrounding tones rather than absolute. Clearly, a woman's low tone may be pronounced at the same pitch as a man's high tone, or indeed higher (as shown in Fok 1974).

As Cantonese is a tonal language where pitch is used to differentiate words, intonation at the level of the sentence is restricted, at least by comparison with English. The lack of sentence intonation patterns is of crucial importance to the pronunciation of Cantonese tones. If an English intonation pattern is supe imposed on a Cantonese sentence, the tone of individual words may be ibscured or even changed completely and may result in incomprehensibi ity. For example, the following question has a falling tone both on the penultimate syllable *yàhn* and the final particle *àh*, which will be lost if it is pronounced with a rising question intonation:

Léih haih Méihgwok yàhn àh?
you are America person PRT
'You're American?'

Despite the constraints imposed by tone, some patterns of intonation can be discerned, especially in the case of questions and sentence particles, which may be pronounced with a variety of intonation patterns (18.1.1). These patterns are not well understood; Kwok and Luke (1986) and K-H. Cheung (1986) are among the few sources to discuss them.

One characteristic intonation pattern is the sharp rise found in **echo questions** (see 17.1.7 for the relevant discussion).

Another distinctive pattern is an emphatic response to a question which often involves pitch change within a word:[11]

A: Léih sek-m̀h-sek léih māmìh a?   B: Sē-ēk!
   you love-not-love your mummy a?   love
   'Do you love your mummy?'   'Sure I do!'

This rising intonation pattern on *sek* is clearly distinct from both the high rising tone and the changed tone. Its exact pattern depends on the basic tone of the syllable on which it is superimposed; on a mid level tone such as *sek*, it rises strongly before levelling out at the end. Note that the vowel is lengthened considerably in order to carry this pattern.

The same pattern is used in providing assurances:

A: Ngóh béi dī yéh léih jouh dāk-m̀h-dāk   a?
   I   give CL thing you do   okay-not-okay PRT
   'I'm giving you something to do, okay?

B: Dā-āk!
   okay
   'Sure!'

A: Léih wúih-m̀h-wúih fāan   làih   Hēunggóng a?
   you will-not-will return come Hongkong PRT
   'Will you be coming back to Hongkong?'

B: Wū-ūih!
   will
   'I certainly will!'

Another pattern, with a lengthened vowel and rising intonation, may be applied in question words such as *dím*, where the rising tone is exaggerated (17.6):

Dí-ím syun a?   Dí-ím gáai   a?
how do   PRT   how explain PRT
'What shall I do?'   'Why?'

1.5 VARIATION AND CHANGE IN PRONUNCIATION

As mentioned in many of the above sections, there is variation between individual speakers, social groups and age groups in many aspects of pronunciation. Such variation is a fact of all languages, but is particularly striking in Cantonese, partly due to the lack of a widely recognized standard form of the language, in particular of a phonetically based written form, to limit the variation. There is often said to be 'confusion' of sounds, as indicated by alternative forms such as *ngōnchyùhn* for *ōnchyùhn* 'safe', *Ngāujāu* for *Āujāu* 'Europe' which are 'incorrect' in the sense that these words originally did not have the initial *ng* (see note 4). Some of these forms are the result of **hypercorrection**, as they typically result from speakers using what they perceive to be 'correct' or prestige pronunciation. While the younger generation of speakers (relative to the time of writing) has generally lost the initial *ng* across the board, many speakers still retain it and may have free variation or their use of one or the other may be determined by the relevant registers, e.g. use *ng* in formal registers and careful speech and zero initial in informal registers and casual speech.

Many speakers have strong views about 'correct' pronunciation, and some words such as *léih* may be corrected to *néih* by some teachers. Recent studies (Yeung 1980, Bauer 1982, Bourgerie 1990) have shown that this variation is quite systematic, following variables such as age, class and gender. This distribution in many cases clearly indicates sound change in process. For example, at the time of writing, very few speakers of the younger generation use *néih* for 'you'; assuming that these speakers will not switch from *léih* to *néih* as they grow older, it is likely that the next stage of sound change will occur whereby all speakers will use *léih*. To this extent, to correct the pronunciation *léih* is attempting to reverse an inevitable change.

Note that these sound changes often appear to be random and unsystematic, as they affect individual words differently. For example, many speakers will pronounce the second person pronoun as *léih* but use *n* in *nīdouh* 'here'. Such a pattern is in fact characteristic of sound change in progress: rather than affecting all the words concerned at one fell swoop, it affects one word at a time, eventually affecting the whole vocabulary and completing the sound change.[12]

The main changes and sources of variation are as follows:

(a) *n → l*, as in *nám → lám* 'think': this change is so advanced that the words concerned are generally shown as *l* in this book. *n* is heard primarily in formal registers such as singing and reading of written texts. The *n/l* alternation was first discussed in Wong (1941) and the phenomenon has been around for several decades (see 1.1.3).

(b) *gwo- → go-*, as in *gwok → gok* 'country': this change is also very widespread. However, it is subject to considerable stylistic variation, with many speakers using *gw* in formal or careful style and *g* elsewhere. One consequence of this change is that the syllable *gwo*, with its many grammatical functions, becomes homophonous with the classifier *go* (see 1.1.1).

(c) *kwo-* → *ko-*, as in *kwòhng* → *kòhng* 'crazy' is a parallel change (see 1.1.1).

(d) *-k* → *-t*, as in *baak* → *baat* 'hundred' and *bāk* → *bāt* 'north' (see 1.1.2).

(e) *k* → *h*, in the pronoun *kéuih* (see 5.1).

(f) *ng-* → [Ø], as in *ngóh* → *óh* 'I', *ngáahn* → *áahn* 'eye': many younger speakers do not pronounce this initial in casual speech, typically replacing it with a glottal stop. For other speakers, there is free variation between the two, e.g. *ngāam-ngāam* or *āam-āam* 'just now', *ngūk* or *ūk* 'house' and the tendency to use hypercorrect forms with initial *ng* for words which do not have it originally for sociolinguistic reasons (see 1.1.3).

(g) *ng* → *m*, as in *ńgh* → *ḿh* 'five' (distinguished by its low rising tone from the negative *m̀h* 'not'). This change appears to predominate among speakers who do not use initial *ng-* (see 1.1.4).

(h) *-ng* → *-n*, as in *sāang* → *sāan* 'produce': this change is widespread especially when preceded by the long vowel *aa*. It occurs more sporadically after short *a* and other vowels, e.g. *sāng-mihng* 'life' may be pronounced as *sān-mihng*. This change causes many words to become homonyms, e.g. *sāang* 'alive' sounds identical to *sāan* 'hill' and *sān sāng-mihng* 'new life' would be pronounced as *sān sān-mihng* (see 1.1.3).

Note that the last three changes (f–h) all involve replacement of the velar nasal *ng*. If brought to completion, they would eventually lead to the loss of this sound from the language.

2 WORD STRUCTURE: MORPHOLOGY AND WORD FORMATION

Morphology is concerned with the internal structure of words – their form and composition. Cantonese would be described typologically as an **isolating** language, following a tradition developed in the nineteenth century and popularized by Sapir (1921), whereby languages are classified as inflectional, agglutinating or isolating in their word structure. Chinese in general, as Sapir noted, is one of the best examples of the isolating type: there is little, if any, inflection, and each syllable is a meaningful form (**morpheme**) in its own right.

None the less, the paucity or simplicity of morphology in Chinese has often been exaggerated, partly as a result of comparison with European languages and partly through the perception that each written character represents an independent word. The idea that words are single syllables has been termed the Monosyllabic Myth by de Francis (1984). While there are few inflections or derivational affixes, reduplication and compounding have been neglected. Reduplication refers to the process whereby a morpheme is repeated so that the original morpheme together with its repetition form a new word. Reduplication is particularly complex, applying to several parts of speech and performing a number of distinct grammatical functions. Compounding is also a very productive means of forming nouns, verbs and adjectives. Broadly defined, it refers to the process that puts two or more morphemes together to form a single word. Some morphemes are free, i.e. they can occur independently as a word while others are bound, i.e. they cannot occur independently but have to attach to another morpheme. There are three main means by which words are formed in Cantonese:

(a) affixation (**prefixes** and **suffixes**: 2.1)
(b) reduplication (doubling of words or syllables: 2.2)
(c) compounding (combination of independent forms to form a complex word: 2.3)

2.1 PREFIXES AND SUFFIXES

Prefixes and suffixes are usually **bound** forms which do not occur independently. Prefixes are attached to the beginnings of morphemes and suffixes to the ends of morphemes. However, what we consider as prefixes and suffixes in Cantonese may sometimes appear as independent forms. Thus they are quite versatile compared with affixes in other languages. Cantonese has relatively few prefixes and a small number of suffixes used to derive related words from stems. These are listed and illustrated in alphabetical order below.

2.1.1 PREFIXES

a- is a prefix used with names and kinship terms, denoting familiarity (20.3):

> a-Lái 'Mr Lai' (familiar: note changed tone of the surname *Làih*)
> a-Yīng (familiar form of names such as Méih-Yīng)
> a-màh 'grandmother'
> a-gō 'elder brother'
> a-yī 'aunt' (also used generically by children for adult female friends)

fáan- 'anti-', 'counter-' forms verbs, adjectives and nouns:

> fáan-gīk
> counter-attack
> 'counter-attack' (verb)

> fáan-waih
> turn-stomach
> 'feel-sick' (verb)

> fáan-mín
> turn-face
> 'change countenance, turn against someone' (verb)

> fáan-gwāt
> turn-bone
> 'disloyal, treacherous' (adj.)

> fáan-buhn
> turn-disloyal
> 'rebellious' (adj.)

> fáan-ginyíh 'counter-proposal' (noun)
> fáan-haauhgwó 'counter-effect' (noun)
> fáan-mihn 'opposite side, reverse' (noun)

hó- '-able' forms adjectives:

> hó-lìhn 'pitiable'   hó-làhng 'possible'
> hó-wu 'detestable'   hó-kaau 'reliable'
> hó-ngoi 'lovable, cute'   hó-pa 'dreadful'

hóu- 'good' and *làahn-* 'difficult' with verbs of perception form adjectives with positive and negative connotations respectively:

hóu-tái 'good to look at/see'   làahn-tái 'ugly'
hóu-tēng 'good to hear'   làahn-tēng 'bad-sounding'
hóu-sihk 'good to eat'   làahn-sihk 'bad-tasting'
hóu-màhn 'nice-smelling'   làahn-màhn 'smelly'
hóu-siu 'funny, amusing'

làahn- also forms negative adjectives meaning 'un . . . able':

làahn-chāk 'unpredictable'   làahn-mòhng 'unforgettable'
làahn-díng 'unbearable'   làahn-wán 'hard to find'

yih- 'easy' forms adjectives with the converse meaning:

yih-wán 'easy to find'   yih-tái 'easy to read, readable'

lóuh- means 'old' literally but when used as familiar terms of address (20.2), the literal meaning is lost:

lóuh-báan 'boss'   lóuh-yáuh 'mate, buddy'
lóuh-gūng 'husband, hubby'   lóuh-pòh 'wife, honey' (colloquial)

The negative prefix *m-* is added to adjectives and verbs:

m-syūfuhk 'uncomfortable, sick'
m-geidāk 'forget' (lit. 'not remember')
m-hahpgaak 'not qualified'
m-gin 'lose' (lit. 'not see')

The prefix *m-* is distinct from the negative *m̀h* marking sentence negation, although the distinction may be difficult to make in individual cases (see 13.1). For example, verbs prefixed with *m-* may take the aspect marker *jó* which is incompatible with *m̀h* (11.2.4):

Ngóh	mgin-jó	jek	gáu.	Léih	mgeidāk-jó	àh?
I	lose-PFV	CL	dog.	you	forget-PFV	PRT

'I lost my dog.'   'Have you forgotten?'

yáuh + noun, literally 'having [a property, attribute]' is a very productive means of forming adjectives:

yáuh-chín   yáuh-tīn-fahn
have-money   have-heaven-portion
'rich'   'talented, gifted'

yáuh-líu   yáuh-hohkmahn
have-material   have-knowledge
'substantial'   'learned, cultured'

yáuh-meih-lihk	yáuh-yìhng
have-charm-power	have-style
'charming'	'stylish' (person)

All these forms can take degree modifiers such as *hóu* 'very', *géi* 'quite', etc.:

hóu	yáuh-chín	géi	yáuh-tīn-fahn
very	have-money	quite	have-heaven-portion
'very rich'		'quite talented, gifted'	

móuh, the negative from of *yáuh* (15.4), forms adjectives similarly:

móuh-yuhng	móuh-líu-dou
not-have-use	no-material-arrive
'useless'	'vacuous' (person)

2.1.2 SUFFIXES

The major suffixes are listed according to their word class.

Noun suffixes

-deih is the plural suffix forming pronouns, but is *not* used with nouns, with the exception of *yàhn* (see 5.1):

ngóh-deih 'we/us'	kéuih-deih 'they'
léih-deih 'you (plural)'	yàhn-deih '(other) people'

-douh means 'degree' forming abstract nouns denoting measurements when attached to adjectives:[1]

gōu-douh	chèuhng-douh
tall-degree	long-degree
'height'	'length'
làahn-douh	jī-mìhng-douh
difficult-degree	known-name-degree
'level of difficulty'	'degree of fame'

-faat, which as a noun means 'law', serves as a suffix meaning 'way, method':

góng-faat	lám-faat
speak-way	think-way
'way of speaking'	'way of thinking'
tái-faat	jouh-faat
see-way	do-way
'point of view'	'way of doing things'

baahn-faat	yuhng-faat
solve-way	use-way
'solution, way out'	'usage, way of using'

-faat also appears in a discontinuous sequence with *dím* (*yéung*) 'how' and *gám* (*yéung*) 'this way' in describing or questioning a state of being or the way an action is performed.

Ngóh	hóu	séung	tái	háh	kéuih	**dím**	leng	**faat**.
I	much	want	see	DEL	her	how	pretty	way

'I very much want to see how beautiful she really is.'

Kéuih	**dím**	jínggú	léih	**faat**	a?
S/he	how	trick	you	way	PRT

'In what way did he trick you?'

-gā '-ist' is a personal suffix, denoting a specialist in a field:

jyūn-gā	síusyut-gā
special-ist	novel-ist
'specialist, expert'	'novelist'

wá-gā	yāmngohk-gā
picture-ist	music-ian
'painter'	'musician'

yúhyìhn-hohk-gā	souhohk-gā
linguistics-ist	mathematics-ian
'linguist'	'mathematician'

The suffix *-gā* suggests a certain distinction, so these terms are not applied lightly; *wágā*, for example, suggests a professional artist rather than an amateur. *jyūngā* may be preceded by the field of expertise, e.g. *gaauyuhk jyūngā* 'education expert'.

-gaau '-ism' forms names of religions (cf. below, discussion of *-jyúyi* '-ism' which forms different ideologies):

Faht-gaau	Gēidūk-gaau
Buddha-ism	Christ-ism
'Buddhism'	'Christianity'

Húng-gaau	Douh-gaau
Confucius-ism	Tao-ism
'Confucianism'	'Taoism'

Yandouh-gaau	Mōmùhn-gaau
India-ism	Mormon-ism
'Hinduism'	'Mormonism'

-gēi 'machine' is a productive suffix which continues to form new words:

sái-yī-gēi
wash-clothes-machine
'washing machine'

sāu-yām-gēi
receive-sound-machine
'radio'

dihnsih-gēi
television-machine
'television set'

luhkyíng-gēi
video-record-machine
'video cassette recorder'

yíng-díp-gēi
laser-disc-machine
'laser-disc player'

chyùhnjān-gēi
fax-machine
'fax machine'

-hohk forms names of fields of study:

séhwúi-hohk 'sociology'
jit-hohk 'philosophy'
sou-hohk 'mathematics'

sāmléih-hohk 'psychology'
mahtléih-hohk 'physics'
yúhyìhn-hohk 'linguistics'

-jái is a diminutive suffix, *X-jái* meaning 'little X':

bìhbī-jái 'baby'
syū-jái 'booklet'

māau-jái 'kitten'
tói-jái 'little table'

lóuhpòh-jái 'little wife' (also slang for 'girlfriend')
lóuhgūng-jái 'husband, hubby' (also slang for 'boyfriend')

-jái is also suffixed to names, typically suggesting intimacy or familiarity as with the names of children and teen idols:

Faat-jái (the film star Chow Yun-Faat)
Wah-jái 'Andy Boy' (the singer Andy Lau Dak Wah)

-jé is an agentive suffix also used in Mandarin (*-je*), indicating a person who performs an action:

sihwāi-jé
protest-person
'demonstrator, protester'

tàuhjī-jé
invest-person
'investor'

hohk-jé
learned-person
'scholar'

daai-kwán-jé
carry-germ-person
'carrier of a disease'

-jí is the Cantonese cognate of Mandarin *-zi*, but is not used as widely as *-zi* in Mandarin, which serves primarily to give a word two syllables:

Cantonese	Mandarin	
tói	zhuō-zi	'table'
dang	dèng-zi	'stool'
hàaih	xié-zi	'shoe'
maht	wà-zi	'sock'
beih(-gō)	bí-zi	'nose'

-jí appears obligatorily in a small number of words:

leuht-jí 'chestnut'	yin-jí 'swallow'
júng-jí 'seed'	sī-jí 'lion'
lìhn-jí 'lotus-seed'	faai-jí 'chopstick'
ké-jí 'eggplant'	faat-jí 'solution, method'
(yāt) fahn-jí 'a member'	daai-jí 'scallop'

With another group of words, *-jí* is optional:

sāam hòuh-(jí) 'three dimes'
laih-(jí) 'example'
móuh-mihn-jí *or* móuh-**mín** 'no face' (note the tone change)

-jyúyi forms names of ideologies or principles:

guhngcháan-jyúyi	séhwúi-jyúyi
commune-ism	society-ism
'communism'	'socialism'
héung-lohk-jyúyi	yùhnméih-jyúyi
enjoy-pleasure-ism	perfect-ism
'hedonism'	'perfectionism'

-léui is the female counterpart of *-jái* for human terms:

bìhbī-léui 'baby girl'	sailouh-léui 'girls' (children)
fā-léui 'bridesmaid'	
(lit. 'flower-girl')	

-lóu is a colloquial suffix for males, combining with nouns or adjectives:

gwái-lóu	yáuh-chín-lóu
devil-guy	have-money-guy
'(western) foreigner'	'rich guy'
daaih-lāp-lóu	fūng-séui-lóu
big-piece-guy	wind-water-guy
'big shot'	'geomancer'

-pòh is the female counterpart of *-lóu*:

gwái-pòh	mùih-yàhn-pòh
devil-woman	mediate-person-woman
'foreign (western) woman'	'matchmaker'

daaih-tóuh-pó
big-stomach-woman
'pregnant woman' (note tone change: *pòh* → *pó*)

baat-pòh (vulgar)
eight-woman
'nosy woman, gossip' (cf. baat-gwa 'nosy')

-séh denotes an organization:

chēut-báan-séh 'publisher'
léuih-hàhng-séh 'travel agency'

-sī denotes professions, contrasting with *-gā* (see above) which implies greater or more specialized expertise:

chyùh-sī	kèh-sī
kitchen-ist	ride-er
'chef'	'jockey'
gaau-sī	fēigēi-sī
teach-er	plane-ist
'teacher'	'pilot'
wuihgai-sī	chitgai-sī
account-ist	design-er
'accountant'	'designer'

-sing as an independent word means 'nature' or 'sex'; it combines with different parts of speech to form abstract nouns denoting the nature or state of being of the stem:

-sing attached to adjectives:
ngàih-hím 'dangerous' → ngàih-hím-sing 'danger'
juhng-yiu 'important' → juhng-yiu-sing 'importance'
yìhm-juhng 'serious' → yìhm-juhng-sing 'seriousness'

-sing attached to verbs:
gei-dāk → (hóu) gei-sing '(good) memory'
daahn → daahn-sing 'bounciness'

-sing attached to nouns:
móuh 'mother' → móuh-sing 'motherly nature'
yàhn 'person' → yàhn-sing 'human nature'
sau 'beast' → sau-sing 'beastly (animal) nature'
muhk 'wood' → muhk-sing 'wooden nature'
séui 'water' → séui-sing 'aquatic nature'[2]

-sing also forms adjectives in other cases (see adjectival suffixes).

-tàuh corresponds to Mandarin *-tou*, being related to *tàuh* 'head' and applying to various head-shaped items. As with the suffix *-jí* above, the distribution in Cantonese and Mandarin does not always coincide. In many words which in Mandarin require the suffix *-tou*, the Cantonese *-tàuh* is optional; in others, both Mandarin and Cantonese require the suffix:

Cantonese	Mandarin	
gwāt(-tàuh)	gútou	'bone'
muhk(-tàuh)	mùtou	'wood'
sehk(-tàuh)	shítou	'stone'
jūng(-tàuh)	zhōngtou	'hour'
maahn-tàuh	mántou	'steamed bread'
wuh-táu	yùtou	'taro' (root vegetable)
(note tone change)		

-tàuh is also used to form place expressions and localizers, as an alternative to *mihn/bihn* (7.1):

Cantonese	Mandarin	
nī-tàuh	zhèi-tou	'this end'[3]
gó-tàuh	nèi-tou	'that end'
ngoih-tàuh	wàitou	'outside'
chìhn-tàuh	qiántou	'in front'
léuih-tàuh	lítou	'inside'

Many words with *-tàuh* combine with *yáuh* to form adjectives:

yáuh   tái-tàuh
have   see-head
'presentable'

yáuh   lám-tàuh
have   think-head
'full of (good) ideas'

yáuh   pāai-tàuh
have   style-head
'stylish, classy'

yáuh   lòih-tàuh
have   come-head
'have fancy background'

yáuh   cheuk-tàuh
have   feature-head
'full of attractive features, marketable'

The fact that Cantonese makes less extensive use of the suffixes *-jí* and *-tàuh* than Mandarin does of *-zi* and *-tou* relates to the contrast in tones and final consonants. Mandarin has lost many of the final consonants which are preserved in Cantonese, and has four tones as opposed to six in Cantonese. Hence, the problem of **homophony** (identical-sounding words) is more severe in Mandarin; the addition of suffixes compensates for this (Li and Thompson 1981: 44). Cantonese is thus not under as much pressure to avoid homophony by having disyllabic words as Mandarin is.

Adjectival suffixes

-déi is a suffix used with reduplicated adjectives and stative verbs. Used as an adjective, the resulting form has a diminutive meaning similar to '-ish':

hùhng-húng-déi	chèuhng-chéung-déi
red-red-ish	long-long-ish
'reddish'	'pretty long'
hàhn-hán-déi	gēng-gēng-déi
itchy-itchy-ish	scared-scared-ish
'a little itchy'	'a bit scared'
mìhng-míng-déi	jī-jī-déi
understand-understand-bit	know-know-bit
'understand roughly'	'know a bit' (about facts)
seun-séun-déi	sīk-sīk-déi
believe-believe-bit	know-know-bit
'believe a bit'	'know a bit' (about a person)

Note the tone change of the second reduplicated element (1.4.2).

Reduplicated adjectives with the suffix *-déi* may also be used as adverbs (10.1.3):

Léih **hóu-hóu-déi** fan lā.
you good-good-ish sleep PRT
'Sleep well.'

Ngóh **màh-má-déi** jūngyi nī sáu gō jēk.
I so-so-ish like this CL song PRT
'I'm not too keen on this song.'

-sīk 'style' forms adjectives applied to furniture, cooking, etc:

Jūng-sīk 'Chinese-style'   Taai-sīk 'Thai-style'
sāi-sīk 'Western-style'   Faat-sīk 'French-style'

-sīk 'coloured' is used with colour terms when they actually denote colours:

hāk-sīk 'black'   hùhng-sīk 'red'
làahm-sīk 'blue'   luhk-sīk 'green'

The suffix *-sīk* is not used in the numerous metaphorical and idiomatic uses of colour words, such as *hāk* meaning 'dark, secret' as in *hāk síh* 'black market' and *hùhng* 'hot, fashionable' as in *daaih hùhng yàhn*, literally 'big red person', i.e. 'star' (in entertainment circles, politics, etc.).

-sing combines with different stems to form adjectives functioning like English *-y* in *lucky* and *-al* as in *seasonal* (see also *-sing* forming abstract nouns under 'Noun suffixes', above):

-sing attached to adjectives:

ngok 'malign' → ngok-sing láu
                 malignant tumour
                 'malignant tumour'

ngok-sing   chèuhnwàahn
vicious   cycle
'vicious cycle'

maahn 'slow' →   maahn-sing   behng
slow   disease
'chronic disease'

-sing attached to nouns:[4]

lihksí-sing   ge   sìhhāk
histor-ic   LP   moment
'a historic moment'

chyùhn-kàuh-sing   ngàihgēi
whole-world   crisis
'a global crisis'

geihseuht-sing (ge) mahntàih
technique   LP   problem
'technical problems'

gwaijit-sing ge   behng
season   LP   illness
'seasonal illness'

Verbal suffixes

-fa '-ize, -ify' is a causative suffix forming verbs from nouns and adjectives:

-fa with nouns:

fó-fa
fire-suffix
'incinerate, cremate'

dihnlóuh-fa
computer-ize
'computerize'

kātūng-fa
cartoon-ize
'cartoonize'

heikehk-fa
drama-ize
'dramatize'

-fa with adjectives:

yihndoih-fa
modern-ize
'modernize'

méih-fa
beauty-ify
'beautify'

luhk-fa
green-ify
'green-ify'

cháu-fa
ugly-ize
'make ugly'

These compounds are used especially in formal registers such as broadcasting, often with the *jēung* construction (comparable to Mandarin *bǎ*: 8.3.1) because they are not used transitively:[5]

Jingfú **jēung** Hēunggóng mahntàih **gwokjai-fa**.
government put Hongkong problem international-ize
'The government is internationalizing the Hongkong question.'

Dímgáai **jēung** gin sih **fūkjaahp-fa**?
why put CL matter complicate
'Why complicate the matter?'

Verb forms with the suffix -*fa* can also function as nouns, corresponding to nominalizations in English:

Jūnggwok ge yihndoih-fa   tàuhjī ge dōyùhn-fa
China LP modern-ize   investment LP plural-ize
'China's modernization'   'pluralization of investments'

In addition, the aspect markers *gán, jyuh, jó, gwo, hōi* (see ch. 11) would be regarded as suffixes under most criteria. In particular, they are **bound** forms (i.e. they may not occur without a verb), and may not be separated from the verb.[6] Verbal particles (11.3), by contrast, do not behave consistently as suffixes: although typically occurring directly after the verb which they modify, they may be separated from it by the negative *m̀h* or the modal *dāk*:

Ngóh **bōng** m̀h **dóu** léih.   *or*   Ngóh **bōng** léih m̀h **dóu**.
I help not V-PRT you   I help you not V-PRT
'I can't help you.'   'I can't help you.'

A few verb–particle combinations *must* be separated in this way, e.g. *syū . . . héi* and *díng . . . seuhn* 'tolerate':

Kéuihdeih **syū** dāk **héi**.
they lose can up
'They can afford to lose.'

Ngóh díng m̀h seun gó jahm meih.
I bear not V-PRT that CL smell
'I can't stand that smell.'

The verbal particles described in 11.3 are thus clearly not suffixes, although often written as such in the Yale system.

2.1.3 INFIXES

In colloquial Cantonese certain words may be infixed inside a morpheme (stem). The expletive *gwái* 'devil, ghost', used to emphasize adjectives

(9.1.2), may be infixed into not only single morphemes but also morpheme boundaries, compound words and phrases:

-gwái with a single morpheme:

> leuhnjeuhn → leuhn-gwái-jeuhn 'downright clumsy'
> gūhòhn 'mean, stingy' → gū-gwái-hòhn 'downright stingy'
> yuhksyūn 'ugly' → yuhk-gwái-syūn 'downright ugly'

-gwái between a stem (e.g. a verb) and another affix (e.g. aspect marker):

> kéuih   séi-gwái-jó   hóu   loih   la.
> s/he   die-devil-PFV   very   long   PRT
> 'He died a long time ago.' (Didn't you know?)

> Dī   mihn   béi   kéuih   sihk   gwái   saai   la.
> CL   noodles   by   him   eat   devil   all   PRT
> 'The noodles have been eaten up by him.'
> (Too bad, nothing left for you.)

-gwái with compound words:

> dō-yùh   →   dō-gwái-yùh
> much-extra   much-devil-extra
> 'a waste of time'   'a damn waste of time'

> māt-yéh   →   māt-gwái-yéh lèihga?
> what-stuff   what-devil-stuff PRT
> 'what'   'what on earth is this?'

> bīn-douh   →   bīn-gwái-douh?
> which-place   which-devil-place
> 'where'   'where on earth?'

Other expletive words, many more offensive than the relatively mild *gwái*, may be infixed similarly. *Gwái* is very versatile and can be used in many other contexts such as questions for rhetorical effects:

> Gwái   jī   mē?
> devil   know   PRT
> 'Only the devil knows.' (i.e. I don't know.)

> Gwái   m̀h   jī   àh?
> devil   not   know   PRT
> 'Only the devil doesn't know.' (i.e. Everybody knows.)

> Gwái   tùhng   lèih   heui!
> devil   with   you   go
> 'Only the devil will go with you.' (i.e. I won't go with you)

mātyéh 'what' (17.3.2) may be inserted into compound words, especially verb–object compounds, with the meaning 'What do you mean?' or 'What's the point?' to achieve a certain rhetorical effect:

pīn-sām 'biased' → Pīn-mātyéh-sām a?
'What do you mean, biased?'

duhk-syū 'study' → Duhk-mātyéh-syū a?
'What's the point in studying?'

matyéh (often shortened to *mī'eh* or *māt*) can also be followed by *gwái* in all contexts; moreover, the whole complex infix *māt-gwái-yéh*, whereby *gwái* is between *māt-* and *-yéh*, can be infixed productively. The following orders illustrate the different possibilities:

Cheung-māt(yéh)-gwái-gō?
sing-what-devil-song
'What do you mean, singing?'

Cheung-māt-gwái-yéh-gō?
sing-what-devil-stuff-song
'What do you mean, singing?'

Pīn-māt(yéh)-gwái-sām   a?
incline-what-devil-heart   PRT
'What do you mean, biased?'

Pīn-māt-gwái-yéh-sām   a?
incline-what-devil-stuff-heart PRT
'What do you mean, biased?'

In some other rhetorical expressions, *gwái* can be substituted for *mātyéh* with a different sentence-final particle:

Gwāan léih mātyéh sih   a?
concern you what   business PRT
'It's none of your business.'

→ Gwāan léih gwái sih   àh?
concern you devil business PRT
'It's none of your business.'

2.2 REDUPLICATION

Reduplication, the doubling of a word or syllable, is a characteristic and productive feature of Cantonese. It is particularly important in the modification of adjectives (9.2). However, many word classes can be reduplicated:

Classifiers (6.2.1, 14.1.2):

Jek-jek (māau) dōu leng.
CL-CL   (cat)   all pretty
'They (the cats) are all pretty.'

Stative verbs (8.1.2): *sīk* 'know' → *sīk-sīk-déi* 'know a little':

A: Léih sīk-m̀h-sīk   waaht-syut a?
you know-not-know   slide-snow PRT
'Do you know how to ski?'

B: Sīk-sīk-déi   je.
know-know-ish   PRT
'Just a little.'

Directional verbs (8.3.2): *séuhng-lohk* 'rise-fall' → *séuhng-séuhng-lohk-lohk*:

Nī   pàaih dī gúpiu séung-séung-lohk-lohk,
these days   CL share rise-rise-drop-drop

hóu làahn góng ga. (radio)
very hard   say   PRT
'These days shares are going up and down, it's hard to say.'

Adjectives (9.2):

sòh → sòh-só-déi   wàhn → wàhn-wán-déi
        silly-silly-ish   dizzy-dizzy-ish
        'rather silly'   'a little dizzy'

sāpseui → sāp-sāp-seui 'trivial' *or* sāp-sāp-seui-seui 'miscellaneous'

Compare the following:

Yāt go yuht gāau sei baak   mān   gúnléih
one CL month pay four hundred dollars management

fai, hóu **sāp-sāp-seui** jē.
fee very trivial   PRT
'Paying four hundred dollars of management fee per month is
nothing.'

Ngóh yáuh hóu dō   **sāp-sāp-seui-seui** ge yéh yiu dám.
I   have very many miscellaneous   LP stuff need dump
'I have a lot of miscellaneous stuff that I need to dump.'

As these examples show, the functions of reduplication are heterogeneous.
It typically serves to modify the meaning of the word, as in the case of
adjectives, but reduplication of classifiers denotes quantification.
Reduplication also occurs in A-not-A questions (17.1.2).

Reduplication often causes a change of tone. Reduplicated adjectives
with the suffix -*déi* take the changed tone on the second reduplicated
syllable (1.4.2):

fèih → fèih-féi-déi
fat   fat-fat-ish
         'rather fat'

A diminutive form of verbs is also formed by reduplication and tone
change, in this case affecting the first reduplicated syllable. These forms

are equivalent to (or contractions of) the construction [verb – *yāt* – verb] (see 11.2.6):

> si-yāt-si → sí-si
> try-one-try
> 'have a try'

> sou-yāt-sou → sóu-sou
> brush-one-brush
> 'have a brush'

> sóu-yāt-sóu → sóu-sóu
> count-one-count
> 'have a count'

Similarly with *léuhng* 'two':

> tái-léuhng-tái 'take a couple of looks'
> góng-léuhng-góng 'exchange a couple of words'

Reduplication also occurs in the construction [adjective – *yāt* – adjective] which serves to emphasize the adjective, and the contraction of *yāt* causes the first adjective to change tone:

> chìh yāt chìh → chí-chìh
> late one late
> 'very late'

> Fūng seun chí-chìh dōu meih gei dou.
> CL letter late-late still not mail arrive
> 'The letter hasn't arrived though it's very late already.'

> yeh yāt yeh → yé-yeh
> late night one
> 'very late at night'

> Go léui yé-yeh dōu meih fāan ūkkéi.
> CL daughter late-late still not-yet back home
> 'My daughter still hasn't returned home though it's so late at night.'

> leng yāt leng → léng-leng 'very beautiful'
> Kéuih dábaahn dou léng-leng sīn heui paaktō.
> s/he groom till pretty-pretty then go date
> 'She makes herself up beautifully before going on a date.'

Reduplication also appears in onomatopoeic expressions, often with tone change of the second syllable (see 1.4.2):

> ngàhng-ngáng-sēng
> mumble-mumble-noise
> '(make) a mumbling noise'

gohk-gók-sēng
knock-knock-sound
'(make) a knocking sound'

kàh-ká-sēng
chuckle-chuckle-sound
'(make) a chuckling sound'

These expressions with *sēng* form a very productive pattern and may function syntactically as verbs, nouns or adverbs, etc.:

Léih jouh māt **háidouh ngàhng-ngáng-sēng** a? (verb)
you do what here mumble-mumble-noise PRT
'What are you mumbling for?'

Ngóh yehmáahn tēng dóu **dī gohk-gók-sēng**. (noun)
I evening hear V-PRT some knock-knock-sound
'I heard a knocking sound at night.'

Kéuih **ngàhng-ngáng-sēng** **gám** hàahng yahp làih. (adverbial)
s/he mumble-mumble-noise so walk in come
'He came in making a mumbling noise.'

Go bìhbī siu **dou kàh-ká-sēng**. (resultative complement)
CL baby laugh till chuckle-chuckle-sound
'The baby is chuckling away.'

Further types of reduplication occur in **baby-talk** register, the language addressed to and used by small children; in particular, the object of verb–object compounds may be reduplicated:

heui gāai-gāai
go street-street
'go out'

yám lāai-lāai
drink milk-milk
'drink milk'

buhk lēi-lēi
catch hide-hide
'play hide and seek'

fan-gàauh-gāau *or* gàauh-gāau-jyū
'sleep'

Children also reduplicate common nouns (*wōu-wōu-gáu* 'doggie') and kinship terms, as in *yī-yī* 'auntie', *yèhyé* 'grandpa', etc.

An idiomatic type of reduplication involves the pattern verb – *gwái* – verb – *máh* or adjective – *gwái* – adjective – *máh* which is quite productive in colloquial Cantonese for rhetorical purposes:

Heui-gwái-heui-máh mē? Bīndouh dōu msái heui la. (film)
go-devil-go-horse PRT anywhere also no-need go PRT
'What's the point of going? There's no need to go anywhere.'

Sihk-gwái-sihk-máh mē? Lìhn yāt mān   dōu móuh.
eat-devil-eat-horse   PRT even one dollar also not-have
'No way to eat. Haven't got a dime.'

A: Kéuih yáuh móuh   pèhng dī maaih béi léih a?
   s/he   have-not-have cheap bit sell   to you PRT
   'Did she sell (it) to you at a cheaper price?'

B: Pèhng-gwái-péhng-máh,   juhng gwai-jó   tìm.
   cheap-devil-cheap-horse still expensive-PFV PRT
   'Not only no cheaper but even more expensive.'

2.3 COMPOUNDING

Very broadly defined, compounding is the combination of two or more independent morphemes to form a single new word, the meaning being not always predictable. For example, *chūng-lèuhng* 'wash-cool = shower' and *sihk-yīn* 'eat-cigarette = smoke' are compounds because they refer to single events and behave like single words in the ways described below. In contrast, *chūng chàh* 'make tea' and *sihk yeuhk* 'take medicine' are not considered compounds but treated as a phrase consisting of a verb and a direct object.

In Cantonese, as in English, compounding is a very productive means of forming nouns, adjectives and verbs. There are no cut-and-dry ways to differentiate compounds from non-compounds regardless of what criteria one invokes; the controversial linguistic issues related to compounding in Mandarin are discussed in Li and Thompson (1981). Below we discuss the properties of compounds according to their parts of speech.

Nouns (2.3.1):	ga-kèih	syut-gwaih
	leave-period	snow-cupboard
	'holiday'	'refrigerator'
Adjectives (2.3.2):	gōu-daaih	hāk-baahk
	tall-large	black-white
	'tall and sturdy'	'black-and-white'
Verbs (2.3.3):	gú-gai	hahp-jok
	guess-calculate	unite-work
	'estimate'	'cooperate'

In addition, verb–object compounds such as *diu-yú* 'catch-fish = fishing' are highly productive (see 2.3.3, 8.2.4).

2.3.1 COMPOUND NOUNS

In compound nouns the head noun (of which the compound denotes a type) may appear in either initial or final position. The following examples have their head in the final position:

jáu-dim wine-shop 'hotel'	jáu-làuh wine-flat 'restaurant'
yàhn-lihk person-strength 'man-power'	maht-lihk material-strength 'resources'
hēung-séui fragrant-water 'perfume'	hēung-pín fragrant-leaf 'jasmine (tea)'
hói-góng sea-harbour 'harbour'	hói-gíng sea-view 'sea-view'

Some compound nouns like food and animal terms have their head nouns in the initial positions (see Y-S. Cheung 1969):

yùh-sāang fish-raw 'raw fish'	jyū-yuhk-gōn pig-meat-dry 'pork jerky'
choi-gōn vegetable-dry 'dry vegetable'	ngàuh-yuhk-gōn cow-meat-dry 'beef jerky'
gāi-gūng chicken-male 'rooster'	gāi-lá chicken-female 'chicken'
jyū-gūng pig-male 'male pig'	jyū-lá pig-female 'female pig'

Note that the Mandarin counterparts of the animal nouns have the reverse order, e.g.:

gōng-jī male-chicken 'rooster'	mu-jī female-chicken 'chicken'

Other examples with the head in the initial position:

fùh-sáu	háu-hek
rest-hand	mouth-eat
'handrail, armrest'	'stuttering'

A common feature of compound nouns is the change of tone, whereby if the second element of a compound originally has a low-register or mid level tone, it changes to the mid/high rising tone (see 1.4.2):

jī 'resource' + **liuh** 'material' → jīlíu 'data, information'
jūnggāan 'middle' + **yàhn** 'person' → jūnggāan-**yán** 'middle-man'

As in English *gréen hóuse → gréenhouse*, where the change to a single stress indicates that the compound functions as a single word, the second element of the Cantonese compound loses its original low-register tone to show that it is no longer an independent word.

Compound nouns may also be formed by taking one syllable (not necessarily the first) from each of two bisyllabic nouns:

Hēunggóng Síujé → Góng-jé 'Miss Hongkong'
Ajāu Síujé → A-jé 'Miss Asia'
Hēunggóng Daaihhohk → Góng-daaih 'Hongkong University'
Jūngmàhn Daaihhohk → Jūng-daaih 'The Chinese University'

This is primarily a device of written Chinese, much used in political contexts:

Jūng-Góng mahntàih 'the China–Hongkong question'
(Jūnggwok 'China' + Hēunggóng 'Hongkong')

2.3.2 COMPOUND ADJECTIVES

Adjectives are formed from various combinations:

(a) adjective + noun → adjective:

chī-sām	hāk-sām
crazy-heart	black-heart
'infatuated'	'malicious'
síu-sām	fā-sām
small-heart	varying-heart
'careful'	'philandering'

(b) adjective + adjective: two adjectives may be juxtaposed to form an adjective expressing a combination of characteristics:

gōu-sām	syūn-laaht (tōng)
high-deep	sour-hot (soup)
'profound'	'hot-and-sour (soup)'

sāi-bāk	dūng-làahm
west-north	east-south
'northwest'	'southeast'

Note the order of the points of the compass, east/west coming before north/south.

(c) noun + adjective:

jih-sī	jih-daaih
self-private	self-big
'selfish'	'arrogant'
tóuh-ngoh	háu-hot/géng-hot
stomach-hunger	mouth-thirst/neck-thirst
'hungry'	'thirsty'

2.3.3 VERB–OBJECT COMPOUNDS

The process of **incorporation** of an object (see 8.2.4) in effect creates compound verbs, known as verb–object compounds. The resulting meaning often does not fully reflect that of the object, corresponding to an intransitive verb in English:

duhk-syū	tái-syū
study-book	look-book
'study'	'read'
hàahng-louh	yàuh-séui
walk-road	swim-water
'walk'	'swim'
jau-mèihtàuh	faat-pèihhei
wrinkle-eyebrow	produce-temper
'frown'	'get angry'

In other cases the combination has an idiomatic meaning, which is not predictable from the two parts:

haap-chou
sip-vinegar
'be jealous'

yám-chàh
drink-tea
'have tea' (denotes going to eat dim sum)

jáu-tòhng
leave-lesson
'skip classes'

cheut-māau
out-cat
'cheat' (in examinations, etc.)

hōi-dōu
open-knife
'carry out an operation'

sihk-yúhn-faahn
eat-soft-rice
'live off a woman'

Despite the close relationship between verb and object suggested by their meanings, these compounds may be separated in various contexts:

(a) aspect markers and verbal particles (11.2, 11.3) come between the verb and object:

duhk-gán-syū   duhk-yùhn-syū
study-PROG-book   study-finish-book
'(be) studying'   'finish studying'

yàuh-háh-séui   yàuh-fāan-séui
swim-DEL-water   swim-again-water
'have a swim'   'go swimming again'

(b) certain modifiers to the noun may be inserted:

yàuh-jóu-séui   yám-hah-ńgh-chàh
swim-early-water   drink-afternoon-tea
'go for a morning swim'   'have afternoon tea'

heui-yeh-gāai
go-evening-street
'go for an evening walk'

sihk-gwo yeh-jūk
'have eaten late-night congee'
(idiom: meaning to have served one's apprenticeship in a martial art)

yàuh-gōn-séui
swim-dry-water
'play mahjong' (idiom: refers to motion of mixing tiles)

(c) an expression of duration or frequency may intervene (8.2.5):

duhk léuhng go jūngtàuh **syū**
study two CL hour book
'study for two hours'

jáu géi chi **tòhng**
leave a-few time class
'skip classes a few times'

(d) certain idiomatic verb–object compounds may take a personal object
between the verb and noun:

faat ngóh **pèihhei**
produce me anger
'get angry at me'

cháau kéuih **yàuhyú**
fry him squid
'fire him' (employee)
(alternatively: *cháau kéuih yáu*, with tone change)

dahn kéuih **dōng-gū**
simmer him mushroom
'demote him' (employee)

(e) the compounds may be split up by topicalizing the object (see 4.2), e.g.

duhk-syū 'study':

Syū yātdihng yiu **duhk** dāk hóu sīn wán
book definitely need study ADV well first find

dóu hóu gūng.
V-PRT good job
'You must study well in order to get a good job.'

yìh-màhn 'emigrate':

Chín msái jaahn gam dō, **màhn** jauh yātdihng
money no-need earn so much emigrate then definitely

yiu **yìh**. (film)
need emigrate
'Never mind earning money, we have to emigrate.'

fan-gaau 'sleep':

Chàhm-máahn móuh **gaau** hóu **fan**. (film)
last-night not-have sleep good sleep
'I didn't sleep well last night.'

Verb–object compounds should be distinguished from compound verbs,
which are not separable in any of these ways:

dāam-sām	gwāan-sām
burden-heart	care-heart
'worry'	'be concerned (about)'
tàuh-jī	wán-sihk
throw-resources	seek-eat
'invest'	'make a living'

These compounds may not be separated, except by the infixed *mātyéh* 'what' (2.1.3):

Dāam-mātyéh-sām a? 'Why worry?'
Tàuh-mātyéh-gwái-jī? 'Why on earth invest?'

Certain verbs are variable, e.g. *teui-yāu* 'retire' and *yìhmàhn* 'emigrate' which may be separated or not:

teui-jó-yāu *or* teui-yāu-jó 'has retired'
yìh-jó-màhn *or* yìh-màhn-jó 'has emigrated'

It should be noted that verb–object compounds can function not only as intransitive verbs but also as noun phrases. They can occur in subject and object positions where noun phrases occur:

Chēut-māau   hóu   ngàihhím   ga.
out-cat   very dangerous   PRT
'Cheating is very dangerous.'

Ngóh m̀h séung tàih   chéng-yám   nī   yeuhng yéh.
I   not   want   mention invite-drink this   CL   thing
'I don't want to mention having a banquet.'

When a verb–object compound is separated by a classifier or measure phrase, the idiomatic meanings are often lost:

Ngóhdeih yám-jó   hóu   dō   būi   chàh.
we   drink-PFV very many CL   tea
'We drank many cups of tea.'

Kéuih sihk-jó   léuhng wún   faahn.
s/he   eat-PFV   two   bowl   rice
'She ate two bowls of rice.'

While *yám-chàh* as a verb–object compound means having dim sum idiomatically, *yám géi būi chàh* refers specifically to drinking tea. Similarly, *sihk-faahn* as a verb–object compound denotes having a meal, *sihk géi wún faahn* refers specifically to eating rice.

3 SYNTACTIC CATEGORIES: PARTS OF SPEECH IN CANTONESE

This grammar is arranged primarily by grammatical categories (parts of speech, such as nouns and verbs) and secondarily by functional and notional categories (action and motion, comparison, etc.). This grammatical organization is largely for the convenience of Western readers accustomed to these categories, and some explanation of the categories used is called for here.

Like the monosyllabic character of the language (see ch. 1), the difficulty of distinguishing parts of speech in Chinese has often been exaggerated, sometimes even to the point of denying that Chinese has distinct parts of speech in the Western sense. Cantonese is not very different from English in this respect. The dual status of **coverbs** (3.1.3) as verbs and prepositions has parallels in English: words such as *after* function both as prepositions (as in *after the party*) and as conjunctions (as in *after we left*).[1] Similarly, the fact that some adjectives may be used as verbs, as in *fèih-jó* 'has become fatter' is hardly more remarkable than the fact that English verbs such as *run* and *cut* may be used as nouns, or that *box* or *shell* may be used as verbs. Both English and Cantonese allow limited **conversion** of one part of speech to another. However, the two languages differ with respect to the range of possibilities of conversion. For example, while any verb in Cantonese can appear in subject and object positions without change in form, verbs in English generally take on affixes if they are to appear in these positions: *criticize* → *criticism*; *swim* → *swimming*; *destroy* → *destruction*.

English
   Swimming is good for you.
   He accepts your **criticism**.
   The **destruction** of the city is a sad story.

Cantonese
   Yàuh-séui   deui léih   sāntái hóu.
   swim-water   for   your   body good
   'Swimming is good for your body.'

   Kéuih jipsauh léih   ge **pāipìhng**.
   s/he   accept you   LP criticism
   'She accepts your criticism.'

Cantonese allows an extreme case of conversion involving the use of adjective–noun compounds:

leng 'good-looking' + jái 'boy' → lengjái 'handsome boy'
yìhng 'stylish' + jái 'boy' → yìhngjái 'stylish boy'
lēk 'clever, smart' + léui 'girl' → lēkléui 'clever girl'

The resulting nouns may be used as adjectives, which has no parallels in English:

Léih   go   jái   **géi**   **lengjái**   wo!
your   CL   son   quite   good-looking   PRT
'Your son's pretty good-looking!'

Kéuih   **hóu**   **yìhngjái**   bo!
he   very   stylish   PRT
'He's really got style.'

The compound adjectives may be used as verbs to denote change of state:

Gam   loih   móuh   gin,   lengjái-jó   wo!
so   long   not-have   see   handsome-PFV   PRT
'It's been a while since I saw you, you've become quite good-looking!'

Léih   sèhng   go   lēkléui-jó   wo!   (TV ad.)
you   whole   CL   clever-girl-PFV   PRT
'You've turned into quite a smart little girl!'

Such cases of conversion represent one reason why the parts of speech are difficult to pin down, forming a controversial area in Chinese linguistics.

On the other hand, the use of proper noun as predicative adjective in Cantonese does have parallels in English:

Kéuih   go   yàhn   hóu   a-Kīu   ga!
S/he   CL   person   very   ah-Q   PRT
'She is very ah-Q!' (Ah-Q is a character in Lǔxùn's novel who only cares for spiritual satisfaction despite being regarded by others as stupid)

Syntactically, *hóu a-Kīu* is comparable to *hóu lengjái* and *a-Kīu* can take any degree modifiers that an adjective can take. In English, with respect to style or art, brand names and proper names, for example, can occur in the same predicative positions:

That suit is really YSL!
He's so XO!   (TV ad.)
Jack and Annie are very Los Angeles!

Similar cases are possible in Mandarin, e.g. *tiānkōng fēicháng Xīlà* 'the sky is very Greece'. In these creative usages the proper nouns stand for characteristic properties with which they are conventionally associated.

3.1 COMPARABILITY OF SYNTACTIC CATEGORIES

The extent to which Chinese possesses the same range of parts of speech (syntactic categories) as the Indo-European languages has been the subject of much discussion in linguistics. The Chinese grammatical tradition recognizes a rather different set of categories. However, for English speakers it is useful to describe the language in terms of the familiar categories of European languages. Chao (1947: 41) makes some relevant remarks on this question:

> While Chinese grammar proper should deal only with the grammatical features which are found in the Chinese itself, an English-speaking student cannot help being concerned about how English grammatical categories will be translated in Chinese. This is a perfectly healthy state of mind, provided the student remembers the fact that every grammatical feature of one language does not necessarily correspond to some familiar feature of another language.

Thus, while the chapter and section headings of this book are designed to help the reader to find ways of expressing what is expressed by the relevant English parts of speech, they are not intended as a claim that these categories exist in Cantonese; indeed, there are several cases where the equivalence is questionable. Thus, when we speak of 'adjectives' we refer to the words which are expressed by adjectives in English and which may be thought of as adjectives in learning Cantonese; the use of the familiar term does not, however, imply that they should be regarded as a distinct category in analysing Cantonese on its own terms.

The following sections review the most important of these questions of correspondence. It will be seen that there are alternative views, which occasion some controversy within specific models and theories of grammar. The discussion involves complex linguistic arguments, and hence becomes relatively technical at times; readers not concerned with general linguistics may prefer to pass over these questions and use the familiar parts of speech merely as convenient labels.

3.1.1 VERBS VERSUS ADJECTIVES

The distinction between verb and adjective is not clearly drawn in Chinese. It can be argued that both belong to a single category of predicates, and indeed in traditional Chinese grammar, adjectives are treated as stative verbs. Alternatively, verbs and adjectives may be treated as separate categories; stative verbs are then intermediate between the two, sharing properties with both categories.

In many respects verbs and adjectives behave alike. Both can take aspect markers and verbal particles (see ch. 11):

béi-jó	sau-jó
pay/give-PFV	thin-PFV
'has paid/given'	'has become thinner'
tái-gwo	leng-gwo
see-EXP	pretty-EXP
'have seen before'	'used to be pretty'
wàahn fāan	hōisām fāan
return back	happy back
'return'	'be happy again'
sihk saai	wūjōu saai
eat V-PRT	dirty V-PRT
'eat up'	'all dirty'

These may be seen as cases of **conversion**, involving use of an adjective as a verb to represent a change of state.

The distinction between adjectives and stative verbs is particularly difficult to draw. Words which might seem to be adjectives can take objects like transitive verbs, such as the word *suhk* or *suhksīk* 'familiar' and *gánjēung* 'worried':

Ngóh mhaih hóu suhk kéuih.
I not-be very familiar him
'I don't know him very well.'

Sān Góngdūk yiu hóu suhksīk Jūng–Góng mahntàih.
new governor need very familiar-know China–HK question
'The new governor must be familiar with the China–Hongkong question.'

Kéuih hóu gánjēung dī léui.
s/he very nervous CL daughters
'She's very concerned about her daughters.'

Adjectives used as predicates are normally modified by an adverb such as *hóu* (see 9.1.2). However, this criterion does not distinguish adjectives from stative verbs, such as *jūngyi* 'like' and *tùhngyi* 'agree', which may also be modified with *hóu* providing that they represent gradable concepts:

hóu jūngyi	hóu tùhngyi
very like	very agree
'very much like'	'very much agree'

Further, reduplication of adjectives with *-déi* (9.2.2) also applies to some stative verbs:

Adjectives	Stative verbs
sòh-só-déi 'a little silly'	sīk-sīk-déi, jī-jī-déi 'know a little'
chī-chī-déi(-sin) 'a bit crazy'	mìhng-míng-déi 'understand a little'

Constructions such as questions with extent complements *sèhng* or *sìhng* (17.3.7) occur with either verbs or adjectives:

Tái-háh **sái** **sèhng** dím.
see-DEL wash extent how
'Let's see how well it's washed.'

Tái-háh kéuih **leng** **sèhng** dím.
see-DEL s/he pretty extent how
'Let's see how pretty she is.'

To summarize, if verbs and adjectives are treated as distinct categories, as in this book, then it must be acknowledged that:

(a) Adjectives and verbs share many common characteristics, and may appear in many of the same constructions.
(b) In particular, adjectives denoting states may be used as verbs denoting change of state.
(c) Stative verbs, in the narrow sense used here (see 8.1.2), are intermediate between verbs and adjectives in their grammatical properties.

3.1.2 VERBS AND AUXILIARIES

Whereas English auxiliary verbs such as *can* and *will* are distinguished by morphological and syntactic properties, their Cantonese counterparts behave for the most part like other verbs.[2]

Functionally, there are **modal** auxiliary verbs such as *wúih* 'will, would', *hóyíh* 'can' (12.1). Unlike other verbs, they do not take aspect markers or verbal particles, and must be accompanied by a main verb to form a complete sentence. Auxiliaries are used alone only when a main verb is clearly given in the context:

A: Bīngo **wúih** **jūngyi** nī júng yàhn ge jēk?
who would like this kind person PRT PRT
'Who would like a person like that?'

B: Kéuih jauh **wúih** laak.
s/he then would PRT
'She would.'

A: A-Léun daih-yih-sìh saht **faat-daaht**.
Ah-Leun another-time sure make-money
'Leun is sure to make money in the future.'

B: Kéuih jauh gánghaih séung lā.
he then of-course wish PRT
'He'd like to, of course.'

3.1.3 COVERBS/PREPOSITIONS

Whether prepositions exist in Chinese is also an open question. Functionally, the role of prepositions in expressing relationships between noun phrases is played by two different types of word: 'coverbs' and 'localizers' (see 3.1.4 below). Coverbs are so called because they typically occur together with another verb, the coverb and its object serving to modify the following verb:

Ngóh **tùhng** kéuih **paak-gán-tō**.
I with him date-PROG
'I'm going out with him.'

Kéuih **hái** gódouh **yíng-séung**.
s/he at there take-photo
'She's over there taking a photo.'

Although the coverb functions like a prepositional phrase in English, this pattern resembles the serial verb construction which is a basic feature of Chinese syntax (8.3). The question thus arises whether the coverbs are functioning as prepositions or merely as verbs. The main Cantonese coverbs at issue are:

béi 'to' (giving)	heung 'towards' (direction)
bōng 'for' (helping)	tùhng 'with' (together with)
deui 'to, towards'	waih(jó) 'for the sake of'
gān (jyuh) 'with, following'	wán 'with, using'
gīng 'via' (itinerary)	yuhng 'with' (instrumental)
hái, héung 'at' (location)	

The meanings given above refer to the 'prepositional' functions of the coverbs. Many of them also have distinct meanings as main verbs, e.g. *béi* 'give', *wán* 'look for', *gān* 'follow', *gīng* 'pass by'. Even in those contexts where they correspond to prepositions in English, these words behave like verbs in many respects. Apart from *tùhng*, they may readily occur without a following verb:

Luhk Sāang yìhgā **hái** hohkhaauh.
Luk Mr now at school
'Mr Luk is at school now.'

Go jái sèhngyaht dōu **gānjyuh** kéuih lóuh-dauh.
CL son always all follow his old-dad
'The son always goes around with his dad.'

The coverbs may take aspect markers such as *jó* and verbal particles such
as *dóu*:

Aspect markers (11.1)
Ngóh **tùhng-gán** kéuih góng yéh.
I with-PROG her talk things
'I'm talking to her.'

Léih **hái-gwo** ngóh ūkkéi fan meih?
you at-EXP my house sleep not-yet
'Have you ever slept in my house?'

Ngóh **gān-hōi** kéuih jouh-yéh.
I with-HAB her do-work
'I'm used to working with her.'

Verbal particles (11.3)
Ngóh **tùhng** **m̀h** **dóu** léih heui.
I with not V-PRT you go
'I can't go with you.'

Ngóh dī jái **hái** **saai** ngoihgwok.
my CL boy at all foreign-country
'All my sons are abroad.'

Léih **gān** **màaih** ngóh heui lā.
you with V-PRT me go PRT
'Come along with me.'

They may also be reduplicated in an A-not-A question, like verbs and
adjectives:

Léih tùhng-m̀h-tùhng ngóh heui a?
you with-not-with me go PRT
'Are you going with me?'

The potential construction with *dāk* (12.3.2) may occur with coverbs:

Ngóh **m̀h** **tùhng** dāk léih git-fān. (film)
I not with able you marry
'I can't marry you.'

Ngóh **m̀h** **hái** dāk Hēunggóng chèuhng jyuh.
I not at able Hongkong long live
'I can't live in Hongkong for very long.'

The use of reduplicated adjectives as adverbs (10.1.3) also occurs modifying coverbs:

Léih hóu-hóu-déi deui ngóh (go) múi lā. (film)
you good-good-ish to my (CL) sister PRT
'Be good to my (younger) sister.'

Léih gwāai-gwāai-déi hái ūkkéi lā.
you good-good-ish at home PRT
'Be good and stay home.'

All these properties are typical of verbs rather than prepositions. What they suggest is that in so far as prepositions exist in Cantonese, they are a subclass of verbs which may be used as prepositions. Alternatively, the coverbs may be regarded as verbs in all their manifestations, in which case their characteristic use as 'coverbs' invariably involves a serial verb construction (as argued by McCawley 1992 with respect to Mandarin).

3.1.4 LOCALIZERS/POSTPOSITIONS

The words known in Chinese linguistics as **localizers** are expressions of location which may, and in some cases must, be accompanied by the morphemes *mihn* 'face' or *bihn* 'side' (apart from *deuimihn*, *bihn* or *mihn* are used interchangeably):

seuhng (mihn/bihn) 'above'   hah (mihn/bihn) 'under'
chìhn (mihn/bihn) 'in front of'   hauh (mihn/bihn) 'behind'
yahp-mihn/bihn 'inside'   chēut-mihn/bihn 'outside'
léuih-mihn/bihn 'within, among'   deui-mihn 'opposite'

In general, these expressions serve two main functions:

(a) as adverbs of location (7.1):

Dī fā **hái yahpbihn.**
CL flowers at inside
'The flowers are inside.'

Yahpbihn yáuh hóu dō fā.
inside have very many flowers
'There are lots of flowers inside.'

(b) following a noun phrase, like postpositions. In this function, they are typically used in conjunction with the locative coverb *hái* (3.1.3). Thus the basic expression of location is coverb – noun – localizer:

hái léih hauhbihn   hái hohkhaauh deuimihn
at you behind   at school   opposite
'behind you'   'opposite the school'

Since *mihn* can be used independently as a noun meaning 'face', the localizers which contain them can be argued to be nouns (see Y-H.A. Li 1990). The typical locative structure illustrated above may therefore be analysed as preposition–noun–postposition, verb–noun–postposition, preposition–noun–noun or verb–noun–noun. The use of these constructions is discussed in chapter 7.

3.1.5 CLASSIFIERS

An important part of speech absent in English are the noun classifiers, also known as measure words. In English, measures such as *pound* and *foot* are clearly nouns, and are used only with uncountable (mass) nouns, as in *a pound of flesh* and *a foot of cloth*. Cantonese classifiers are a distinct category of words which are used not only to express quantities of mass nouns, but also in counting and referring to countable nouns:

léuhng	bohng	ngàuh-yuhk	sāam	jek	gáu
two	pound	ox-meat	three	CL	dog
'two pounds of beef'			'three dogs'		

Moreover, in the case of countable nouns, the choice of classifier is determined by the noun, as *jek* goes with *gáu* 'dog'. In addition to these counting and quantifying functions, classifiers are grammatically required in certain contexts such as with demonstratives (6.2.1):

nī	go	mahntàih	gó	dī	hohksāang
this	CL	problem	those	CL	student
'this problem'			'those students'		

Classifiers also have more specialized grammatical functions, such as in possessive constructions (6.3), relative clauses (6.4) and in the expression of quantification (14.1.2).

3.1.6 ADVERBS

Cantonese uses a number of constructions to express adverbial modification; there is no single means of forming adverbs comparable to -*ly* in English. The closest Cantonese comes to forming adverbs from adjectives is the use of reduplicated adjectives, with or without the suffix -*déi* (9.2.2), as adverbs (10.1.3):

maahn-máan	hàahng	hóu-hóu-déi	fan
slow-slow	walk	good-good-ish	sleep
'go slowly'		'sleep well'	

However, since such reduplicated forms are also used as adjectives, reduplication cannot be termed categorically a means of forming adverbs.

Adverbial modification of verbs is also expressed by adjectives in specific constructions:

(a) the construction [verb] – *dāk* – [adjective] (10.1.1):

> Go sīgēi jā dāk taai faai.
> CL driver drive ADV too fast
> 'The driver's going too fast.'

(b) [adjective] – *gám* – [verb] (10.1.2):

> Go sailouhjái hóu daaih-sēng gám góng-yéh.
> CL kid very big-voice so speak-things
> 'The kid spoke very loudly.'

Adverbs which modify the sentence (as opposed to the verb phrase alone) may be divided into two groups according to their placement in the sentence. Adverbs of quantity such as *juhng* 'still' and *dōu* 'also' must come directly before the verb:

> Léih juhng yíhwàih móuh sih àh?
> you still think not-have matter PRT
> 'You still think there's nothing wrong, do you?'

Time words reduplicated to form adverbs of frequency, e.g. *lìhn-lìhn* 'every year' (10.3.4) also come before the verb. A second group of sentence adverbs such as *yìhgā* 'now' and *waahkjé* 'perhaps' are sometimes known as 'movable' adverbs, since they may come either immediately before the verb or at the beginning of the sentence:

> Ngóh yìhgā fāan hohkhaauh la.
> I now return school PRT
> 'I'm going to school now.'

> Yìhgā dī léuihjái yuht làih yuht làhnggon.
> now CL girls more come more capable
> 'Nowadays girls are increasingly capable.'

3.1.7 VERBAL AND SENTENCE PARTICLES

There are two sets of items in Cantonese which are treated here as **particles**:

(a) verbal particles: [verb] – *dóu, yùhn, saai*, etc. (11.3), as in *sāu dóu* 'receive', *sihk yùhn* 'finish eating';
(b) sentence particles: *a, lā, mē* etc. (ch. 18).

The Mandarin words corresponding to the verbal particles (a) are also termed **resultative verbal complements** in Li and Thompson (1981) and some linguistic studies. These particles resemble those found in English

phrasal verbs such as *fill up* and *put off*. Since most of the Cantonese particles concerned also exist as verbs, e.g. *dou* 'arrive' and *fāan* 'return', it might be argued that they do not constitute a distinct syntactic category. However, several particles are *not* used as verbs, for example *hōi* meaning 'away' and *dóu* denoting accomplishment. In this respect, the status of these items is comparable to the particles of English phrasal verbs: many, such as *up* and *off*, are also used as prepositions, but others such as *away* and *out* (in British English) are not.

The rich set of particles (b) which occur primarily at the end of a sentence are one of the most distinctive features of Cantonese. They serve to indicate speech-act types such as questions and requests, attitudinal factors and emotional colouring. These have no direct counterpart in English, although comparable in function to question tags such as *right?* and *do you?* In theoretical frameworks it has been argued that the particles belong to the category COMP (Complementizer; see e.g. Law 1990; Law and Neidle 1992). The category COMP in syntactic theory contains expressions like the English conjunction *that*, which has no counterpart in Cantonese; this complementary distribution lends some plausibility to the analysis of particles as sentence-final complementizers.

3.1.8 CONJUNCTIONS

Spoken Cantonese does not readily conjoin phrases as English does with *and* (many conjunctions used in written Chinese do not occur in speech). Conjunction is typically expressed by juxtaposition of phrases, without explicit marking of their relationship. In these cases, the connection between the conjoined items must be inferred from the content of the phrases and the context. A juxtaposition of two nouns or verbs may be read as conjunction or disjunction:

Léih hái Yīnggwok yáuh-móuh **chānchīk pàhngyáuh** a?
you in England have-not-have relatives friends PRT
'Do you have relatives or friends in England?'

Such juxtaposition is especially typical of fixed expressions, such as the following phrases used of share prices:

máaih	maaih	ga		móuh	héi	dit
buy	sell	price		not-have	rise	fall
'buying and selling prices'				'no rise or fall'		

Similarly, a sentence consisting of two juxtaposed clauses may be interpreted as a conditional sentence (see 16.3):

Léih m̀h séung dōu yiu heui ge la.
you not want also need go PRT PRT
'Even if you don't want to go, you still have to.'

Although there is no general-purpose conjunction corresponding to *that*, there are more specific conjunctions such as *yānwaih* 'because' and *sēuiyìhn* 'although'. These, however, differ substantially from their English counterparts in that they require a matching conjunction in the following main clause:

yānwaih . . . sóyíh 'because . . . so'
sēuiyìhn . . . daahnhaih 'although . . . but'
yùhgwó . . . jauh 'if . . . then'
jauhsyun . . . dōu 'even if . . . still'

These pairs are sometimes known as **double conjunctions**; similar constructions, such as *although . . . but . . .* , are a common feature of Chinese speakers' English. These sentence types and the usage of conjunctions are discussed in chapter 16.

4 SENTENCE STRUCTURE: WORD ORDER AND TOPICALIZATION

As a language with little grammatical morphology, Cantonese relies heavily on word order to express grammatical relations such as subject and object. As a result, word order is fairly rigid, as it is in English for similar reasons. Like other isolating languages, Cantonese has the basic word order [subject–verb–object], or is said to be an SVO language (4.1.1). The main sources of deviation from this rigid order are:

(a) [subject–object–verb] order (4.1.1);
(b) [verb–subject] order or subject–verb inversion (4.1.2);
(c) **right-dislocation**, which involves putting an element last or adding it separately from the rest of the sentence (4.1.3);
(d) **topicalization**: the possibility of making various elements of a sentence the sentence **topic** by placing them first (4.2).

Another typological feature of Cantonese is known as topic-prominence. The distinction between subject-prominent and topic-prominent languages was introduced by Li and Thompson (1976), who consider Mandarin Chinese as a prime example of a topic-prominent language. This distinction is an elaboration of an insight expressed by Chao (1968), who noted that the basic Chinese sentence structure consists not of subject–predicate, but of topic–comment. The **topic** is a phrase which the **comment** says something about. The sentence topic in this sense need not be the subject, and indeed need not bear any grammatical relation to the comment:

Gwo hói àh, deihtit jeui faai.
cross sea PRT underground most fast
'As far as crossing the harbour is concerned, the underground
is fastest.'

The relationship between *gwo hói* 'crossing the harbour' and the undergound being fast is a semantic one of association: this is a typical topic-comment relationship in Cantonese, which in English can only be expressed by an elaborate periphrasis with *as far as* . . . Note also that the topic in the Cantonese example is separated from the comment by the particle *àh* and a slight pause.

The presence of such grammatical constructions makes Cantonese a 'topic-prominent' language. The value of this classification is that it relates several other properties to the role of the sentence topic. A number of grammatical features relate to the role of the topic in the structure of the sentence, including the omission of subject and object pronouns where these refer back to a topic already mentioned or understood (4.2.5) and the constraint that subjects must be definite (see 4.2.4) as well as topicalization constructions themselves (4.2).

4.1 BASIC WORD ORDER

4.1.1 SUBJECT, VERB AND OBJECT

One respect in which Cantonese grammar resembles English is the word order of the simple sentence: subject–verb–object. Since there are no distinctions of case, even in pronouns, the word order alone indicates these grammatical relations:

Ngóh	ngoi	kéuih.	Kéuih	ngoi	ngóh.
I	love	him/her	s/he	love	me
'I love her.'			'She loves me.'		

At the same time, the freedom of word order is rather greater than in English. In particular, several regular patterns deviate from the SVO form:

(a) Subject–object–verb (in secondary topicalization (4.2.3) and in constructions with *dōu* (8.2.3, 14.1)):

Ngóh	Yīnggwok	meih	heui-gwo.
I	England	not-yet	go-EXP
'I haven't been to England.'			

Ngóh	fūk-fūk	wá	dōu	séung	máaih.
I	CL-CL	picture	all	want	buy
'I want to buy all the pictures.'					

(b) Object–(subject)–verb (topicalization of the object: see 4.2)

Gāmyaht	ge	sung	ngóh	yíhgīng	máaih-jó	la.
today	LP	food	I	already	buy-PFV	PRT
'I've already bought food for today.'						

Dī	sāam	maaih	saai	la.
CL	clothes	sell	all	PRT
'The clothes have all been sold.'				

Note that the subject may or may not be present.

As in English, the subject may be separated from the verb by adverbs and other adverbial phrases:

Kéuih	**sèhngyaht**	**dōu**	góng	siu	ge.
s/he	always	all	speak	joke	PRT
'He's always making jokes.'					

Ngóh **hah** **go** **sīngkèih** fong-ga.
I next CL week take-leave
'I'm going on leave next week.'

By contrast, the object (unless topicalized) must follow the verb immediately; the only items which may intervene are aspect markers, verbal
particles and expressions of duration or frequency:

Ngóh faatyihn-**jó** yāt go beimaht. (*jó* = aspect marker)
I discover-PFV one CL secret
'I've discovered a secret.'

Kéuih yíhgīng duhk **yùhn** syū. (*yùhn* = verbal particle)
s/he already study finish book
'She's finished her studies.'

Ngóh hohk-jó **baat** **lìhn** Yīngmán. (*baat lìhn* = duration
I learn-PFV eight years English phrase)
'I've been learning English for eight years.'

Ngóhdeih gin-gwo **géi** **chi** mihn. (*géi chi* = frequency
we see-EXP a-few times face phrase)
'We've met a few times.'

4.1.2 VERB–SUBJECT ORDER

With certain types of intransitive verbs, what appears to be the subject
appears after the verb:

(1) with verbs of motion:

Gāmyaht làih-jó hóu dō daaih lāp-lóuh.
today come-PFV very many big shot-guys
'A lot of big shots came today.'

Yíhchìhn dit-gwo géi go sailouhjái lohk gāai.
before fall-EXP a-few CL children down street
'In the past quite a few children have fallen down onto the street.'

(2) with weather verbs:

Yìhgā **lohk**-gán **yúh**.
now fall-PROG rain
'It's raining now.'

The [subject–verb] order is also available:

Yúh **lohk** dāk hóu daaih.
rain fall ADV very big
'It's raining hard.'

Similarly, both verb-subject and subject-verb orders are possible with the following:

Kàhmyaht **dá** **daaih** **fūng** chēut m̀h dóu gāai.
yesterday blow big wind out not V-PRT street
'Yesterday it was so windy that we couldn't go out.'

Ngoihmihn **fūng dá** dāk hóu daaih.
outside wind blow ADV very big
'The wind is blowing strongly outside.'

(3) with verbs of appearance, disappearance and occurrence:

Gām jīu faatsāng-jó yāt gihn gwaai sih.
this morning happen-PFV one CL strange matter
'Something strange happened this morning.'

Gāmyaht chēutyihn-jó yāt tìuh sāyùh.
today appear-PFV one CL shark
'A shark appeared today.'

(4) with the verb *séi* 'die':

alternatively:

Kéuih séi-jó lóuhdauh.
s/he die-PFV father
'She lost her father.'

Kéuih lóuhdauh séi-jó.
s/he father die-PFV
'She lost her father.'

The inverted order is also used when *séi* is used as an emphatic verbal particle (11.3.2):

Ngoh séi kéuih la!
hunger die her PRT
'She's starving!'

Muhn séi yàhn la!
bore die people PRT
'Everyone's bored to death!'

The above (1–4) are clearly related: all involve verbs which denote a change of state or location. The noun phrase which undergoes the change of state is invariably expressed as the subject in English; however, it may appear in Cantonese either after the verb (as in the (a) examples below) or before the verb (introduced by *yáuh* if indefinite), as in the (b) examples:

(a) Gāmyaht faatsāng-jó yāt gihn gwaai sih.
today happen-PFV one CL strange matter
'Something strange happened today.'

(b) Gāmyaht yáuh yāt gihn gwaai sih faatsāng-jó.
today have one CL strange matter happen-PFV
'Something strange happened today.'

(a) Tòih seuhng chēutyihn-jó yāt go yàhn.
stage upon appear-PFV one CL person
'On the stage appeared a man.'

(b) Yáuh yāt go yàhn chēutyihn-jó hái tòih seuhngmihn.
    have one CL person appear-PFV at stage upon
    'A man appeared on the stage.'

The verbs involved in (1–4) above are known as **ergative** verbs. According to the 'ergative' analysis (see Y-H.A. Li 1990 for Mandarin), the noun phrase bearing the role of **theme** or **experiencer** of the action is the underlying object of the predicate, hence its occurrence after the verb, in object position, in the (a) sentences. In the (b) sentences, the same noun phrase appears as subject, introduced by *yáuh* 'have' if it is indefinite (see 4.2.5).

4.1.3 RIGHT-DISLOCATION

Another departure from the typical SVO word order in colloquial speech is *right-dislocation*. Typically, a noun or pronoun which is the subject of a clause appears at the end of a sentence in a so-called **dislocated** position:

Hóu lēk wo, **léih!**
very smart PRT you
'You're so smart!'

Chīsin gàh, **léih!**
crazy PRT you
'You're crazy!'

Géi leng wo, **dī sāam.**
quite nice PRT CL clothes
'Not bad, those clothes.'

Móuh-líu-dou gé, **bún syū.**
no-substance PRT CL book
'Pretty vacuous, that book.'

As these examples suggest, this word order is typically used in exclamations, when the predicate is placed first for emphasis and the subject added to complete the sentence. The same position may also be used for objects:

Yáuh-móuh máaih a, **ga chē?**
have-not-have buy PRT CL car
'Did you buy that car?'

Note that the dislocated subject or object follows even the sentence particle, which would normally come at the end of the sentence or clause (18.2). This is also a common position for modal verbs and adverbs (see 12.1, 12.2), which are often added as afterthoughts:

Kéuih ngāam-ngāam jung-jó tàuh jéung, saht máaih
s/he just-just win-PFV first prize sure buy

gāan daaih ūk lā, **wúih.** (TV)
CL big house PRT will
'She just won the first prize; she will surely buy a big house.'

A: Léih   gòhgō   hái bīn   a?
   your   brother   is   where   PRT
   'Where's your brother?'

B: Fāan-jó   ūkkéi,   dōsou.
   return-PFV   home   probably
   'Gone home, probably.'

4.2 TOPICALIZATION AND TOPIC PROMINENCE

Chao (1968) and Li and Thompson (1976, 1981) pointed out an important contrast between Chinese and English in the status of subjects and topics. In English, it is a grammatical requirement that every sentence must have a subject. Hence, a subject does not always represent the performer of an action (**agent**) or what the sentence is about (**topic**); when there is no such notional subject present, the expletive or 'dummy' subject *it* is used, as in *It is forbidden to smoke*. In Chinese, there is no pronoun corresponding to *it* in this sense, and many sentences lack an overt subject.[1]

The role of **sentence topic**, however, is central to Chinese grammar. The notion of sentence topic with reference to Chinese is a grammatical notion, referring to a position in the sentence with particular properties (normally the initial position; an exception is secondary topicalization: see 4.2.3). It should be distinguished from the notion of **discourse topic**, which refers to the overall topic of a text or conversation in the everyday sense, and is equally applicable to all languages. Li and Thompson try to relate the sentence topic to the discourse context by requiring that it represent 'old' information, i.e. something already referred to in the text. However, a 'new' topic of discourse may be introduced as a sentence topic. Nor is the sentence topic necessarily what the sentence is 'about', although this is typically the case. A more general definition given by Chafe is useful: 'the topic sets the spatial, temporal or other framework in which the predication holds' (Chafe 1976). That is, the topic specifies the time, place or circumstances to which the rest of the sentence applies.

As Chao (1968) points out, the notion topic–comment includes that of subject–predicate: within Chinese grammar, the subject–predicate construction is a special case of topic–comment. Hence, if no other element is topicalized, the subject becomes the topic by default. In a simple sentence with the order subject–verb–object, such as *ngóh ngoi kéuih* illustrated in 4.1.1, the subject *ngóh* serves simultaneously as the topic.

4.2.1 TOPICALIZATION

Topicalization in general refers to the placement of a word or phrase at the beginning of a sentence or clause, making it the **sentence topic**. The effect is similar to that of the English construction *as for . . .* or *as far as . . . is concerned*. For example:

Chín   ngóh   bōng léih m̀h dóu   laak. (film)
money I   help you not V-PRT PRT
'As far as money's concerned I can't help you.'

In discussions of Chinese syntax sentences with topicalized elements are often glossed in this way, although it often does not result in an idiomatic English translation.

The most common and straightforward form of topicalization is that in which the object of the verb is displaced at the beginning of the sentence:

Nī dī yéh   móuh yàhn   sīk   ge.
this CL stuff no   person knows PRT
'No one knows this stuff.'

Jēung jí   léih fong hái bīn   a?
CL   paper you put at where PRT
'Where did you put the piece of paper?'

Topicalization of an object is also widely used without a subject, where the implicit subject is unknown or generic:

Gám yéung ge yéh   m̀h yīnggōi góng ge.
such type   LP   thing not should say   PRT
'One shouldn't say such things.'

Ga chē jíng   hóu   la.
CL car make good PRT
'The car's been repaired.'

Note that English typically uses the passive to make the object the subject (and thereby topic) of the sentence, where Cantonese simply topicalizes the object. Such topicalizations thus often correspond to passives in English. Li and Thompson (1976) note that the relatively restricted use of the passive is a further characteristic of topic-prominent languages; it should be noted, however, that Cantonese also has some passive constructions which are not possible in English (8.4.1).

One of the main communicative functions of topicalization, in Cantonese as in English, is to contrast the topicalized word or phrase with another which is mentioned or implied in the context:

Syū Baak Dahk ngóh sèhngyaht tēng   ge,   **Syū Maahn**
Schubert   I   always   listen PRT, Schumann

jauh síu dī   la.
then little-er PRT
'I listen to Schubert a lot, Schumann rather less.'

Góngdaaih ngóh kàhmyaht heui-gwo, **Jūngdaaih**
HK-University I yesterday go-EXP Chinese-University

jauh meih heui-gwo.
then not-yet go-EXP
'I went to Hongkong University yesterday, but I haven't been to the Chinese University yet.'

(Note the formation of *Góngdaaih* from *Hēunggóng Daaihhohk* 'Hongkong University': see 2.3.1.)

4.2.2 DOUBLE SUBJECTS AND HANGING TOPICS

One of the more striking 'topic-prominent' features of Cantonese is the possibility of sentence topics having no grammatical relation to the predicate:

Yìhgā ge tīnhei jeui yih sēung-fūng. (TV ad.)
now LP weather most easy catch-cold
'It's easy to catch a cold in this weather.'

The topic *yìhgā ge tīnhei* is not the subject of any action, but indicates the circumstances ('in this weather') to which the predicate 'It's easy to catch cold' applies. A subtype of such sentences are sometimes known as double subject constructions, as they appear to have two subjects:

Hēunggóng làuhga gwai dou séi.
Hongkong flat-price dear till die
'Flat prices in Hongkong are ridiculous.'

Here, *Hēunggóng* is the topic and *làuhga* the subject, *Hēunggóng* setting the frame in which the sentence is to be understood.[2]
Such topics are not the subject or object of a verb, but have a looser connection to the predicate which follows, such as a part–whole relationship:

Chìuhjāu-wá ngóh **yāt geui** dōu m̀h sīk ga. (radio dialogue)
Chiuchow-ese I one phrase also not know PRT
'I don't know a single word of Chiuchow (dialect).'

Here the topic *Chìuhjāu-wá* and the object *yāt geui* are related by a part–whole relationship. Similarly, there is a part–whole relationship between *ńgh tìuh yú* 'five fish' and *géi dō* 'how many' in the following example:

Ńgh tìuh yú làuh géi dō béi Māmìh sihk a?
five CL fish leave how many for mummy eat PRT
'Of the five fish, how many shall I leave for Mummy?'

A type–token relationship holds between *bējáu* and *bīn jek* in the following example:

Bējáu léih jeui jūngyi yám **bīn** **jek** a?
beer you most like drink which CL PRT
'Which kind of beer do you prefer?'

4.2.3 SECONDARY TOPICALIZATION

In another form of topicalization, the topic comes after the subject:

Kéuih **Hēunggóng** jihnghaih sīk Gáulùhng.
s/he Hongkong only know Kowloon
'In Hongkong she only knows Kowloon.'

Note that the **secondary topic** *Hēunggóng* does not have a **grammatical** relation to the verb *sīk*, but has a part–whole relation with the object *Gáulùhng*, very much as in the topic structures illustrated in 4.2.2. Similarly:

Ngóh **Gáulùhng** mhaih géi sīk louh.
I Kowloon not-be quite know road
'I don't know the roads too well in Kowloon.'

Kéuih **jyú** **faahn** jeui lēk haih jīng yú.
s/he cook food most clever is steam fish
'As far as cooking is concerned she's best at steamed fish.'

By virtue of its position, a secondary topic has lesser prominence than an initial topic, but has essentially the same function of setting the range in which the predicate is to be understood.

4.2.4 VERB TOPICALIZATION

When a verb is topicalized, it is typically repeated in the comment; the displaced verb is followed by a pause (comma intonation):

A: Léih dī léui gam lēk, saht háau dóu
your CL daughter so smart, sure pass V-PRT

yahp daaihhohk lā.
enter university PRT
'Your daughters are so smart, they're sure to get into university.'

B: **Mohng** jauh (haih) gám **mohng** lā.
hope then (is) so hope PRT
'Well, that's what we hope.'

This construction is used especially to place two verbs in contrast:

> A: Léih gám-m̀h-gám tái húngbou pín a?
> you dare-not-dare see horror film PRT
> 'Do you dare watch horror films?'

> B: **Gám** jauh gám; **séung** jauh m̀h séung laak.
> dare then dare want then not want PRT
> 'I dare, but I don't want to.'

The copula *haih* may take the place of the repeated verb:

> A: Léih sīk hóu dō Jūngmán bo?
> you know very much Chinese PRT
> 'You know a lot of Chinese?'

> B: **Góng** jauh haih; **tái** jauh mhaih.
> speak then yes read then no
> 'Yes, as far as speaking is concerned, not reading.'

The same construction applies to adjectives:

> A: Léih gau-m̀h-gau chín yuhng a?
> you enough-not-enough money use PRT
> 'Do you have enough money?'

> B: **Gau** jauh mhaih géi **gau** . . .
> enough then not-be quite enough
> 'Well, it's not quite enough . . .'

4.2.5 DEFINITE SUBJECTS AND EXISTENTIAL SENTENCES

Another property related to topicalization is the constraint that subjects must be definite in Chinese. Rather than introducing an indefinite noun phrase as the subject as in *a man came in*, the existential marker *yáuh* is added to introduce a new topic (see 15.5):

> Tàuhsīn yáuh (yāt) go yàhn yahp-jó làih.
> just-now have (one) CL person enter-PFV come
> 'Someone came in just now.'

Not all topics are definite in the sense of the English definite article, however. **Generic** noun phrases are also treated as definite and hence as possible sentence topics:

> Māau hóu jūngyi sihk yú ge.
> cat much like eat fish PRT
> 'Cats like to eat fish.'

Bējáu   móuh   yīk   ge.
beer   not-have   nutrition   PRT
'Beer is not good for you.'

The words *māau* 'cat' and *bējáu* 'beer' used without a classifier (6.2.1) are understood generically, i.e. as referring to cats and beer in general.[3]

Moreover, a classifier with a noun in subject/pre-verbal position also assumes definiteness (see also 6.1 for discussion of the distinction between definite and indefinite noun phrases):

Jek   māau   jáu-jó   yahp-làih.
CL   cat   walk-PFV   enter-come
'The cat came in.'

The same combination in object/post-verbal position, however, can take either definite or indefinite reference:

Jáu-jó   **jek   māau**   yahp-làih.
walk-PFV   CL   cat   enter-come
'A/the cat came in.'

Why subjects should be required to be definite in Cantonese invites comment. The definiteness constraint is one which naturally applies to topics (since a topic for discussion must be an identifiable entity and hence definite), rather than to subjects. A useful way to think of the phenomenon is that in a Chinese sentence there should normally be a topic; if there is no other topicalized element present (such as an object), then the grammatical subject (if overtly present) is made the topic by default. Hence, the constraint that topics should be definite extends also to subjects.

4.2.6 TOPIC CHAINS

The notion of topic chain refers to a series of connected sentences or clauses sharing the same topic.[4] The topic of the first clause may serve as the subject or object of several following clauses:

Gihn sāam   hóu   leng   a,   ngóh jūngyi dou séi.   Léih
CL   blouse   very   pretty   PRT I   like   till death   you

máaih-m̀h-máaih   béi   ngóh   jēk?
buy-not-buy   for   me   PRT
'That blouse is nice, I like (it) very much. Will you buy (it) for me?'

The topic *gihn sāam* 'the blouse' serves not only as the subject of *hóu leng* 'very pretty' but also as the object of *jūngyi* 'like' and of *máaih* 'buy'. The topic of a chain is typically introduced as a sentence topic, as in the above example. It may be introduced, however, by an existential sentence (see 4.2.5 above and ch. 15) or as an object:

Yáuh go hohksāang hóu síng ge, sèhngyaht mahn yéh,
have CL student very bright PRT always ask things

chi-chi háau-síh dōu ló hóu gōu fān ge.
time-time take-exam also get very high mark PRT
'There's a student who's really bright, always asking questions, (she) gets high marks every time (she) takes an exam.'

Here, the indefinite noun phrase *go hohksāang* 'the student' is introduced by the existential verb *yáuh* 'have' and becomes the topic of the following 'chain' of clauses, functioning as the subject of *mahn yéh* 'ask things', *háau-síh* 'take exam' and *ló hóu gōu fān* 'get high marks'.

5 PRONOUNS

5.1 PERSONAL PRONOUNS

Personal pronouns are the only items in Cantonese with distinct plural forms, regularly formed by adding the suffix -*deih*:

ngóh 'I'	ngóhdeih 'we'
léih 'you'	léihdeih 'you (plural)'
kéuih 'he/she/it'	kéuihdeih 'they'

There is no gender distinction between *he*, *she* and *it* in either spoken or written Cantonese (whereas in written Mandarin, male and female *tā* take different radicals). Although *kéuih* is used primarily to refer to people, it may refer to inanimate objects in some restricted contexts (see below).

In addition, the word *yàhn* 'person' can also take -*deih* to mean 'people' (cf. Mandarin *rénjiā*).[1] Despite the suffix -*deih*, *yàhndeih* may have singular or plural reference depending on the context. It is typically used in the following ways:

(a) 'other people', referring to people other than the speaker:

> Yàhndeih gaap-chín sung yéh béi léih. (subject)
> people pool-money send stuff give you
> 'People are pitching in to buy you a gift.'

> Léih yiu sé-seun dōjeh yàhndeih. (direct object)
> you need write-letter thank people
> 'You need to write to thank these people.'

> Dím gáai léih waih yàhndeih hēisāng gam dō? (object of
> how come you for people sacrifice so much coverb)
> 'Why do you sacrifice so much for others?'

(b) ironically or coyly, to refer to oneself or to a third person:

> A: Léih dím gáai m̀h chēut sēng a?
> you how come not speak out PRT
> 'Why don't you say something?'

> B: Yàhndeih pacháu āma.
> people shy PRT
> 'Well, some people are shy.' (i.e. I am shy)

Mother to son (referring to son's girlfriend outside):

Dím gáai m̀h chéng yàhndeih yahp làih chóh a?
how come not invite people enter come sit PRT
'Why don't you invite the guest in?'

-deih cannot be added to other nouns, as the Mandarin plural form *-men* can be added to bisyllabic words, e.g. *xuéshēng-men* 'students' but not **hohksāang-deih*. The Mandarin word *-men*, read in Cantonese as *mùhn*, may be used in formal register, e.g. *tùhnghohk-mùhn* 'fellow students'.

Pronunciation note: ongoing sound changes lead to variation in the pronunciation of all three pronouns:

(a) Many Cantonese speakers do not pronounce the initial consonant *ng-* (1.5). The first person pronoun *ngóh* is therefore often heard as *óh*, usually with a glottal stop before the vowel.
(b) *léih* is still pronounced as *néih* by older speakers and in formal registers. The current pronunciation *léih* is regarded by some language teachers as an error, though clearly part of a sound change in progress from initial *n-* to *l-* (see 1.5).
(c) *kéuih* is often pronounced as *héuih*, with initial *h* substituted for the aspirated [kʰ]. This pronunciation is currently common among younger speakers, and may indicate an incipient sound change (Bourgerie 1990).

The pronouns have a single form for subject or object. There are no separate forms for the genitive (possessive) pronouns corresponding to the English *my/mine*, *your/yours*, *their/theirs*, etc. The first person singular *ngóh* corresponds to 'I' or 'me':

Ngóh jáu la. (*ngóh* = subject)
I leave PRT
'I'm going.'

Mhóu haak ngóh lā! (*ngóh* = direct object)
don't scare me PRT
'Don't frighten me!'

Kéuih sung-jó sāang-yaht láihmaht béi ngóh. (*ngóh* = indirect
s/he send-PFV birth-day gift to me object)
'She gave me a birthday gift.'

To express the genitive/possessive relation, the linking particle *ge* is often used between the pronoun and the possessed entity (6.3):

ngóh ge tàuhfaat   ngóh ge gihnhōng
I LP head-hair   s/he LP health
'my hair'   'my health'

In many cases, the pronoun is followed directly by the classifier:

ngóh jek sáují
I   CL finger
'my finger'

ngóh go jái
I   CL son
'my son'

To express the English *mine* in Cantonese, *ngóh ge* is used:

Nī   ga chē (haih) ngóh ge.
this CL car (is)   mine
'This car is mine.'

Similarly for *yours*, *his*, *hers*, *its* and *theirs*, the corresponding pronoun + *ge* is used: *léih ge*, *kéuih ge* and *kéuihdeih ge*.

léih 'you': there is no distinction between formal and informal 'you' (though see the note above on the pronunciation of *léih*).

kéuih 'he/she': note that there is no gender distinction in the third person:

Kéuih haih ngóh tùhnghohk lèihga.
s/he is   my   classmate PRT
'He/She's my classmate.'

kéuih normally refers to animate (human or animal) nouns but may also refer to inanimate objects and abstract entities:

Ngóh séung **tái   saai kéuih** sīn wàahn. (*kéuih* = the book)
I   want read all it   first return
'I want to finish reading it before I return it.'

Léih yātdihng yiu **maaih-jó kéuih**. (*kéuih* = the car)
you definitely need sell-PFV it
'You really have to sell it.'

A: Ngóh séung si-háh   sihk nī jek ōnmìhn yeuhk.
   I   want try-DEL eat this CL sleeping pill
   'I want to try taking this brand of sleeping pill.'

B: Ngóh dōu haih **sihk-gán   kéuih** ga. (*kéuih* = the same brand)
   I   also am   eat-PROG   it   PRT
   'I've been taking **that one** too.'

This usage is especially common in imperatives:

Faai-faai   cheui-cheui **sihk saai kéuih** lā! (*kéuih* = the food)
quick-quick crisp-crisp eat up   it   PRT
'Hurry up and finish it up.'

Dáng ngóh **gáau   dihm kéuih** lā! (*kéuih* = the task)
let me   manage V-PRT it   PRT
'Let me handle it.'

Kéuih refers to abstract entities in the following:

Nī go gēiwuih taai hóu la, léih yiu
this CL opportunity too good PRT you must

jānsīk kéuih a. (*kéuih* = opportunity)
treasure it PRT
'This is a very good opportunity. You have to treasure it.'

Kéuihdeih mhaih jānhaih tàihchēung màhnjyú, bātgwo
they not-are really advocate democracy but

yuhng kéuih làih ngāak-faahn-sihk ge je. (*kéuih* =
use it come cheat-food-eat PRT PRT democracy)
'They're not really advocating democracy but using it to make a living.'

Note that *kéuih* referring to inanimate things and abstract entities is found primarily in object, rather than subject, position.

In colloquial speech, *kéuih* referring to objects is also used pleonastically to reinforce a noun:

Léih sihk màaih **tùh yú** kéuih lā.
you eat up CL fish it PRT
'Eat up the fish.'

Giu A-Yīng sái saai **dī sāam** kéuih lā.
ask Ah Ying wash all CL clothes it PRT
'Ask Ying to wash all the clothes.'

Mgōi cheung-sáan jēung **yāt baak mān jí** kéuih ā.
please change CL one hundred dollar note it PRT
'Please change this one hundred dollar note into smaller notes.'

Daaihgā yám-sing **kéuih** lā!
everyone drink-cheer it PRT
'Cheers, everyone!'

Note that *kéuih* in this sentence is not immediately preceded by any noun as in the other examples and does not refer to any particular cause of the toast either. This pleonastic use of *kéuih* also occurs in the idiomatic expressions, *wah jī kéuih* (see 16.5) and *séi-jó kéuih*:

Ngóh bātyùh séi-jó-**kéuih** hóu gwo la.
I rather die-PFV-it good than PRT
'I'd rather die.'

Giu Daai-Sòh faai dī séi-jó-**kéuih** bá lā. (film)
ask big fool quick bit die-PRF-it PRT PRT
'Tell Big-Fool to go to hell quickly.'

A name followed by *kéuihdeih* 'they' forms a collective expression:

Paul kéuihdeih chéng ngóhdeih yám-chàh.
Paul they invite us drink-tea
'Paul and his family have invited us for dim sum.'

The meaning of this expression is flexible: it could be 'Paul and his family', 'Paul and his friends', 'Paul and his colleagues', etc. It may be contracted, as in *Bóulòh-deih* (using *Bóulòh* as a Cantonese pronunciation of *Paul*).

Pronouns which occur in the relativized positions in relative clauses are known as **resumptive pronouns**. See 6.4.1 for the relevant discussion.

5.1.1 OMITTED PRONOUNS

As shown in chapter 4, the subject or object of the sentence can readily be omitted where it is already established as the topic of the discourse. Subjects and objects may be omitted in Cantonese under either of two main conditions:

(a) The omitted subject or object has been the topic of a previous sentence, question or dialogue:

A-Yīng gām-lín bātyihp ge la. Yìhgā bok-mehng
Ah-Ying this year graduate PRT PRT now strive

wán gūng.
find job
'Ying's graduating this year. (She)'s looking hard for a job now.'

A: Léih jūng-m̀h-jūngyi sihk Chìuhjāu choi a?
you like-not-like eat Chiuchow food PRT
'Do you like Chiuchow food?'

B: Gánghaih jūngyi lā!
of-course like PRT
'Yes, of course I do.'

(b) The reference is clear from the context. This applies especially to first and second person subjects, and also to third person subjects which are present at the time of speaking:

Āiya, móuh sāmgēi tēng-syū a! (expressing the speaker's
PRT not-have heart hear-book PRT feelings)
'I don't feel like listening to lectures!'

Wáan-gán   māt   a?   (addressing child at play)
play-PROG   what   PRT
'What are you playing (with)?'

Dím   gáai   wúih   gám   ga?   (referring to an object or situation)
how   come   would   so   PRT
'Why is it like this?'

5.2   REFLEXIVE PRONOUNS

5.2.1   *JIHGÉI*

The reflexive pronoun *jihgéi* is invariable in form, serving all persons ('myself, yourself, itself, ourselves', etc.); it must have an antecedent in its own clause or in the main clause if it is in an embedded clause:

Ngóh   hōichí   líuhgáai   **jihgéi**. (film)
I   begin   understand   self
'I'm beginning to understand myself.'

Sailouhjái   m̀h   sīk   bóuwuh   **jihgéi**.
children   not   know   protect   self
'Children don't know how to protect themselves.'

A-Màh   wah   **Mìhng-jái**   m̀h   sīk   jiugu   **jihgéi**.
grandma   say   Ming-boy   not   know   take-care   self
'Grandma says Ming doesn't know how to take care of himself'
or 'Grandma says Ming doesn't know how to take care of her.'

Note that in this last example *jihgéi* may take as antecedent either the embedded clause subject *Mìhng-jái* 'Ming' or the main clause subject *a-Màh* 'grandma'; the latter usage is known as long-distance coreference (see below).

We may distinguish two functions of *jihgéi*: the true reflexive pronoun, as in the above examples, and an emphatic function, where it reinforces a pronoun or noun phrase (C-C. J.Tang 1989). These two usages are discussed in turn below.

As a reflexive, *jihgéi* is **subject-oriented**, i.e. it tends to pick a subject as its antecedent:

Ngóh   tùhng   kéuih   góng-jó   jihgéi   heui.
I   with   him   say-PFV   self   go
'I told him I would go myself.'

This sentence would *not* mean 'I told him to go himself' because *kéuih* here is the object of the coverb *tùhng* and *jihgéi* refers back to a subject.

In its emphatic function, *jihgéi* reinforces a noun phrase; it can occur in almost any position where a noun phrase can occur:

A-Mìhng jihgéi wúih lám   baahn-faat, msái   leih dāam-sām.
Ah-Ming self   will think solution   no need you worry
'Ming himself will think of a solution, you don't need to worry.'

Léih jūngyi Wàh-jái jihgéi   dihnghaih kéuih dī chín   a?
you like   Wah   self   or   his   CL money PRT
'Do you like Wah himself or his money?'

Another common function of *jihgéi* is to indicate 'by oneself' or 'alone':

Léih lám-jyuh   jihgéi   heui àh?
you think-CONT   self   go   PRT
'You're planning to go on your own?'

Dáng ngóh jihgéi   gáau-dihm lā.
let   me   self   manage   PRT
'Let me manage by myself.'

Idiom: the pattern *jihgéi* – [verb] – *jihgéi* appears in various set expressions:

Léih mhóu jihgéi ngāak jihgéi la.
you don't self   cheat self   PRT
'Don't deceive yourself.'

Jihgéi jī   jihgéi sih.
self   know self   affair
'Only you know about your own affairs.'

5.2.2 PRONOUN + *JIHGÉI*

jihgéi is also used together with the personal pronouns, with an emphatic meaning very much like the English; however, the construction pronoun + *jihgéi* prefers to appear in subject position:

Ngóh jihgéi jauh móuh   sówaih,   bātgwo ngóh lóuhpòh
I   self   then not-have objection   but   my   wife

m̀h jai   wo.
not willing PRT
'I don't mind at all myself but my wife is not willing.'

Kéuih jihgéi msíu-sām   johng-jó-chē   m̀h yīnggōi laaih
s/he   self   not careful   bump-PFV-car   not should blame

yàhndeih.
others
'He crashed his car due to his own carelessness and shouldn't blame others.'

This emphatic usage can also appear in serial verb constructions, i.e. between two verbs:

Ngóh yuhng ngóh jihgéi (làih) jouh sahtyihm.
I use I self (come) do experiment
'I do experiments with myself (as a guinea pig).'

Dáng kéuih jihgéi lám baahnfaat lā!
let her/him self think solution PRT
'Let her think of a solution herself.'

Both *jihgéi* and pronoun + *jihgéi* can appear in genitive/possessive constructions:

Ngóh sé-jó bún gwāanyū **jighéi ge syū**.
I write-PFV CL about self LP book
'I've written a book about myself.'

Nī dī haih **léih jihgéi ge** sih.
this CL is you self LP matter
'This is your own business.'

5.2.3 SYNTAX OF REFLEXIVE PRONOUNS

The syntax of the Cantonese reflexives differs substantially from the English. A reflexive pronoun may be the subject of an embedded clause:

Ngóh gokdāk jihgéi hóu sòh.
I feel self very silly
'I feel pretty silly.'

Moreover, a reflexive can refer back to a subject outside the clause in which it appears:

A-Lìhng fāat muhng Wah-jái jūngyi jihgéi.
Ah-Ling have dream Wah-boy like self
'Ling dreamed that Wah liked her.'

In these examples, it is clear that the antecedent of *jihgéi* is the subject of the main clause (*a-Lìhng*), rather than of the subordinate clause. These are known as **long-distance** reflexives; note that English uses a personal pronoun rather than a reflexive here. Some sentences are potentially ambiguous, as the reflexive may refer either to the local (nearest) or to the long-distance antecedent:

A-sèuh wah **dī hohksāang** deui jihgéi móuh seunsām.
Ah-sir say CL student towards self not-have confidence
'The teacher says students lack confidence in him' *or*
'The teacher says students lack confidence in themselves.'

Sālaih daai Máhleih fāan jihgéi gāan fóng.[2]
Sally bring Mary return self CL room
'Sally brought Mary back to her [Sally's or Mary's] room.'

(Note that this example is ambiguous in English too: *her* could refer to Sally or Mary.) In the following sentence, however, *jihgéi* cannot refer to the indirect object but only to the higher- and lower-clause subjects:

A-Jān wah a-Sāan béi-jó a-Jī yāt bún jihgéi ge yahtgei.
Ah-Jan say ah-Saan give-PFV ah-Ji one CL self LP diary
'Jan says that Saan gave Ji a diary about her/herself.'

In this Cantonese sentence, the reflexive *jihgéi* can only refer to either *a-Jān* or *a-Sāan* but not *a-Jī*, the indirect object. However, *kéuih jihgéi* in place of *jihgéi* in the same position could refer to any of the three antecedents. This asymmetry shows that while *jihgéi* is subject-oriented, pronoun + *jihgéi* does not exhibit **subject-orientation**.

5.3 RECIPROCALS: 'EACH OTHER'

There is no reciprocal pronoun corresponding to 'each other'. The reciprocal adverbs *béichí* or *wuhsēung*, also used in Mandarin, may be used in formal contexts:

Sing-Gīng wah yiu béichí sēung-ngoi.
Bible say need mutually each-other-love
'The Bible says we should love one another.'

Léuhng-gūng-pó yīnggōi wuhsēung chīnjauh.
two-husband-wife should mutually accommodate
'Couples should accommodate each other.'

In colloquial speech, a reciprocal construction is formed by repeating the clause with the subject and object reversed:

Ngóh béi-mín kéuih kéuih béi-mín ngóh.
I give-face him he give-face me
'He and I respect each other.'

Go-go chóh saai háidouh, léih mohng ngóh, ngóh mohng léih.
CL-CL sit all here you stare me I stare you
'Everyone is sitting around, staring at each other.'

Léih hóyíh bōng ngóh ngóh hóyíh bōng léih.
you can help me I can help you
'We (you and I) can help each other.'

6 THE NOUN PHRASE

The noun phrase consists of a noun and those items which accompany or modify it. The order of the elements of the noun phrase is as follows:

demonstrative – numeral – classifier – adjective – (*ge*) – noun

The linking particle *ge* (glossed as LP in the examples), which occurs in several types of noun phrase, comes between the modifying expressions and the noun itself (it may be omitted in some cases: see 6.3, 6.4):

gó   sāam   jek   hóu   dākyi   **ge**   gáu-jái
that   three   CL   very   cute   LP   puppy
'those three cute puppies'

nī   léuhng   júng   gwo-sìh   **ge**   lám-faat
this   two   kind   over-time LP   think-way
'these two outdated ways of thinking'

The overall structure of a simple noun phrase is thus similar to the English, with the difference that a noun classifier is required in many contexts (see 6.2). Note that the noun (the head of the noun phrase) always comes at the end of the phrase, after all the expressions which modify it.[1] These characteristics are also seen in the following more complex types of noun phrase:

Possessive constructions (6.3):
gó   sāam   go   sailouhjái   ge   **fuhmóuh**
those   three   CL   children   LP   parents
'those three children's parents' or 'the parents of those three children'

géi   go   yáuh-chín-lóu   ge   **chòihcháan**
few   CL   have-money-guy   LP   property
'a few rich guys' property' or 'the property of a few rich guys'

Relative clauses (6.4):
jā-chē   fāan   hohk   ge   **hohksāang**
drive-car   return   school   LP   student
'**students** who drive to school'

ngóh   chéng   ge   gūngyàhn
I   hire   LP   maid
'the maid I hire'

6.1 DEFINITENESS AND DEMONSTRATIVES

Cantonese has no articles equivalent to *a* or *the*. The word *yāt* 'one' may be used like an indefinite article, referring to an indefinite object or person:

Yáuh (**yāt**) **ga chē** jó-jyuh   go chēut-háu.
have (one) CL car block-CONT CL exit-mouth
'There's a car blocking the exit.'

A-Yīng yiu wán (**yāt**) **go leuhtsī**.
Ah-Ying need find (one) CL lawyer
'Ying has to find a lawyer.'

However, the word *yāt* is optional: *ga chē* or *go leuhtsī* would be sufficient here. To a large extent, the classifiers (6.2) perform the functions of the English articles in individuating entities. When the noun phrase is a subject or a topicalized object, the presence of a classifier denotes a **definite** person or object (see also 4.2.5 on the definiteness of topics):

Ga chē jó-jyuh   go chēut-háu.
CL car block-CONT CL exit-mouth
'The car is blocking the exit.' (*not* 'A car is blocking the exit')

Go leuhtsī yiu hóu lēk sīn dāk.
CL lawyer need very smart only-okay
'The lawyer had better be pretty smart.' (*not* 'a lawyer')

By contrast, a noun with classifier following the verb may be definite or indefinite:

Ngóh tīngyaht wúih wán **go leuhtsī**.
I tomorrow will contact CL lawyer
'I'll contact a/the lawyer tomorrow.'

Ngóh yiu faai dī máaih fāan **gāan ūk**.
I need fast-ish buy V-PRT CL house
'I want to hurry up and buy a/the house.'

6.1.1 DEMONSTRATIVES

The demonstratives *nī* 'this' and *gó* 'that' are used for **deictic** functions such as pointing or referring back to noun phrases. Note that they must be accompanied by the appropriate classifier (see 6.2):

nī go behngyàhn   gó jēung tói
this CL patient   that CL table

nī gāan hohkhaauh   gó deui fūfúh
this CL school   that CL couple

The linking particle *ge* is sometimes pleonastically following the demonstrative and classifier, as in *nī go ge jitmuhk* 'this programme', *gó júng ge gámgok* 'that kind of feeling'. This usage generalises the function of *ge* in marking prenominal modification, as seen with attributive adjectives (9.1.2), possessives (6.3) and relative clauses (6.4.1).

Note: *nī* 'this' may also be pronounced as *lī*, following the general change from initial *n-* to *l-* (1.5). Other alternative forms of *nī* are *lēi* as in *lēi dī* 'these' and *yī* as in *yīdouh* 'here'.

---

nī and *gó* can also occur with time expressions pointing to or referring back to a specific period in time:

nī pàaih/páai	gó pàaih/páai	gó jahn(sìh)/ján
this period	that period	that period
'these days'	'those days'	'those days'

Note that **nī jahn/ján* does not occur.

In addition, *gām* and *gám* have a demonstrative value in expressions of time and manner respectively:

gām chi 'this time' gám yéung 'this way'
gām-lín 'this year' gám (yéung) ge sih 'such matters'

A classifier with head noun without a demonstrative in subject position may be used with a demonstrative force:

Go jái hóu baakyim.
CL boy very naughty
'Our son is very naughty.'

Tìuh yú géi sānsīn wo.
CL fish quite fresh PRT
'This fish is quite fresh.'

This is also true of the classifier *dī*, which applies to plural or uncountable items (6.2.2):

Dī yàhn jouh māt a?
CL people do what PRT
'What are those people up to?'

Dī sāam dán hái bīndouh a?
CL clothes put at where PRT
'Where shall we put these clothes?'

Dī hohksāang hóu láahn ge.
CL student very lazy PRT
'Those students are really lazy.'

6.1.2 DEMONSTRATIVES IN APPOSITION

A demonstrative noun phrase is often used in apposition to a noun, a time or place expression. In fact, the types of phrases that can have an apposition relation with a demonstrative noun phrase are quite versatile (see below). This pattern is especially common following a proper noun:

A-Sìhng **nī go sēui yàhn** je-jó chín m̀h wàahn ge.
a-Sing this CL bad person borrow-PFV money not return PRT
'That A-Sing is a bad guy who borrows but does not return money.'

Síu Waih **nī go méng** hóuchíh hóu suhk gám.
Siu Wai this CL name seem very familiar so
'The name Siu Wai seems familiar.'

Múih yaht sei dím **nī go sìhgaan** ngóh saht yám-chàh ga.
every day four o'clock this CL time I sure drink-tea PRT
'Every day at four, I always drink tea.'

Sahpbaat seui **nī go lìhngéi** haih jeui gaamgaai ge.
eighteen age this CL age is most embarrassing PRT
'Age eighteen is the most embarrassing age.'

Hái Hēunggóng **nī go séhwúi**, sīk yàhn hóu gányiu ge.
in Hongkong this CL society know people very important PRT
'In Hongkong society, connections matter a lot.'

Compare the expletive use of demonstratives with place names as in *Gáulùhng góbihn* 'over in Kowloon' (7.1).

A verb–object compound (2.3.3) used in a generic sense may also be followed by such a demonstrative phrase:

Hohk yúhyìhn **nī gihn sih** hóu fūkjaahp ge.
learn language this CL matter very complicated PRT
'Learning languages is a complicated matter.'

Ngóh deui tiu-móuh **nī yeuhng yéh** móuh
I towards dancing this CL thing not-have

māt hingcheui.
any interest
'I have no interest in (this) dancing.'

Moreover, a clause can also take such a demonstrative phrase:

Meih git-fān sāang-jái **gám ge sih** móuh
not-yet marry produce-baby this CL matter not-have

māt chēutkèih jē.
any surprise PRT
'To have a baby without getting married is not surprising at all.'

Reduplicated adjectives often occur with a demonstrative phrase:

Kàuh-kàuh-kèih-kèih **nī** **júng** **taaidouh** dím hóyíh
sloppy-sloppy this kind attitude how can

jipsauh a?
accept PRT
'How can one accept this kind of sloppy attitude?'

6.2 NOUN CLASSIFIERS

Classifiers (also called **measure words** in works on Chinese) are an important element in the syntax of nouns. Each noun is assigned a particular classifier, much as nouns are assigned genders in many European languages. While gender is loosely based on sex, classifiers are based on distinctive features of shape, natural kind and function. There are over sixty different classifiers,[2] and the choice of classifier is often not predictable from the meaning of a noun: hence, dictionaries typically provide the appropriate classifier(s) in the entry for the noun. There are often two or more alternative classifiers for the same noun (6.2.4).

The nearest equivalent to classifiers in English are words used in counting which are specific to certain classes of nouns: *fifty **head** of cattle*, *two **pairs** of shoes* but *a **brace** of pheasants*. In Cantonese too, a major function of classifiers is in counting or enumerating, as in *baat léung gām* 'eight taels of gold' and *léuhng jek dáan* 'two eggs'. However, they are also used more generally in individuating nouns, as in *nī jek dáan* 'this egg' (see 6.2.1).

It is useful to distinguish two types of classifier:[3]

(a) **measure** or **mensural classifiers**, which denote quantities of an item, such as *dī* denoting plurality or uncountable substances, or the collective *bāan* referring to a group of people (6.2.2);

(b) **type** or **sortal classifiers** which belong with the noun and classify it in terms of some intrinsic feature, e.g. *tìuh* denoting long, thin objects such as fish (6.2.3).[4]

In general, measure classifiers are used with uncountable nouns denoting substances or collectively, to refer to quantities of objects; sortal classifiers are used with countable nouns referring to individual objects. However, this distinction is not absolute, and some nouns can be used in either countable or uncountable senses. Thus *bou* 'cloth' as a countable noun may take the sortal classifier *faai* denoting a flat surface as in *nī faai bou* 'this cloth', while as an uncountable noun referring to the material 'cloth', it can either take a measure classifier such as *chek* 'foot' or be left without a classifier:

Léih yiu géi dō chek bou a?
you need how many feet cloth PRT
'How many feet of cloth do you need?'

Jouh nī gihn sāam yiu yuhng hóu dō bou.
make this CL dress need use very much cloth
'It takes a lot of material to make this dress.'

6.2.1 SYNTAX AND USAGE OF CLASSIFIERS

A classifier accompanies the noun obligatorily in many contexts. In general, whenever a noun phrase refers to a **specific** object, it is accompanied by the classifier. Unlike in Mandarin, the classifier and noun may be used without any demonstrative adjective or numeral:

Jī bāt hóu hóu sé.
CL pen good good write
'This/that pen is good to write with.'

In this usage, the presence of the classifier indicates a specific object: without it, the noun *bāt* would be understood generically, i.e referring to pens in general:

Yuhng hùhng bāt sé hóu dī.
use red pen write good a-bit
'It's better to write with a red pen'.

The following contexts require a classifier:

(a) following a numeral or quantifier:

léuhng jek gáu   múih ga chē
two   CL dog   each CL car
'two dogs'   'each car'

With the relative quantifiers *dō* 'many, much', *síu* 'few, little', *daaih dō sou* 'the majority (of)', *dō/síu gwo yātbun* 'more/less than half', etc. the classifier is optional, especially with more abstract types of nouns:

géi dō (go) mahntàih
quite many (CL) problem
'quite a few problems'

hóu dō (júng) yúhyìhn
very many (CL) language
'many languages'

hóu síu yàhn
very few people
'very few people' (here the classifier *go* for *yàhn* 'people' is always left out)

Fēisèuhngjī síu syū góng nī júng duhngmaht ge.
extremely few book talk this kind animal PRT
'Extremely few books talk about this kind of animal.'

Note that the classifier is required with concrete objects in questions, for example:

Léih yiu géi dō jī bāt a?
you need how many CL pen PRT
'How many pens do you need?'

Compare with the following:

Ngóh yáuh hóu dō (jī) bāt.
I have very many (CL) pen
'I have many pens.'

Note that the classifier is not needed for uncountable entities:

Léih yáuh géi dō chín hái go dói douh a?
you have how much money be-at CL pocket there PRT
'How much money do you have in your pocket?'

Kéuih kàhmmáahn yám hóu síu jáu.
s/he last night drink very little wine
'He drank very little wine last night.'

(b) following the demonstratives *nī* and *gó*:

nī go yàhn   gó fūk wá
this CL person   that CL picture
'this person'   'that picture'

(c) with *bīn* 'which' or *bīn . . . dōu* 'any':

bīn tou hei?
which CL film
'which film?'

Bīn gāan (jáulàuh) dōu dāk.
which CL (restaurant) also okay
'Any (restaurant) will do.'

Certain categories of noun do not take specific (i.e. sortal) classifiers:

(a) time expressions such as *yaht* 'day', *lìhn* 'year':

gó yaht 'that day' (but: gó **go** láihbaai 'that week')
múih lìhn 'each year' (but: múih **go** yuht 'each month')

(b) abstract entities such as *màhnjyú* 'democracy':

Màhnjyú deui ngóhdeih jeui gányiu ge.
democracy to us most important PRT
'Democracy is most important to us.'

The only classifiers used with such nouns are **generic** classifiers, as in *nī júng màhnjyú* 'this kind of democracy' (*nī go màhnjyú* does not exist).

Idiom: with the adjectives *daaih* 'big' and *sai* 'small', classifiers are used predicatively:

Nī   gāan fóng   hóu   **daaih gāan.**
this CL   room   very big   CL
'This room is a big one.'

Wa!   Gam   **sai**   **jek!**
wow! so   small   CL
'What a tiny one!' (of an animal)

Note that the noun itself need not be expressed where its identity is clear from the context. The construction may also be used attributively:

Ngóh **gam daaih go** léui dōu meih   tái-gwo
I   so   big   CL   girl still not-yet see-EXP

Jūng   yī   ge.
Chinese doctor PRT
'As old as I am, I've never seen a Chinese doctor (herbalist).'

This construction occurs with any of the classifiers, but not with adjectives other than *daaih* and *sai*. The phrases *sai lāp* and *daaih jek* are used idiomatically to describe people's size or physique (note the unusual use of these classifiers referring to people):

Kéuih mùihmúi hóu   **sai**   **lāp** ge.
s/he   sister   very small   CL   PRT
'Her sister is very small.'

Ngóh gòhgō   hóu   **daaih jek** ge.
my   brother very big   CL   PRT
'My [elder] brother's pretty well-built.'

An important function of classifiers is to serve as a substitute for a noun, like the English pronoun *one*:[5]

Ngóh hóu   jūngyi **nī** go.
I   much like   this   one
'I like this one a lot.'

> **Gó** **jek** géi dō chín a?
> that one how much money PRT
> 'How much is that one?'

Similarly, where classifiers are reduplicated with the meaning 'every one' (14.1.2), the noun itself may be omitted, the classifier serving to identify it in context:

> Go-go (yàhn) dōu séung máaih láu.
> CL-CL (people) all want buy flat
> 'Everyone wants to buy a flat.'

> Mhaih jek-jek (gúpiu) dōu wúih sīng ge.
> not-be CL-CL (share) all will rise PRT
> 'Not all (shares) are going to rise.'

Classifiers are also used in possessive constructions (6.3) and relative clauses (6.4).

6.2.2 MEASURE (QUANTITY) CLASSIFIERS

These classifiers denote quantities or amounts of items and substances. Some function like collective nouns, while others are names of containers. They are sometimes referred to as **measure words** rather than classifiers, but share the syntax of classifiers as described in 6.2.1 above. The simplest type of classifier are measures of weight, quantity or size, such as *bohng* 'pound' and the Chinese measures *gān* 'catty', *léung* 'tael', etc. Their usage resembles that of English measures:

> Mgōi béi **yāt gān** choisām ngóh.
> please give one catty choisum me
> 'A catty of choisum, please.' (a Chinese vegetable)

> Nī dī yú sāam mān **yāt léung**.
> this CL fish three dollar one tael
> 'These fish are three dollars a tael.'

The remaining measure classifiers may be divided into three types: **collective**, **container** and **generic** classifiers.

Collective classifiers

These resemble English collective nouns:

bāan denotes a 'group', 'bunch' or 'gang' of people:

> nī bāan hohksāang 'this class of students'
> gó bāan léuihjái 'that bunch of girls'

It is also used for air flights and for referring to the bus or train scheduled to arrive/depart:

Léih daap bīn   bāan gēi   a?
you catch which CL   plane PRT
'Which flight are you taking?'

Hah bāan chē yiu   sahp fānjūng hauh sīnji dou.
next CL   bus need   ten minutes later then arrive
'The next (scheduled) bus arrives ten minutes later.'

kwàhn is a more formal classifier for 'group'.

bāt 'amount' is used to denote a sum of money:

gó bāt chín 'that (sum of) money'
kéuih bāt jaai 'his debt'

chāan is used to denote a meal:[6]

yāt   chāan faahn
one   CL   rice
'a meal'

chāu 'bunch' implies a group of objects linked together:

géi chāu tàihjí 'a few bunches of grapes'
daaih chāu sósìh 'a big bunch of keys'

daahp denotes a 'pile':

yāt daahp boují 'a pile of newspapers'
yāt daahp seun 'a pile of letters'

daat 'patch':

yāt daat deih 'a patch of land'
yāt daat jīk 'a patch of stain'

dēui 'heap, mound' implies a conical shape:

yāt dēui sāanggwó 'a pile of fruit'
yāt dēui laahpsaap 'a heap of rubbish'

deui is used for items which come in pairs:

léuhng deui faaijí 'two pairs of chopsticks' (singular: yāt **jek** faaijí)
jeuk deui sān hàaih 'wear a pair of new shoes' (singular: yāt **jek** hàaih)
yāt deui fūfúh 'a couple' (husband and wife)

However, not all objects which are treated as pairs in English are so treated in Cantonese. For example, a pair of trousers does *not* take *deui*, but is *tìuh fu*, the classifier denoting a long, thin object, while a pair of scissors is *yāt bá gaaujín*, using the classifier for tools and instruments.

dī is used, like English *some*, to denote a quantity of either countable things or uncountable substances:

góg dī chē
'those cars'

dī séui
'the/some water'

dī saimānjái
'the/some children'

dī wùhjīu-fán
'the/some pepper (powder)'

dihk 'drop' applies to liquids:

yāt dihk hyut 'a drop of blood'
géi dihk yúh 'a few drops of rain'

fāan goes with the following noun, usually abstract in nature to refer to a collective unit in formal registers:

yāt fāan syutwah/jūnggūk 'these words/advice as a whole'
yāt fāan sāmgēi/lóuhlihk 'this effort/hard work as a whole'

gauh 'lump' suggests a solid mass of no particular shape:

yāt gauh sehk 'a lump of rock'
nī gauh laahpsaap 'this lump of rubbish'

gyuht 'portion':

yāt gyuht yàhn mgin-jó 'a portion of people have disappeared'

hyūn 'circle, round' applies to games:

dá géi hyūn màhjéuk 'play a few rounds of mahjong'

jah 'bunch' suggests an irregular group:

sèhng jah yàhn 'a whole bunch of people'
yāt jah jeukjái 'a flock of birds'

jaat 'bunch, bundle' denotes a bundle of items tied together:

máaih yāt jaat fā 'buy a bunch of flowers'
paai yāt jaat boují 'deliver a bundle of newspapers'

peht 'patch' applies to shapeless masses:

nī peht làih 'this patch of soil'
yāt peht yéh 'a lump of stuff' (referring to an ugly thing or person)

pōu 'round' (also *pùhn*) is used in games:

jūk yāt pōu/pùhn kéi 'play a game of chess'
wáan géi pōu/pùhn 'play a few games' (e.g. on a video game)

tāan 'patch' is used for liquids:

yāt tāan séui 'a patch of water, puddle'

tou serves as a collective classifier meaning 'set':

tou sāam 'suit' (contrast: gihn sāam 'piece of clothing')
sihk tou chāan 'eat a set meal'

It also applies to certain nouns as a type classifier (*tou hei* 'film').

Container classifiers

Nouns denoting commodities and products such as food and drink take the appropriate container as the measure classifier:

būi 'cup'	jām būi chàh 'pour a cup of tea'
dihp 'dish'	giu dihp choi 'order a dish of vegetables'
doih 'bag'	yāt doih laahpsaap 'a bagful of rubbish'
gwun 'can'	léuhng gwun bējáu 'two cans of beer'
hahp/háp 'box'	géi hahp yuhtbéng 'a few boxes of moon-cake'
	(*hahp* does not change tone as classifier)
jā 'jar, jug'	giu yāt jā bējáu 'order a jug of beer'
jēun 'bottle'	yám jēun heiséui 'have a (bottle of) soft drink'
làahm 'basket'	yāt làahm gāiddan 'a basket of eggs'
lùhng 'basket'	sāam lùhng chāsīu-bāau 'three baskets of pork buns'
'cage'	yāt lùhng jeukjái 'a cage of birds'
pùhn 'basin'	yāt pùhn sáan sā 'a basin of scattered sand' (idiom)
	yāt pùhn séui 'a basin of water' literally, also 'ten thousand dollars' (slang)
túng 'bucket'	géi túng séui 'a few buckets of water'
wún 'bowl'	léuhng wún faahn 'two bowls of rice'

Note that these container classifiers may also function as nouns in their own right, in which case they themselves take the classifier *go* (*go būi* 'a/the cup') or *jek* (*jek díp* 'a/the dish') and take the changed tone where applicable (*go háp* 'the box'). A few are also used as sortal classifiers, e.g. *yāt hahp luhkyíng-dáai* 'a video tape', so classified because it typically comes in a box.

Any noun which can function as a container may be used as a classifier in this way. For example, body parts may be used as collective/container classifiers:

sèhng   mihn   fūi
whole   face   dust
'a faceful of dust'

yāt   tàuh   yīn
one   head   smoke
'a head full of smoke' (i.e. in a state of turmoil)

yāt   ngaak   hohn
one   forehead   sweat
'a forehead full of sweat'

yāt   sān   jáu-meih
one   body   wine-smell
'a body smelling of wine all over'

yāt   sān   ngáih
one   body   ant
'a body full of ants' (i.e. trouble all over)

The class of container classifiers is thus open-ended, very much as the suffix *-ful* may be added to English nouns. Nouns such as *ūk* 'house' and *tói* 'table', which would not be listed as classifiers, may function syntactically as container classifiers:

sèhng   tói   syū
whole   table   book
'a tableful of books'

sèhng   ūk   léuihyán
whole   house   woman
'a whole houseful of women'

sèhng   deih   laahpsaap
whole   floor   rubbish
'a whole floor of rubbish'

Similarly: yāt wohk póuh, lit. 'a wok full of bubbles' = 'a handful of trouble' (idiom)[7]

Generic classifiers

This group of classifiers, denoting types and kinds, are intermediate between measure and type classifiers, often functioning in both ways. For example, the generic classifier *júng* is the type classifier for nouns such as *yúhyìhn* 'language' but with other nouns denotes 'a kind of' as in *yāt júng fā* 'a kind of flower':

júng 'kind'	hóu dō júng yúhyìhn 'many languages'
	nī júng fā 'this kind of flower'
	gó júng behng 'that (kind of) disease'
leuih 'genre, species'	nī leuih duhngmaht 'this (species of) animal'
	yāt leuih mahntàih 'one genre of problem'
yeuhng 'kind'	nī yeuhng yéh 'this thing'
	sāam yeuhng sung 'three dishes'

Note: the noun with *yeuhng* is often omitted:

Giu	**sāam**	**yeuhng**	dāk	ge	la,	hó?	(at restaurant)
order	three	kind	okay	PRT	PRT	PRT	

'Three dishes will be enough, right?'

Kéuihdeih	góng	làih	góng	heui	dōu	haih	**gó**	**géi**
they	talk	come	talk	go	all	is	this	few

yeuhng	ge	je.
kind	PRT	PRT

'They talk over and over about the same few things.'

tíng 'kind' may have a negative connotation:

Gó	tíng	yàhn	seun	m̀h	gwo	ge.
that	kind	person	trust	not	worth	PRT

'People like that are not trustworthy.'

Nī	tíng	gēi	hóu	yih-waaih	ga.
this	CL	machine	very	easy-broken	PRT

'This kind of machine easily goes out of order.'

fún 'pattern, design' is used as a generic classifier for clothes, etc.:

gó fún sāam 'that [design of] dress'
nī fún ngáahn-géng 'this pair of glasses [design]'

jek as a generic classifier means 'model, variety':

nī jek jáu 'this (variety of) wine'   nī jek chē 'this model of car'
gó jek pàaihjí 'that brand'   gó jek máih 'that kind of rice'

jek is also used in colloquial Cantonese to refer to a type of people or objects where the head noun is often left out:

Ngóh	jūngyi	gōu-gōu-daaih-daih,	sī-sī-màhn-màhn
I	like	tall-tall-big-big	gentlemanly

gó	jek.	(conv.)
that	type	

'I like the tall, gentlemanly type (of guy).'

Kéuih	ga	gēi	haih	ji	pèhng	gó	jek.	(conv.)
Her	CL	machine	is	most	cheap	that	type	

'Her machine is the cheapest type.'

6.2.3 SORTAL (TYPE) CLASSIFIERS

These classifiers, rather than denoting measures or quantities, reflect intrinsic features of the nouns with which they belong. As with gender in

European languages, the choice of classifier is to some extent predictable from the meaning of the noun, especially where the shape of the object plays a role. Other cases seem idiosyncratic and must be learnt individually; many dictionaries provide the classifier under the entry for the noun. Some nouns may take two or more classifiers according to the sense in which they are used (see 6.2.4).

go is the most common and neutral classifier. It is used with all words denoting people (but see 6.2.4 for alternative classifiers):

> yāt go chyùhsī 'a chef'
> sāam go hohksāang 'three students'

go is also used for individual items which do not call for a more specific classifier. Thus abstract nouns which refer to non-concrete entities lacking physical features, generally take *go*:

> yāt go yuhnmohng 'a wish'
> nī go tīujin 'this challenge'
> yāt go gēiwuih 'an opportunity'
> nī go kyutdihng 'this decision'

but: *nī **gihn** sih* 'this matter', *gó **gihn** ngon* 'that (legal) case', *yāt **chàhng** yisī* 'a level of meaning', *yāt **tiuh** mehng* 'a (physical) life'; also the more abstract meaning of destiny as in:

> Léih **tiuh** mehng jānhaih fú   la!
> your CL   life   really   bitter PRT
> 'Your life is really bitter.'

Certain abstract nouns take special classifiers and *yāt* 'one':

> yāt **sin** hēimohng   yāt **sin** sāng-gēi
> one line hope   one line live-chance
> 'a ray of hope'   'a chance of survival'

Note that abstract entities such as *pìhng ōn* 'peace, safety' and *gihnhōng* 'health' do not take any classifier (6.2.1).

Many of the more common classifiers define nouns in terms of shape:

faai denotes flat-surfaced objects which are typically vertically oriented, such as slices of foods:

> yāt faai ngàuhpá 'a steak'
> yāt faai mihnbāau 'a slice of bread'
> yāt faai yùhsāang 'a piece of sashimi'
> gó faai bōlēi 'that window pane'

but with oranges, *káaih* is used; compare:

yāt káaih cháang 'a slice of orange'
yāt faai cháang-pèih 'a slice of orange skin'

buhng is the classifier for a wall denoting a flat surface (this should be distinguished from the *buhng* in *yāt buhng chèuih* 'a strong pungent smell' (see below):

yāt buhng chèuhng 'a wall'

jēung denotes flat objects which typically lie in a horizontal position (contrast *faai* referring to vertically oriented flat surfaces):

jēung tói 'table'	jēung dang 'seat, bench'
jēung jí 'sheet of paper'	jēung fēi 'ticket'

fūk applies to rectangular items:

fūk wá 'painting'   fūk séung 'photograph'
fūk bou 'a [square piece of] cloth' (also *pāt bou* 'roll of cloth')

gauh denotes a lump-like or irregularly shaped object:

gauh sehk 'stone'
gauh chaatgāau 'rubber, eraser'

gihn 'piece', applies to some abstract nouns as well as to commodities:

gihn sáusīk 'piece of jewellery'	gihn daahngōu 'piece of cake'
gó gihn ngon 'that case' (legal)	nī gihn sih 'this matter'

gihn applies to most pieces of clothing, except the elongated items *fu* 'trousers' and *kwàhn* 'skirt' which take *tìuh*.

jek has a variety of meanings:

(a) animal: yāt jek gāi 'a chicken', léuhng jek gáu 'two dogs';
(b) round object: léih jek sáubīu 'your wrist watch', léuhng jek gāidáan 'two eggs';
(c) one of a pair: yāt jek yíhwáan 'one earring', nī jek hàaih 'this shoe'.

jek also serves as a generic classifier meaning 'variety' as in *nī jek jáu* 'this (variety of) wine' (6.2.2).

jī applies to cylindrical items:

jī bāt 'a pen'
yāt jī fā 'a stem of flowers'
jī dék 'flute'
géi jī jáu 'a few bottles of wine' (also *jēun* 'bottle')

joh applies to some large items:

yāt joh gongkàhm 'a (grand) piano'
yāt joh sāan 'a mountain'

lāp denotes small objects:

yāt lāp láu 'a button'   géi lāp yeuhkyún 'a few pills'
yāt lāp tóng 'a sweet, candy'   yāt lāp dáu 'a bean'

tìuh applies to long, thin objects and animals:

tìuh louh 'road'   tìuh sèh 'snake'
tìuh tàuhfaat 'strand of hair'   tìuh yú 'fish'

A few classifiers are associated with functional features:

bá applies to tools and instruments (but not musical instruments):

bá jē 'umbrella'   bá sēng 'voice'
bá dōu 'knife'   bá só 'lock'

ga classifies vehicles and other large machines:

ga   chē   ga   yī-chē
CL   car   CL   clothes-machine
'car'   'sewing machine'

ga   fēigēi   ga   séung-gēi
CL   fly-machine   CL   photo-machine
'aeroplane'   'camera'

fahn denotes a 'copy' or 'part':

máaih fahn boují 'buy a newspaper'
léuhng fahn gūng 'two jobs'
chīm fahn bóudāan 'sign an insurance policy'
fahn yàhn-gūng 'salary'

A special use of *fahn* followed by *yàhn* is as follows:

Ngóh fahn yàhn ji   móuh   sówaih ge. (film)
I   CL person most not-have care   PRT
'As a person, I couldn't care less (about many things).'

Kéuih gó   fahn yàhn móuh   māt   dím, jihnghaih
s/he   that CL person not-have what how   just

gūhòhn dī   jē.
stingy bit PRT
'As a person, he is alright but just a bit stingy.'

Note that whereas *fahn* in the first sentence can be replaced by the classifier *go*, it cannot in the second sentence unless the preceding demonstrative *gó* 'that' is left out.

A number of sortal classifiers are more specific in meaning, applying to only a few nouns:

bouh	'machine'	léih bouh séunggēi 'your camera'
	'volume'	nī bouh síusyut 'this novel'
		yāt bouh jihdín 'a dictionary'
bún	'volume'	sé bún syū 'write a book'
		máaih bún jaahpji 'buy a magazine'
chàhng	'storey'	jōu chàhng láu 'rent a flat'
dāan	'bill'	yāt dāan sāangyi 'an item of business'
douh	'place'	sāan douh mùhn 'close the door'
		yāt douh deihfōng 'a certain place'
dán/duhng	'pillar'	yāt duhng daaihhah 'a mansion block'
fūng	'message'	sé fūng seun 'write a letter'
gāan	'block, building'	géi gāan ngūk 'several houses'
		nī gāan jáulàuh 'this restaurant'
geui	'phrase'	yāt geui syutwah 'a turn of phrase'
gyún	'roll'	yāt gyún fēilám 'a roll of film'
jahm	'smell'	hóu daaih jahm meih 'a strong smell'
jahn	'burst'	géi jahn jaauhyúh 'a few showers'
		yāt jahn fūng 'a burst of wind'
lūk	'plank'	yāt lūk muhk 'a piece of wood'
pàahng	'row'	yāt pàahng ngàh 'a row of teeth'
pàaih	'bar'	yāt pàaih jyūgūlīk 'a chocolate bar'
pō	'stem, trunk'	pō syuh 'tree'
		pō choi 'stem of vegetable'
pīn	'text'	sé pīn màhnjēung 'write an article'
sáu	'hand'	nī sáu gō 'this song'
		gó sáu sī 'that poem'
wàih	'round'	dehng géi wàih tói 'reserve a few (round) tables'

6.2.4 ALTERNATIVE CLASSIFIERS

For many nouns two or more alternative sortal classifiers may be used. To some extent this is due to variation between individuals, social groups and varieties of Cantonese in the choice of classifier. For example, *yāt lāp cháang* 'an orange' is used by some speakers while others use *go*, the age and dialect background of speakers being important factors here. In many cases, the choice depends on the kind of item referred to or the way the noun is being used:

jā jī chēung 'hold a gun' (classified by cylindrical shape)
yuhng bá chēung 'use a gun' (classified by function as tool/weapon)

nī ga dihnlóuh 'this computer' (classified as machine)
nī bouh dihnlóuh 'this computer' (classified as model)
nī go dihnlóuh 'this computer' (classified as object)

kéuih bá háu 'her mouth' (as instrument for speaking)
kéuih go háu 'her mouth' (as part of body)

yāt dihk ngáahnleuih 'a tear-drop'
yāt hok ngáahnleuih 'a bowl of tears' (idiom)[8]

ga syùhn 'ship' (as large vehicle)
jek syùhn 'boat' (as small object)
tìuh syùhn 'ship' (long, thin; literary usage)

yāt go douhléih 'a principle'
daaih tìuh douhléih 'a major rationale' (emphasizing the extent)

yāt tou hei 'a film' (tou 'set')
yāt chēut hei 'a film'

An extreme case is the noun *yéh* 'thing' which may take almost any classifier, according to the kind of thing referred to:

gó go yéh 'that thing' (object; idiomatically also of people)
gó jek yéh 'that thing' (animal, e.g. insect; also of children, husbands, etc.)
gó yeuhng yéh, gó gihn yéh 'that thing' (matter, affair)
góng géi geui yéh 'say a few things' (words)

Such cases illustrate that the classifiers are not merely determined by individual nouns, but are applied meaningfully to classes of nouns. It is also possible to use a classifier other than the usual one for the noun concerned, in order to derive particular implications. For example, the neutral classifier for people is *go* but *wái* is used in order to convey politeness and respect towards the individual referred to:

Ngóh séung gaaisiuh   nī **wái** tùhngsih béi daaihgā   sīk.
I   wish introduce this CL colleague for everyone know
'I'd like to introduce this colleague to everyone.'

Conversely, *tìuh*, which normally classifies long thin items, is used of people in some slang expressions:

gó	tìuh	yáu (slang)	ngóh	tìuh	jái (vulgar)
that	CL	friend	my	CL	boy
'that guy'			'my boyfriend'		

léih tìuh léui (slang)	léih tìuh choi (vulgar)
you CL girl	you CL vegetable
'your girlfriend'	'your girlfriend'

The use of a classifier normally used only of objects and animals (see *tìuh*, 6.2.3) has a demeaning effect, hence the slang usage. Similarly, when animal terms are used to refer to people for jocular or derisive purposes, the classifier *jek* may be used as for animals:

ngóh jek (máhlāu) jái	jek gāi	jek ngaap
my CL (monkey) boy	CL chicken	CL duck
'my monkey of a boy'	'prostitute'	'male prostitute'

6.3 POSSESSIVE CONSTRUCTIONS

The possessor invariably comes before the item possessed, as in English *my mother's castle*. One possessive construction resembles that in Mandarin, with *ge* performing the function of Mandarin *de*:

gaausauh ge baahngūngsāt	hohksāang ge gājéung
professor POSS office	student POSS parents
'the professor's office'	'the student's parents'

dīk is the Cantonese reading for Mandarin *de*, and is used in formal Cantonese, for example in songs:

Ngóh dīk yāt sāang
dear POSS one life
'my whole life'

Also as in Mandarin, the possessive marker *ge* may be left out with kinship terms and certain other nouns where there is a close (**inalienable**) link between the possessor and the noun, especially where the possessor is a pronoun:

ngóh sailóu 'my younger brother'
kéuihdeih ūkkéi 'their home'
ngóh ngoihgā 'my husband's family'
léih (gāan) gūngsī 'your company'

An alternative possessive construction uses the classifier before the possessed noun in place of *ge* (except for those nouns which do not take any classifiers):

ngóh gāan ūk	ngóh jek geuk
my CL house	my CL foot
'my house'	'my foot'

kéuih	bún	syū
her	CL	book

'her book'

léih	go	boksih	hohkwái
your	CL	PhD	degree

'your PhD degree'

Note that the possessor is not restricted to pronouns in this construction:

lóuhbáan	ga	chē
boss	CL	car

'the boss's car'

fèih-lóu	go	daaih	tóuhláahm
fat-guy	CL	big	tummy

'Fatty's big tummy'

A demonstrative is often added in this construction:

léih	(gó)	dī	pàhngyáuh
you	those	CL	friends

'those friends of yours'

Potentially, there is thus a choice between four possessive constructions:

(a) léih ge pàhngyáuh
you LP friend
'your friend(s)'

(b) léih pàhngyáuh
you friend
'your friend'

(c) léih go pàhngyáuh
you CL friend
'your friend'

(d) léih gó go pàhngyáuh
you that CL friend
'that friend of yours'

The *ge* structure (a) belongs to more formal registers, the others (b–d) being more colloquial.

The possessive constructions serve broader functions than merely indicating possession. The phrase in the 'possessor' position may be associated less directly with the noun; note that verb phrases, for example, can appear in this position:

sihk ge yéh
eat LP thing
'things for eating'

jeuk ge sāam
wear LP clothes
'clothes for wearing'

yuhng ge sìhgaan
use LP time
'the time used'

wáan ge yàuhhei
play LP games
'games for playing'

jyú	yéh	ge	wohk		gāau	seui	ge	chín
cook	thing	LP	wok		pay	tax	LP	money

'woks for cooking'   'money for paying tax'

Strictly speaking, the verb phrases in these constructions do not have a possessor–possessed relationship with the head noun but they are associated in some way. Hence this construction is termed **associative** by Li and Thompson (1981). As with the possessive use of *ge*, the classifier construction is an alternative:

sihk	gó	dī	yéh		Yīnggwok	gó	go	gaausauh
eat	that	CL	thing		England	that	CL	professor

'things for eating'   'that professor in Britain'

Other constructions involving the structure [*ge* head noun] include adjectival passives (8.4.3) and relative clauses (6.4).

6.4 RELATIVE CLAUSES

Relative clauses are clauses which modify a noun phrase. **Restrictive** relative clauses serve to restrict the reference of a noun phrase, as in *The teachers I know are underpaid*, which suggests that the comment only applies to certain teachers, namely those known to the speaker. Relative clauses in Chinese have the reverse order of the English: the head noun comes at the end, as in all noun phrases. The order is thus:

(a) relative clause – *ge* – noun
(b) relative clause – (*gó*) – CL – noun

The structure is similar to that for possessive construction described in 6.3 above, with the same choice between *ge* and classifier before the head noun.

Relative clauses in spoken Cantonese tend to be of limited length, and some types of complex relative clause used in English rarely occur; on the other hand, the use of resumptive pronouns permits some types of relative clause which are not possible in English (6.4.2). There are no relative pronouns as such, although the particle *ge* used in one type of relative (6.4.1) functions like English *that*. In another type of relative, the demonstrative + classifier is used in place of *ge* (6.4.2). There are thus two forms of relative clause, corresponding to the two types of possessive construction discussed in 6.3:

(a) (Gó dī)   sīk   Gwóngdūng-wá **ge**   hohksāang háau
    (those CL)   know   Cantonese   that   students   examine

    dāk   hóu   dī.
    ADV   well   a-bit
    'The students who know Cantonese did a bit better.'

(b) Sīk   Gwóngdūng-wá **gó**   **dī** hohksāang háau
    know   Cantonese   those   CL   students   examine

    dāk   hóu   dī.
    ADV   well   a-bit
    'The students who know Cantonese did a bit better.'

These two types are treated separately in the following sections, as they have different ranges of application.

Cantonese does not have any direct counterparts to the non-restrictive relative, as in *The postman, who is a friend of mine, arrived.* However, existential and presentative sentences (15.5) are similar to the existential relative as in *There are people who believe in democracy.* The **free relative clause** as in *Who dares, wins* is discussed in 6.4.3, although it bears no structural resemblance to the restrictive relatives discussed in 6.4.1 and 6.4.2.

6.4.1   RELATIVES WITH *ge*

This type of relative clause is similar in form to the *ge* possessive (6.3) and attributive adjective constructions (9.1). Corresponding to the relative clause construction with *de* in Mandarin, it allows relative clauses in which the noun is understood as the subject or object of the predicate:

sīk   ngóh ge   yàhn
know   me   that   people
'people that know me'   (*yàhn* = subject of *sīk*)

ngóh   sīk   ge   yàhn
I   know   that   people
'people that I know'   (*yàhn* = object of *sīk*)

Where the head noun is not the subject or direct object of the predicate, a **resumptive pronoun** must be used in the relative clause to refer forward to the head noun. This may be done optionally in the case of a direct object:

ngóh chéng **(kéuihdeih)** sihk-faahn ge   pàhngyáuh
I   invite (them)   eat-food   that   friends
'friends that I invite for dinner'

Such resumptive pronouns are required when the head noun represents an indirect object, object of preposition/coverb, or object of comparison within the relative clause:

ngóh sung fā béi **kéuihdeih** ge behngyàhn (indirect object)
I send flower to them that patients
'the patients I sent flowers to'

ngóh tùhng **kéuihdeih** kīnggái ge hohksāang (object of coverb)
I with them chat that students
'the students that I chat with'

ngóh jaahn chín dō gwo **kéuihdeih** ge yàhn (object of
I earn money more than them that people comparision)
'The people who I make more money than'

Where the head noun is the possessor of a noun within the relative clause, the pronoun is optional:

(**kéuihdeih**) tìuh kwàhn hóu dyún ge sailouh-léui (genitive
their CL dress very short that little girls relative)
'the little girls whose dress is very short'

As with the possessive construction, *dīk* (Mandarin *de*) may be used in place of *ge* in formal registers of Cantonese:

Yùhngyih sauhsēung dīk léuihyán. (song title)
easy get-hurt that woman
'Women who are easily hurt.'

6.4.2 RELATIVES WITH CLASSIFIER

As for the possessive construction (6.3), an alternative form of relative clause uses a classifier and, optionally, a demonstrative:[9]

Ngóhdeih hái Faatgwok sihk **dī yéh** géi hóu-sihk ga.
we in France eat CL food quite good-eat PRT
'The food we ate in France was pretty good.'

Léih béi ngóh **gó dī séung** hóu leng.
you give me those CL pictures very nice
'The pictures you gave me are very nice.'

This construction is extremely common, being preferred in colloquial Cantonese to the more formal *ge* construction. It also enables relative clauses to be constructed which would be awkward or impossible using *ge*, such as those with a demonstrative phrase as the head:[10]

Gaau léih tàahn kàhm **gó** **go**? (film)
teach you play piano that CL
'The one who teaches you piano?'

Kéuihdeih jyuh **gódouh** hóu m-fōngbihn.   (conv.)
they   live there   very not-convenient
'Where they live is very inconvenient.'

Relative clauses in which the head noun functions as an indirect object, such as *the patient we sent flowers to*, can readily be formed in this way:

Ngóhdeih sung fā   béi **kéuih** gó go behngyàhn hóu
we   send flower to him that CL patient   well

fāan saai la.
back all PRT
'The patient we sent flowers to has recovered completely.'

Note that a resumptive pronoun, *kéuih* appears in the relative clause, referring forward to the noun *behngyàhn* 'patient', as described in 6.4.1 above. Similarly, where the antecedent of the relative clause is the possessor, the pronoun *kéuih* must be used in the relative clause:

Ngóhdeih tái-gwo **kéuih** fūk séung **gó** **go yàhn** làih-jó.
we   see-EXP his   CL picture that CL person come-PFV
'The person whose picture we saw has arrived.'

Ngóh johng dóu **kéuih** ga chē **gó** **go léuihyán** hóu
I   bump PRT her   CL car that CL woman   very

hóu yàhn ge.
nice person PRT
'The woman whose car I bumped into was nice.'

Even the object of a comparative may be made the antecedent, resulting in a construction barely possible in English:

Ngóh wah léih leng   gwo **kéuih** gó go léuihjái
I   say you beautiful than her that CL girl

jouh-jó Hēunggóng Síujé.
do-PFV Hongkong Miss
'The girl I said you were more beautiful than has become Miss Hongkong.'

Note that simpler relatives, in which the antecedent is the subject or object of the relative clause, do not call for the pronoun:

Ngóh yiu   wán   gó   go   yàhn   m̀h   háidouh.
I   need seek that CL   person not   here
'The person I'm looking for is not here.'
(*not* *Ngóh wán **kéuih** gó go yàhn)

6.4.3   FREE RELATIVE CLAUSES

Free relative clauses in English are those containing a wh-phrase in place of
head noun, as in *I'll give you what you want* and *You can do whatever you
like*. They are 'free' in the sense that what the clause refers to is left
unspecified. In Cantonese, there are two types of free relative, corresponding broadly to those with and without *-ever* in English. The first type
resembles the relative clauses discussed in 6.4.1 above, but without a head
noun after *ge*:

Ngóh séung góng ge   dōu   móuh   góng dou.
I   want   say   LP   still not-have   speak V-PRT
'What I want to say I didn't say.'

Léih m̀h   ngoi ge   ngóh ngoi.
you   not   want LP   I   want
'What you don't want, I want.'

Heui hōi-wúi   ge   yíhgīng jáu   saai.
go   have-meeting   LP   already leave   all
'Those who are going to the meeting have all left.'

Ngóhdeih gaau-gwo   ge   dōu   háau dāk   hóu   hóu.
we   teach-EXP   LP   all   exam ADV   well well
'Those we've taught did very well in the exam.'

The second type of free relative uses a question word, corresponding to the
English forms 'whoever', 'whatever', etc. (see 17.3 for a list of the
Cantonese question words). The question word is repeated in the main
clause, giving a parallel sentence structure in which it serves as subject or
object of both clauses:

Bīngo yáuh chín,   **bīngo** béi.
who   has   money who   pays
'Whoever has the money pays.'

Yìhgā dī   léuihjái jūngyi jeuk **mātyéh**, jauh jeuk **mātyéh**.
now   CL   girls   like   wear what   then wear what
'Nowadays girls wear whatever they want.'

    Léih séung béi **géi** **dō**,   jauh béi **géi** **dō**.
    you want pay how much then pay how much
    'You pay however much you want.'

Note the use of *jauh* (16.2.2) to connect the two clauses.

    The shortened forms *māt* 'what', *dím* 'how' and *bīn* 'where' are often used in this construction, as in indirect questions which have a similar structure (17.4):

    Léih séung sihk māt, ngóhdeih   sihk māt.   (conv.)
    you wish eat what we   eat what
    'We'll eat whatever you want to eat.'

    Ngóh jūngyi dím, jauh dím. (film)
    I   like   how then how
    'I do things however I like.'

    Yàhndeih giu kéuih   heui bīn, kéuih jauh heui bīn.
    people   tell him/her go   where s/he then go   where
    'He goes wherever he's told to go.'

Similar indefinite constructions are used in concessive clauses (16.2.4).

7 PREPOSITIONS AND EXPRESSIONS OF LOCATION

As discussed in chapter 3, prepositions do not form a clearly distinct class of words in Cantonese. The **coverbs**, which play a major role in expressing location, behave in most respects like a subclass of verbs: they may take aspect markers and verbal particles, and many may be used independently as the main verb in a sentence (see 3.1.3). Functionally, however, they play the role of prepositions and may usefully be viewed as such. Like English prepositions, they serve primarily to express spatial relations of location, direction, etc. (7.1), and additionally to indicate non-spatial relationships such as those of time and purpose (7.2). The coverbs/prepositions are used together with the **localizers** (3.1.4) to express more specific spatial relationships.

7.1 LOCATION

The most basic terms expressing location are compounds based on the demonstratives *nī* and *gó* (6.1):

nīdouh 'here'	gódouh 'there'
nībihn 'over here, this way'	góbihn 'over there, that way'
nīsyu 'here'	gósyu 'there'
nītàuh 'around this area'	gótàuh 'around that area'

These terms are used in the following ways:

(a) after a preposition/coverb such as *hái* 'at' or *yàuh* 'from':

> Dī   sāam   dán-jó   hái   gódouh.
> CL   clothes   put-PFV   at   there
> 'The clothes are over there.'

> Yàuh   nīdouh   heui   Jūngwàahn   géi   yúhn   a?
> from   here   go   Central   how   far   PRT
> 'How far is it from here to Central?'

(b) after a verb of motion:

> Ngóhdeih   yiu   heui   góbihn   pàaih-déui.
> we   need   go   there   queue-line
> 'We have to go and queue up over there.'

Ngóh hóu síu làih nītàuh.
I very little come here-abouts
'I rarely come to this area.'

(c) as sentence topics, followed by *yáuh/móuh* 'there is (not)':

Nītàuh móuh māt chē-sēng ge.
this-area not-have any car-noise PRT
'There's hardly any traffic noise in this area.'

Gódouh yáuh sāanggwó maaih.
there have fruit sell
'There's fruit for sale over there.'

Note: (i) *gódouh* refers to a specific place, unlike the *there* subject in the English translation which is a non-referential or 'dummy' subject; (ii) a preposition is not used before the demonstrative at the beginning of the clause.

(d) together with a place name:

hái Gáulùhng góbihn   hái Yīnggwok gódouh
at Kowloon that-side   at England there
'over in Kowloon'   'over in England'

Colloquially, *douh* may stand for *gódouh*:

Jī sósìh **hái** ngóh go dói **douh**.
CL key at my CL bag there
'The key's in my bag.'

7.1.1 SPATIAL LOCATION: COVERBS AND LOCALIZERS

hái 'be at/in' corresponds to Mandarin *zài* as the general-purpose marker of location: 'be located' would be a more accurate gloss, as it might be translated as 'on', 'in' or 'at' according to the context. As a coverb (3.1.3), *hái* may function as a verb rather than a preposition, although often corresponding to a preposition in English.

hái is used in a number of different constructions to indicate location in space:

(a) *hái* alone occurs with names of places:

Kéuih yìhgā m̀h **hái** **Hēunggóng**.
s/he now not be-at Hongkong
'She's not in Hongkong at the moment.'

Kéuih yíhgīng **hái yīyún** yāt go láihbaai.
s/he already at hospital one CL week
'She's already been in hospital for a week.'

(b) followed by another verb in a serial construction, *hái* is best translated as a preposition:

> Kéuih dākhàahn jauh **hái** ūkkéi **tái**-syū.
> s/he at-leisure then at home read-book
> 'He's at home reading when he has time.'

> Ngóhdeih **hái** Gáulùhng **jyuh-jó** sāam lìhn.
> we at Kowloon live-PFV three year
> 'We've been living in Kowloon for three years.'

(c) with a localizer alone, used as an adverb:

> Ga chē hái chēutbihn.
> CL car at outside
> 'The car's outside.'

> Kéuih lóuhgūng hái ngoihmihn yáuh go léuihyán.
> her husband at outside has CL woman
> 'Her husband has a mistress.'

(d) with a noun phrase followed by a localizer, in the pattern *hái* – [noun phrase] – [localizer], which is a very productive construction. The coverb *hái* serves as a general-purpose preposition of location while the localizer expresses the specific spatial relationship involved:

> Léih deui hàaih **hái** jēung tói **hahbihn**.
> your pair shoes be-at CL table under
> 'Your shoes are under the table.'

---

háidouh or *háisyu* 'be here' is used, for example, on the telephone:

A: Chéng mahn Chàhn sāang hái-m̀h-háidouh a?
request ask Chan Mr here-not-here PRT
'Is Mr Chan there, please?'

B: Deuim̀jyuh, Chàhn sāang m̀h háidouh wo.
sorry Chan Mr not be-here PRT
'I'm sorry, Mr Chan is not here.'

háidouh is also used together with verbs in a progressive sense (11.2.2):

A-Mā háidouh chē-sāam.
A-Mum be-here sew-clothes
'Mum's busy sewing (with sewing machine).'

héung (not to be confused with *heung* 'towards', 7.1.3) is a variant of *hái*:

Léih ūkkéi héung bīndouh a?
your home at where PRT
'Whereabouts is your home?'

The localizers used with *hái* or *héung* in constructions (c) and (d) above are as follows:

yahpbihn and *léuihmihn* 'inside' (*léuihmihn* corresponds to Mandarin *lǐmiàn*, but *léuih* cannot be used alone like Mandarin *lǐ*):

Fūng seun hái go háp yahpbihn.
CL letter be-at CL box inside
'The letter's inside the box.'

Hái ngóh (ge) sām léuihmihn jí yáuh yāt go beimaht.
at my (LP) heart inside only has one CL secret
'There's only one secret in my heart.'

chēutbihn and *ngoihmihn* 'outside':

Kéuih hái jáudim chēutbihn dáng ngóh.
s/he at hotel outside wait me
'She is waiting for me outside the hotel.'

Ngoihmihn lohk-gán yúh.
outside fall-PROG rain
'It's raining outside.'

chìhnmihn 'in front (of)' and *hauhbihn* 'behind':

Hái ga Bēnsí chìhnmihn yáuh go leng-léui.
at CL Benz in-front has CL pretty-girl
'There's a pretty girl in front of the Mercedes.'

Chē-jaahm hái nī tìuh gāai hauhbihn.
car-stop be-at this CL street behind
'The bus stop is behind this street.'

seuhng or *seuhngmihn/bihn* 'on (top of)' and *hah*(*mihn/bihn*) 'below':

Go gōsīng hái tòih seuhngmihn hōisām dou haam.
CL singer at stage on-top happy till cry
'The singer was so happy that she cried on the stage.'

Jēung tói hahbihn móuh yéh ge.
CL table under not-have thing PRT
'There's nothing under the table.'

deuimihn (not *deui or *deuibihn) 'opposite':

Hái séjihlàuh deuimihn yáuh gāan jáulàuh.
at office opposite have CL restaurant
'There's a restaurant opposite the office.'

jūng essentially means 'middle' as in *Jūnggwok* 'the Middle Kingdom = China' but is used in Modern Standard Chinese and formal Cantonese to mean 'in':

Ngóhdeih yāt sāng jūng yáuh msíu kwanlàahn.
our one life middle have not-few difficulty
'There are many difficulties in our lives.'

The spatial meaning 'in the middle' is expressed by *jūnggāan*:

Go gongkàhm fong hái haak-tēng jūnggāan.
CL piano put at guest-hall middle
'The piano is placed in the centre of the living room.'

jīgāan 'between' is used with *tùhng* coordinating two places or parties:

Kéuih jyuh hái Gáulùhng-tòhng tùhng Gáulùhng-sìhng jīgāan.
s/he live at Kowloon Tong and Kowloon City between
'She lives between Kowloon Tong and Kowloon City.'

Ngóhdeih léuhng go jīgāan ge kéuihlèih yuht lèih
we two CL between LP distance more come

yuht yúhn.
more far
'The distance between the two of us is growing farther and farther.'

The place expression [noun-localizer] may begin a clause, followed by the existential verb *yáuh* 'have' or *móuh* 'not-have', forming an existential locative construction (note that no preposition is used here):

Go dói yahpbihn móuh saai chín.
CL bag inside not-have all money
'There's no money in the bag.'

Sing Gīng léuihmihn yáuh go gusih . . .
Holy Book within have CL story
'There's a story in the Bible . . .'

káhn 'near' may occur with or without an object:

Ngóhdeih léuhng go jyuh dāk hóu káhn.
we two CL live ADV very near
'The two of us live close together.'

Ngóhdeih jyuh dāk hóu káhn hóibīn.
we live ADV very near seaside
'We live near the sea.'

7.1.2 DISTANCE AND MOVEMENT

lèih 'away from' indicates the distance between two places:

Daaihhohk lèih léih ūkkéi géi yúhn a?
university from your home how far PRT
'How far is the university from your home?'

hái . . . làih/heui expresses distance or motion 'from X to Y', assuming that one is located at point X:

Hái Lèuhndēun heui Gimkìuh yiu yāt go jūngtàuh.
at London go Cambridge need one CL hour
'It takes an hour to get from London to Cambridge.'

Hái Jūngwàahn heui Sām Séui Bóu yáuh syùhn daap ge.
at Central go Sam Shui Po have ferry catch PRT
'There's a ferry from Central to Sham Shui Po.'

yàuh 'from' is used mainly in the following ways:

(a) to express distance:

Yàuh Gáulùhng dou Sātìhn yiu sāam go jih. (see 21.3)
from Kowloon to Shatin need three CL unit
'It takes fifteen minutes from Kowloon to Shatin.'

(b) referring to time:

yàuh gām-yaht hōichí
from today begin
'beginning from today'

Ngóhdeih yàuh sai dou daaih dōu haih gam
we from small until big also be so

hóu pàhngyáuh.
good friend
'We've been good friends since we were small.'

(c) indicating the source of responsibility or sponsorship:

Sóyáuh faiyuhng yàuh ngóh fuhjaak.
all expenses from me responsible
'I'm responsible for all the expenses.'

Nī   go   jitmuhk   haih   yàuh   Wíhng   Ōn   gūngsī
this CL   programme   is   from   Wing   On   company

dahkyeuk bo-chēut.   (TV)
specially broadcast
'This programme is broadcast specially by the Wing On company.'

chùhng 'from' (Mandarin *cóng*) is a formal equivalent of *yàuh*, used to introduce a source of movement, or a starting point in time:

chùhng   ngoihgwok   làih   ge   hohkjé
from   abroad   come   LP   scholar
'scholars coming from abroad'

chùhng   luhksahp   lìhndoih   hōichí
from   sixty   decade   begin
'from the 1960s onwards'

7.1.3 DIRECTION

góbihn 'that way' and *nībihn* 'this way' may be used to indicate direction:

Go   cháak   jáu-jó   heui   góbihn.
CL   thief   run-PFV   go   that-way
'The thief ran off that way.'

heung means 'towards' in a directional sense (contrast *deui*, 7.2.1):

Ngóh   heung   deihtit   góbihn   hàahng.
I   towards subway   that-way walk
'I'm walking in the direction of the subway (MTR).'

Go   fūng   heung-gán   dūngmihn   chēui.
CL   typhoon   towards-PROG   east-side   blow
'The typhoon is blowing towards the east.'

gīng (*gwo*) in a serial verb construction expresses the relation 'via':

Ngóhdeih   gīng   Yandouh   heui   Yīnggwok.
we   via   India   go   England
'We're going to England via India.'

Ga   chē   gīng   seuihdouh   heui   Hēunggóngjái.
CL   car   via   tunnel   go   Aberdeen
'The car goes to Aberdeen via the tunnel.'

Note that *gīng* is also widely used as a verb, meaning 'pass (by)':

Gīng-m̀h-gīng Máhlaih yīyún a?
pass-not-pass Mary hospital PRT
'Do you pass by the Queen Mary hospital?'
(used on buses, minibuses, etc.)

7.1.4 PLACEMENT

With transitive verbs denoting placement, a locative prepositional phrase
(as seen in 7.1.1) follows the object:

Mgōi léih fong dī yéh hái tói seuhngmihn.
please you put CL thing at table top-side
'Please put those things on the table.'

Ngóh gwa fūk wá hái gódouh.
I hang CL picture at here
'I'm hanging the picture over there.'

Dī chín ngóh jāi hái go háp douh.
CL money I keep at CL box there
'I'm keeping the money in the box.'

Note that the *hái*-phrase is completed by a localizer such as *seuhngmihn* or
a demonstrative such as *douh* (7.1.1).

An alternative structure for verbs of placement is the serial construction
with *jēung* (8.3.1):

Ngóh **jēung** go fā-jēun **báai hái gódouh**.
I take CL flower-bottle put at here
'I'm putting the vase over there.'

7.2 NON-SPATIAL RELATIONSHIPS

In addition to indicating location in space and time, prepositions/coverbs
and postpositions/localizers may indicate other relationships between noun
phrases.

7.2.1 COVERBS

deui means 'towards' in a non-directional sense, for example with reference to personal relationships and feelings:

Ngóh ngoihmóu deui ngóh hóu hóu ge.
my mother-in-law towards me very good PRT
'My mother-in-law treats me nicely.'

Ngóh deui chín móuh pīngin ga. (film)
I towards money not-have prejudice PRT
'I don't have anything against money.'

Hēunggóng-yàhn deui baatgwa sānmán hóu
Hongkong-people towards gossip news very

yáuh hingcheui.
have interest
'Hongkong people are very interested in gossip.'

dou with time expressions means 'until' or 'by':

Ngóhdeih dou yìhgā dōu meih si-gwo gam kùhng.
we until now still not-yet try-EXP so poor
'We've never been so poor until now.'

Ngóh dou gām sìh gāmyaht juhng m̀h mìhng.
I till this time today still not understand
'To this day, I still don't understand.'

gān, which as a verb means 'follow', also functions as a preposition meaning 'with':

Ngóh hah chi gān léih heui máaih sung.
I next time with you go buy food
'I'll go and buy groceries with you next time.'

Other prepositions formed from *gān* are *gānjyuh* 'with, following' and *gāngeui* 'according to':

Léih gānjyuh ngóh hàahng.
you following me walk
'Follow me.'

gāngeui jyūngā ge fānsīk
according expert LP analysis
'according to expert analysis'

jiu or *jiujyuh* have a similar meaning, 'following' or 'according to':

Jiu gai yīnggōi yáuh chīu gwo yāt baak
according calculate should have more than one

maahn jihng ge.
million remain PRT
'According to calculations there should be over a million left.'

Nī go góngsī sèhngyaht jiujyuh bún syū góng.
this CL lecturer always following CL book talk
'This lecturer always lectures according to the textbook.'

jiu is often used with the particle *fāan* 'back, in return' (11.3.1):

Ngóhdeih jiu   fāan gauhlín ge fōngfaat heui chàuh fún.
we   follow back old-year LP method go   raise fund
'We'll go with last year's way to raise funds.'

Idiom: *jiu* can be used as an adverbial before a verb with the meaning
'carry on . . . regardless':

Yám jeui-jó   kéuih dōu jiu   yám.
drink drunk-PFV s/he also continues drink
'He goes on drinking even when he's drunk.'

Hóu dō   yàhn mìhng jī   yáuh ngàihhím dōu
very many people even know have danger   also

jiu   sihk yín.
continue smoke cigarette
'People carry on smoking even when they know it's dangerous.'

Gáuchāt   jīhauh móuh jiu   tiu, máh
ninety-seven after dance continue dance horse

jiu   páau.
continue race
(tiu-móuh 'dance', páau-máh 'race-horse')
'After 1997, the dancing and horse-racing will continue as before.'

A: Ńgh ' dím   bun juhng jouh-m̀h-jouh a?
   five o'clock half still do-not-do   PRT
   'Do we still work after five-thirty?'

B: Jiu   jouh.
   continue do
   'Carry on.'

---

tùhng 'with' expresses personal relationships:

Ngóh tùhng Wòhng Sāang mhaih hóu suhk   ge je.
I   with Wong Mr   not-be very familiar PRT PRT
'I don't know Mr Wong very well.'

A-Wíhng lám-jyuh   tùhng kéuih gòhgō gáau sāangyi.
Ah-Wing think-CONT with his   brother deal business
'Wing is thinking of setting up a business with his [elder] brother.'

tùhng is also used to coordinate nouns (16.1.1) and in comparisons (9.3.3).

Idiom: *tùhng . . . móuh gwāan* (or *gwāanhaih*) 'have nothing to do with':

Nī   gihn sih   tùhng ngóhdeih móuh   gwāanhaih ge.
this CL matter with us   not-have connection PRT
'This has nothing to do with us.'

tùhng in this usage may also take a clause as its object:

Go gachìhn **tùhng bīngo jouh** móuh   gwāan   ge.
CL price   with   who   does not-have connection PRT
'The price has nothing to do with who does the job.'

---

waih or *waihjó* means 'for' in the sense 'for the sake/benefit of':

Ngóh   waih léih cheung sáu gō.
I   for you sing   CL song
'I'll sing a song for you.'

Kéuih waihjó gó go léuihyán mātyéh dōu háng   jouh.
he   for   that CL woman what   all willing do
'He'll do anything for that woman.'

yānwaih 'because (of)' may function as a preposition as well as a conjunction:

Ngóh mhaih yānwaih chín   bōng léih ge.
I   not-be because money help you PRT
'I help you not because of the money.'

Kéuih haih **yānwaih mihnjí** sīnji gyūn   gam dō   chín.
s/he   is   because face   then donate so much money
'She donates so much money for appearance's sake.'

yānwaih may be used together with nouns denoting reasons, a usage which is redundant in English but consistent with the pattern of *yānwaih . . . sóyíh* as a conjunction (16.2):

Ngóh m̀h wúih **yānwaih nī go yùhnyān** lèih-hōi   kéuih.
I   not would because this CL reason   leave-away him
'I wouldn't leave him for THAT reason.'

Note that the English here is potentially ambiguous, while in Cantonese the position of the *yānwaih* phrase relative to the negation determines the meaning:

Ngóh **yānwaih nī go yùhnyān** m̀h wúih lèih hōi kéuih.
I   because this CL reason   not would leave apart him
'I wouldn't leave him, for that reason.'

kèih jūng 'among others' is a literary phrase also used in speech:

Kèih jūng   yāt go jyūngā haih Jūngmàhn Daaihhohk
rest among   one CL expert   is   Chinese   University

ge gaausauh.
LP professor
'One of the specialists is a professor at the Chinese University.'

It is commonly used to refer back to a previous clause or sentence:

Yáuh géi   go   hohkjé sé-gwo   gwāanyū Jūngmán
have some CL   scholar write-EXP concern Chinese

yúhfaat ge syū, kèih jūng jeui chēutméng
grammar LP book rest among most famous

ge haih Jiuh Yùhn-Yahm.
LP is   Chao Yuen-Ren
'A number of scholars have written books about Chinese grammar, among whom the best-known is Chao Yuen-Ren.'

7.2.2 NON-SPATIAL LOCALIZERS/POSTPOSITIONS

Some words which behave syntactically like localizers or postpositions (see 7.1.1) express non-spatial relationships. Localizers marking location in time are formed with the prefixes *jī* and *yíh*:

jīchìhn/yíhchìhn 'before'   jīhauh/yíhhauh 'after'
jīloih/yíhloih 'within'   jī-ngoih/yíh-ngoih 'beyond'

The two alternatives *jīchìhn/yíhchìhn* 'before' and *jīhauh/yíhhauh* 'after' are not interchangeable in all environments, although they overlap. The forms with *jī* are used after a noun phrase, like postpositions:

Syú-ga   **jīchìhn** ngóh yiu sé   hóu   bún syū.
summer-holiday before I   need write V-PRT CL book
'I need to finish writing the book before the summer holiday.'

Yīnggōi tái hóu **gáu-chāt**   **jīhauh** ge faatjín.
should look good ninety-seven beyond LP development
'One should be optimistic about developments beyond 1997.'

Chāamháau syū yiu   **léuhng yaht jīloih** wàahn.
reference   book should two   day   within return
'Reference books should be returned within two days.'

These words are also used as conjunctions after a clause (16.2.1):

Ngóh bātyihp   jīhauh wúih wán gūng ge   la.
I   graduate after will find job   PRT PRT
'I'll find a job after I graduate.'

By contrast, the related words *yíhchìhn* 'before' and *yíhhauh* 'after' function as adverbs (10.3.3):

Yíhchìhn kéiuh gaau   Jūngmán ge.
before   s/he teach Chinese PRT
'He used to teach Chinese.'

Yíhhauh   ngóh dōu   m̀h séung tēng dóu
afterwards   I   still not want hear V-PRT

léih   bá   sēng.
your CL   voice
'From now on I don't want to hear your voice again.'

yíhseuhng 'above' and *yíhhah* 'below' are used with figures to express lower and upper limits respectively:

Sāamsahp seui yíhseuhng   Yāt bāak   mān   yíhhah
thirty   year above   one hundred   dollar below
'aged thirty and above'   'below $100'

Similarly, *yíh-ngoih* 'beyond' may refer to limits in time or space:

Yāt baak   gūngléih yíh-ngoih sāu   m̀h
one hundred   kilometre beyond   receive   not

dóu   yahmhòh seunhouh.
V-PRT   any   signal
'Beyond a range of 100 km you can't receive any signal.'

8 THE VERB PHRASE

This chapter deals with the basic syntax of verb phrases: types of verb (8.1), objects (8.2) and serial verb constructions (8.3). Passive, causative and resultative constructions are treated in sections 8.4 and 8.5. The aspect markers and verbal particles are treated separately in chapter 11, modal (auxiliary) verbs in chapter 12.

Cantonese verbs do not vary in form according to number, person or tense. There are no verbal inflections, apart from the aspect markers, which behave for the most part as suffixes (11.2.1).

8.1 TYPES OF VERB

Cantonese verbs are traditionally divided into categories as follows:

copular verb	haih 'be'
stative verbs	jūngyi 'like', jyuh 'live', lám 'think'
action verbs	jouh 'do', heui 'go', yūk 'move'
auxiliary verbs	yiu 'need', wúih 'will/would', séung 'want'

The distinctions between auxiliary and other verbs, and between stative verbs and adjectives are not categorical ones, as discussed in chapter 3.

8.1.1 THE VERB HAIH 'BE'

The copular verb *haih* 'to be', like other Cantonese verbs, is invariable in form, hence *haih* may translate as 'am', 'are', 'were', etc. It should be distinguished from the locative coverb *hái* 'be at' with a high rising tone (see 7.1). As the name *copula* suggests, the main function of *haih* is to join two noun phrases:

Gó dī yàhn haih ngóh ge pàhngyáuh.
that CL people are my LP friend
'Those people are my friends.'

Gó fūk wá haih ngóh ge.
that CL picture is my LP
'That picture is mine.'

Note that in neutral contexts *haih* is *not* used to connect nouns with adjectives (9.1):

Gó fūk séung hóu leng.
that CL photo very nice
'The picture's nice.'

In general, *haih* would not be used except as a focus marker in an emphatic sentence or to refute a claim:

Gó fūk séung **haih** hóu leng bo.
that CL photo is very nice PRT
'The picture is really nice.'

A: Kéuih mhaih hóu leng-jái jē.
    he isn't very good-looking PRT
    'He isn't very good-looking.'

B: Kéuih **haih** hóu leng-jái léh.
    he is very good-looking PRT
    'He is really good-looking.'

In most cases *haih* can be omitted without affecting the sense or structure of a sentence:

Nī go (haih) ngóh sailóu lèihge.
this CL (is) my brother PRT
'This is my [younger] brother.'

Dī choi (haih) sahp mān (yāt) gān.
CL vegetable (is) ten dollar (one) catty
'These vegetables are ten dollars a catty.'

Gó bún syú (haih) ngóh ge.
that CL book (is) my LP
'That book is mine.'

Idiom: in (*haih*) *ngóh ge* meaning 'it's on me' *haih* is conventionally omitted:

Nī chāan ngóh ge. (TV ad)
this meal my LP
'This meal's on me.'

In addition to its basic role as copula, *haih* has a number of grammatical functions:

(a) In the emphatic construction *haih* . . . *ge*, which should be distinguished from the possessive *ge* (6.3). Like Mandarin *shì* . . . *de* and the 'cleft' construction in English, it emphasizes the word after *haih*:

Gó bún syū **haih** ngóh dehng **ge.**
that CL book is I order PRT
'It was I who ordered that book.'

Gám ge jouhfaat **haih** léih sīnji lám dóu **ge.**
such LP do-way is you only think V-PRT PRT
'Only you could have thought up that kind of method.'

Note that *ge* is replaced by *ga* in questions, due to contraction with the question particle *a* (18.1.1):

Nī fūk wá **haih** bīngo sung **ga?**
this CL picture is who give PRT
'Who was it that gave us this picture?'

Since the *haih . . . ge* also allows omission of *haih*, the sentence particle *ge* (18.3.2) may be seen as a case of this construction with *haih* omitted.

(b) in A-not-A form, *haih-mhaih*, to ask yes/no questions (17.1.3):

Haih-mhaih móuh saai máih a?
be-not-be not-have all rice PRT
'Are we out of rice?'

(c) as an affirmative answer to certain types of question, notably particle questions (17.1.8, 17.1.9):

A: Léih sīk kéuih ge mē?   B: Haih a.
   you know him PRT PRT   is PRT
   'You know him, do you?'   'Yes.'

A: Léih móuh saai chín àh?   B: Haih a.
   you not-have all money PRT   is PRT
   'Don't you have any money?'   'No.'

(d) to introduce predicative complements, like English *as*, with the verbs *syun haih* 'count as' and *dong . . . haih* 'treat as, regard as':

Sāam baak mān **syun** **haih** géi pèhng.
three hundred dollar count is pretty cheap
'Three hundred dollars counts as pretty cheap.'

Ngóh **dong** kéuih **haih** sailouhjái lèihge je.
I regard him as child PRT PRT
'I regard him as just a child.'

(e) in quantified sentences with *dōu*, meaning 'every' (14.1):

Haih yàhn **dōu** jī kéuih daaih-jó tóuh.
is person all know she big-PFV belly
'Everyone knows she's pregnant.'

Idiom: *haih* . . . *dōu* expresses stubbornness or determination:

Kéuih **haih** dōu yiu jihgéi heui.
s/he is also need self go
'He insists on going himself.'

Kéuih mìhng jī lohk-yúh **haih** dōu m̀h daai jē.
s/he clear know fall-rain is also not carry umbrella
'He won't carry an umbrella even when it's raining.'

8.1.2 STATIVE VERBS

The term **stative verb** is used in both a broad and a narrow sense. In the broad sense, traditional in Chinese grammar, stative verbs include what we treat as adjectives (see ch. 9). As discussed in chapter 3, there is no clear distinction between stative verbs and adjectives. In a narrower sense, more usual in linguistics and grammars of other languages, stative verbs in this sense are those which are clearly verbs, but share certain properties with adjectives. Clear examples are *jīdou* 'know' and *tùhngyi* 'agree', which may be modified by *géi* 'quite' and *hóu* 'very much':

Ngóh mhaih géi jīdou kéuihdeih séung dím.
I not-be quite know they want how
'I'm not quite sure what they have in mind.'

Kéuihdeih mhaih hóu tùhngyi.
they not-be very agree
'They don't really agree.'

Many stative verbs are intermediate between verbs and adjectives; *gēng*, for example, resembles both the verb *fear* and the adjective *afraid*. It behaves as a verb in taking an object, but like an adjective in allowing reduplication (9.2.2):

Yàhn-yàhn dōu gēng nī júng behng.
person-person all afraid this CL disease
'Everyone is afraid of this disease.'

Ngóh gēng-gēng-déi jēk.
I afraid-afraid-ish PRT
'I'm a bit afraid.'

Several of them take objects, while the corresponding English adjectives cannot:

Ngóh hóu **suhk** kéuih ūkkéi-yàhn.
I very familiar his home-people
'I know his family very well.'

Nī gihn sāam ji **ngāam** léih la!
this CL shirt most right you PRT
'This shirt suits you perfectly.'

[Nī jek sái-tàuh-séui] ngāam saai síu-pàhngyáuh! (TV ad.)
[this CL wash-head-water] right PRT small-friend
'[This shampoo's] just the thing for children!'

Like adjectives, however, they may be modified by *hóu* and other modifiers (9.1.3) and may be reduplicated with *déi* (9.2.2).

8.1.3 VERBS OF PERCEPTION

Perception verbs are formed by combining a sensory verb with a verbal
particle or other verb. Note the systematic distinction between the simple
verb denoting perceptual activity and the compound verbs with *dóu* or *gin*
which denote actual perception of a stimulus:

tái 'look, watch'	tái dóu, tái gin 'see'
tēng 'listen'	tēng dóu, tēng gin 'hear'
gin 'see'	gin dóu 'see, notice'
mohng 'watch, stare'	mohng dóu, mohng gin 'see, watch'
màhn 'smell, sniff'	màhn dóu 'smell' (transitive)
gok dāk 'feel'	gok dāk dóu 'feel' (formal)

The verb and particle in these combinations, although usually written as
single words in the Yale system, are all potentially separable, the negative
m̀h and the modal particle *dāk* coming between them:

tái m̀h gin 'cannot see'	tái dāk gin 'can see'
gámgok m̀h dóu 'cannot feel'	màhn dāk dóu 'can smell'

dāk is often redundant with perception verbs as *tái dóu* alone, for example,
may have the modal meaning 'can see', but *dāk* may be added for
emphasis:

Hóu yúhn dōu màhn (dāk) dóu.
very far also smell (can) V-PRT
'You can smell it a long way off.'

Gam yúhn, léih tái-m̀h-tái dāk gin a?
so far you look-not-look can see PRT
'Can you see so far away?'

dāk chēut with verbs of perception denotes the ability to 'tell' in the sense of recognizing what is perceived:

Ngóh **tēng dāk chēut** kéuih mhaih Gwóngdūng-yàhn.
I listen can out s/he not-be Cantonese-person
'I can tell (by listening) that she's not Cantonese.'

Léih **sihk-m̀h-sihk dāk chēut** yahpbihn yáuh dī mātyéh a?
you eat-not-eat can out inside have some what PRT
'Can you taste what's in this?'

m̀h chēut is the negative counterpart of *dāk chēut* (see 12.3.3):

A: Kéuih luhksahp-géi seui ga la.
   s/he sixty-some years PRT PRT
   'He's in his sixties.'

B: **Tái m̀h chēut** wo!
   look not out PRT
   'You wouldn't know!'

Ngóh **màhn m̀h chēut** haih mātyéh meih leihge.
I smell not out be what flavour PRT
'I can't tell what the flavour is.'

Idioms with tái:
tái-háh or *tái-gwo* 'it depends' is followed by an indirect question:

A: Yiu géi loih a?
   need how long PRT
   'How long will it take?'

B: Tái-háh bīngo jouh lā.
   see-DEL who does PRT
   'It depends who does it.'

A: Léih géisìh chéng ngóh sihk-faahn a?
   you when invite me eat-food PRT
   'When are you going to invite me to dinner?'

B: Tái-gwo sìn.
   see-EXP first
   'We'll see . . .'

tái làih is used to make an inference based on appearances:

Tái làih léih gām chi yātdihng faat-daaht la. (film)
see come you this time definitely make-money PRT
'It looks like you're sure to make money this time.'

Idioms: *tái hóu* 'be optimistic' may be used intransitively or transitively:

Léih juhng tái-hóu àh?
you still look-good PRT
'Still optimistic, are you?'

Ngóh jauh m̀h tái-hóu lak.
I then not look-good PRT
'But I'm not optimistic.'

Chèuhng sin làih tái hóyíh tái-hóu gáu-chāt
long term come look can look-good ninety-seven

jíhauh ge faatjín.
after LP development
'In the long term one can be optimistic about developments after 1997.'

tái hōi also means 'be optimistic', the particle *hōi* 'away' meaning to look away from a problem or difficult situation:

Léih tái hōi dī lā!
you look V-PRT a-bit PRT
'Why not look on the bright side?'

tái chúhng 'regard as important' and its converse *tái hēng* or
tái síu 'underestimate' have a similar syntax:

Jūnggwok-yàhn tái chúhng gwāanhaih ge.
Chinese-person look important connection PRT
'The Chinese place great importance on connections.'

Léih mhóu tái síu kéuih a.
you don't look small him PRT
'Don't underestimate him.'

tái dāi and *tái m̀h héi* 'look down on' apply similarly to people:

Ngóh jīdou léih tái m̀h héi ngóh. (film)
I know you look not up me
'I know you look down on me.'

tēng dāk mìhng 'understand (what one is hearing)' has a similar syntax:

Hēimohng léih tēng dāk mìhng.
hope you hear can understand
'I hope you understand.'

Léih tēng-m̀h-tēng dāk mìhng kéuih góng māt a?
you hear-not-hear can understand s/he say what PRT
'Can you understand what he's saying?'

Complement clauses of perception verbs, describing witnessed events, directly follow the verb without any conjunction:

Ngóh tái-jyuh go bìhbī **fan-gaau**.
I look-CONT CL baby sleep
'I'm watching the baby sleep.'

Ngóh sèhngyaht tēng dī hohksāang **gám góng**.
I always hear CL students so talk
'I often hear the students talking like that.'

Léih yáuh-móuh gin dóu kéuih **hàahng yahp làih** a?
you have-have-not see V-PRT her walk enter come PRT
'Did you see her come in?'

Note that the verb in the complement clause does not change in form: the progressive form -gán is not used, for example, in such complement clauses.

8.1.4 VERBS OF COGNITION

These verbs indicate mental activity or perception:

jīdou 'know' (facts)
sīk 'know' (a person or skill)
lám 'think'
yíhwàih 'think' (usually erroneously)
yihngwàih 'think, consider'

gokdāk 'feel' (opinion)
geidāk 'remember'
yihngdāk 'recognize'
mgeidāk 'forget'
(sēung-)seun 'believe' (have confidence)

The syntax of these verbs is straightforward: there being no conjunction corresponding to *that*, a verb of cognition is simply followed by a clause:

Ngóh gokdāk léih yīnggōi síusām dī.
I feel you should careful little
'I think you ought to be more careful.'

Ngóh geidāk kéuih géi lēk gé.
I remember s/he quite clever PRT
'I remember that she's pretty bright.'

Note: sīk means 'know' applied to people, as in the phrase *sīk yàhn* 'to have connections' and also to knowledge of how to do things (*sīk yàuh-séui* 'to know how to swim'; see 12.1.2). *jī* applies to facts or information, as in *Jī-m̀h-jī hái bīndouh?* 'Do you know where it is?' When *jī* is followed by only a pronoun as follows, *m̀h jī kéuih* can be interpreted as an elliptical form of *m̀h jī kéuih jouh mātyéh*:

A: A-Táam jouh mātyéh a?
   Ah-Tam do what PRT
   'What's the matter with Tam?'
B: M̀h jī kéuih wo.
   not-know him PRT
   'Oh, I don't know about him.'

8.2 OBJECTS OF THE VERB AND TRANSITIVITY

The verb phrase, in linguistic theory, includes the object. In Cantonese, the relationship between verb and object is particularly close (see verb–object compounds, 8.2.4) and objects may be of several distinct kinds.

8.2.1 DIRECT AND DIRECTIONAL OBJECTS

Many verbs of motion which are intransitive in many languages may take directional objects in Cantonese. There is no need for a preposition between a directional verb and its object: (see ch. 7 and 3.1.3 for discussion of Cantonese prepositions/coverbs)

heui Méihgwok
go America
'go to America'

làih Hēunggóng
come Hongkong
'come to Hongkong'

yahp fóng
enter room
'go into a room'

chēut mùhnháu
out entrance
'go out of the door'

Verbs of posture take objects denoting locations:

Léih chóh nī jēung yí lā.
you sit this CL chair PRT
'Sit on this chair.'

Fan jihgéi ge chòhng syūfuhk dī.
sleep self LP bed comfortable more
'It's more comfortable to sleep in one's own bed.'

Many verbs may take either a direct or a locative object, e.g. *duhk* 'study' and *sihk* 'eat':

Direct object
Léih duhk bīn fō ga?
you study which subject PRT
'Which subject are you studying?

Ngóh sihk-gwo Bākgīng choi.
I eat-EXP Beijing food
'I've eaten Pekinese food.'

Object of location
Léih duhk bīn gāan hohkhaauh a?
you study which CL school PRT
'Which school do you go to?'

Ngóh sihk-gwo Bākgīng Làuh.
I eat-EXP Beijing House
'I've eaten at the Beijing Garden.'

8.2.2 INDIRECT OBJECTS

Verbs like *béi* 'give' may take two consecutive objects, as in English. In Cantonese, however, the indirect object follows the direct:

Ngóh béi chín léih. (*not* *ngóh béi léih chín)
I give money you
'I'll give you the money.'

Note that Cantonese differs from both English and Mandarin in the order of the two objects. However, the indirect object may come first when the direct object is especially long:[1]

Ngóh béi léih géi chín mān tùhngmàaih
I give you a-few thousand dollar plus

yāt jēung gēipiu.
one CL air-ticket
'I'll give you a few thousand dollars plus an air ticket.'

This construction is used primarily with the verbs *béi* 'give' and *je* meaning 'lend':

Ngóh je-jó yāt chīn mān kéuih.
I lend-PFV one thousand dollars him/her
'I lent him one thousand dollars.'

Note that if the indirect object precedes the direct, *je* may mean 'borrow':

Ngóh je-jó kéuih yāt chīn mān.
I borrow-PFV him one thousand dollars
'I borrowed a thousand dollars from him' *or* 'I lent him a thousand dollars.'

Some speakers use the double object construction with additional verbs such as *sung* 'send, give as a present' and *wàahn* 'return':

Kéuih   sung   bún   syū   ngóh.
s/he   send   CL   book   me
'She gave me a book (as a gift).'

Faai   dī   wàahn   fāan   tìuh   sósìh ngóh.
quick   a-bit   return   back   CL   key   me
'Return the key to me quickly.'

In general, verbs of giving such as the above with the exception of *béi* appear in a serial verb construction (see 8.3), typically with *béi* as the second verb:[2]

Ngóh   sailóu   **gei**-jó   fūng   seun   **béi** ngóh.
my   brother   mail-PFV   CL   letter   to   me
'My brother mailed me a letter.'

Yīnggōi   **sung**   fā   **béi**   kéuih.
should   send   flower   to   her
'We should send her flowers.'

Ngóh   **maaih**   ga   chē   **béi**   léih.
I   sell   CL   car   to   you
'I'm selling you the car.'

A third verb may be added after the indirect object, often appearing redundant in English:

Ngóh   **gei**   dī   jīlíu   **béi**   léih   **tái**.
I   send   some   information   to   you   see
'I'll send you some information.'

Léih   **góng béi**   kéuih   **tēng**   sìn.
you   say   to   him   hear   first
'You tell him first.'

In these constructions, *béi* is optional.

Another set of verbs may take two objects with a fixed order, the first indirect and the other a direct object:

gaau 'teach':

Móuh   yàhn   gaau   ngóh   Jūngmán.
not-have   person   teach   me   Chinese
'There's no one to teach me Chinese.'

mahn 'ask':

Ngóh   sīn   mahn   léih   yāt   go   mahntàih.
I   first   ask   you   one   CL   question
'I'll ask you a question first.'

faht 'punish':

> Léih chìh dou   yàhndeih wúih faht léih chín   ge.
> you late arrive people   will fine you money PRT
> 'They'll fine you if you're late.'

Many verbs which take two objects in English (*call, consider* etc.) are expressed using serial verb constructions. The verb *jouh* 'do' is used as the second verb:

> Yàhndeih **giu** kéuih **jouh** fèihlóu ge.
> people   call him   as   fatty PRT
> 'He's known as fatty.'

This construction with *giu* is also used in giving one's name, with *jouh* optional:

> Ngóh   giu   (jouh)   Chàhn   Síu   Bóu.
> I   call   (as)   Chan   Siu   Bou
> 'My name is Chan Siu Bou.'

dong 'regard as, treat as' takes either *haih* + noun phrase or a full clause as its complement:

> Yàhndeih **dong**   ngóh   **haih gūngyàhn**   lèihge.
> people   regard me   as   work-person PRT
> 'I'm being treated as a servant.'

> Léih **dong**   ngóh   **móuh dou**   àh? (idiom)
> you   regard me   not   here PRT
> 'Are you treating me as a nobody?'

8.2.3 QUANTIFIED OBJECTS

Where the object, direct or indirect, is quantified, followed by the quantifier *dōu*, it is placed before the verb:

> Ngóh   léuhng   deui   (hàaih)   dōu jūngyi.
> I   two   pair   (shoes)   all like
> 'I like both pairs (of shoes).'

> Ngóhdeih   sèhng   tìuh   (yú)   sihk   saai.
> we   whole   CL   (fish)   eat   V-PRT
> 'We've eaten the whole fish.'

> Kéuih   go-go   (hātyī)   dōu béi   chín.
> s/he   CL-CL   (beggar)   all   give   money
> 'He gives money to every beggar.'

Note that the noun itself may be omitted, leaving behind the classifier, when its identity is clear from the context. The special syntax of quantified phrases is discussed further in chapter 14.

8.2.4 VERB–OBJECT COMPOUNDS

In many fixed verb–object combinations the object is said to be 'incorporated' into the verb (2.3.3). These are written with hyphenation to show this relationship:

tái-syū	cheung-gō
read-book	sing-song
'read'	'sing'
gin-gūng	yám-yéh
see-work	drink-stuff
'go to an interview'	'have a drink'

tái alone merely means 'look' (8.1.3), while *cheung* 'sing' is rarely used without an object. Similarly, the verbs *sé* 'write' and *jā* drive' are not readily used intransitively as in English, but are typically accompanied by an object as in the following cases:

Ngóh yiu **sé-seun** béi ngóh gòhgō.
I need write-letter to my brother
'I have to **write** to my [elder] brother.'

Ngóhdeih **jā-chē** heui Jīm Dūng.
we drive-car go Tsimshatsui East
'We'll **drive** to Tsimshatsui East.'

Note that the object in these constructions is generic or indefinite: it is not understood as referring to a particular object.

Despite the close relationship between verb and object, the two parts may be separated as follows:

(a) The aspect markers and verbal particles (see ch. 11) come between the verb and object:

A-mā tái-gán-syū. Ngóh tàuhsīn lohk-jó-gāai.
Mum read-PROG-book I just-now down-PFV-street
'Mum is reading.' 'I went outside just now.'

Kéuih jā-gwaan-chē ge la.
s/he drive-used-car PRT PRT
'She's used to driving.'

(b) The object may be topicalized (4.2.1), leaving the verb 'stranded':

Léih dī lóuhyáuh go-go dōu git-saai-fān, yáuh dī
your CL mates CL-CL all get-all-married have some

juhng lèih-jó-fān tìm, léih jauh lìhn **fān** dōu
also divorce-PFV PRT you then even married also

meih **git**! (*git-fān* 'get married') (film)
not-yet get
'Your friends are all married, some are already divorced, but you're not
even married yet!'

(c) A noun or pronoun serving as the object of the compound may
intervene between its two parts:

chaat-hàaih 'flatter':

Kéuihdeih gám góng haih séung **chaat léih hàaih** ge je.
they so talk is want polish your shoes PRT PRT
'They're just saying that to flatter you.'

bōng-sáu 'help out':

Léih hó-m̀h-hóyíh **bōng ngóh sáu** a?
you can-not-can help me hand PRT
'Could you give me a hand?'

púng-chèuhng 'support':

Léih bíuyín ngóh saht wúih **púng léih chèuhng**.
you perform I sure will support your show
'I'll be sure to support you at your performance.'

Note that the intervening pronouns here may be seen as the possessor of
the object of the compound verb, as in English *He's pulling your leg*.

(d) An adverbial noun phrase expressing duration or frequency (8.2.5)
may intervene:

Ngóh múih yaht yiu **jā bun go jūngtàuh chē** fāan-gūng.
I every day need drive half CL hour car return-work
'I have to drive for half an hour a day to get to work.'

Kéuihdeih yāt go láihbaai **yám géi chi chàh**.
they one CL week drink a-few times tea
'They go for tea [and dim sum] a few times a week.'

8.2.5 ADVERBIAL OBJECTS

A noun phrase expressing the frequency or duration of an action may be
used as adverbial objects

Go bìhbī kāt-jó **léuhng sēng**.
CL baby cough-PFV two sound
'The baby coughed twice.'

Ngóh fuhmóuh làih jyuh **yāt go láihbaai**.
my parents come live one CL week
'My parents are coming to stay for a week.'

If the verb is transitive, it tends to be repeated before the time expression:[3]

Ngóh **sái** nī gihn sāam **sái-jó léuhng chi**.
I wash this CL shirt wash-PFV two times
'I've washed this shirt twice.'

Ngóhdeih **jyuh** jáudim **jyuh-jó yāt go láihbaai**.
you-PL live hotel live-PFV one CL week
'We stayed in the hotel for a week.'

yāt 'one' together with a noun may form an adverbial phrase. The phrase resembles a classifier and is sometimes known as a **verbal measure phrase**:

Léih sek ngóh **yāt daahm** ā.
you kiss me one bite PRT
'Give me a kiss.'

Yīnggōi dá kéuih **yāt háh**.
should hit him one slap
'We should give him a slap.'

Léih bōng ngóh **yāt go mòhng** ā.
you help me one CL favour PRT
'Do me a favour.'

These phrases are often formed from body parts:

Léih tek kéuih **yāt geuk**.
you kick him one foot
'Give him a kick.'

Ngóh séung tái bìhbī tái dō **yāt ngáahn**.
I wish look baby look more one eye
'I want to take another look at the baby.'

8.3 SERIAL VERBS

The **serial verb** construction is one of the most important and productive patterns in Cantonese syntax. Although almost unknown in European languages, it resembles constructions like *go see a movie, come fly with us* and similar combinations in American English. It is essentially a simple concatenation of verbs:

Bātyùh ngóhdeih **heui tái hei**.
rather we go see film
'Let's go and see a film.'

Ngóh tīngyaht **fēi heui gin-gūng**.
I tomorrow fly go see-work
'I'm flying to an interview tomorrow.'

Note that the Cantonese in this example has three verbs while English has one.

Serial verb constructions express many of the relationships which are expressed by prepositions in English and other European languages. For example, the sentence *I'll phone for you* cannot readily be rendered literally in Cantonese because there is no preposition corresponding to 'for' (the coverb *waih* has the more specific meaning 'for the sake of': 7.2.1). Instead, two verbs are used:

Ngóh **bōng** léih **dá-dihnwá**.
I help you call-phone
'I'll phone for you.'

Note that although *bōng* in isolation means 'help', the addressee here is not expected to participate actively; rather, the speaker is offering to perform the action single-handedly. This contrast illustrates a difference between the English complementation structure as in 'help you (to) phone' and the Chinese serial construction which is closer to 'help you by phoning'.

8.3.1 SERIAL CONSTRUCTIONS EXPRESSING ACTIONS

Actions which are expressed by a verb and a preposition in English are typically expressed in Cantonese by a serial construction containing two or more verbs. The so-called 'coverbs' (see 3.1.3 and ch. 7) are very widely used in serial constructions, playing the role of prepositions in English. For example, the relation 'from' may be expressed by the coverb *tùhng* 'with/accompany':

Jeui hóu tùhng ngàhnhòhng je chín.
most good with bank borrow money
'It's best to borrow money from the bank.'

Such constructions can be ambiguous as to the relation expressed by *tùhng*:

Ngóh tùhng léih máaih ga chē.
I with you buy CL car
'I'll buy a car for/from/with you.'

The meaning may be clarified by the addition of adverbs such as *yātchàih* 'together' which would give the meaning 'with'.

yuhng 'use' expresses the instrumental sense of 'with', followed by *làih* 'come' or *heui* 'go' and the verb:

Nī	go	**yuhng**	**làih**	jouh	mātyéh	ga?
this	CL	use	come	do	what	PRT

'What's this for?'

Kéuihdeih	**yuhng**	dī	chín	**heui**	máaih	láu.
they	use	CL	money	go	buy	flat

'They're buying a flat with the money.'

wán 'look for' is also used in serial constructions with an instrumental meaning:

Léih	**wán**	dī	yéh	**kám-jyuh**	kéuih	ā.
you	find	CL	thing	cover-CONT	it	PRT

'Get something to cover it with.'

jēung 'put' is used in serial constructions indicating placement (see 7.1.4):[4]

Kéuih	**jēung**	dī	wūjōu	sāam	jāuwàih	**pehk**.	(TV ad.)
s/he	take	CL	dirty	clothes	around	throw	

'He throws his dirty clothes all over the place.'

Ngóhdeih	**jēung**	gó	bāt	chín	**fān**	léuhng	fahn.
we	take	that	sum	money	split	two	part

'We'll split the money in two.'

jēung is the nearest equivalent to the *bǎ* object structure in Mandarin. Unlike *bǎ*, however, it is not used with all transitive verbs, but is primarily restricted to cases where motion takes place as in the above example. It is also applicable in metaphorical cases of movement or removal, such as exchanging places:

Yàhndeih	yìhgā	**jēung**	gúlóuh	**dong**	**sìh-hīng**.
people	now	put	old-fashioned	treat	fashionable

'People are treating old-fashioned stuff as fashionable.'

Yiu	**jēung**	dī	mhōisām	ge	yéh	gút-yāt-sēng
need	put	CL	unhappy	LP	stuff	one-voice

tān-jó	kéuih.	(film)
swallow-PFV	it	

'You should take the unhappy things and swallow them in one gulp.'

Note the seemingly redundant use of *kéuih* as the object of the second verb (see 5.1 and H-N. S. Cheung 1992).

jouh 'do' as the second verb in a serial construction introduces predicative complements, corresponding to *as*:

Hóyíh **yuhng** dī gauh sāam **jouh** maat-deih-bou.
can use CL old clothes do wipe-floor-cloth
'We can use these old clothes as floor cloths.'

Kéuihdeih **syún**-jó go Hēunggóng-yàhn **jouh** jyújihk.
they elect-PFV CL Hongkong-person for chairman
'They elected a Hongkong person as chairman.'

Note that the aspect marker may occur on the first or the last verb of the series, according to the construction. It follows the first verb with most serial constructions, but with *jēung* it follows the second verb:

Kéuihdeih **ló-jó** gó bāt chín **heui máaih** láu.
they take-PFV that CL money go buy house.
'They used the money to buy a house.'

Go sīnsāang **jēung** ngóhdeih léuhng go **fāan-hōi-jó**.
CL teacher place us two CL separate-PFV
'The teacher separated the two of us.'

8.3.2 DIRECTIONAL VERBS AND VERBS OF MOTION

Serial constructions are also involved in expressing motion. These constructions are based on seven **directional verbs**:[5]

yahp 'in'   chēut 'out'
séuhng 'up'   lohk 'down'
gwo 'over'   fāan 'back'
màaih 'close'

Although usually best translated as prepositions, these are verbs in their own right, and can be used transitively with directional objects (see 8.2.1):

yahp/chēut fóng 'enter/leave the room'
yahp/chēut yún 'enter/leave hospital'
yahp jihk 'become naturalized'
chēut gwok 'go abroad'
séuhng/lohk syùhn 'get on/off a boat'
séuhng/lohk gēi 'get on/off a plane'
séuhng/lohk chē 'get into/out of a car'
séuhng/lohk tòhng 'attend/leave class'
gwo máhlouh 'cross the road'
gwo seuihdouh 'go through the tunnel'

fāan Hēunggóng 'return to HK'
fāan ūkkéi 'go home'
màaih wái 'take one's seat'
màaih sān 'approach the body' i.e. 'come near someone'

Some of these verbs may also take direct objects, especially in some fixed verb–object compounds (2.3.3, 8.2.4):

yahp-chín 'deposit money' (into a bank account)
yahp-yáu 'fill up with petrol'
chēut-syū 'publish a book'
chēut-tàihmuhk 'come up with (examination) topics'
lohk-dehng 'put down a deposit'
lohk-fo 'unload goods'

Most of the directional verbs are also used as directional particles following the verb (11.3.1), but with some differences of meaning and structure. In the serial verb construction, the directional verbs combine with the verbs of motion, *heui* 'go' and *làih* 'come':

yahp heui 'go in'	yahp làih 'come in'
chēut heui 'go out'	chēut làih 'come out'
séuhng heui 'go up'	séuhng làih 'come up'
lohk heui 'go down'	lohk làih 'come down'
gwo heui 'go over'	gwo làih 'come over'
fāan heui 'go back'	fāan làih 'come back'
màaih heui 'go closer'	màaih làih 'come closer'

In this construction, the aspect markers come between the directional verb and the verb of movement:

A-Màh   fāan-jó   làih.   (*not* *fāan làih-jó)
Grandma   return-PFV come
'Grandma has come back.'

Hóuchíh   yáuh   yàhn   yahp-gwo   làih.
seem   have   person   enter-EXP   come
'Someone seems to have come in.'

The order here contrasts with Mandarin, where the aspect marker follows the second verb (*huí lái le* 'has come back'). Similarly, verbal particles such as *dou* (11.3) come between the directional verb and the motion verb:

Ngóh   ńgh   fānjūng   hauh   jauh   **fāan   dou**   **làih**.
I   five minutes   after then   back   arrive come
'I'll be back in five minutes.'

The addition of *dou* here adds the meaning of arrival: without it, the sentence would mean that the speaker (for example, on the telephone) will merely set out in five minutes' time:

Ngóh ngh fānjūng hauh jauh **fāan làih**.
I   five minutes after then back come
'I'll come back in five minutes.'

Similarly, the particle *dihng* adds the meaning 'in readiness':

Fóchē jauh dou la, ngóhdeih **chēut dihng heui** sīn.
train soon arrive PRT, we   exit ready go first
'The train's arriving, let's go out ready.'

To express the manner of movement, a third verb may be added before the directional verb, producing a sequence of three verbs:

jáu	yahp	heui		pàh	chēut	làih
run	in	go		climb	out	come
'rush in'				'climb out'		
tiu	séuhng	heui		dit	lohk	làih
jump	up	go		fall	down	come
'leap up'				'fall down'		
būn	gwo	heui		hàahng	màaih	làih
move	cross	go		walk	close	come
'move over'				'come closer'		

Note that the last verb in this construction is always *heui* 'go' or *làih* 'come', the choice depending on one's point of reference, much as in English; other verbs cannot be substituted. Aspect markers and verbal particles follow the first verb of the series:

Dī sailouhjái **jáu-jó** **yahp** heui.
CL children run-PFV in   go
'The children came running in.'

Kéuihdeih yìhgā **hàahng-gán** lohk làih.
they   now   walk-PROG down come
'They're walking down now.'

Ngóhdeih yiu **būn** **fāan** gwo heui.
we   need move back over go
'We have to move back over there again.'

The same construction may form the complement of a transitive verb phrase:

daai dī haakyàhn yahp heui
bring some guests in   go
'bring some guests in'

līng jī bējáu chēut làih
take CL beer out come
'take out a bottle of beer'

būn dī gīp séuhng heui
move CL case up go
'bring up the cases'

ló fūk wá lohk làih
take CL picture down come
'take the picture down.'

Note: lohk-heui as a verbal complement means 'continue' (11.3.1):

Kéuihdeih yāt louh **góng lohk-heui.**
they one road talk continue
'They just carry on talking.'

Léih tàahn lohk-heui lā.
you play continue PRT
'Carry on playing (the piano).'

Idioms of motion: [verb] – *làih* – [verb] – *heui*, in which the same verb is repeated, expresses motion 'to and fro' or 'up and down':

Léih hàahng làih hàahng heui jouh māt a?
you walk come walk go do what PRT
'What are you walking up and down for?'

Taaihūng-yàhn sèhngyaht fēi làih fēi heui.
space-man always fly come fly go
'The spacemen are always flying to and fro.'

(*taaihūng-yàhn* 'spacemen' refers to those who 'commute' between Hongkong and abroad, often while acquiring a foreign passport.) This idiom may be used to translate 'around' or 'about':

Dī sailouhjái sèhngyaht tiu làih tiu heui.
CL children always jump come jump go
'The children are always leaping about.'

It is also used more metaphorically:

Ngóh lám làih lám heui dōu m̀h mìhngbaahk.
I think come think go still not understand
'I've thought it over and over and still don't understand.'

Góng làih góng heui dōu móuh gitleuhn.
talk come talk go still no conclusion
'They talk and talk and still there's no conclusion.'

Idioms: *jāuwàih heui* 'go around' suggests random movement:

Dī   léuihjái   jāuwàih   heui   máaih   sāam.
CL   girls   around   go   buy   clothes
'The girls are going around buying clothes.'

heui . . . *làih* is a serial verb construction denoting return from a trip:

Ngóh   ngāam-ngāam   **heui-gwo**   Bākgīng   (**làih**).
I   just-just   go-EXP   Beijing   (come)
'I've just been to Beijing.'

Kéuihdeih   **heui**   **yùhn**   Oujāu   **fāan**   **làih**.
they   go   finish   Australia   return   come
'They're just back from a trip to Australia.'

joi làih (*gwo*/*yāt chi*), literally 'come again', means 'do/try again':

Joi   làih   gwo.   (used in practising pronunciation)
again   come   over
'Once more.'

Ngóhdeih   joi   làih   yāt   chi.   (instruction at a rehearsal)
we   again   come   one   time
'Let's try one more time.'

8.4 PASSIVES

Cantonese has a passive structure similar to that in Mandarin, distinguished by the word *béi*. Note that the 'by-phrase' (*béi* + noun) must precede the verb:

Yíhchìhn   gó   go   beisyū   **béi gīngléih**   cháau-jó.
before   that   CL   secretary   by   manager   sack-PFV
'The previous secretary was sacked by the manager.'

In spoken Cantonese the passive construction must contain a noun phrase after *béi* representing the agent of the action, unlike in Mandarin where the agent phrase may be omitted (e.g. *Tā bèi kāichú le* 'He was sacked'). If the agent is unknown or generic, the word *yàhn* 'person' is used after *béi* to represent the agent:

Dī   cháang   **béi yàhn**   máaih   saai.
CL   oranges   by   people   buy   all
'The oranges have all been bought.'

Léih **béi yàhn**   ngāak-jó   la.
you   by people cheat-PFV PRT
'You've been cheated.'

Similarly, if the agent is unknown but clearly non-human, it will be expressed as *yéh* 'thing':

Ngóh yauh **béi yéh**   ngáauh chān.
I   again by thing bite   PRT
'I've been bitten again.'

Passives without an agent are occasionally used under the influence of Mandarin, for example in news reporting or in a literary context:

Júngguhng yáuh ńgh go   chaahkyàhn **beih**   **bouh**.
altogether have five CL   thief   PASS   arrest
'Altogether five thieves were arrested.'

Kéuih ge   tīnchòih yātjihk   **beih**   **màaihmuht-jó**.
her   LP   talent   until-now PASS   bury-PFV
'Her talent has always been buried.'

Note that the passive marker *beih* here has a different form, with a low level tone (the usual spoken form *béi* originates as *beih* with a changed tone).

The passive is used rather less in spoken Cantonese than in English. One reason is that the object can readily be topicalized (4.2.1), often resulting in a sentence best translated with an English passive. A common sentence type begins with the object as topic, followed by a modal verb and no subject:

Gó   tou hei   yātdihng yiu   tái.
that CL film must   need   see
'That film has to be seen.'

Another factor restricting the use of the passive is that the *béi* passive entails that the subject is affected by the action, typically in an adverse or unpleasant manner. English passives such as *I was remembered* and *I was given a present*, for example, cannot be rendered in Cantonese because there is no such adverse effect on the subject *I*. However, the *béi* passive is sometimes used with verbs that do not involve any element of adversity, for example:

Kéuih hóu   jūngyi béi yàhn   jaan.
s/he   very like   by people praise
'She likes very much to be praised.'

The development of clearly non-adversative passives in Mandarin, i.e. verbs which do not clearly involve an element of adversity, has been attributed to the influence of English, especially translation (Chao 1968; Chappell 1986).

8.4.1 INDIRECT PASSIVES

While the use of the passive is relatively restricted in Cantonese in some respects, there are also some passive constructions which have no exact counterparts in English. The term **indirect passive** (drawn from Japanese grammar, where analogous constructions exist) indicates that the subject does not correspond to the direct object of an active sentence, as with the simple passives illustrated in 8.4.[6] These sentences are difficult to translate, the nearest equivalent being the *have . . . participle* construction:

Kéuih béi yàhn tāu-jó chín.
s/he by person steal-PFV money
'He had some money stolen (from him).'

In this structure, the **experiencer** adversely affected by the action is the subject of the sentence (as in ordinary passives), but is not understood as the object of the verb: the verb *tāu* retains its direct object (*chín* 'money').[7] Note that there is no corresponding active sentence: the nearest active equivalent would be *Yáuh yàhn tāu-jó kéuih dī chín*, which differs in that *kéuih* is the possessor of the object *chín*. Similar examples include:

Ngóh béi yàhn tō-jó ga chē. (film)
I by people tow-PFV CL car
'I had my car towed away.'

Kéuih béi yàhn jīdou saai kéuih dī beimaht.
s/he by people know all her CL secrets
'She had all her secrets discovered.'

Verb–object compounds (2.3.3, 8.2.4) may be passivized in this way, retaining the object:

Kéuihdeih léuhng go sèhngyaht béi yàhn **góng-hàahn-wá**.
they two CL always by people say-idle-talk
'Those two have people gossiping about them all the time.'

Kéuih gēng béi yàhn **cháau-yàuh-yú**.
s/he fear by people fry-squid
'He's afraid of getting the sack.'

Another form of indirect passive involves a clause after the verb:

Ngóh si-gwo béi yàhn wah m̀h sīk Yīngmán.
I try-EXP by people say not know English
'I have had people say I couldn't speak English.'

Sìhng-jái   sèhngyaht   béi   yàhn   jaan   kéuih lengjái.
Sing-boy   always   by   people   praise   him handsome
'Young Sing is always being praised for his good looks.'

In this case, a corresponding active sentence is possible (*Yáuh yàhn wah ngóh m̀h sīk Yīngmán* 'People say I cannot speak English').

8.4.2 RESULTATIVE PASSIVES

Similar to the indirect passive is the resultative construction, in which a resultative verbal particle (11.3.2) or adjective following the passive verb indicates a state resulting from the action:

Nī   hahp luhkyíngdáai   yíhgīng   béi   yàhndeih   **tái**   **waaih-jó**.
this CL   video-tape   already   by   people   watch   bad-PFV
'This video-tape has deteriorated from being watched.'

Nī   go   jái   béi   fuhmóuh   **jung   waaih   saai**.
this CL   son   by   parent   spoil   bad   PRT
'The son has been spoilt to death by his parents.'

Deui   hàaih   béi   ngóh   **jeuk   laahn-jó**.
CL   shoes   by   me   wear   broken-PFV
'These shoes have worn out (through my wearing them).'

Dī   hóisīn   búnlòih   hóu   pèhng   ge,   hauhlàih béi
CL   seafood   originally   very   cheap   PRT   later   by

yàhn   **sihk   gwai-jó**.
people eat   expensive-PFV
'The seafood used to be cheap, but has become expensive as a result of its popularity.'

Note that many of these constructions cannot readily be translated with a corresponding English passive. This follows from the difference in the productivity of resultative verb compounds in Cantonese and English. As with the indirect passive, the subject is affected not just by the verb but by the whole predicate, consisting here of [verb + particle] or [verb + adjective].

Resultative passives may also be formed with *dou* 'to the extent that' introducing a complement clause (8.5.3):

Kéuih   béi   yàhn   ngāak   dou   po-jó-cháan.
s/he   by   people cheat   until   bankrupt-PFV
'He was cheated to the point of bankruptcy.'

Ngóh   béi   dī   jái   gīk   dou   sāang   hā   gam   tiu.
I   by   CL   kids annoy   until   live   shrimp   so   jump
'I was made hopping mad by my kids.'

Kéuih béi yàhn dá dou lóuhpòh dōu m̀h
s/he by people beat until wife also not

yihng dāk kéuih.
recognize able him
'He was beaten so that not even his wife could recognize him.'

8.4.3 ADJECTIVAL PASSIVES

The passive verb together with the *béi* phrase can function as an adjectival phrase modifying a head noun; *ge* is used to link the two together:

béi ngàhnhòhng chéuisīu-jó ge wuhháu
by bank cancel-PFV LP account
'the account cancelled by the bank'

béi lóuhbáan cháau-jó ge beisyū
by boss fire-PFV LP secretary
'the secretary fired by the boss'

The structure of the adjective passive resembles that of the relative clause (see 6.4.1). Compare the following:

béi yàhn tāu-jó ge chē
by people steal-PFV LP car
'the cars which were stolen'

dī cháak tāu-jó ge chē
CL thieves steal-PFV LP car
'the cars (which were) stolen by the thieves'

8.5 CAUSATIVE AND RESULTATIVE CONSTRUCTIONS

8.5.1 CAUSATIVE CONSTRUCTIONS

Causative constructions take two distinct forms, according to the type of situation or event caused. Causation of a state of affairs is expressed by the verb *jíng* 'make' or *lihng* 'cause', followed by an adjective and the object:

Mgōi léih bōng ngóh **jíng** **yiht** dihp choi ā.
please you help me make hot dish vegetable PRT
'Could you heat up the dish of vegetables for me, please?'

Kéuih msíusām **jíng** **daaih** yàhndeih go tóuh. (film)
he not-careful make big other's CL tummy
'He carelessly made her pregnant.'

Chín   hóyíh   **lihng**   léih   **hōisām**   mē?
money   can   make   you   happy   PRT
'As if money could make you happy!'

. . .   **lihng**   léih   **jīngsàhn**   saai!   (TV ad.)
    make   you   energetic   all
'It fills you up with energy!'

Note the difference of word order between the two causative verbs: *jíng* – [adjective] – [object] but *lihng* – [object] – [adjective].

To express causation of an event ('make something happen') a periphrastic construction with *dou* is used:

jíng dou . . . 'make . . .' is a colloquial causative construction:

Kéuih   gám   yéung   góng,   jíng   dou   yàhndeih   móuh
s/he   so   way   speak   make   that   people   not-have

saai   sāmgēi.
all   enthusiasm
'He makes everyone lose their enthusiasm, talking like that.'

lihng dou . . . is used in more formal contexts:

Fuhmóuh   yiu   lihng   dou   sailouhjái   hōi-hōi-sām-sām
parent   need   cause   that   children   happy-happy

fāan-hohk.   (TV)
return-school
'Parents should see to it that their children go to school happily.'

This use of *dou* resembles the resultative complement construction (8.5.3).

8.5.2 RESULTATIVE COMPOUNDS

Another form of resultative construction involves combining two verbs to form a resultative predicate. The verbs combined may be transitive or intransitive, but the resulting combination is transitive (specifically, causative):

giu 'call' + *séng* 'wake up' → *giu séng* 'wake up'

Léih   gei-jyuh   giu   séng   ngóh   a.
you   remember   call   wake   me   PRT
'Remember to wake me up.'

chòuh 'make a noise' + *séng* 'wake up' → *chòuh séng* 'wake up'

Léih   mhóu   **chòuh séng**   ngóh   a.
you   don't   noisy   wake   me   PRT
'Don't wake me up (by making a noise).'

Go bìhbī **haam séng** kéuih màhmā.
CL baby cry wake her mother
'The baby cried and woke her mother up.'

Gó jek láaih-fán hóu yùhngyih **sihk fèih** dī bìhbī.
that CL milk-powder very easy eat fat CL babies
'That milk powder easily makes babies fat.'

Many of the resultative particles (11.3.2) may express causation similarly:

Nī dī hei **gaau-waaih** saai dī sailouhjái.
these CL films teach-bad all CL children
'These films exert bad influences on the children.'

Ngóh **jeuk laahn**-jó deui hàaih.
I wear out-PFV pair shoes
'I've worn out this pair of shoes.'

Ngóh hóu faai jauh **gwun-jeui**-jó kéuih.
I very quickly then pour-drunk-PFV him
'I got him drunk by making him drink a lot.'

8.5.3 RESULTATIVE AND EXTENT COMPLEMENTS

A construction which enables an adjective or a clause expressing a result to follow as the complement to a verb is [verb – *dou*]. *dou* 'until' introduces a complement, typically an adjective (sometimes with an aspect or particle) expressing the end result or extent of an action or process:

Léih **háahng dou guih** jauh yāusīk-háh lā.
you walk till tired then rest a-while PRT
'If you get tired of walking, then have a rest.'

Ngóhdeih yám-yéh **yám dou báau** saai.
we drink-things drink until full V-PRT
'We drank ourselves full.'

Būi séui **dóu dou múhn**-sé-jó.
CL water pour till full-flow-PFV
'The glass of water is overflowing as a result of the pouring.'

Note the repetition of the verb where the verb already has an object, as in *yám-yéh* above. This repetition is required in order for the *dou* phrase to follow the verb directly (cf. *dāk* above and 10.1.1).

In addition to a resultative adjective, *dou* may be followed by a clause which may be interpreted as a result of the action encoded by the main verb; the relationship between the main verb and the clause may also be interpreted in terms of a causing event and resultant state:

Kéuih   góng-syū   góng   **dou**   **yàhndeih**   **fan-saai-gaau**.
s/he   talk-book   talk   till   people   fall-all-asleep
'His lecturing puts everyone to sleep.'

Kéuih   haam   **dou**   **ngóh**   go   sām   lyuhn   saai.
s/he   cry   till   my   CL   heart disarray all
'His crying put my heart in total disarray.'

Note that the same construction with *dou* is used as a complement to adjectives (9.1.3), representing a further parallel between verbs and adjectives. Some idiomatic complements with *dou* also resemble those with adjectives (9.1.3):

Yiht   dou   ngóh   séi!   (adj.)
hot   till   I   die
'I'm sweltering!'

Ngóhdeih   **siu**   dou   lūk   déi!   (verb)
we   laugh   till roll ground
'We were laughing ourselves silly.'

Chèuhng   dou   tō   déi.   (adj.)
long   till drag floor
'(It's) so long as to drag on the floor.'

Kéuih   fan   dou   m̀h   jī   séng.   (verb)
s/he   sleep   till not   know   wake
'She slept so well that she forgot to wake up.'

An alternative resultative construction has the form [verb – *dāk* – adjective], based on a Mandarin construction with *de*. This construction resembles the adverbial construction with *dāk* (10.1.1), but describes the result rather than the manner of an action:

Dī   sāam   **sái**   **dāk**   hóu   gōnjehng.
CL   clothes wash   ADV   very clean
'Those clothes have washed nice and clean.'

Kéuih   **sihk**   **dāk**   hóu   báau.
s/he   eat   ADV   very full
'She was full as a result of eating.'

In transitive sentences where the object follows the verb, the verb phrase is repeated, as in adverbial constructions with *dāk* (10.1.1):

Kéuih   jouh   yéh   jouh   dāk   hóu   hōisām.
s/he   do   thing   do   ADV   very happy
'She's very happy in her work.'

9 ADJECTIVAL CONSTRUCTIONS: DESCRIPTION AND COMPARISON

As discussed in chapter 3, the distinction between adjective and verb in Cantonese is not a categorical one. Hence, what are thought of as adjectives in the European grammatical tradition are often described as 'stative verbs' in Chinese linguistic works. As predicates, adjectives behave very much like verbs: the verb 'to be' is not used with adjectives (8.1.1), and some adjectives may take aspect markers like verbs (see 9.1.1 and ch. 11). Nevertheless, it remains useful to distinguish adjectives from verbs. The distinctive properties of adjectives described in this chapter are:

(a) Predicative adjectives are normally preceded by *hóu* (or another modifying adverb: see 9.1.3):

> Kéuih   nī   pàaih   **hóu**   **hōisām**.
> s/he   these   days   very   happy
> 'She's happy these days.'

Without *hóu* the sentence (*Kéuih nī pàaih hōisām*) would be incomplete.[1]

(b) adjectives may undergo reduplication, modifying their meaning (see 9.2; some of these patterns are also applicable to stative verbs):

> fē-fē-déi 'brownish'   gōu-gōu-sau-sau 'tall and thin'

(c) adjectives may take comparative constructions such as *dī* and *gwo* (9.3):

> Nīdouh   **jihng**   **dī**.
> here   quiet   a-bit
> 'It's quieter here.'

> Chóh   deihtit   **faai**   **gwo**   chóh   bāsí.
> sit   underground   fast   than   sit   bus
> 'It's quicker by underground than by bus.'

9.1 SYNTAX OF ADJECTIVES

As in English, we may distinguish predicative and attributive uses of adjectives. Predicative adjectives behave very much like verbs, following the subject without a copular verb. Attributive adjectives always precede the noun which they modify.

9.1.1 PREDICATIVE ADJECTIVES

Predicative adjectives do not require the copular verb 'to be'. However, a predicative adjective is usually preceded by a modifier such as *hóu*, which as an adjective means 'good.' *hóu* in this function may be regarded as merely an adjective marker, its meaning being much weaker than English 'very'. A predicative adjective with *hóu* makes a complete sentence:

Léih go jái hóu gōu.   (*not* haih hóu gōu)
you CL son very tall
'Your son is tall.'

The adjective alone occurs only in certain restricted contexts, such as in answer to an A-not-A question containing the adjective:

A: Nī   bún   syū   gwai-m̀h-gwai   a?
   this   CL   book   expensive-not-expensive   PRT
   'Is this book expensive?'

B: Gwai   a.
   expensive   PRT
   'Yes, it is.'

Used as predicates, adjectives may take aspect markers and verbal particles in the same way as verbs:

Léih go jái **gōu-jó** hóu dō wo.
you CL son tall-PFV very much PRT
'Your son has got a lot taller.'

Kéuih yíhchìhn chàhnggīng **leng-gwo,** yìhgā jauh
s/he before once beautiful-EXP now then

cháuyéung-jó.
ugly-PFV
'She used to be beautiful, but she's become ugly now.'

Ngóh sāang yùhn jái hóu faai **sau fāan**.
I give-birth V-PRT child very fast thin V-PRT
'I soon got slim again after giving birth.'

These usages may be seen as conversion of adjectives denoting states into verbs expressing change of state (see also 3.1.1).

9.1.2 ATTRIBUTIVE ADJECTIVES

Attributive adjectives always precede the noun, normally followed by the linking particle *ge*:

Léih	mǎmìh	haih	go	**hóu**	**hou-haak**	**ge**	**yàhn**.
your	mummy	is	CL	very	hospitable	LP	person

'Your mum's a really hospitable person.'

Chūngmìhng	**ge**	**hohksāang**	sīn	sīk	daap	ge.
clever	LP	student	only	know	answer	PRT

'Only the clever students know the answer.'

Note that the same *ge* appears in other structures which modify nouns, such as possessive constructions and relative clauses, serving to link the modifying expressions to the noun (6.3, 6.4). All these noun phrases therefore have a similar structure, with the head noun itself at the end of the phrase.

As in the case of the possessive construction (6.3), *ge* may be omitted in certain contexts. It must be omitted, in particular, in fixed combinations when the property denoted by the adjective is an inherent characteristic of the noun. For example, *leng léui* 'beautiful woman' might be translated as 'a beauty'. Similarly:

baahk jáu 'white wine'   hùhng chàh 'black tea' (lit. 'red tea')
lēk léui 'bright girl'   chéun jái 'foolish boy'

Note that when the adjective in these phrases is modified by a degree word such as *hóu* 'very', *géi* 'rather' and *ji* 'most', *ge* must be present (as pointed out by H-N.S. Cheung 1972):

baahk maht 'white socks'   hóu baahk **ge** maht 'very white socks'
gauh sāam 'old clothes'   géi gauh **ge** sāam 'rather old clothes'
leng ūk 'beautiful house'   ji leng **ge** ūk 'the most beautiful house'

9.1.3 MODIFICATION OF ADJECTIVES

A predicative adjective must normally be modified by one of a number of adverbs of degree. The following adverbial expressions are used to modify adjectives:

géi 'quite'   fēisèuhng (jī) 'extremely'
gam 'so'   mjī géi 'incredibly'
gau 'enough'   taai, gwotàuh 'too' (see 9.3.4)
béigaau 'rather, relatively'   jeui, ji 'most' (see 9.3.5)

If no other modifier is present, *hóu* is used by default, as illustrated in 9.1.1.

In negative sentences either *m̀h* takes the place of *hóu*, or the negative copula *mhaih* may be used together with one of the above modifiers. For example, to express the idea 'not very' or 'not really', *mhaih* is followed by *hóu* or *géi* 'quite':

Nī   bún   syū   mhaih   hóu   gwai   jē.
this CL   book not-be very expensive PRT
'This book's not very expensive.'

Gám   yéung mhaih   géi   gūngpìhng.
such way   not-be quite   fair
'It's not quite fair this way.'

The word *dou* expressing degree, or 'to the extent that . . .' (8.5.3) may introduce a clause or another adjectival phrase to serve as a complement to an adjective:

Hóu   dou   léih   gú   m̀h   dóu!   (TV ad.)
good till you   guess not   succeed
'Better than you can imagine!'

Jānhaih pèhng dou   léih   m̀h   seun!   (radio ad.)
really   cheap till you   not   believe
'You won't believe the prices!'

Léihdeih léuhng go   chan   dou   jyuht.
you-PL   two   CL   match till absolute
'You two are perfectly matched.'

This construction with *dou* is a Cantonese counterpart to the Mandarin use of *de* to mark extent (Li and Thompson 1981: 626); *dāk*, the Cantonese equivalent of *de*, is not used in this way. Thus *Tā píqì hǎo de chū-le-míng* 'He's famous for his good temper' would be expressed in Cantonese as *Kéuih pèihhei hóu dou chēut saai méng* or *Kéuih chēutméng pèihhei hóu*.
   dou séi, literally 'to death' is used to emphasize adjectives:

yáuh-chín   dou   séi
have-money   till die
'extremely rich'

chèuhng-hei dou   séi
long-winded till die
'very long-winded'

dākyi dou   séi
cute   till die
'extremely cute'

fēi héi, literally 'fly up' (i.e. take off) is used to indicate the extreme case denoted by the adjective:

leng   dou   fēi   héi   gwai   dou   fēi   héi
pretty till take off   expensive till take off
'mind-blowingly beautiful'   'mind-blowingly expensive'

bāt-dāk-líuh has a counterpart in Mandarin, *bùdéliǎo* which also encodes an extreme extent:

làahn   dou bāt-dāk-líuh
difficult till extreme
'incredibly difficult'

tìhm   dou bāt-dāk-líuh
sweet   till extreme
'extremely sweet'

Some adjectives combine idiomatically with a particular verb as complement to *dou*:

làahn dou wàhn
hard till dizzy
'mind-bendingly difficult'

muhn dou baauja
bored till explode
'bored stiff'

leng   dou dám yāt sēng
pretty till dam one sound
'extremely beautiful' (idiomatic)

Note that *dám yāt sēng* is an onomatopoeic expression describing the sound produced when something falls into the water.

dou gám (yéung) 'to such an extent' is used to elaborate on adjectives in exclamatory fashion:

Wa, go   pìhnggwó laahn dou gám yéung gé!
wow CL apple   bad   to   such extent PRT
'Wow, the apple's so badly rotten!'

The complement to *dou* may also be omitted or preposed as in:

Léih tái-háh   kéuih, hōisām dou . . .!
you look-DEL   him   happy   till
'Look at him, so happy!'

Hàahng m̀h yūk la,   guih dou!
walk   not move PRT tired till
'I can't move, I'm so tired.'

dou gihk where *dou* introduces the extent complement and *gihk* means 'to the extreme' is used to give emphasis to predicative adjectives:

Nī   bún syū gwai   dou gihk.
this CL book expensive till extreme
'This book is extremely expensive.'

Nī   tou hei   muhn   dou gihk.
this CL   movie boring till extreme
'This movie is extremely boring.'

The expletive *gwái* is also used to emphasize adjectives:

gwái gam leng
devil so   beautiful
'damned good-looking'

gwái gam gūhòhn
devil so   stingy
'damned stingy'   (also: *gū-gwái-hòhn*: see 2.1.3)

gwái may combine with another emphatic expression such as *séi* 'dead':

gam gwái séi   leng   *or*   gwái séi   gam leng
so   devil dead beautiful   devil dead so   beautiful
'dead gorgeous'

It may also be infixed between the syllables of an adjective (2.1.3):
màhfàahn 'troublesome' → màh-gwái-fàahn 'dead troublesome'

Idiom: gau saai emphasizes an adjective in an appreciative way, using
gau 'enough' with the verbal particle *saai* 'all' (11.3.3):

Léihdeih làih   màaih jauh **gau**   **saai yihtlaauh** la!
you-PL   come   along then enough   all   lively   PRT
'If you come too it'll be nice and lively.'

Léih yìhgā **gau**   **saai duhklahp**   wo!
you now   enough   all independent   PRT
'You're all independent now!'

9.2 REDUPLICATION OF ADJECTIVES

Reduplication (doubling) is one of the few morphological devices available
to Cantonese (2.2), and is much used to modify the meaning of adjectives.
Reduplication of an adjective takes several different forms, serving to
modify its meaning in a number of ways. Reduplicated adjectives are also
used adverbially (see 10.1.3).

Reduplication of adjectives is highly idiomatic, in that it is not possible to
predict exactly which adjectives may be reduplicated, which form the
reduplication will take, or how the meaning of the adjective will change.
Nevertheless, some typical patterns of form and function emerge.

9.2.1 ADJECTIVE – ADJECTIVE

The simplest form of reduplication merely repeats the adjective, with an intensifying effect:

daaih-daaih-go or *dáai-daaih go* 'really big'

> Kéuih lóuh-gūng **dáai-daaih go** chóh háidouh, léih gin m̀h dóu mē?
> Her husband big-big CL sit here, you see not V-PRT PRT
> 'Her husband, the big guy, is sitting right there, can't you see?'

múhn-múhn ge or *mún-múhn ge* 'really full'

> Go kàuhchèuhng chóh dou **mún-múhn ge**.
> CL ball-stadium sit till full-full PRT
> 'The seats in the stadium are all filled up.'

Note the optional tone change: for some speakers, the first of the reduplicated adjectives takes the rising changed tone as in *daaih* → *dáai-daaih*. This change resembles that in verb reduplication, e.g. *si-yāt-si* → *sí-si* 'have a try' (2.2).

This form of reduplication often suggests an element of intimacy:

sai-sai jek māaujái	síu tìhm-tím
small-small CL kitten	little sweet-sweet
'a little tiny kitten'	'sweetheart, sweetie'

In the case of bisyllabic adjectives, both syllables are reduplicated separately, in the form [AABB]:

chīngchó 'clear' → chīng-chīng-chó-chó 'nice and clear'
jīngsàhn 'energetic' → jīng-jīng-sàhn-sàhn 'all full of energy'
yīnngahn 'intimate' → yīn-yīn-ngahn-ngahn 'pretty intimate'
póutūng 'ordinary' → póu-póu-tūng-tūng 'pretty ordinary'
syūfuhk 'comfortable' → syū-syū-fuhk-fuhk 'pretty comfortable'

Certain combinations occur only in reduplicated form:

hīng-hīng-ngóh-ngóh 'intimate, in love'

Two such adjectives may be reduplicated together, typically for emphasis. The following phrase from a radio station disc jockey illustrates a combination of two bisyllabic reduplicated adjectives, *hīngsūng* 'relaxing' and *gáandāan* 'simple':

hīng-hīng-sūng-sūng gáan-gáan-dāan-dāan
'nice and light and easy and relaxing'

Similarly, in a comic film a rather uncouth character was described ironically as:

sī-sī-màhn-màhn wān-wān-yàuh-yàuh 'nice and kind and gentle'
(sīmàhn 'gentle' + wānyàuh 'tender')

Some idioms take the form AAB, e.g. *sāpseui* → *sāp-sāp-seui* 'trivial':

Nī bāt chín sāp-sāp-seui ge jē.
this CL money rather-trivial PRT PRT
'This is a pretty trivial amount of money.'

Several reduplicated expressions of this form are used as adverbs (10.1.3).

9.2.2 ADJECTIVE – ADJECTIVE – *DÉI*

In a second form of reduplication, an adjective is repeated and followed by the suffix *-déi*. Whereas [AA] or [AABB] reduplication confers an emphatic or vivid meaning, the form [A-A-*déi*] serves to qualify or moderate the meaning of the adjective, like the English suffix *-ish*:

fèih-féi-déi 'rather fat, chubby'
lyuhn-lyún-déi 'a bit messy'

Nī jēung yí waaih-wáai-déi ge.
this CL chair broken-broken-ish PRT
'This chair is a bit broken.'

Note that the tone of the second reduplicated word changes to the modified tone (see 1.4.2) except where it originally has a high tone (*sān-sān-déi* 'new-ish').

Idiom: *màh-má-déi* 'so-so' is a common colloquial reduplicated form. Like other [adj – adj – *déi*] reduplicated forms, it can be used as an adjective or as an adverb (10.1.3):

A: Dím a, léih?
how PRT you
'How are you doing?'
B: Màh-má-déi jēk.
so-so-ish PRT
'So-so.'

As an adverb, it modifies adjectives or stative verbs:

Chàhm máahn chāan faahn **màh-má-déi hóu-sihk** jēk.
last night CL meal so-so-ish good-eat PRT
'The dinner last night was mediocre.'

Ngóh **màh-má-déi jūngyi** nīdouh jēk.
I so-so-ish like here PRT
'I'm not too keen on this place.'

Note that the disparaging particle *jēk* (18.3.5) often accompanies the idiom.

A common function of this construction is to modify colour terms:

góga hùhng-húng-déi ge chē
that CL red-red-ish LP car
'that reddish car'

go tīn làahm-láam-déi
CL sky blue-blue-ish
'the sky is bluish'

When this reduplication occurs with a bisyllabic adjective, only the first syllable is reduplicated:

chīsin → chī-chī-déi-sin pacháu → pa-pa-déi-cháu
'crazy' 'a bit crazy' 'shy' 'rather shy'

Note that reduplicated forms with -déi are also used as adverbs (10.1.3).

9.2.3 A-B-B ADJECTIVES

Another, rather less productive, form of reduplication occurs with an adjective and a reduplicated noun or adjective. In this case, only the second noun or adjective is repeated, giving adjectives of the form [A-B-B]:

chī-lahp-lahp
glue-stick-stick
'sticky, gooey'

yùhn-lūk-lūk
round-wheel-wheel
'rounded'

dung-bīng-bīng
cold-ice-ice
'freezing cold'

chau-bāng-bāng
smelly-poo-poo
'smelly, high'

waaht-lyūt-lyūt
soft-bare-bare
'smooth as a baby's bottom'

These combinations occur only in the reduplicated form: there is no word *chīlahp* or *chaubāng*, for example. As these examples suggest, the ABB form of reduplication typically produces perceptual adjectives, describing how things feel, look or smell. A prominent function of this type is to produce compound colour terms made up of a colour and a modifying noun:

baahk-syūt-syūt
white-snow-snow
'snow-white'

hāk-māng-māng *or* hāk-mā-mā
black-dark-dark
'pitch dark'

Like AABB adjectives, adjectives of the ABB pattern may be combined one after the other for emphasis:

Kéuih   pèihfū   baahk-syūt-syūt   waaht-tyūt-tyūt.
s/he   skin   white-snow-snow   soft-bare-bare
'Her complexion is lovely and white and soft.'

For example, an emigrant expressing nostalgia about Hongkong combined three reduplicated adjectives to produce the following appreciative description:

Yàuhjagwái   yiht-laaht-laaht   hēung-pan-pan
fried-doughnut   warm-hot-hot   fragrant-smell

cheui-bōk-bōk.   (radio int.)
crispy-crispy
'The doughnuts are piping hot, appetizing and crispy.'

9.3 COMPARISON OF ADJECTIVES

There is no single comparative form of adjectives; several forms of comparison are used, according to the context and nature of the comparison:

(a) *dī* is used where the object of comparison is not explicitly mentioned, but implied by the context:

Gāmyaht yiht dī.   Síu-Yin yìhgā leng   dī.
today   hot   a-bit   Siu-Yin now   pretty a-bit
'It's hotter today.'   'Siu-Yin is prettier now.'

This structure, however, may also have the meaning 'rather' or 'a bit too', for example in rhetorical questions (17.1.2):

Kwā-m̀h-kwājēung dī   a?   Léih hāan fāan dī   lā!
ex-not-exaggerate a-bit PRT   you   spare back a-bit PRT
'Isn't it rather over the top?' 'Why not spare yourself the
                                  trouble?'

To make the comparative meaning explicit, it may be reinforced by the adverb *béigaau* 'rather':

Gāmyaht béigaau yiht dī.
today   rather   hot   a-bit
'Today is rather hotter.'

(b) Where two items are to be explicitly compared, the usual means of comparison is with the word *gwo*:

Gāmyaht yiht gwo   kàhmyaht.
today   hot   than yesterday
'Today is hotter than yesterday.'

Síu-Yin leng gwo yíhchìhn.
Siu-Yin pretty than before
'Siu-Yin is prettier than she used to be.'

As a verb, *gwo* literally means 'cross' or 'pass'; it comes to express comparison by the same route as the English verb *surpass*. Note that the object of comparison can be omitted where it may be understood from the context:

A: Bóumáh yáuh-móuh Alfa gam faai a?
   BMW have-not-have Alfa so fast PRT
   'Is a BMW as fast as an Alfa?'

B: Hólàhng **faai gwo** tìm.
   perhaps fast than too
   'Maybe even faster.'

Yùhgwó léih lám-jyuh máaih láu làih tàuhjī, bātyùh
if you think-CONT buy flat come invest rather

máaih gúpiu **hóu gwo**.
buy shares good than
'If you're thinking of buying a flat as an investment, you'd do better to buy shares.'

(c) An alternative marker of explicit comparison is *béi*, based on the Mandarin comparative construction with *bĭ*. This has the formal flavour of Mandarin-based syntax:

A-Wàhn béi kéuih mùihmúi leng.
A-Wan than her sister pretty
'Wan is prettier than her (younger) sister.'

Ngóhdeih kàuh-déui béi yíhchìhn kèuhng-jó. (news report)
we ball-team than before strong-PFV
'Our team is stronger than it was.'

Note that the word order in this construction is the reverse of the English, the object of comparison ('sister' and 'before' in the above examples) preceding the adjective. The adjective need not take a comparative form, but may be followed by *dī*, a degree modifier such as *hóu dō* 'much' or an aspect marker as in *kèuhng-jó* 'has become stronger'.

béihéi 'compared to' is an alternative, used together with *dī* or a degree expression such as *hóu dō* following the adjective:

Nī gāan gūngsī **béihéi** kèihtā gūngsī gōukāp **dī**.
this CL store compare other store high-class a-bit
'This department store is more high-class than the others.'

Léih go dihnlóuh **béihéi** kèihtā gēi gwai **hóu do**.
you CL computer compare other machine expensive very much
'Your computer is much more expensive than other models.'

A *béihéi*-phrase can also be added as an 'afterthought':

Nī gāan jáulàuh m̀h syun gwai, **béihéi daih yih dī**. (conv.)
this CL restaurant not count expensive, compare other CL
'This restaurant is reasonable, compared to some.'

9.3.1 DEGREES OF COMPARISON

All the above constructions may be modified by the addition of degree adverbs, such as *hóu dō* 'much' and *síu-síu* 'a little' and *dī-dī* 'a bit':

Nī jek gwai (gwo gó jek) hóu dō.
this CL dear (than that CL) very much
'This one is far more expensive (than that one).'

Yúhyìhnhohk làahn (gwo màhnhohk) síu-síu.
Linguistics hard (than literature) little-little
'Linguistics is slightly harder (than literature).'

Cheung-gō gó go leng dī-dī.
sing-song that CL pretty some-some
'The one who's singing is a bit prettier.'

Note that the object of comparison (*gwo* + noun phrase) may be omitted where its identity is clear from the context, so that the only overt indicator of a comparison is the degree adverb following the adjective.

Other degree expressions such as *sahp púih* 'ten times' (often used hyperbolically, as in English) and *yāt bun* 'half' may be added similarly:

Kéuih lēk gwo ngóh sahp púih.
s/he smart than me ten times
'She's ten times smarter than I am.'

Nī dī hàaih hái Yīnggwok máaih pèhng yāt bun.
this CL shoe in England buy cheap one half
'These shoes are half the price in England.'

Note that *gwai yāt púih* means 'twice as expensive' (cf. 100 per cent more).

The adverb *juhng* 'still' preceding the adjective expresses the emphatic comparison 'even more':

Daap dihnchē juhng maahn (gwo daap bāsí).
catch tram still slow (than catch bus)
'It's even slower by tram (than by bus).'

The object of comparison may again be omitted here, as *juhng* indicates the comparative meaning. *juhng gang gā* is more emphatic still:

Léih m̀h góng béi kéuih tēng, kéuih **juhng gang gā lāu**.
you not say to him hear s/he still more add angry
'He'll be angrier still if you don't tell him.'

The progressive comparison 'more and more' is expressed by *yuht làih yuht*:

Dī hohksāang yuht làih yuht chā.
CL student more and more bad
'These students are getting worse and worse.'

'the more . . . the more' is expressed by *yuht . . . yuht*:

Léih go léui **yuht daaih yuht leng**.
your CL daughter more big more pretty
'Your daughter is looking prettier and prettier as she grows older.'

Yáuh dī yàhn **yuht** yáuhchín **yuht** mhōisām.
have CL people more have-money more unhappy
'Some people get more unhappy, the richer they are.'

9.3.2 EQUAL COMPARISONS

Equal comparisons (*as* [adjective] *as* . . .) may be expressed by the verb *hóuchíh* 'resemble' together with the adverb *gam* 'as, so':

Kéuih hóuchíh gājē gam leng.
she just-like sister as pretty
'She's as pretty as her (elder) sister.'

yātyeuhng gam 'just as . . . ' is a more emphatic form of equal comparison. The object of comparison may be expressed using *tùhng*:

Ngóh **tùhng léih** yātyeuhng gam kùhng.
I with you one-same as poor
'I'm just as broke as you are.'

Gó gāan jáudim **tùhng nī gāan** yātyeuhng gam gwai.
that CL one-same with this CL one-same so expensive
'That hotel is just as expensive as this one.'

Note the use of the classifier phrase *nī gāan* to mean 'this one' (6.2.1).

tùhng . . . chā-mdō 'about as . . . as' is used similarly, with or without *gam*:

Ngóh go jái **tùhng** kéuih go léui **chā-mdō**
my CL son with her CL daughter almost

gam daaih.
as big
'My son is about the same age as her daughter.'

Léih dī   tàuhfaat **tùhng** kéuih **chā-mdō dyún**.
you CL   hair   with   him/her almost   short
'Your hair is about as short as hers.'

9.3.3 NEGATIVE AND INTERROGATIVE COMPARISONS

Negative comparatives require the negative existential verb *móuh* (15.4)
and the adverb *gam* 'so':

Kéuih móuh   gājē   gam leng.
she   not-have sister as pretty
'She's not as pretty as her [elder] sister.'

The interrogative counterpart is formed with the corresponding A-not-A
question, i.e. *yáuh-móuh*:

Kéuih yáuh-móuh   gājē   gam leng   a?
she   have-not-have sister as pretty PRT
'Is she as pretty as her [elder] sister?'

The positive form of this construction, *yáuh . . . gam*, is used in rhetorical
questions (17.3.4) and to contrast with *móuh . . . gam*:

Ngóh **bīndouh yáuh** kéuih gam lēk   a?
I   where   have him   so clever PRT
'I'm nothing like as clever as him.'

Kéuih hólàhng **yáuh** léih gam leng, daahnhaih
s/he maybe have you so pretty but

móuh   léih gam lēk.
not-have you so clever
'She may be as good-looking as you, but she's not as clever.'

Yáuh kéuih gam pèhng, móuh   kéuih gam
have it   so cheap not-have it   so

jeng! (radio ad. for restaurant)
great
'Anywhere that's as cheap is not as great!'

An alternative form of negative comparison is the phrase *m̀h gau* 'not
enough':

Ngóh m̀h gau   kéuih (gam) lēk.
I   not enough s/he (as) smart
'I'm not as smart as her.'

The adverb *gam* 'as' may appear optionally in this construction.

> *Idiom*: *m̀h chíh dāk* is an emphatic form of negative comparison
> (cf. *hóu-chíh* 'resemble' as in 9.3.2):
>
> Ngóh m̀h chíh dāk léih gam daaih jek.
> I   not like able you so   large CL
> 'I can't match you for size.'

[adjective] *gihk*, where *gihk* is a resultative particle meaning 'to the limits,
extreme' with a concessive sense is typically matched by *dōu* 'still' in the
following clause:

Kéuih sēui gihk   dōu m̀h gau   léih sēui.
s/he   bad   extreme   also not enough you   bad
'Bad though he is, he is not as bad as you are.'

Ngóh sau   gihk   dōu jeuk m̀h dóu   gó
I   slim extreme   also wear not V-PRT that

tìuh kwàhn.
CL   dress
'As slim as I can be, I still can't fit into that dress.'

[adjective] *gihk yáuh-hahn* is a fixed expression meaning 'not all that
[adjective]':

Kéuih sēui gihk   yáuh-hahn.
s/he   bad   extreme   have-limit
'Bad though she may be, she's not all that bad.'

Kéuih lēk   gihk   yáuh-hahn.
s/he   smart extreme   have-limit
'She's not that smart.'

Verbs can also occur with *gihk* and *gihk yáuh-hahn* (see 11.3.2).

9.3.4 EXCESSIVES

The basic excessive construction uses *taai* 'too' followed by an adjective:

Gám   yéung taai màhfàahn   la!
such way   too   troublesome PRT
'It's too much trouble that way!'

The comparative marker *gwo* may be added:

Nī   bún syū   taai (gwo)   sām   la.
this CL   book too   (excess) hard PRT
'This book is too difficult.'

An alternative is *gwotàuh* following the adjective (formed from *gwo* 'over' and *tàuh* 'head', like *over the top* in English):

Nī   bún   syū   sām   gwotàuh.
this CL   book hard excessively
'This book is excessively difficult.'

Dī   tōng   tìhm   gwotàuh.
CL   soup   sweet   excessively
'The soup is too sweet.'

[adjective] *dāk jaih* is an idiomatic expression of excess:

Nī   gihn   sāam   chèuhng   dāk jaih.
this CL   dress long   a-bit-much
'This dress is a bit (too) long.'

Sāam   baak   mān   gwai   dāk jaih.
three hundred   dollar   expensive   a-bit-much
'Three hundred dollars is rather expensive.'

Chìh-m̀h-chìh   dāk jaih   a?
late-not-late   a-bit-much   PRT
'Isn't it rather late for that?'

9.3.5 SUPERLATIVES

Superlative constructions are formed with *jeui* 'most' preceding the adjective:

Nī   dī   láu   haih   nī   kēui   jeui   gwai   ge   lak.
these CL   flat   are   this   area   most   expensive   PRT   PRT
'These flats are the most expensive in the area.'

The word order with *jeui* is often inverted, *jeui* + adjective coming before *haih* in order to focus the subject:

Jeui   cháam   haih   móuh   chín   sái.
most   poor   is   not-have   money   spend
'The biggest pity is not having any money to spend.'

Jeui   sēui   haih   léih!
most   bad   is   you
'It's all your fault!'

The range within which a superlative is to be understood can be established by a noun phrase preceding the superlative adjective:

Kéuih haih chyùhn Hēunggóng jeui yáuhchín gó go.
s/he is whole Hongkong most rich that CL
'He's the richest in all Hongkong.'

Yīnggwok jeui chēutméng ge gōsīng haih bīngo a?
Britain most famous LP song-star is who PRT
'Who is Britain's most famous singer?'

The superlative may also be preceded by a numeral or by the phrase *gam dō* + classifier, meaning 'of them all':

Sāam jímúi jeui lēk haih bīngo a?
three sister most clever is which PRT
'Which is the brightest of the three sisters?'

Léih sīk gam dō yīsāng bīngo jeui lēk a?
you know so many doctor which most clever PRT
'Which is the best doctor you know?'

gam dō also expresses the experiential superlative, as in *the most . . . I've ever known*:

Ngóh tái-gwo **gam dō hei** jeui hóu siu haih
I see-EXP so many film most good laugh is

gó tou.
that CL
'That was the funniest film I've seen.'

Ngóh háau-gwo **gam dō chi** síh jeui làahn
I take-EXP so many time exam most difficult

haih nī chi.
is this time
'This is the hardest exam I've ever taken.'

Note that English uses relative clauses here, while Cantonese uses a topicalized clause with the experiential aspect marker *gwo* (11.2.5).

ji is an idiomatic alternative to *jeui*, typically having a hyperbolic function of exaggeration. While *jeui* implies 'the most . . . ' within a certain range, *ji* suggests 'the most . . . of all (time)' or 'the most . . . ever'. It is much used in advertising, in preference to *jeui*:

Ji gányiu haih gáan dāk ngāam. (radio ad.)
most important is choose ADV right
'The most important thing is to make the right choice.'

ji is also used ironically or sarcastically:

Yùhnlòih léih haih ji síngmuhk gó go. (film)
after all you are most smart that-CL
'Oh, I see, you're the smartest.'

9.4 COMPLEMENTATION: COMPLEX STRUCTURES WITH ADJECTIVES

The complementation of adjectives – the question of what structures may follow individual adjectives – poses some problems. Most adjectives which are followed by infinitive (*to*) or gerundive (*-ing*) complements in English can be treated relatively straightforwardly. Many adjectives may simply be followed by a clause:

Ngóh hóu hōisām gin dóu léih.
I   very happy   see PRT you
'I'm glad to see you.'

Kéuih mhóuyisi tùhng léih góng.
s/he   embarrassed with   you   talk
'He's embarrassed to talk to you.'

However, while these structures present no problem to the English speaker, the apparent resemblance is often misleading. There is no infinitive form in Cantonese, and the above structures are probably to be analysed as serial constructions (see 8.3). One sign of the difference is that the order of the adjective and complement can be reversed in Cantonese:

(a) Ngóh hóu hōisām léihdeih gam yúhn dōu làih
    I   very happy   you-PL so   far   also come

    taam ngóh.
    visit me
    'I'm so glad you've come to visit me from so far away.'

(b) Léihdeih gam yúhn dōu làih   taam ngóh, ngóh hóu
    you-PL   so   far   also come visit me   I   very

    hōisām.
    happy
    'I'm so glad you've come to visit me from so far away.'

9.4.1 ADJECTIVES OF EASE AND DIFFICULTY

This class of adjectives deserves special attention in that their complementation works differently from English. In an English sentence such as *He is hard to tolerate*, the subject of the sentence is understood as the object of the complement verb (*tolerate*). In Cantonese, the sentence subject is understood as the subject of the complement verb:

Kéuih hóu làahn mìhngbaahk (nī go mahntàih).
s/he very hard understand (this CL question)
'He has difficulty understanding (this question).'

Although the literal gloss is 'he very hard understand', the sentence would not normally mean what 'He is hard to understand' does in English. However, a structure superficially like the English one does occur as a result of topicalization of the object:

Dī Jūngmàhn jih hóu yùhngyih mgeidāk ge.
CL Chinese character very easy forget PRT
'Chinese characters are easy to forget.'

As a result, sentences may be ambiguous, depending on whether the topic is understood as the subject or object of the clause:

Kéuih hóu yùhngyih jauh wán dóu ge la.
s/he very easy then find V-PRT PRT PRT
'He'll have no problem finding (it).' or 'He is easy to find.'

The English meaning as in 'hard to understand' or 'easy to forget' may be expressed unambiguously:

(a) by using an impersonal structure without a subject (note that there is no counterpart to the expletive pronoun it in Chinese: see ch. 5):

Jānhaih hóu làahn múhnjūk kéuih.
really very hard satisfy him
'He's really hard to satisfy.'

Hóu yùhngyih mgeidāk dī Jūngmàhn jih.
very easy forget CL Chinese character
'It's easy to forget Chinese characters.'

(b) alternatively, the adjective may be followed by a passive béi phrase (8.4):

Ngoihgwok-yàhn hóu yùhngyi béi yàhn ngh-wuih.
foreign-person very easy by people mis-understand
'Foreigners are easily misunderstood.'

Léih yìhga hóu làahn béi yàhn ngāak dóu.
you now very hard by people cheat V-PRT
'You're difficult to cheat now.'

There is a small class of adjectives which behave like làahn 'difficult' in the example above:

yùhngyih 'easy':

Saimānjái hóu yùhngyih fanjeuhk.
children very easy fall asleep
'Children fall asleep easily.'

fōngbihn 'convenient':

Ngóh gāmyaht m̀h fōngbihn làih.
I today not convenient come
'It's not convenient for me to come today.'

dākhàahn 'free, at leisure':

Léih dāk-m̀h-dākhàahn tēng dihnwá?
you free-not-free listen phone
'Are you free to answer the phone?'

hólàhng 'possible':

Kéuihdeih m̀h hólàhng jihgéi jouh saai.
they not possible self do all
'They can't possibly do it all themselves.'

Note that although these adjectives behave differently from the corresponding English adjectives, a similar construction occurs in English with other adjectives such as *likely* and *certain*, as in *We are likely to be free* or *John is certain to win*. Thus, the construction (sometimes known as Subject Raising) is not entirely unfamiliar to the English speaker; the difficulty posed by the Cantonese structure is to learn which adjectives behave in this way.[2]

Idiom: *hóu làahn dāk* means that something does not happen easily:

Léih go jái chéui-jó go gam hóu ge
your CL son marry-PFV CL so good LP

sān-póuh, hóu làahn dāk ga!
daughter-in-law very difficult able PRT
'Fancy your son marrying such a good daughter-in-law!'

Another idiomatic expression with *làahn* is *làahn-gwo* 'have a hard time' or 'be heart-broken':

Ngóh gójahnsí hóu làahn-gwo.
I that-time very hard-time
'I was having a hard time then.'

The above construction is liable to be confused with the use of *làahn* and *yih* to form adjectives such as *làahntái* 'bad-looking' with verbs of perception (see 2.1.1). With these compounds, unlike the constructions discussed above, the subject is understood as the object of the perception verb:

Nī   sáu   gō   hóu   làahntēng   ge.
this CL   song ADJ   hard-hear   PRT
'This song is awful.'

Note that the meaning is not 'hard to hear' but 'bad-sounding', indicating that these are lexicalized compounds.[3]

9.4.2 EVALUATIVE CONSTRUCTIONS

dái 'worthy' is used in colloquial speech to mean 'deserving', and may be followed by a complement verb:

Jek   māau hóu   dái   sek   ge.
CL   cat   very   worthy   love PRT
'The cat's so lovable.'

Léih wah léih haih-mhaih dái   laauh ā?
you   say you   be-not-be   worthy   scold PRT
'Don't you think you deserve to be scolded?'

Idiom: dái séi 'worthy to die' is a hyperbolic use of *séi* (cf. also 9.1.3). It may mean 'serves you right' or 'you asked for it':

Léih gám   yéung   góng yéh,   jānhaih dái séi!
you   so   manner   say   things really   worth-die
'You asked for it, talking that way.'

dái séi in a positive sense may also be a compliment:

Nī   tou hei   ge   deui-baahk hóu   yāumahk
this CL   film   LP   dialogue   very funny

dái séi.   (film review)
worth-die
'This film's dialogue is funny and sharp.'

dái dāk lám 'selfless' is also a compliment:

Ngóh sīk   gam   dō   yàhn   jeui dái-dāk-lám
I   know   so   many people most worth-able-think

haih léih!
is   you
'You're the most self-effacing person I know!'

---

jihkdāk 'worth(while)' behaves like the adjectives *làahn* and *yùhngyih* (9.4.1): 'These are not worth buying' in Cantonese may be rendered by topicalization of the object:

Nī   fahn boují   m̀h jihkdāk   máaih.
this CL   newspaper   not worthwhile   buy
'This newspaper's not worth buying.'

m̀h dái máaih 'not worth buying' would be equivalent.

10 ADVERBIAL CONSTRUCTIONS

Cantonese lacks a systematic means of forming adverbs from adjectives, although one function of reduplicated adjectives is as adverbs (10.1.3). Instead, adverbial modification is expressed by adjectives, in conjunction with adverbial constructions (10.1.1, 10.1.2).

Predicate adverbs (10.1) are those which describe the manner of an action, and apply to the verb or verb phrase. Sentence adverbs (10.3) describe the circumstances of events and states, such as time and probability; they apply to the whole sentence. The syntax of the two types is very different.

10.1 ADVERBS MODIFYING THE VERB PHRASE

Modification of the verb or verb phrase is expressed using adjectives, together with adverbial constructions taking three main forms:

(a) verb – *dāk* – adjective (10.1.1);
(b) adjective – *gám* – verb (10.1.2);
(c) reduplicated adjective – (*déi*) – verb (10.1.3).

Since each of these patterns involves adjectives, to a large extent the syntax of adjectives described in chapter 9 also applies to these adverbial constructions. Similarly, comparison of adverbs is based on that of adjectives (10.2).

10.1.1 *DĀK*

The most general adverbial construction resembles that in Mandarin, with *dāk* corresponding to Mandarin *de*. The [verb] – *dāk* construction is followed by an adjective, preceded by the adjective marker *hóu* or another modifier, as discussed in (9.1.2):

Kéuih hohk dak hóu faai.
s/he learn ADV very fast
'He learns fast.'

Gó dī sīnsāang **gaau dāk géi hóu** wo.
those CL teacher teach ADV quite well PRT
'Those teachers teach pretty well.'

The adjective may be modified in any of the ways illustrated in chapter 9, for example by *gam* 'so' or by reduplication of the adjective:

Kéuih **jyuh dāk syū-syū-fuhk-fuhk**,   m̀h wúih
s/he   live ADV comfortable-comfortable   not will

būn   ge   la.
move PRT PRT
'She's living nice and comfortably, she won't move.'

The adverbial construction with *dāk* is most typically used in a generic or habitual sense, as in the above examples which do not refer to any particular occasion. By contrast, the similar use of *dāk* in resultative complements (8.5.3) does refer to a particular occasion:

Dím gáai wúih **háau   dāk   gam chā** ga?
how   come would examine   ADV   so   bad   PRT
'How come he did so badly in his exam?'

With transitive verbs where the object is present, the verb is repeated in the *dāk* construction:

Kéuih **jā**   chē **jā**   dak   hóu faai.
s/he   drive car drive ADV   very fast
'She drives very fast.'

Kéuih **chau**-jái **chau** dāk   hóu hōisām.
s/he   care-child care   ADV   very happy
'She enjoys looking after the child.'

The repetition results from the constraint that both the object and the adverbial *dāk* must directly follow the verb.

With a few adjectives, notably *faai* 'fast' and *maahn* 'slow', *dāk* is not needed:

Léih hàahng faai dī dāk-m̀h-dāk   a?
you   walk   fast-ish okay-not-okay   PRT
'Can you walk a bit faster?'

A colloquial alternative to the *dāk* construction is a topic–comment sentence, where the verb phrase is followed directly by an adjective:

Ngóh lóuhgūng jyú   faahn hóu lēk   ge.
my   husband   cook food   very smart PRT
'My husband is a very good cook.'

Kéuih sé   jih   leng-m̀h-leng a?
s/he   write character nice-not-nice   PRT
'Does he write characters well?'

10.1.2 *GÁM*

An alternative adverbial construction uses an adjective followed by the adverbial *gám* 'in this way' before the verb. *gám* is to be distinguished from *gam* 'so' with mid level tone (see 9.1.3):

Ngóh mhaih **yìhngjān gám** hohk.
I   not-be genuine   thus learn
'I'm not studying (it) seriously.'

Kéuih **hóu lāu gám** sāu-jó   sin.
s/he very mad thus close-PFV line
'He put the phone down furiously.'

This construction is often used with reduplicated adjectives:

Ngóh gin dóu   kéuih **sòh-só-déi**   **gám** siu.
I   see V-PRT him   silly-silly-ish thus smile
'I saw him smiling stupidly.'

Kéuih **daaih-daaih-lihk**   gám tek go bō.
s/he great-great strength   thus kick CL ball
'He kicks the ball very hard.'

Due to its structural similarity to the English pre-verbal adverb, the construction with *gám* may also be used to import an English adverb into a Cantonese sentence:

Ngóh séung **seriously** gám tóuleuhn nī   go mahntàih.
I   wish serious   thus discuss this CL problem
'I want to seriously discuss this problem.'

gám may be used elliptically as a predicate, together with *haih* or an auxiliary, meaning 'be like that':

Dī sailouhjái **haih gám** ge laak.
CL children   are so   PRT PRT
'Children are like that.'

Léih **mhóu gám** lā!   Dím gáai **wúih gám** gé?
you don't so   PRT   how come will so   PRT
'Don't be like that!'   'Why is it like this?'

This use of *gám* corresponds to *dím* in questions (see 17.3.7).

gám is also used with the verb *hóuchíh* 'seem, resemble' in two ways:

(a) the *hóuchíh* phrase may function as an adverb with *gám*:

Go sailouh **hóuchíh** daaih yàhn **gám** góng yéh.
CL child   just-like big   person so   talk things
'The child's talking like an adult.'

> *Idioms with* gám: [verb] *sìhng gám* (or *sèhng gám*) is a demonstrative phrase used to emphasize the extent of an outcome or result:
>
> Dím   gáai   wúih   **bin**   **sìhng**   **gám**   gé?
> how   come   would   change   result   so   PRT
> 'Why has it come out this way?'
>
> Ngóh   gú   m̀h   dóu   wúih   **gáau**   **sìhng**
> I   guess   not   succeed   would   manage   result
>
> **gám**!   (TV drama)
> so
> 'I never imagined it would turn out like this!'

The corresponding question construction, [verb] *sìhng dím?* is used to form manner and extent questions (17.3.7).

jauh gám, meaning 'just' or 'simply', is often used in instructions:

> Léih   jauh   gám   hàahng yahp heui   jauh   dāk   ge   laak.
> you   then   so   walk   in   go   then okay   PRT PRT
> 'You simply walk in like this. It'll be fine.'
>
> Léih   m̀h   hóyíh   jauh   gám   jáu   ge   wo.
> you   not   can   then   so   leave   PRT   PRT
> 'You can't just leave like that.'

haih gám 'that's all' is used to terminate a conversation:

> Haih   gám   sīn.   (tel.)
> is   so   first
> 'That's all for now.'

(b) *gám* is added pleonastically at the end of the clause:

Kéuih   **hóuchíh** mhaih   géi   múhnyi   **gám**.
s/he   seem   not-be   quite   satisfied   so
'She doesn't seem to be very satisfied.'

Kéuih   jeuk   sāam   **hóuchíh**   hohksāang   **gám**.
s/he   wear   clothes   resemble   student   so
'He dresses like a student.'

Adverb idioms with gam: *gam* (distinct from *gám* with high rising tone) is found in some idioms. *lyuhn/lyún gam* [verb] is to act in a random or disorganized manner; note that *gam* is optional:

Ngóh jauh **lyuhn (gam) gáan** yāt go.
I therefore random (thus) choose one CL
'So I chose one at random.'

Kéuih **lyuhn (gam) góng** yéh ge je.
s/he random (thus) talk things PRT PRT
'He's just talking nonsense.'

Note that *gam* may be omitted, as in the corresponding Mandarin idiom *luàn jiǎng* 'talk nonsense'. *Máahng gam* [verb] is to do something like mad:

Dī yàuhhaak làih dou Hēunggóng máahng gam
CL tourist come to Hongkong crazy thus

máaih yéh.
buy things
'When tourists get to Hongkong they buy like crazy.'

Ngóh máahng gam wán dōu wán m̀h dóu
I crazy thus search also search not succeed

tìuh sósìh.
CL key
'I look for the key like crazy and still can't find it.'

kòhng 'crazy', used as an adverb, has a similar meaning to *máahng gam*:

Nī dī tīnhei yiu kòhng yám-séui.
this CL weather need crazy drink water
'You have to drink like mad in this weather.'

Ngóhdeih kòhng lám nī go mahntàih.
we crazy think this CL problem
'We're racking our brains over this problem.'

10.1.3 REDUPLICATED ADVERBS

Reduplicated adverbs, typically formed from adjectives, are used before the verb in three patterns:

(a) with the suffix *-déi* (see 9.2.2):

Léih **tāu-tāu-déi** jíng yéh sihk àh?
you steal-steal-ish make things eat PRT
'You've been secretly preparing food, have you?'

(b) with certain adjectives, the reduplicated form alone:

Kéuih ge behng **maahn-máan** hóu fāan la.
s/he LP illness slow-slow good back PRT
'Her illness is gradually improving.'

Ngóh **mìhng-mìhng** tái dóu léih tùhng go léuihyán yātchàih.
I clear-clear see V-PRT you with CL woman together
'I clearly saw you with a woman.'

(c) together with *gám* (10.1.2):

Kéuih **sai-sai** sēng **gám** góng.
s/he small-small voice so speak
'He spoke in a quiet voice.'

Note that the reduplication may result in a changed tone on the second adjective, hence *maahn + maahn → maahn-máan* but *tāu-tāu-déi* as *tāu* already has a high tone.

These reduplicated adverb constructions are used especially in imperative sentences, in preference to the adverbial constructions with *dāk* and *gám* (see 19.1):

Léih **gwāai-gwāai-déi** kéih háidouh dáng lā.
you good-good-ish stand here wait PRT
'Be good and stand here waiting.'

Maahn-máan hàahng a. (used as a farewell greeting)
slow-slow walk PRT
'Go slowly.'

Two reduplicated adjectives in the form AABB (cf. 9.2.1) serve to emphasize a suggestion or instruction:

Léih **faai-faai cheui-cheui** sé yùhn bún syū lā!
you fast-fast crisp-crisp write finish CL book PRT
'Hurry up and finish your book!'

Reduplication of adjectives is highly idiomatic, and several reduplicated idioms of the AAB pattern (9.2.3) are used specifically as adverbs, for example:

Kéuih **jihng-jíng-gāi** jáu-jó.
s/he quiet-quiet-chicken leave-PFV
'He quietly went and left.'

Léih **làh-lá-sēng** jāp hóu dī yéh.
you la-la-voice collect up CL stuff
'Hurry up and clear up this stuff.'

Kéuih **kàhm-kám-chēng** sihk saai dī yéh jauh jáu-jó.
s/he rush-rush eat all CL things then leave-PFV
'He ate up his food in a rush and left.'

10.2 COMPARISON OF ADVERBS

Comparison of adverbs is based on that of adjectives. Since the adverbial constructions described in section 10.1 call for the use of adjectives, the syntax of adjectival comparison (see 9.3) applies. Thus, the basic comparative construction with *gwo* combines straightforwardly with the adverb construction with *dāk*:

Kéuih waahk wá waahk dāk hóu gwo ngóh.
s/he paint picture paint ADV good than me
'She paints better than I do.'

Yàhndeih dá-gēi dá dāk juhng lēk gwo léih.
people play-machine play ADV even clever than you
'Other people play (video games) even better than you do.'

Negative and interrogative comparisons are expressed by *móuh* and *yáuh-móuh* respectively (see 9.3.3), followed by *gam* 'so [adjective]':

Ngóh **móuh** léih góng dāk **gam hóu**.
I not-have you speak ADV so good
'I don't speak as well as you.'

Léih **yáuh-móuh** léih gòhgō hohk dāk **gam faai** a?
you have-not-have your brother learn ADV so fast PRT
'Do you learn as fast as your [elder] brother?'

Note the word order here, with (*yáuh-*)*móuh* preceding the verb.

The comparative use of *dī* (9.3) is applicable where the object of comparison is not explicitly stated:

Kéuih yìhgā cheung-gō cheung dāk hóu tēng dī.
s/he now sing-song sing ADV good listen a-bit
'She's singing a bit better now.'

Léih hó-m̀h-hóyíh góng dāk maahn dī a?
you can-not-can speak ADV slow a-bit PRT
'Could you speak a bit slower?'

The excessive constructions with *taai* (*gwo*) and *dāk jaih* combine similarly with *dāk*:

Sìhgaan gwo dāk taai faai.
time pass ADV too fast
'Time passes too quickly.'

Kéuih jā dāk faai dāk jaih.
s/he drive ADV fast a-bit
'He's driving a bit too fast.'

The superlative *jeui* or *ji* (9.3.5) may be applied to adverb constructions, with the order of the verb phrase and subject often inverted:

Gām chi haih A-Chán **háau dāk jeui hóu**.
this time is Ah-Chan exam ADV most good
'Chan did best in the exam this time.'

Gam dō màhjeuk-yáu **dá dāk ji lēk** haih
so many mahjong-er play ADV most clever is

kéuih a-mā.
her mother
'The best mahjong player of all is her mother.'

Hái gódouh **cheung dāk ji lām**, ji
at there sing ADV most cosy most

syūfuhk. (radio ad. for karaoke lounge)
comfortable
'It's the most comfortable place for singing.'

The construction *yuht . . . yuht . . .* 'the more . . . the more . . . ' may either follow the adverbial construction with *dāk* or occur on either side of the verb:

Kéuihdeih jouh dāk **yuht faai yuht hóu**.
they do ADV more fast more good
'The faster they can do it the better.'

Léih **yuht jóu** làih **yuht hóu**.
you more early come more good
'The earlier you come the better.'

Comparative idioms: *jeuhn* 'as . . . as possible' is used specifically with adverbs. Note that as for sentence adverbs (see 10.3), the whole adverbial phrase comes between the subject and the verb:

Léih **jeuhn faai** gáau dihm lā!
you best fast manage V-PRT PRT
'Finish up as soon as possible.'

jeuhn-leuhng is used adverbially to mean 'as well as one can' or 'to the best of one's ability', for example in expressing encouragement:

Ngóh wúih jeuhn-leuhng bōng léihdeih ge la.
I will as-possible help you-PL PRT PRT
'I'll do my best to help you.'

The comparative *gwo* may be used to compare two clauses with respect to an adverb:

Kéuih góng Gwóngdūngwá lēk gwo ngóh
s/he speak Cantonese clever than I

góng Yīngmán.
speak English
'He speaks Cantonese better than I speak English.'

Léih chūng-lèuhng faai gwo ngóh sái tàuh. (conv.)
you take-shower fast than I wash head
'You take a shower faster than I can wash my hair.'

This construction also appears in the idiom:

Ngóh sihk yìhm dō gwo léih sihk máih.
I eat salt more than you eat rice

The meaning is similar to the English idiom 'I've seen more . . . than you've had hot dinners'.

10.3 SENTENCE ADVERBS: MODIFYING THE SENTENCE

Sentence adverbs are distinguished from verbal adverbs in that they modify the whole sentence rather than the verb phrase or predicate alone. Time adverbs, for example (10.3.3), concern the circumstances of events and states rather than the manner in which they occur. Modal adverbs, which describe the possibility and probability of events, are discussed in 12.2.

10.3.1 POSITION OF SENTENCE ADVERBS

There are three positions for sentence adverbs:

(a) between the subject/topic and the verb:

Ngóh **waahkjé** m̀h làih dāk.
I perhaps not come able
'I might not be able to come.'

Ngóhdeih **hóu chói** móuh máaih dou gáan ūk.
we good luck not-have buy V-PRT CL house
'Fortunately we didn't buy the house.'

(b) at the beginning of the sentence:

Hóu chói ngóhdeih jóu dī làih.
good luck we early rather came
'Lucky we came early.'

This option is often used when there is already a manner adverb before the verb:

Waahkjé léih   léuih-pàhngyáuh **dahkdāng** máaih yéh
perhaps your girl-friend   specially buy   thing

sung béi léih.
give to you
'Maybe your girlfriend went out of her way to buy something for you.'

Yìhgā dī   yàhn **yuht** **làih** **yuht** jūngyi sái-séui-sī.
now   CL people more and   more like   wash-water-silk
'Nowadays people like washable silk more and more.'

(c) at the end of the sentence, by way of afterthought:

Kéuih juhng duhk-gán-syū,   **gójahnsí**.
s/he   still   study-PROG book   then
'She was still a student, at that time.'

Sailóu   heui-jó wáan, **dōsou**.
brother go-PFV   play   probably
'Little brother has gone to play, probably.'

This option is restricted to casual conversation (see 4.1.3).

10.3.2 ADVERBS OF QUANTITY

dōu, in addition to its many functions in quantifying expressions (14.1.1), serves as an adverb meaning 'also' or 'too':

A: Léih bóu-juhng a.   B: Léih **dōu**   haih.
   you take-care   PRT   you also   be
   'Take care.'   'You too.'

gau 'enough' may be used with a similar meaning:

A: Ngóh hóu   guih a.   B: Ngóh **gau**   haih lok.
   I   very tired PRT   I   enough   am   PRT
   'I'm tired.'   'So am I.'

dōu may also mean 'anyway', especially in negative sentences:

Ngóh dōu   m̀h   sīk   kéuih gé.
I   also not   know   him   PRT
'I don't know him, anyway.'

Ngóhdeih dōu   lám-jyuh jáu   ge   la.
we   also intend·   leave PRT   PRT
'We were going to leave anyway.'

wàahngdihm has a similar meaning:

> Léih wàahngdihm yiu   chēut heui, bātyùh seuhnbín
> you anyway   need out   go   rather on-the-way
>
> bōng ngóh gei màaih seun.
> help me   send V-PRT letter
> 'You have to go out anyway, you might as well post the letters for me.'

jihnghaih and *jíhaih* 'only, just' are often followed by the particle *je/jē* (18.3.5):

> Ngóhdeih jihnghaih tái-háh   ge je.
> we   only   look-DEL PRT PRT
> 'We're just taking a look.'
>
> Jíhaih yāt chi jē.
> only one time PRT
> 'It's only once . . . '

dāk may also mean 'only', but is used with noun phrases:

> Dāk sāam go yàhn làih jàh?
> just three CL people come PRT
> 'Only three people came?'
>
> Jihng dāk ngóh tùhng ngóh a-gō   háidouh.
> only just me   with my   brother here
> 'Only me and my [elder] brother are here.'

10.3.3 ADVERBS OF TIME

In the absence of tense, adverbs of time take on a particular importance in specifying the time to which a sentence refers. They may be usefully divided according to past, present and future, although they clearly do not form a tense system as such. Note that the adverb in the Cantonese examples is often redundant in the English translation, due to the tense of the verb.

Past time adverbs

búnlòih 'originally':

> Ngóhdeih búnlòih   móuh lám-jyuh fāan Hēunggóng.
> we   originally not   intend return Hongkong
> 'We weren't planning to come back to Hongkong.'

yíhchìhn 'before, formerly':

Gwok yīsāng yíhchìhn jyuh Sāan Déng.
Kwok doctor before live Peak
'Dr Kwok used to live on the Peak.'

gójahnsìh or *gójahnsí* 'then, at that time':

Ngóh gójahnsí juhng meih háau dóu chē-pàaih.
I that-time still not-yet pass PRT vehicle-licence
'At that time I still hadn't got my driving licence.'

chō-chō, *chō tàuh*, *hōi tàuh* 'at first':

Ngóh chō-chō m̀h jūngyi kéuih, hauhlàih
I at-first not like him afterwards

maahn-mán jūngyi.
slow-slow like
'I used not to like him, but gradually got to like him.'

bātlāu 'until now, always' is used together with *dōu*:

Léih bātlāu dōu gam chūngmìhng ge.
you until-now also so clever PRT
'You've always been so clever (until now).'

Present time adverbs

yìhgā or *gāján* 'now':

A-Fúng yìhgā jyuh Sāatìhn.
Ah Fung now live Shatin
'Fung lives in Shatin now.'

juhng or *juhng haih* 'still':

Léih juhng gei-m̀h-geidāk ngóh a?
you still re-not-remember me PRT
'Do you still remember me?'

Léih deui Hēunggóng chìhntòuh juhng haih gam
you towards Hongkong future still are so

yáuh-seunsām àh?
have-confidence PRT
'You're still so confident about Hongkong's future, are you?'

yìhngyìhn 'still' is more formal:

Ngóhdeih yìhngyìhn wúih gaijuhk lóuhlihk.
we still will continue strive
'We will still continue to do our best.'

jaahmsìh 'for the time being' expresses the short-term or provisional future:

Ngóhdeih jaahmsìh msái chéng gūngyàhn.
we time-being not-need employ maid
'We don't need to employ a maid for the moment.'

Future time adverbs

dousìh 'by that time':

Dousìh ngóhdeih jauh jīdou dím ge lak.
that-time we then know how PRT PRT
'We'll know how it is by then.'

A: Heui dou gódouh dím a?
    go arrive there how PRT
    'What do we do when we arrive?'

B: Dousìh ji syun lā.
    that-time only plan PRT
    'We'll plan that when the time comes.'

gānjyuh 'next':

Ngóhdeih gānjyuh góng daih-yih go tàihmuhk.
we following talk another CL topic
'Next we'll talk about another topic.'

yāt-jahn-gāan 'in a moment':

Kéuihdeih yātjahngāan heui sung-gēi.
they in-a-moment come accompany-plane
'In a moment they're going to see someone off (at the airport).'

yàuh yìhgā hōichí 'from now on':

Ngóh yàuh yìhgā hōichí m̀h tùhng léih
I from now begin not with you

góng yéh.
speak stuff
'From now on I'm not going to talk to you.'

daih yih sìh 'in future' (often reduced to *daih sìh*):

Daih-yih sìh mhóu máaih nī jek pàaihjí.
another time don't buy this CL brand
'In future we shouldn't buy this brand.'

sīn as a time adverb means 'first of all', often together with the
delimitative aspect marker *háh* (11.2.6):

Ngóhdeih sīn tái-háh dím joi
we first look-DEL how again

lám baahnfaat.
think solution
'We'll see how it goes first and then think of a solution.'

Used following a time expression, *sin/sīnji* or *ji* means 'only' or 'not
until' (see also 16.3.2 for their use in conditionals):

Ngóh **tīngyaht** **sīnji** jīdou chéng-m̀h-chéng dóu ga.
I tomorrow first know apply-not-apply succeed leave
'I won't know until tomorrow whether I can take leave.'

In this function *sīnji* is not restricted to time, but is also used to
contrast two phrases:

Kéuih sīnji sīk, ngóh m̀h sīk.
s/he only know I not know
'Only she knows, I don't.'

sīnji/sīn/ji emphasizes the preceding word or phrase, which may be an
expression of time or of some other circumstance:

Ngóh tīngyaht sīnji béi dihnwá léih lā.
I tomorrow only give telephone you PRT
'I won't call you until tomorrow.'

Yiht-laaht-laaht sīnji hóu sihk gáma.
warm-hot-hot only good eat PRT-PRT
'It only tastes good when it's hot, you know that.'

sìn is also used as a sentence particle (18.3.5).

10.3.4 ADVERBS OF FREQUENCY

Adverbs of frequency are formed using the means of quantification such as
dōu (14.1.1), *múih* (14.1.4) and reduplication (14.1.2).

tūngsèuhng or *gīngsèuhng* 'usually':

Tūngsèuhng dōu haih yuhng nī go baahnfaat.
usually all is use this CL do-manner
'It's usually done this way.'

sèhngyaht (dōu), although usually translated as 'always', is often used hyperbolically:

Léih sèhngyaht (dōu) wah móuh   sìhgaan.
you always   (all)   say not-have time
'You always say you don't have time.'

hóu síu (14.4) as an adverb has the meaning 'rarely':

Yīnggwok hóu síu   yáuh gam yiht ge   tīnhei.
England   very little   have   so   hot LP   weather
'The weather's not often as warm as this in England.'

Reduplicated time expressions (14.1.2) form adverbs of frequency:

Lìhn-lìhn   dōu yáuh hingjūk   a-màh   sāangyaht.
year-year all   have   celebrate   grandma   birthday
'There's a celebration for Grandma's birthday every year.'

A-Kèuhng yaht-yaht dōu yiu   paai   boují.
Ah-Keung day-day   all   need deliver newspaper
'Keung has to deliver newspapers every day.'

Kéuih chi-chi   dōu haih gám ge   wo.
s/he   time-time all   is   so   PRT PRT
'She's like this every time.'

múih 'each' (14.1.4) also combines with time expressions to form adverbs of frequency. Unlike reduplicated adverbs, these forms may be modified by numerals or quantifiers such as *géi* 'a few':

múih chi 'every time'	múih sāam chi 'every third time'
múih yaht 'each/every day'	múih léuhng yaht 'every two days'
múih go láihbaai 'every week'	múih léuhng go láihbaai 'every two weeks'
múih go yuht 'each month'	múih géi go yuht 'every few months'
múih lìhn 'each/every year'	múih bun lìhn 'every six months'
múih gaak yāt lìhn 'every other year'	

As time adverbials, these phrases come before the verb:

Ngóhdeih **múih léuhng lìhn** yiu   būn   yāt   chi   ūk.
we   each two   year need move one   time house
'We have to move house once every two years.'

. . . *yāt chi* 'once (in . . .)' is an alternative expression of frequency, which may combine with *múih*:

Ngóh yāt go láihbaai yiu tái **yāt chi** yīsāng.
I one CL week need see one time doctor
'I have to see the doctor once a week.'

Múih sāam go yuht yiu béi **yāt chi** leihsīk.
each three CL month need pay one time interest
'You have to pay interest every three months.'

Compare the question form *géiloih . . . yāt chi* meaning 'how often?'
(17.3.5).

10.4 ADVERBIAL PHRASES

The following phrases function as time and manner adverbs:

chìhn 'ago' may either follow the time expression, as in English, or precede
it:

Ngóh **géi lìhn chìhn** gin-gwo kéuih.
I few year before meet-EXP him
'I met him a few years ago.'

Kéuihdeih haih **chìhn géi go yuht** sīn hōichí
they are before a-few CL months first begin

paak-tō ge je.
date PRT PRT
'They only started dating a few months ago.'

hauh 'later' is the converse of *chìhn* but consistently follows the time
expression:

léuhng lìhn **hauh**	géi fān-jūng **hauh**
two years after	a-few seconds after
'two years later'	'a few seconds later'

dahkdāng means 'specially' or 'deliberately':

Kéuih dahkdāng làih taam ngóhdeih.
s/he specially come visit us
'She's coming specially to see us.'

Kéuih dahkdāng jíng-gú ngóh.
s/he specially play-trick me
'He deliberately played a trick on me'

The converse is *m-gokyi* 'unintentionally':

Ngóh m-gokyi chái chān kéuih.
I un-intentional tread V-PRT him
'I didn't mean to step on him.'

Idiom: *chìhn yāt pàaih/páai* 'a while ago', has the fixed order:

Ngóh chìhn yāt pàaih johng dóu kéuih.
I before a while bump V-PRT him
'I ran into him a while ago.'

Compare the expression *nī pàaih/páai* 'these days'.

yáuh yāt pàaih 'it's been a while' is used with *móuh* (13.3, 15.4) to refer to non-occurrence of an event in the recent past:

A-Wóng yáuh yāt pàaih móuh chēut-yihn-gwo.
Ah-Wong have one while not-have appear-EXP
'Wong hasn't put in an appearance for some time.'

yáuh pàaih or *yáu pàaih* 'it'll be a while' suggests an indefinite period, typically extending into the future:

Kéuihdeih **yáuh pàaih** dōu meih git-dāk-fān.
they have while still not-yet marry-able
'It'll be a while before they can get married.'

A: Géisìh bātyihp a, léih?
   when graduate PRT you
   'When are you going to graduate?'

B: Juhng yáuh pàaih lā.
   still have while PRT
   'It'll be a while yet.'

---

yāt [classifier] *yāt* [classifier] is a reduplicated construction meaning 'one by one' or 'one after another', usually used together with *dāk* (10.1.1) or *gám* (10.1.2):

Dī seun **yāt fūng yāt fūng** daahp dāk hóu jíngchàih.
CL letter one CL one CL pile ADV very tidy
'The letters are piled tidily one on top of the other.'

Nī dihp choi yiu **yāt daahm yāt daahm** gám sihk.
this CL food need one bite one bite so eat
'This dish should be eaten one mouthful at a time.'

yāt go gān yāt go 'one after the other' has a similar meaning:

Dī   yàuhhaak   hóu   yáuh-dihtjeuih gám **yāt go   gān   yāt**
CL   tourists   very have-order   so   one CL   follow one

go hàahng yahp heui.
CL   walk   in   go
'The tourists went in one by one in an orderly fashion.'

yāt chi gwo 'all in one go':

Ngóhdeih séung **yāt chi   gwo** būn   saai dī   yéh.
we   wish one time pass move all   CL   things
'We want to move everything in one go.'

10.4.1 VIEWPOINT ADVERBS

These phrases present a point of view to begin a sentence.

góng jān 'to tell you the truth' is used to confide opinions:

Góng jān ā,   ngóh m̀h wúih ga   béi kéuih ge.
speak true PRT I   not will marry to   him   PRT
'To tell you the truth, I wouldn't marry him.'

. . . *làih góng* 'as far as . . . is concerned' establishes a topic of
conversation:

Gīngjai làih   góng, Hēunggóng gáau   dāk   mcho.
economy come   speak Hongkong   manage ADV   not-bad
'As far as the economy is concerned, Hongkong is doing pretty well.'

Yahtbún choi   làih   góng, nī   gāan jáudim syun
Japan   food   come   speak this CL   hotel count

haih yāt-làuh.
is   first-rate
'As far as Japanese food is concerned, this hotel is excellent.'

. . . *làih tái* has a similar function:

Chèuhng sin   làih   tái, máaih láu   hóyíh bóu
long   term come   see   buy   flat can   preserve

jihk.   (radio int.)
value
'From a long-term point of view, buying a flat can be a good
investment.'

jiu ngóh tái 'as I see it':

Jiu ngóh tái, gām-máahn yīnggōi jouh dāk   yùhn.
as   I   see   tonight   should   do   able finish
'As I see it, we should be able to finish up tonight.'

11 ASPECT AND VERBAL PARTICLES

As is well known, Chinese grammar lacks distinctions of tense as such: that is, the notions past, present and future are not encoded grammatically by forms of the verb. There is, however, a relatively complex system of verbal aspect, distinguishing notions such as events, states and processes. Through the close relationship between these aspectual notions and time, the aspect markers contribute to the expression of time relations (11.1), together with adverbs of time (10.3.3).

Aspect is a subjective notion in the sense that it enables the same situation to be viewed and described in different ways. Aspects can be seen as 'viewpoints' which can be taken on a situation; hence, the same situation may be described using two or more different aspect markers, for example the progressive *gán* (11.2.2) and the continuous *jyuh* (11.2.3):

Ngoihbihn	lohk-gán	yúh.	Ngoihbihn	lohk-jyuh	yúh.
outside	fall-PROG	rain	outside	fall-CONT	rain
'It's raining outside.'			'It's raining outside.'		

The progressive *gán* describes the action of rain falling, while *jyuh* presents the weather as a continuing situation. The choice of aspect marker is determined partly by the context and partly by the speaker's own choice of how to present the situation. A further element of choice is introduced by the fact that unlike tense in English, aspect markers are in most cases grammatically optional, i.e. they may be omitted (see 11.2.1).

The Cantonese system of aspect corresponds broadly to that in Mandarin as shown in Table 11.1. Despite this approximate correspondence, aspect is an area where the two languages differ significantly. The Cantonese markers of aspect all follow the verb, behaving essentially as suffixes. Cantonese also has a habitual marker *hōi* which Mandarin lacks, and there are important differences in the usage of individual aspects.

In addition to aspect markers as such, Cantonese has numerous verbal particles whose functions are closely related to those of aspect (see 11.3). Many of these are peculiar to Cantonese, in particular the quantifying particles *saai* and *màaih* (11.3.3) and the adversative/habitual *chān* (11.3.4).

Table 11.1 Aspect markers in Mandarin and Chinese

	Mandarin	*Cantonese*
Perfective	VERB – le	VERB – jó
Experiential	VERB – guò	VERB – gwo
Progressive	zài VERB	VERB – gán
Continuous	VERB – zhe	VERB – jyuh
Delimitative	VERB – yī – VERB	VERB – háh
Habitual		VERB – hōi

11.1 ASPECT AND THE EXPRESSION OF TIME

In the absence of explicit tense marking, temporal relations are expressed by a combination of adverbials, aspect markers and contextual factors. Time adverbs such as *búnlòih* 'originally' and *yíhchìhn* 'before', for example, anchor the time reference of a sentence in the past (see 10.3.3):

Ngóh búnlòih jyuh Gáulùhng ge.
I originally live Kowloon PRT
'I used to live in Kowloon.'

The basic meaning of the aspectual particles concerns not the time of an action, but the way it is viewed: as a state of affairs, an event or an action in process; these aspectual meanings are discussed individually in section 11.2. Nevertheless, in the absence of specific indications of time, the aspect markers imply reference to certain times:

gán is normally used of ongoing actions, i.e. in the absence of any indication to the contrary, it is understood as referring to the present:

Wòhng síujé góng-gán dihnwá.
Wong Miss talk-PROG telephone
'Miss Wong is on the phone.'

jyuh denotes a state of affairs, typically present or timeless:

Dī wàhn jē-jyuh go taaiyèuhng.
CL cloud block-CONT CL sunlight
'The clouds are blocking out the sunlight.'

gwo, like the present perfect in English, implies that the situation took place prior to the point of speech or reference:

Ngóh hohk-gwo Dākmán ge.
I study-EXP German PRT
'I have studied German before.'

It combines with past time adverbs such as *chàhnggīng* 'before':

Kéuih   chàhnggīng   ló-gwo   jéung.
s/he   previously   take-EXP   award
'She has received an award before.'

jó, which indicates an event, also normally implies past time reference:

Ngóh   mgin-jó   tìuh   sósìh.
I   lose-PFV   CL   key
'I've lost the key.'

It combines with adverbs of recent past such as *ngāam-ngāam* 'just' or *tàuhsīn* 'just now':

Lóuhbáan   ngāam-ngāam   chēut-jó   heui.
boss   just-just   out-PFV   go
'The boss has just gone out.'

These temporal implications may be thought of as default interpretations which hold when other things are equal. The aspect markers should not be equated with tense; in particular, *jó* and *gwo* should not be regarded as past tense markers. For example, *jó* is used in imperative sentences and complement clauses referring to the present or future:

Sihk-jó   kéuih   sīn.   Ngóh   séung   maaih-jó   ga   chē.
eat-PFV   it   first   I   wish   sell-PFV   CL   car
'Eat it up.'   'I want to sell the car.'

Conversely, sentences referring to the past do not *require jó* or *gwo*:

Ngóh   kàhmmáahn   tùhng   ngóh   ūkkéi-yàhn   sihk-faahn.
I   last-night   with   my   home-people   eat-food
'I had dinner with my family last night.'

Note also that the time reference of aspect markers is *relative* rather than absolute. That is, the temporal meaning of *jó* and *gwo* may not be past in an absolute sense, but only relative to some other reference time. This is seen clearly in subordinate clauses:

Kéuihdeih   yiu   heui-gwo   ngoihgwok   sīn   jīdou   haih   dím   ge.
they   need   go-EXP   abroad   first know   is   how   PRT
'They'll only know what it's like when they've been abroad.'

In such cases, the verb modified by *gwo* is actually referring to the future: it is past only relative to the main verb, *jīdou*. Similarly, a verb with *jó* may refer to the anticipated completion of a future event:

Ngóhdeih   sihk-jó-faahn   sīn   heui   máaih   yéh.
we   eat-PFV-food   first go   buy   things
'After eating we'll go shopping.'

11.2 ASPECT MARKERS

The aspect markers *gán*, *jyuh*, *jó*, *gwo*, *háh* and *hōi* are bound forms, behaving essentially as suffixes: in their functions as aspect markers, they may not be separated from the verb, which distinguishes them from verbal particles (11.3).

11.2.1 SYNTAX OF ASPECT MARKERS

In general, aspect markers are grammatically optional, i.e. for every context in which one occurs it is possible to have the same sentence without the aspect marker. This is seen clearly in the case of the progressive *gán* which, unlike the English progressive, may freely be omitted:

Ngóhdeih yìhgā góng(-gán) nī go mahntàih.
we now talk(-PROG) this CL problem
'We're talking about this problem now.'

In certain syntactic contexts, however, the aspect marker is strongly preferred, if not obligatory. The perfective *jó* is required where the verb has a quantified object and refers to the past:

Ngóh kàhmmáahn sé-jó léuhng fūng seun.
I last-night write-PFV two CL letter
'I wrote two letters last night.'

This may be contrasted with a similar context without a quantified object, in which *jó* is not required:

Kéuih kàhmmáahn dá-dihnwá béi ngóh.
s/he last night call-telephone to me
'She gave me a call last night.'

The position of aspect markers is complicated in the case of complex verbs (those of more than one syllable). Such compounds fall into three kinds:

(a) In the case of typical verb–object compounds (2.3.3), the two parts are separable, the aspect marker coming between them:

Kéuihdeih yìhgā **paak-gán-tō**.
they now date-PROG-date
'They're dating at the moment.'

Kéuih yíhgīng **fan-jó-gaau**.
s/he already fall-PFV-asleep
'She's already gone to sleep.'

(b) In a second group of compound verbs, the two parts cannot be separated:

Ngóh   faatgok-jó   yāt   yeuhng yéh.
I   discover-PFV   one   CL   thing
'I've discovered something.'

(c) A third group of verbs may either be separated or not:

yìh-jó-màhn or yìhmàhn-jó 'emigrated'
teui-jó-yāu or teuiyāu-jó 'retired'

While aspect markers are normally suffixed to the verb they modify, *gwo* may be attached to a phrase:

Ngóh   meih   yáuh gēiwuih tēng gwo.
I   not-yet   have chance   hear EXP
'I haven't had the chance to hear it yet.'

gwo here modifies the whole phrase *yáuh gēiwuih tēng* rather than the verb *tēng* alone.

The aspect markers often appear in constructions with an apparently passive meaning:[1]

Chàhng láu   yíhgīng héi-gán.
CL   building already build-PROG
'The building is already being built.'

This is not a passive structure, but results from topicalization of the object *chàhng láu* 'the building' with the subject understood as a generic 'they' (see 4.2). Similarly with the perfective marker *jó*:

Nī   bún syū   dehng-jó   ge   lak.
this CL book order-PFV   PRT   PRT
'This book has been ordered.'

Note that Cantonese would not use the *béi* passive here because the object concerned (*nī bún syū* in the above example) is not adversely affected by the action (see 8.4).

Idiom: yuh-jó 'as expected' is an idiom of this form:

A: Jūnggwok yauh   yèhng-jó wo.
    China   again win-PFV   PRT
    'China won again.'

B: Yuh-jó   ge   lak!
    predict-PFV   PRT   PRT
    'Exactly as expected!'

11.2.2 PROGRESSIVE: *GÁN, HÁIDOUH*

The most familiar of the aspects to the English speaker is the progressive, marked by the particle/suffix *gán*. Its meaning is similar to that of the English progressive *-ing* form. In its use, however, the Cantonese particle is much more restricted than the English progressive form. It applies only to activities described as ongoing:

Kéuihdeih léuhng go paak-gán-tō.
they two CL date-PROG
'The two of them are dating.'

Chàhn Sāang taan-gán saigaai.
Chan Mr enjoy-PROG world
'Mr Chan is having a good time.'

gán applies to the present if there is no indication otherwise, but may apply to the past in conjunction with past time adverbs:

Gójahnsìh nī duhng láu juhng **héi-gán**.
that-time this CL flat still build-PROG
'At that time this block of flats was still being built.'

háidouh, which literally means 'to be here/there', is an alternative means of describing an action in progress. Its use as a progressive marker is probably influenced by the Mandarin *zài* which means either 'to be situated' or 'to be doing'. *háidouh* precedes the verb:

Ngóh háidouh gói gyún.   Léih háidouh jouh māt a?
I be-here correct paper   you be-here do what PRT
'I'm grading papers.'   'What are you doing?'

háidouh is commonly used to reinforce *gán* in expressing progressive meaning:

Kéuih háidouh góng-gán dihnwá.
s/he be-here talk-PROG telephone
'She's (talking) on the phone.'

11.2.3 CONTINUOUS: *JYUH*

While the progressive marker *gán* is used for dynamic ongoing activities, implying change over time, *jyuh* describes a continuous activity or state without change:

Ngóh séung yíhhauh sèhngyaht pùih-jyuh léih. (film)
I want afterwards always accompany-CONT you
'From now on I want always to be with you.'

It is closely associated with particular verbs, with which it denotes a continuous activity or state. The following combinations are especially common:

deui-jyuh 'face':

Gāan	ūk	deui-jyuh	go	hói.
CL	house	face-CONT	CL	sea

'The house faces the sea.'

gón-jyuh 'be in a hurry':

Léih	haih-mhaih	gón-jyuh	ló	chē	a?
you	be-not-be	hurry-CONT	take	car	PRT

'Are you in a hurry to get the car?'

gwa-jyuh 'miss':

Ngóh	wúih	hóu	gwa-jyuh	léih	ga.
I	will	much	miss-CONT	you	PRT

'I'll miss you a lot.'

jā-jyuh 'keep hold of':

Mgōi	léih	bōng	ngóh	jā-jyuh	tìuh	sósìh.
please	you	help	me	hold-CONT	CL	key

'Would you hold on to my key for me, please?'

jó-jyuh 'block, obstruct'

Ga	chē	jó-jyuh	yàhndeih.
CL	car	block-CONT	people

'The car is causing an obstruction.'

mohng-jyuh 'stare at':

Léih	mohng-jyuh	ngóh	jouh	mātyéh?
you	stare-CONT	me	do	what

'What are you staring at me for?'

In a few cases the combination verb – *jyuh* has a slightly different meaning from the simple verb, e.g. *lám-jyuh* 'intend' vs. *lám* 'think':

Ngóhdeih	lám-jyuh	būn	ūk.
we	think-CONT	move	house

'We're thinking of moving.'

jyuh *in serial constructions*

An important function of *jyuh* is in serial constructions (see 8.3), marking the first of two verbs denoting simultaneous activities:

Kéuih mohng-jyuh ngóh siu.
s/he stare-CONT me smile
'He smiled while looking at me.'

Go bìhbī deui-jyuh ngóh haam.
CL baby face-CONT me cry
'The baby was crying in my face.'

Other functions of jyuh

jyuh has certain other functions in addition to its continuous meaning. In negative sentences, it is used as a particle at the end of the clause, meaning 'yet':

Kéuih m̀h séung gitfān jyuh.
s/he not want marry yet
'She doesn't want to get married yet.'

(Léih) mhóu jáu jyuh a.
(you) don't go yet PRT
'Don't leave yet.'

A similar meaning 'for the time being' occurs in positive sentences with the adverbial particle *sìn*:

Léihdeih sihk jyuh sìn.
you-PL eat PRT PRT
'You carry on eating.'

Léih tùhng go bìhbī wáan jyuh sìn.
you with CL baby play PRT PRT
'You carry on playing with the baby.'

11.2.4 PERFECTIVE: *JÓ*

The perfective aspect is basically used to report an event, seen as a whole or as completed. Typically, such an event is one situated in the past; however, *jó* should not be thought of as a past tense marker. It has a range of meaning which overlaps with both the English perfect and the simple past. We may distinguish three typical usages of *jó*:

(a) the **resultative** meaning, which may be translated by the English perfect, where the event has a result:

Ngóh ga chē waaih-jó.
I CL car broken-PFV
'My car's broken down.'

(b) in reporting past events without any such result, [verb] – *jó* corresponds to the simple past:

Gūngsī   gauhlín   jaahn-jó   msíu   chín.
company   last-year   earn-PFV   not-little   money
'The company made a good deal of money last year.'

(c) to express a period of time up to and including the present:

Léihdeih   git-jó-fān   géi   loih   a?
you-PL   marry-PFV   now   long   PRT
'How long have you been married?'

Ngóh   ga   chē   jā-jó   léuhng   lìhn   géi.
I   CL   car   drive-PFV   two   years   some
'I've been driving the car for over two years.'

Note that this usage may correspond to the perfect progressive in English. A similar sentence with *gwo* in place of *jó* would imply that the state of affairs no longer holds (11.2.5).

jó does not occur in negative sentences. Instead, the negative existential *móuh* is used before the verb (13.3, 15.4):

Ngóh   **ló-jó**   chín.   →   Ngóh   **móuh**   **ló**   chín.
I   get-PFV   money   I   not-have   get   money
'I got some money.'   'I didn't get any money.'

To express the failure to achieve an objective, a verbal particle such as *dou* (see 11.3) may be used in place of *jó* in a negative sentence:

Ngóh   móuh   ló   dou   chín.
I   not-have   get   V-PRT   money
'I didn't receive any money.'

jó forms perfective questions with *meih* (17.1.4):

Léih   gāau-jó   seui   meih   a?
you   hand-PFV   tax   not-yet   PRT
'Have you paid your taxes yet?'

jó is used in serial constructions to express a sequence of actions (contrast *jyuh* which expresses simultaneous actions in a similar construction: 11.2.3):

Ngóhdeih   git-jó-fān   jauh   heui   douh   maht-yuht.
we   marry-PFV   then   go   spend   honeymoon
'After getting married we're going on our honeymoon.'

11.2.5 EXPERIENTIAL: *GWO*

The meaning of this particle suggests experience, or something having occurred 'at least once before'. It corresponds closely to the experiential meaning of the present perfect in English, as in:

Léih sihk-gwo yùhchi meih a?
you eat-EXP shark-fin not-yet PRT
'Have you ever eaten shark's fin?'

Kéuih duhk-gwo daaihhohk, yīnggōi hóu yùhngyih wán
s/he study-EXP university should very easy find

dóu gūng.
V-PRT job
'She's been to university, she should be able to find a job easily.'

Another meaning of *gwo*, like the English perfect, is described as 'indefinite past' meaning. The notion of experience is not directly applicable if the subject is not human, for example:

Hóuchíh lohk-gwo yúh wo.
seem fall-EXP rain PRT
'It seems to have been raining.'

Ga dihnlóuh waaih-gwo géi chi.
CL computer break-EXP few time
'This computer has crashed a few times before.'

gwo *versus* jó

The experiential *gwo* contrasts in meaning with the perfective *jó*, although both may be translated with either the English perfect or the past tense according to the context. The contrast typically hinges on whether a result of the event holds (perfective) or not (experiential):

Ngóh yíhgīng sāan-jó mùhn.
I already shut-PFV door
'I've already closed the door (and it's still closed).'

Ngóh yíhgīng sāan-gwo yāt chi mùhn.
I already shut-EXP one time door
'I've already closed the door once (and it's open again).'

Similarly, with expressions of duration, *jó* is used where the situation still applies (is still relevant) and *gwo* where it does not:

Léih hái Hēunggóng jyuh-jó géi loih a?
you in Hongkong live-PFV how long PRT
'How long have you lived in Hongkong?'

Léih hái Hēunggóng jyuh-gwo géi loih a?
you in Hongkong live-EXP how long PRT
'How long did you live in Hongkong (before leaving)?'

However, due to the subjective nature of aspectual choice, alternatives are often possible in the same context. For example, *jó* could be used in place of *gwo* in the above example, referring to the complete period of time involved.

jó and *gwo* also combine with different adverbs, *jó* with adverbs referring to the recent past such as *ngāam-ngāam* 'just' and *gwo* with distant past adverbs such as *yíhchìhn* 'before':

Nī bún syū ngóh ngāam-ngāam tái-jó.
this CL book I just-just read-PFV
'I've just read this book.'

Nī bún syū ngóh yíhchìhn tái-gwo.
this CL book I before read-EXP
'I've read this book before.'

Other functions of gwo

In addition to its aspectual function, *gwo* serves several other grammatical functions:

(a) as a directional verb, *gwo* means 'cross' (8.3.2):

Ngóh hóu síu **gwo** **heui** Hēunggóng góbihn.
I very little cross go Hongkong that-side
'I rarely go over to Hongkong Island.'

Léih dākhàahn jauh **gwo** **làih** kīng-gái lā.
you free then over come chat PRT
'Come over and chat when you have time.'

(b) as a verbal particle (see 11.3) *gwo* means either 'past' or 'over again', as in *sé gwo* 'rewrite' (cf. American English *write over*):

Nī tou hei chīn-kèih mhóu **cho** **gwo**.
this CL film thousand-pray don't miss past
'Don't miss this film.'

Gó fūng seun yiu **sé** **gwo**.
that CL letter need write PRT
'That letter needs to be rewritten.'

See also the idiom [verb] *dāk/m̀h gwo* (12.3.1).

(c) as a transitive verb, *gwo* means 'cross' or 'spend (time)':

Yìhgā hóyíh **gwo** **máhlouh**.
now can cross road
'We can cross the road now.'

Léihdeih heui bīndouh **gwo** **sānlìhn** a?
you-PL go where spend New Year PRT
'Where are you going to spend New Year?'

(d) as a comparative marker (9.3).

11.2.6 DELIMITATIVE: *HÁH*

This particle has the meaning 'do . . . for a while', or 'have a . . . '. It is
typically used with verbs denoting activities, with or without an object:

hàahng-háh 'take a walk'   tái-háh 'have a look'
kīng-háh-gái 'have a chat'   hàahng-háh-gūngsī 'do some shopping'
yám-háh-yéh 'have a drink'   tái-háh-syū 'do some reading'

Ngóh hóu guih a, séung yāusīk-háh.
I very tired PRT want rest-a-bit
'I'm tired, I need to take a rest.'

In this function, *háh* resembles the reduplicated construction [verb] – *yī* –
[verb] in Mandarin (termed **delimitative** by Li and Thompson),[2] which may
also be used in Cantonese. Thus, equivalent to *kīng-háh*, we have:

kīng-yāt-kīng   lám-yāt-lám
chat-one-chat   think-one-think
'have a chat'   'have a think'

Note that this construction is often contracted, with the loss of *yāt* and a
change of tone (2.2):

siu-yāt-siu → síu-siu
smile-one-smile
'have a smile'

A reduplicated verb followed by *háh* implies repetition or prolongation
of the action. This usage often corresponds to the perfect progressive in
English:

Ngóh **lám-lám-háh**,   dōu haih mhóu   būn   ūk.
I think-think-DEL also is not-good move house
'I've been thinking, it's best not to move house.'

This construction may also express two simultaneous actions, where the
reduplicated verb denotes an activity interrupted by another event:

Go bìhbī **sihk-sihk-háh** láaih fan-jeuhk-jó.
CL baby eat-eat-DEL milk fall-asleep-PFV
'The baby fell asleep while drinking milk.'

Ngóh hàahng-hàahng-háh-gūngsī johng dóu   go
I   walk-walk-DEL-shop   bump V-PRT CL

gauh tùhnghohk.
old   classmate
'I ran into an old classmate while shopping.'

Idioms: [verb] – *háh . . . sìn* is to do something temporarily, for example while waiting or to kill time:

Ngóh chēut heui hàahng-háh sìn.
I   out   go   walk-PRT   first
'I'm going out for a walk.'

Mgōi léih chóh-háh sìn.
please you sit-PRT   first
'Please take a seat for a while (until I'm ready).'

Note: when used at the end of a sentence as a particle, *sìn* has a high falling tone (18.3.5).

jáam-háh-ngáahn 'in the blink of an eyelid' serves as an adverbial phrase:

Sìhgaan hóu   faai gwo, jáam-háh-ngáahn yauh
time   very fast pass blink-DEL-eye   again

gwo-jó   yāt lìhn.
pass-PFV one year
'Time flies, in the blink of an eye another year has passed.'

11.2.7 HABITUAL: *HŌI* AND *GWAAN*

The aspect marker *hōi* denotes a habitual, customary activity. Unlike the English *used to* construction, it is not restricted to past time, and in fact is typically used of the present:

Kéuih tái-hōi   Jūng   yī   ge.   (conv.)
s/he   see-HAB   Chinese doctor PRT
'She usually goes to a Chinese doctor.'

Kéuih jouh-hōi   jūngdím   ge.   (conv.)
s/he   work-HAB   part-time PRT
'She normally works part-time.'

To express past habitual actions, *hōi* combines with past time adverbs such as *yíhchìhn* 'before' and *gójahnsí* 'then':

Kéuih	yíhchìhn	jā-hōi	Bēnsí	ge.
s/he	before	drive-HAB	Benz	PRT

'She used to drive a Mercedes.'

hōi is often used in relative and subordinate clauses, where the main clause expresses a departure from a customary habit:

Ngóhdeih	**heui-hōi**	gó	gāan	jáugā	jāp-jó-lāp.
we	go-HAB	that	CL	restaurant	close-PFV-down

'The restaurant we usually go to has closed down.'

Mòuhleuhn	bìhbī	**sihk-hōi**	mātyéh,	luhk	go	yuht	daaih
no-matter	baby	eat-HAB	what	six	CL	month	old

béi	kéuih	sihk . . .	(TV ad.)
give	her	eat	

'Whatever your baby is used to eating, when she's six months old give her . . .'

Note: *hōi* is also used as a directional particle, with the meaning 'away' (11.3.1), which is clearly distinct from the habitual meaning.

The stative verb *gwaan* is also used to indicate habitual aspect, with the more specific meaning 'be accustomed to':

Ngóh	yìhgā	jouh	gwaan	taaitáai.
I	now	do	used	wife

'I'm used to being a housewife now.'

Yám	gwaan	nī	jek	séui	jauh	m̀h wúih	yám	póutūng	séui.
drink	used	this	CL	water	then	not will	drink	ordinary	water

'When you're used to this kind of water you won't drink ordinary water.'

gwaan is not strictly an aspect marker, as it is also used independently as a stative verb:

Léih	**gwaan-jó**	Hēunggóng	sāngwuht	meih	a?
you	used-PFV	Hongkong	lifestyle	not-yet	PRT

'Have you got used to the Hongkong lifestyle yet?'

Moreover, *gwaan* may combine with an aspect marker (see note 5), and may function as a verbal particle in the potential construction (12.3.3):

Ngóh	**jyuh gwaan-jó**	daaih	ūk,	**jyuh m̀h gwaan**	sai	ūk.
I	live used-PFV	big	house	live not used	small	house

'Once I'm used to living in a big house I won't be used to a small one.'

11.3 VERBAL PARTICLES

In addition to the aspect markers, there is a rich range of verbal particles indicating notions such as result (effect on an object) and phase of action (beginning, continuing or ending).[3] These particles are comparable in form and function to the particles of English phrasal verbs such as *up*, which denotes direction in *pick up* but completion in *eat up* (see 3.1.7).

These particles may be divided by their functions into categories:

(a) directional particles (11.3.1):

chēut 'out'	hōi 'away'
dāi 'down'	lohk 'down'
fāan 'back'	màaih 'close(r)'
gwo 'over, past; again'	séuhng 'up'
héi 'up'	yahp 'in'

(b) resultative particles (11.3.2):

báau 'full up'	hóu 'completion'
cho 'wrongly'	jihng 'remain'
dihm 'decisively'	mìhng 'clear'
dihng 'ready'	sèhng 'success'
dóu 'accomplishment'	séi 'to death'
dou 'arrival'	wàhn 'thoroughly'
gihk 'to the limits'	waaih 'bad, broken'
	yùhn 'to the end'

(c) the quantifying particles: *saai*, *màaih* and *tīm* (11.3.3);

(d) adversative/habitual *chān* (11.3.4).

These particles are closely related to aspect in function, and are treated as aspect markers in some descriptive works such as Kwok (1972). For example, the perfective *jó* and the particle *dóu* are close in meaning in some cases:

Ngóh	ngāam-ngāam	**sāu-jó**	chín.
I	just-just	receive-PFV	money

'I've just received the money.'

Ngóh	ngāam-ngāam	**sāu**	**dóu**	chín.
I	just-just	receive	V-PRT	money

'I've just received the money.'

The particle *dóu* indicates a successful accomplishment, and would be used where the money has been expected, while the perfective *jó* indicates an event without any such presupposition. This contrast is clear in the corresponding question, where *dóu* would be used to check that the money has been received:

Léih	sāu	dóu	chín	meih?
you	receive	V-PRT	money	not-yet

'Have you received the money?'

Note also that the particles may form questions with *meih*, like *jó* and *gwo* (17.1.4); this represents another similarity between verbal particles and aspect markers.

Verbal particles differ syntactically from aspect markers in two main respects:

(a) Verbal particles may be separated from the verb by the modal *dāk* (12.3.1) and the negative *m̀h* (12.3.3):

Kéuihdeih saht **sihk dāk saai**.
they   sure eat can all
'They can definitely finish it (eat it up).'

Ngóh gēng gāmyaht **heui m̀h dóu**.
I   fear today   go   not succeed
'I'm afraid I won't be able to get there today.'

Aspect markers such as *jó* may not occur in these constructions.[4] In view of this separability the particles are written separately in this book, while the aspect markers are treated as suffixes.

(b) Verbal particles may be combined with certain aspect markers:[5]

Bún syū **sé hóu jó** laak.
CL book write up PFV PRT
'The book has been written up.'

The particles *hóu* and *hōi* here are followed by the aspect markers *jó* and *gwo*. By contrast, aspect markers may not be combined with one another, e.g. there is no such combination as [verb] – *jyuh* – *gán* or [verb] – *jó* – *gwo*.

Verb–particle constructions are also clearly distinct from serial verb constructions (8.3). Although many of the particles also exist as verbs, such as *dou* 'arrive' and *fāan* 'return', others such as *hōi* 'away' and *dóu* 'successfully' do not. The particles thus form a distinct syntactic category (see also 3.1.7).

The examples given are intended to be illustrative of typical patterns; as these constructions are highly productive, it is not feasible to list all the possible combinations and nuances of meaning. In English, similarly, dictionaries of phrasal verbs exist to list verb–particle combinations, and such a dictionary is necessarily incomplete to the extent that new verb–particle combinations are always possible, and indeed are continually being formed.

11.3.1 DIRECTIONAL PARTICLES

These particles basically denote direction, although many of them have additional, figurative or metaphorical meanings which are not predictable from the combination of verb and particle. In this they resemble verbal particles in English (contrast *sit up* with *freshen up*). They are alternatives to the use of directional verbs (8.3.2), and many of the same words are used in both constructions: thus *fāan* appears both in the verb–particle construction *heui fāan* and the serial verb construction *fāan heui*, both meaning 'go back'. Despite this overlap, the particles differ from directional verbs syntactically and semantically: *dāi*, *héi* and *hōi* do not occur in the construction with *heui/làih*, while those which do, such as *fāan* and *gwo* have a greater range of meanings when used as particles. The particles are illustrated below in alphabetical order.

chēut 'out' is used in several figurative senses:

Ngóhdeih yātdihng yiu **lám** **chēut** go baahnfaat.
we   definitely need think out   CL solution
'We really must think up a solution.'

Léih dím yéung **gaau** **chēut** bāan gam lēk
you   how manner teach   out   class so   smart

ge hohksāang ga?
LP student   PRT
'How do you produce such a clever group of students?'

chēut is also used as a particle with perception verbs (8.1.3).

dāi indicates downward motion, as in *fong dāi*, *jāi dāi* 'put down':

Go bìhbī m̀h jūngyi yàhndeih **fong** **dāi** kéuih.
CL baby not like   people   put   down   him
'The baby doesn't like being put down.'

Dáng ngóh **sé** **dāi** go dihnwá sìn.
let   me   write down CL telephone PRT
'Let me write down the telephone number.'

Also idiomatically in colloquial slang:

Léih séung jouh-dāi ngóh àh? Móuh gam yih!
you   want do-down   me   PRT not   so   easy
'You want to do me in/knock me down? Not so easy!'

In expressions like *jihng dāi* 'remain' and *làuh dāi* 'stay behind', *dāi* has the meaning 'behind':

Léih làuh dāi pùih   ngóh lā.
you   stay behind accompany me   PRT
'Would you stay behind to keep me company?'

fāan used as a particle has the primary meaning 'back' or 'in return', as when it is used as a directional verb:

Léih géisìh **fēi fāan** Hēunggóng a?
you when fly back Hongkong PRT
'When are you flying back to Hongkong?'

Léih sung yéh béi ngóh, ngóh **sung fāan** yéh béi léih.
you send thing to me I send back thing to you
'You gave me a present, so I'm giving you one in return.'

It may indicate resumption of an activity or a return to a state which has been interrupted:

Kéuih **gaau-fāan-syū** jīhauh sèhng go sau saai.
s/he teach-back-book after whole CL slim all
'She has lost a lot of weight since she resumed teaching.'

Léih **jouh-fāan-yéh** hóu gwo hái ūkkéi chau-jái.
you do-back-work better than at home raising-child
'It's better for you to go back to work than stay home to raise kids.'

Gāmyaht **lyúhn fāan** dī la.
today warm ˙back some PRT
'It's a bit warmer again today.'

More idiomatically, *fāan* may be used reflexively to denote acquisition or retention of an item 'for oneself':

Ngóh géi séung **máaih fāan** yāt go. (conv.)
I quite wish buy back one CL
'I rather fancy buying myself one.'

Léih jīkhāak **sānchíng fāan** yāt jēung lā! (TV ad.)
you at-once apply back one CL PRT
'Why not apply for one [a credit card] straight away?'

gwo has two distinct meanings as a verbal particle, in addition to its use as the experiential aspect marker (11.2.5) and as a directional verb (8.3.2):

(a) 'by, past' as in *cho gwo* 'miss out on', *je gwo* 'let by':

Chīnkèih mhóu cho gwo nī go gēiwuih! (ad.)
absolutely don't miss-past this CL chance
'Don't miss this chance, whatever you do!'

Mgōi je gwo!
please let past
'Excuse me (please let me past).'

(b) 'over again':

Ngóhdeih yiu yàuh tàuh hōichí **jouh gwo**.
we need from head begin do over
'We have to start again from the beginning.'

Dī   sāam   sái   dāk   m̀h   gōnjehng   yiu   **sái**   **gwo**.
CL   clothes wash   ADV   not   clean   need wash   over
'These clothes are not washed properly and need washing again.'

Note that the above usages of *gwo* do not occur in the potential constructions with *dāk/m̀h* because the combination (verb) *dāk/m̀h gwo* has an
idiomatic meaning (12.3.1).

héi 'up' has a spatial meaning as in *ló héi* 'pick up':

Kéuih jīkhāak   **līng**   **héi** go   dihnwá.
s/he   at-once   lift   up   CL   phone
'He picked up the phone straight away.'

Léih   **gwa**   **héi**   gihn   sāam   ā.
you   hang   up   CL   clothing PRT
'Hang up this shirt, will you?'

héi may mean 'upwards' in a figurative sense, as in *tái héi* 'look up to,
respect':

Só   yáuh   ge   tùhngsih   dōu   **tái**   **héi**   kéuih.
all   have   that colleagues all   look   up   her
'All her colleagues respect her.'

Referring to time, *héi* denotes completion within a certain time limit:

Ngóhdeih   tīngyaht   saht   **jouh**   **dāk**   **héi**.
we   tomorrow   sure   do   can   up
'We can certainly finish up tomorrow.'

In *tàih héi* and *lám héi* the particle denotes turning one's conversation or
thoughts to something which has been out of the picture for a while
(cf. English *bring up a topic*):

Léih   mhóu   joi   **tàih**   **héi**   nī   gihn   sih.
you   don't again bring   up   this CL   matter
'Don't mention this matter again.'

Ngóh   gin   dóu   nī   bún   syū   jauh   **lám**   **héi**   léih.
I   see   V-PRT this CL   book   then   think   V-PRT   you
'I think of you whenever I see this book.'

In modal constructions *dāk héi* may have the meaning 'can afford to . . . '
(see 12.3.1):

Gam   dō   chín   ngóhdeih   **siht-m̀h-siht**   **dāk héi**   sìn?
so   much   money   we   lose-not-lose   can afford   PRT
'Can we afford to lose so much money?'

hōi 'away' is used with both intransitive and transitive verbs:

Léih mhóu **hàahng hōi** jyuh.
you don't walk away yet
'Don't walk away yet.'

Kéuihdeih mséung **lèih hōi** Hēunggóng.
they not-wish leave away Hongkong
'They don't want to leave Hongkong behind.'

Note: *hōi* also serves as a marker of habitual aspect (11.2.7).

lohk 'down' is used as a particle primarily in the potential constructions with *dāk* (12.3.1) and *m̀h* (12.3.3):

Gam dō yéh dím **báai dāk lohk** a?
so many things how place able down PRT
'How can we fit so many things in?'

Gam yiht, ngóh **sihk m̀h lohk** yéh.
so hot I eat not down things
'I can't eat when it's so hot.'

lohk-heui, which as a directional verb means 'go down' (8.3.2), has the meaning 'continue' in the verb particle position:

Ngóhdeih gūngsī gám yéung **siht lohk-heui** mdāk ge.
our company such way lose continue not-okay PRT
'Our company can't afford to continue losing money like this.'

Similarly, *séuhng-làih* would mean 'come up' as a directional verb, but *héi-séuhng-làih* as a verbal complement means 'begin' (Mandarin *qǐlái*):

Kéuih hóu dahtyìhn gám **haam héi-séuhng-làih**.
s/he very sudden so cry rise-up-come
'She suddenly started crying.'

màaih as a verbal particle means 'closed' or 'together', relating to its use as a directional verb (8.3.2) rather than as a quantifying particle (11.3.3):

Léih **mēi màaih** ngáahn jauh m̀h tung ge lak.
you close V-PRT eye then not hurt PRT PRT
'Close your eyes and it won't hurt.'

Ngóh jūngyi tùhng léih **hái màaih** yātchàih. (film)
I like with you be V-PRT together
'I want to be with you.'

séuhng 'up' is occasionally used as a particle, for example to contrast with *lohk* 'down':

Dī gúpiu béi yàhn cháau séuhng cháau lohk.
CL share by people speculate up speculate down
'The share prices are moved up and down by speculators.'

séuhng also appears in a few verbs borrowed from Mandarin such as *ngoi-séuhng* 'fall in love' and *yím-séuhng* 'get infected':

Yíhm-séuhng ngoi-jī behng ge yàhn yuht làih
infect-up AIDS disease LP people more come

yuht dō. (news)
more many
'The number of people infected with AIDS is on the increase.'

yahp 'in' occurs with verbs denoting acquisition:

Ngóhdeih máaih yahp hóu dō wòhnggām.
we buy in very much yellow-gold
'We bought up a lot of gold.'

Kéuih kāp yahp hóu dō duhk hei.
s/he breathe in very much poison gas
'She has inhaled a lot of poisonous gas.'

11.3.2 RESULTATIVE PARTICLES

These particles are used together with a transitive verb to indicate an effect on the object, and they form compounds with the verb. Many of them exist independently as verbs or adjectives; some, however, such as *hóu* with the meaning 'finish', do not occur independently. They may also be used in passive form, subject to the general restrictions on the use of the passive (8.4, 8.4.2).

báau 'full up' basically applies to eating, but also figuratively to other activities:

Bìhbī **sihk báau** láaih la.
baby eat full milk PRT
'The baby's had enough milk.'

Léih **tái báau** dihnsih meih?
you watch full television not-yet
'Have you seen enough television?'

cho as a particle means 'wrongly' or 'by mistake', as in *dá cho dihnwá* 'call the wrong number' and *yihng cho yàhn* 'mistake someone's identity':

Deui-mjyuh, ngóh **yihng cho yàhn.**
sorry I recognize wrong person
'Sorry, I mistook you for someone else.'

Ngóhdeih tàuhsīn **hàahng cho louh.**
we just-now walk wrong road
'We went the wrong way just now.'

Ngóh hauhfui **sīk cho-jó** léih.
I regret know wrong-PFV you
'I regret that I ever made the mistake of knowing you.'

dihm 'decisively' denotes an activity reaching a conclusion, as in *gáau dihm* 'settle, deal with', *góng dihm* 'settle a matter (by talking)':

Léih **lám** **dihm** meih a? (TV ad.)
you think settle not-yet PRT
'Have you made up your mind yet?'

Ngóhdeih léuhng go **kīng** **m̀h** **dihm**.
we two CL chat not settle
'The two of us can't come to an agreement.'

dihng 'ready' denotes an action done in advance or in preparation:

Léih juhng yiu **jāp** **dihng** yéh heui léuihhàhng.
you still need pack ready things go travel
'You still have to get things ready for the trip.'

Ngóh jauhlàih yiu sāang jái, yìhgā **máaih** **dihng**
I soon need bear child now buy ready

sāam sīn.
clothes first
'I'm having a child soon so I'm buying clothes in preparation.'

dóu is an important particle indicating accomplishment or successful completion of an action:

Ngóh ngāam-ngāam **bok** **dóu** hah yāt bāan gēi.
I just-just connect V-PRT next one CL plane
'I only just caught the next flight.'

Ngóhdeih nīdouh **sāu** **m̀h** **dóu** daaihluhk tòih.
we here receive not V-PRT mainland channel
'We can't receive the mainland [television] channels here.'

dóu is also used to form verbs of perception, such as *tái dóu* 'see' (8.1.3). It should be distinguished from *dou* denoting arrival as in *heui dou* or *làih dou* 'arrive':

Géi dím **fēi** **dou** Sāam Fàahn Síh a?
how time fly arrive San Francisco PRT
'What time do we arrive in San Francisco?'

Note *chìh dou* 'be late' and *jóu dou* 'be early':

Ngóh gām jīu hóu jóu héi-sān, sóyíh **jóu** **dou**.
I this morning very early get-up so early arrive
'I got up early this morning so I arrived early.'

gihk 'hard, at most, to the limits' typically takes a concessive clause with *dōu* 'still':

Ngóh lám gihk **dōu** m̀h mìhng léih góng māt.
I think hard also not understand you say what
'However hard I try, l still can't understand what you're saying.'

Ngóh sihk gihk **dōu** m̀h fèih ge.
I eat at most also not fat PRT
'I don't get fat even though I eat a lot.'

In a fixed expression, [verb] *gihk yáuh-haahn* means there is a limit to
the action or state denoted by the verb.

Kéuih bōng gihk yáuh-haahn. Léih yiu jihgéi
s/he help at most have-limit you need self

séung baahnfaat.
think solution
'There's only so much that she can do to help. You'd better think of a
solution yourself.'

Léih ge beimaht, ngóh jī gihk yáuh-haahn.
your LP secret I know at most have-limit
'As much as I know about your secrets, there's still a lot that I don't
know.'

Adjectives can also occur together with this particle (9.1.3).

hóu 'finish' refers to the completion of an action:

Kéuih ge leuhnmàhn meih **sé** **hóu**.
s/he LP thesis not-yet write up
'He hasn't finished his thesis yet.'

Jyú **hóu** faahn meih a?
cook finish food not-yet PRT
'Have you finished cooking?'

jihng 'remain' as a particle indicates the result 'left over':

Kàhmyaht **sihk** **jihng** hóu dō sung.
yesterday eat remain very much food
'Yesterday there was a lot of food left over.'

Yìhgā **séi** **jihng** ngóh yāt go.
now die remain me one CL
'Now I'm the only one left alive.'

laahn 'broken':

Deui hàaih **jeuk** **laahn-jó** la.
pair shoes wear broken-PFV PRT
'These shoes are worn out.'

Jek gáu **ngáauh laahn-jó** douh mùhn.
CL dog bit broken-PFV CL door
'The door is broken as a result of the dog's biting it.'

mìhng 'clear, understood' goes with perception verbs and verbs of speaking:

Léih tēng mìhng a-Sèuh góng māt jīhauh joi
you listen understood Sir say what then again

gáai béi ngóh tēng.
explain to me hear
'After you've listened and understood what the teacher is saying, would you explain it to me then?'

Ngóhdeih góng mìhng git-jó-fān jauh jīkhāak
we speak clear marry-PFV then immediately

yìhmàhn ge.
emigrate PRT
'We've said very clearly that after we get married we emigrate immediately.'

múhn 'full' indicates the state of being filled to capacity:

Mgōi yahp múhn kéuih ā.
please enter full it PRT
'Fill it up, please.' (filling fuel tank)

Ga chē chóh múhn saai.
CL car sit full all
'The car is full.'

sèhng denotes successful accomplishment (see also 10.1.2, 17.3.7):

Gūnghéi léih, jūngyū git-sèhng-fān la!
congratulate you finally marry-succeed PRT
'Congratulations! You finally managed to get married.'

Kéuihdeih géi fānjūng jauh góng sèhng dāan sāangyi.
they few minutes then talk succeed CL business
'They manage to strike a (business) deal in a few minutes.'

séi 'to death' is much used hyperbolically:

Ngóh béi léih gīk séi!
I by you annoy dead
'You're driving me crazy!'

Ngoh séi go bìhbī la! (note the word order: see 4.1.2)
hungry die CL baby PRT
'The baby's starving.'

waaih means 'bad' or 'broken':

Léih gám yéung wúih **tái waaih** deui ngáahn ga.
you such way will look bad pair eye PRT
'You'll wear out your eyes that way.'

Gám yéung wúih **gaau waaih** saai dī hohksāang ga.
this way will teach bad all CL students PRT
'The students will be taught all the wrong lessons this way.'

wàhn 'thoroughly' may be used in a concessive sense together with *dōu*:

Ngóh **wán wàhn** dōu m̀h gin kéuih.
I seek thorough also not see him
'I've looked everywhere and I still can't find him.'

Wàhn may also serve to quantify the object of the verb; in this function it resembles *saai* (11.3.3), with which it may combine:

Ngóhdeih yāt go yuht loih **heui wàhn** (saai) Āujāu
we one CL month within go thorough (all) Europe

gam dō (go) gwokgā.
so many (CL) countries
'We travelled through all the countries in Europe in one month.'

yùhn 'finish, to the end' in addition to denoting completion, also serves to indicate temporal relationships between clauses (16.2.1):

Léih gaau-yùhn-syū meih a?
you teach-finish-book not-yet PRT
'Have you finished teaching?'

Léih yuhng yùhn go dihnchìh hóyíh wuhn ge.
you use finish CL battery can change PRT
'When you've used up the battery you can change it.'

Most of the above verb–particle combinations may be used in the modal (potential) constructions with *m̀h* and *dāk* (12.3), e.g. *tēng m̀h dóu* 'can't hear', *heui dāk sèhng* 'manage to go':

Ngóh gú gām-máahn **heui dāk sèhng**.
I guess tonight go not succeed
'I think we'll manage to go tonight.'

Ngóhdeih seuhng chi hōi-wúi **hōi m̀h sèhng**.
we last time hold-meeting hold not succeed
'Last time we weren't able to hold the meeting.'

Certain additional particles are used exclusively in the potential forms: thus *chit* appears in *gón dāk chit* 'manage to arrive on time' and *gón m̀h chit* 'fail to arrive on time' but the combination *gón chit* alone does not occur.

11.3.3 QUANTIFYING PARTICLES

The particles *saai* and *màaih* behave syntactically like other verbal particles, but have a distinct quantifying function. *tīm* has a syntax of its own
which is different from *saai* and *màaih*. They are all peculiar to Cantonese,
having no direct counterparts in Mandarin.[6] The logical properties of *saai*
are discussed in Lee (1987).

saai 'all, completely' has as its primary function to quantify either the
subject of an intransitive or the object of a transitive verb:

Intransitive			*Transitive*				
Dī	yàhn	jáu	saai.	Ngóhdeih sihk saai dī			sāanggwó.
CL	people	leave	all	we	eat	all CL	fruit
'Everyone's left.'				'We've eaten up all the fruit.'			

In a transitive sentence with a plural subject, *saai* may refer either to the
object or to the subject, or to both at once:

Kéuihdeih heui-gwo saai Āujāu.
they go-EXP all Europe
'They've been everywhere in Europe.'
or 'They've all been to Europe.'
or 'They've all been everywhere in Europe.'

In its quantifying function *saai* may combine with other quantifiers such as
dōu and *chyùhnbouh* (14.1.1):

Yùhgwó **go-go** **dōu** jáu **saai**, bīngo léih
if CL-CL all leave all who care

Hēunggóng a? (TV ad.)
Hongkong PRT
'If everyone leaves, who will take care of Hongkong?'

Nī gāan yīyún dī bìhbī **chyùhnbouh** yám **saai**
this CL hospital CL baby whole-lot drink all

nī jek láaih-fán.
this CL milk-powder
'All the babies in this hospital drink this brand of milk powder.'

saai may also be used adverbially, with an emphatic rather than quantifying
function:

(a) with an adjective, denoting a change of state:

Léih tái-háh, gāan fóng **gōnjehng** **saai** la.
you look-DEL CL room clean all PRT
'Look, the room's all nice and clean (now).'

Kéuih làuh-jó chèuhng tàuhfaat sèhng go **leng** **saai**.
s/he grow-PFV long hair whole CL pretty all
'She looks really nice now she's let her hair grow long.'

(b) to emphasize a verb–object idiom:

Gó go yàhn jānhaih **lèih-saai-póu**.
that CL person really leave-all-score
'That man is completely off-the-wall (outrageous).'

Ngóhdeih go-go **ngāau-saai-tàuh** dōu lám m̀h
we CL-CL scratch-all-head still think not

dóu baahnfaat.
V-PRT means
'We've all been scratching our heads and we still can't see
a solution.'

Idioms: *gau saai* (*gau* 'enough') emphasizes an adjective:

Ngóhdeih yìhgā gau saai kùhng la!
we now enough all poor PRT
'Now we're really broke!'

tek saai geuk is an idiom meaning to be overstretched or frantically
busy:

Ngóh yāt go yàhn jyú-faahn béi sahp
I one CL person cook-food for ten

go yàhn sihk, jānhaih **tek** **saai** **geuk** la.
CL person eat really kick all feet PRT
'I'm cooking for ten people on my own, really stretched.'

Note that the meaning of the idiom is the opposite of the English *kick
one's feet* meaning to be idle or have nothing to do.

---

màaih 'in addition' or 'along' has a similar syntax to *saai*, modifying the
subject of an intransitive or the object of a transitive verb:

Intransitive

Lìhn Bill dōu **làih** **màaih**.
even Bill also come V-PRT
'Even Bill came along.'

M̀h gau yàhn wo, bātyùh léih wáan màaih lā.
not enough people PRT rather you play V-PRT PRT.
'There aren't enough people, why don't you join us?'

Transitive

Ngóh **ló** **màaih** fahn boují heui tái.
I take V-PRT CL newspaper go read
'I'm taking along a newspaper to read.'

Léih **dáng** **màaih** ngóh lā!
you wait also me PRT
'Wait for me too!'

In its quantifying function *màaih* denotes expansion of a domain to include the last of a series of items or to bring certain ongoing actions to completion:

Kéuih **jouh** **màaih** gām lìhn jauh jáu ge lak.
s/he work V-PRT this year then leave PRT PRT
'She's going to work for the rest of this year and then leave.'

Yùhgwó **móuh** **màaih** nī go gēiwuih, ngóh
if not-have also this CL chance I

jauh cháam la.
then desperate PRT
'If I lose this last chance I'll be in trouble.'

The meaning of accumulation is seen in the phrases *gā màaih* and *lìhn màaih* 'including':

Gā **màaih** gām go yuht ge yàhngūng, jauh gau
add also this CL month's salary then enough

máaih ga chē.
buy CL car
'Including this month's salary, it'll be enough to buy a car.'

Nī ga chē **lìhn** **màaih** seui yiu baatsahp maahn.
this CL car include also tax need eighty ten-thousand
'This car costs $800,000 including tax.'

Nī géi lìhn ngóh **jaahn màaih** dī chín
this few years I earn V-PRT CL money

dōu m̀h gau yìhmàhn.
still not enough emigrate
'The money I've been saving up these few years is still not enough to emigrate.'

màaih has two other distinct uses:

(a) as a directional verb, meaning 'approach' or 'close' (8.3.2):

Ga syùhn **màaih-gán** **ngohn**.
CL ship approach-PROG shore
'The ship is approaching the shore.'

Léih **màaih-jó** **dāan** meih a? (at restaurant etc.)
you close-PFV bill not-yet PRT
'Have you paid the bill?'

Léih mhóu **màaih** **làih** a. (see 8.3.2)
you don't close come PRT
'Don't get any closer.'

(b) as a resultative particle meaning 'close' or 'together' (see 11.3.2).

Idiom: *góng/wah m̀h màaih* 'can't say for sure' only exists in the
negative form where the meaning of *màaih* is different from its usual
meanings:

Saisih ge yéh wah m̀h màaih ge, móuh
world-matter LP thing say not sure PRT no

yàhn jī tīngyaht wúih dím.
person know tomorrow will how
'One can't say for sure about things in the world; no one knows
what's going to happen tomorrow.'

Both *saai* and *màaih* may occur following a directional or resultative
particle (11.3.1, 11.3.2):

Pīn màhnjēung sé **hóu** **saai** la.
CL article write up all PRT
'The article is all written up.'

Ngóhdeih **hái** **fāan** **màaih** yātchàih.
we are back also together
'We're back together again.'

màaih and *saai* may also occur together (in this order):

Yùhgwó kéuih dī pàhngyáuh **làih** **màaih** saai, jauh
if s/he CL friend come along all then

gau saai yihtlaauh.
enough all lively
'If her friends all come along, it'll be nice and lively.'

Idiom: the combination [verb] *màaih saai* may be used with a pejorative meaning, implying that someone does everything (*saai*) even including (*màaih*) the outrageous or excessive:

Kéuih **sihk màaih saai** gó dī gaakyeh sung,
s/he eat V-PRT all that CL leftover food

m̀h gwaai dāk móuh yìhngyéuhng.
not surprising not-have nutrition
'She even eats all the leftover food, no wonder she's in bad shape.'

Dī sailouhjái **jouh màaih saai** dī faahnfaat ge yéh.
CL children do also all CL illegal LP thing
'The children get up to all sorts of illegal things.'

Below the use of *tīm* is discussed. However, note that the positions it occurs in are very different from those of the particles *saai* and *màaih*; in particular, it cannot occur immediately after a verb. Syntactically *tīm* does not behave as a verb particle, however, it does serve some quantifying function. *tīm* has the meaning 'add' as a verb:

Tīm dīng faat chòih! (greeting used at Chinese New Year)
add male make money
'Have a son and make more money.'

Juhng yiu tīm faahn àh?
still need add rice PRT
'You need more rice?'

When functioning as a quantifying element, *tīm* has a related meaning, 'more'. The position where *tīm* can occur is very restricted: it only occurs after a complement phrase (usually with a quantifier or numeral):

Yāusīk yāt jahn **tīm** joi hàahng.
rest one moment V-PRT again walk
'Let's rest a bit more for a while and walk again.'

Ngóh yám yāt wún tōng **tīm** sīn jáu.
I drink one bowl soup V-PRT then leave
'Let me eat a bowl of soup and then leave.'

tīm can also function as a sentence particle in sentence-final positions. See chapter 18.

11.3.4 ADVERSATIVE/HABITUAL *CHĀN*

The verbal particle *chān* is peculiar to Cantonese. It has two distinct meanings: the adversative meaning 'to one's disadvantage/misfortune' and the habitual meaning 'whenever'.

The syntax of adversative *chān* resembles that of *saai* and *màaih* in that it modifies either the subject of an intransitive or the object of a transitive verb. With intransitive verbs, the disadvantage is to the subject:

Léih síusām, mhóu láahng chān.
you careful don't cold V-PRT
'Be careful not to catch a cold.'

Similarly:

ngoh chān 'go hungry'
dung chān 'get cold'
pūk chān 'trip up'

With transitive verbs, the adversative meaning of *chān* applies to the object, which must be a person (animate object) rather than a thing:

Mhóu haak chān kéuih wo.
don't scare V-PRT her PRT
'Don't frighten her.'

Ngóh yáuh-móuh cháai chān léih a?
I have-not-have tread V-PRT you PRT
'Did I tread on you?'

chān naturally occurs in passive constructions, emphasizing the effect of the action on the subject:

Ngóh jek sáují béi douh mùhn gihp chān.
I CL finger by CL door jam V-PRT
'My finger got nipped by the door.'

Ngóh béi mān ngáauh chān.
I by mosquito bite V-PRT
'I've been bitten by a mosquito.'

It is also used reflexively with body parts:

hám chān go tàuh
bump V-PRT CL head
'bump one's head'

chān rarely combines with aspect markers or other verbal particles. The perfective *jó*, for example, is redundant, as *chān* already conveys the notion of result:

Léih haak   chān   (jó)   kéuih.
you   scare V-PRT   (PFV)   her
'You scared her.'

Habitual *chān*

A distinct use of *chān* is in habitual contexts, with the meaning 'whenever'.
This differs from habitual *hōi* (11.2.7) in that it occurs only in the first of
two consecutive clauses:

Go bìhbī siu   chān   go háu   jauh maak dou
CL baby   laugh V-PRT   CL mouth   then open till

hóu   daaih.
very big
'Every time the baby laughs, his mouth opens wide.'

Kéuih háau-chān-síh   dōu ló   jeui gōu   fān   ge.
s/he   take V-PRT exam   all get most high mark PRT
'Whenever she takes an exam she gets the highest marks.'

Kéuih góng-chān-dihnwá   dōu m̀h   tìhng dāk   ge.
s/he   say V-PRT phone   all not   stop   able PRT
'Every time he talks on the phone, he can't stop.'

Note that the particle *chān* in the first clause is matched by the quantifier
dōu (14.1.1) in the second. It may also occur reinforcing *chi-chi* and *múih
chi* 'whenever':

Kéuih **chi-chi**   **aai-chān-gāau** dōu yiu   yèhng ge.
s/he   time-time   argue-V-PRT   all must win   PRT
'Whenever she argues, she has to win.'

Ngóhdeih **múih** **chi** **làih** **chān**   dōu sihk yāt-yeuhng
we   every   time   come V-PRT all eat   one-same

ge   yéh.
LP   thing
'Whenever we come, we eat the same thing.'

12 MODALITY: POSSIBILITY AND PROBABILITY

The notion of modality includes possibility, ability and related concepts. Modality is expressed in Cantonese not only by modal verbs (12.1) and adverbs (12.2), as in English, but also, often more idiomatically, by a number of syntactic constructions (12.3). There is no subjunctive mood or anything comparable in Cantonese. Imperatives, which are sometimes treated as a form of modality, are discussed in chapter 19.

12.1 MODAL VERBS

As in English, there is a small class of modal verbs or **auxiliaries** which behave differently from ordinary verbs. The main modal verbs are:

wúih 'will/would'   yīnggōi 'should, ought to'
hóyíh 'can, may'   yiu, sēuiyiu 'want, need'
sīk, híu 'know how'   msái, msēuiyiu 'no need'
làhnggau 'be able'   séung 'wish'

As modal verbs these must co-occur with another verb, although some of them (sīk, (sēui-)yiu, msái)[1] may also be used alone as main verbs. These modals normally precede the main verb:

Ngóh   yìhgā   yiu   hōi-wúi.
I   now   need   hold-meeting
'I have to attend a meeting now.'

They may be separated from the verb by an adverb:

Dī   syū   yīnggōi   jīkhāak   wàahn.
CL   books   should   immediately   return
'We should return those books immediately.'

Colloquially, modal verbs are often heard attached at the end of a clause as an 'afterthought' (4.1.3). Note that such modals even come after the sentence particle:

Hóu   faai   jouh   yùhn   ga   la,   **yīnggōi**.
very   fast   do   finish   PRT   PRT   should
'We should be finished very soon.'

Modals may be used in an impersonal sense, without a subject:

Ngóh gokdāk m̀h yīnggōi lyuhn gam sái chín.
I feel not should random so spend money
'I feel one shouldn't go around spending money wildly.'

Msái gam kwājēung ge.
no-need so exaggerate PRT
'There's no need to exaggerate so.'

Modal verbs may be classified according to the modal notions they denote, such as possibility, necessity and obligation.

12.1.1 POSSIBILITY AND PERMISSION

wúih has a complex set of meanings relating to possibility or probability. Although most closely glossed as 'will' or 'would,' it should not be thought of as a future tense as such. Firstly, reference to the future is made largely by adverbs (10.3.3) and does not *require wúih*. Moreover, the verb *wúih* itself has a number of related functions, of which predicting the future is only one:

(a) futurity or prediction:

Ngóh wúih hóu gwa-jyuh léih ge.
I will very miss-CONT you PRT
'I'm going to miss you a lot.'

(b) conditional (see also 16.3):

Ngóh m̀h wúih gám góng ge.
I not would thus say PRT
'I wouldn't put it like that.'

(c) willingness:

Léih wúih-m̀h-wúih bōng ngóh a?
you would-not-would help me PRT
'Would you do me a favour?'

(d) habitual action or occurrence:

Léih wúih-m̀h-wúih lám héi kéuih a?
you would-not-would think up her PRT
'Do you (sometimes) think about her?'

(e) Alternatively, *wúih* may have the meaning 'know how to', this being one of the meanings of the corresponding Mandarin auxiliary *huì*:

Kéuih wúih góng hóu dō júng yúhyìhn.
s/he able speak very many CL languages
'He can speak several languages.'

hóyíh means 'can' or 'may' in the sense of something being possible or permissible. It has two senses, according to the distinction between deontic and epistemic modality:

(a) permission (deontic: giving or requesting permission):

Léih hóyíh yuhng-jyuh ngóh ga dihnlóuh sīn.
you can use-CONT my CL computer first
'You may use my computer for the time being.'

Ngóh hó-m̀h-hóyíh jóu jáu dī a?
I can-not-can early leave a-bit PRT
'May I leave a bit early?'

(b) possibility (epistemic: referring to an eventuality which may occur):

Léih hóyíh daap bāsí heui Màhnfa Jūngsām.
you can catch bus go Cultural Centre
'You can take a bus (to get) to the Cultural Centre.'

Jauhsyun léih m̀h sīk, dōu hóyíh gú-háh.
even-if you not know also can guess-DEL
'Even if you don't know the answer, you can have a guess.'

Note: permission and possibility may also be expressed by the potential constructions with *dāk* (12.3.1, 12.3.2), and impossibility by the [verb] – *m̀h* – [particle] construction (12.3.3). These alternatives are often more idiomatic than *hóyíh*.

The retrospective meaning 'could have' may be expressed by *hóyíh* together with *búnlòih* 'originally':

Léih **búnlòih** **hóyíh** sānchíng nī fahn gūng ge.
you originally can apply this CL job PRT
'You could have applied for this job.'

Ngóhdeih **búnlòih** **hóyíh** chóh syùhn gwo làih ge.
we originally can sit boat over come PRT
'We could have come over by boat.'

jéun 'allow' may also express permission:

Haauhjéung jéun ngóhdeih jóu jáu.
headmaster allow us early leave
'The headmaster is allowing us to leave early.'

The negative form *m̀jéun* (*bāt jéun* in formal and written Cantonese) expresses prohibition. It is usually used impersonally, without a subject:

Nīdouh m̀jéun tìhng-chē.
here not-allow stop-car
'You're not allowed to stop (the car) here.'

> Gām-máahn mjéun góng sāangyi wo.
> to-night not-allow talk business PRT
> 'No talking about business tonight, okay?'

Such prohibitions apply to everyone present or concerned.

12.1.2 ABILITY

sīk 'know' is used for *can* in the sense of being able to do something:

> Léih sīk-m̀h-sīk yàuh-séui a?
> you know-not-know swim PRT
> 'Can you swim?'

> Ngóh m̀h sīk jā-chē ga.
> I not know drive-car PRT
> 'I can't drive.'

sīk is also used together with *dāk*, meaning 'know how to':

> Léih gājē hóu **sīk** **dāk** tàuhjī ga.
> your sister very know can invest PRT
> 'Your sister really knows how to invest.'

> Léih m̀h **sīk** **dāk** fān ge mē?
> you not know can distinguish PRT PRT
> 'Don't you know how to tell the difference?'

híu refers to the knowledge of how do do something:

> Léih gaau ngóh laak, ngóh **m̀h híu** dím jouh.
> you teach me PRT I not know how do
> 'I've no idea how to go about it, you'll have to teach me.'

wúih (12.1.1) may also mean 'know how to' in formal and written Cantonese (cf. Mandarin *huì*).

làhnggau 'be able' is a formal word referring to a person's ability:

> Nī go saigaai jí yáuh léih làhnggau mìhngbaak ngóh.
> this CL world only have you capable understand me
> 'You're the only person in the world capable of understanding me.'

12.1.3 NECESSITY

yiu as a main verb may mean either 'want' or 'need'. As an auxiliary, *yiu* has the meaning 'need' or 'have to':

Ngóhdeih gām-máahn yiu chēut heui sihk. (conv.)
we tonight need out go eat
'We have to eat out tonight.'

Jouh nī hòhng yiu dáng hóu loih sīnji jaahn dóu
do this line need wait very long only earn V-PRT

daaih chín.
big money
'In this business you have to wait a long time to make big money.'

yiu may be reinforced by a modal adverb such as *yātdihng*, meaning 'must':

Léihdeih léuhng go **yātdihng yiu** gin-háh-mihn.
you-PL two CL definitely must meet-DEL-face
'You two really must get together.'

Nī fūng seun **yātdihng yiu** léih chīm méng
this CL letter definitely need you sign name

sīn yáuh-haauh.
first have-validity
'This letter must have your signature in order to be valid.'

Note that the epistemic sense of *must* (meaning that, by inference, something must be the case) is expressed by *yātdihng haih* (12.2.2):

Kéuih **yātdihng haih** mgéidāk-jó lak.
s/he definitely is forget-PFV PRT
'He must have forgotten.'

Léih **yātdihng haih** sé cho deihjí lak.
you definitely is write wrong address PRT
'You must have written the address wrongly.'

The compound form *sēui-yiu* unambiguously expresses need:

Múih go sailouhjái dōu sēui-yiu fuhmóuh ge
each CL child all need parent LP

gwāansām. (TV int.)
care
'Every child needs a parent's care.'

Sēui-m̀h-sēui-yiu chyùhnbouh máaih saai a?
need-not-need-want whole buy all PRT
'Do we need to buy the whole lot?'

Idioms with yiu: *jí yiu* 'all you need to do' is typically used impersonally, with no subject mentioned, for example in advertising:

Jí   yiu   dá yāt go dihnwá   jauh dihm ge   la.
just need hit one CL telephone then done PRT PRT
'All it takes is one phone call and it's done.'

Sentences with *yiu* or *yīnggōi* (12.1.4) may be reinforced by the
phrase *sīn dāk*, used to give advice or admonition:

Léih yiu   hohk dāk   faai dī   sīn   dāk   ga!
you   need learn ADV   fast a-bit only okay PRT
'You really need to learn a bit faster, you know.'

This idiom is also used in imperatives (19.1). *sīn hóu* is a similar
pattern, which emphasizes the importance of following the advice
given:

Léih yiu   góng jān   wá   sīn   hóu.
you   need speak true words only good
'You need to tell the truth, okay?'

The negative counterpart of *yiu* as a modal is *msái* or *msēui-yiu* 'need
not':

Nī   geui yéh   msái   joi   gói   la.
this CL   thing no-need again correct PRT
'There's no need to correct this sentence again.'

Msēui-yiu joi   góng lohk-heui la.
not-need again talk continue PRT
'There's no need to go on talking.'

msái is replaced by *yiu* in replies to A-not-A questions:

A: **Sái-msái**   ngóh hōi-chē   làih jip   léih a?
   need-not-need I   drive-car come meet you PRT
   'Do you need me to pick you up in the car?'

B: **Yiu** a.
   need PRT
   'Yes.'

The positive form *sái* occurs in notionally negative contexts such as rhetorical questions:

Juhng **sái** góng mē?   (radio ad.)
still need say   what
'Need any more be said?'

Sái   mmāt   douhhip   jēk?   (see 17.3.6)
need   what   apologize PRT
'There's no need to apologize.'

12.1.4 OBLIGATION

yīnggōi, like *should* in English, has two distinct meanings according to whether the modality is deontic or epistemic:

(a) obligation (deontic: indicating a requirement):

Léih   yīnggōi   síusām   dī.
you   should   careful   a-bit
'You should be more careful.'

Ngóh gokdāk m̀h yīnggōi yáuh júngjuhk kèihsih   ge.
I   feel   not should have race   discrimination PRT
'I feel there shouldn't be racial discrimination.'

(b) probability (epistemic: making a prediction):

Ngóhdeih yīnggōi chā-mdō sei   dím   dou.
we   should   about   four   o'clock   arrive
'We should be there about four.'

Yīnggōi móuh   mahntàih ga   la.
should   not-have problem   PRT   PRT
'There shouldn't be any problem.'

yīnggōi may refer retrospectively to the past, with the meaning 'should have'; in this case, an adverb such as *búnlòih* 'originally' or *yāt-jóu* 'much earlier, at the outset' may be added to indicate reference to the past (see 10.3.3):

Ngóh búnlòih   yīnggōi gāmyaht   fāan-hohk.
I   originally should today   return-school
'I was supposed to go to school today.'

Ngóh yīnggōi yāt-jóu   góng béi léih   tēng.
I   should one-early   say to   you   hear
'I should have told you much earlier.'

12.1.5 VOLITION: WISHES AND DESIRES

séung 'want' expresses a wish or desire:

Dī hohksāang séung fong-yùhn-ga   sīn   háau-síh.
CL student   want   take-finish-leave only   take-exam
'The students don't want to have their exams till after the holiday.'

Ngóh mhaih géi séung joi tō lohk-heui.
I not-be quite want again drag continue
'I don't really want this to keep dragging on.'

Note: *yiu* as a main verb may mean 'want', but as a modal auxiliary it expresses necessity (12.1.3). Similarly, the combination *séung yiu* 'want' also expresses desire, but is a transitive verb rather than an auxiliary:

Kéuih séung yiu dō go bìhbī-léui.
s/he wish need more CL baby-girl
'He'd like to have another baby girl.'

Like English *want*, *séung* may be followed either by a verb phrase with the same subject as in (a) below, or by a full clause with a change of subject (b):

(a) Ngóh séung tàuh léih yāt piu.
I wish vote you one vote
'I want to vote for you.'

(b) Ngóh séung léih tàuh ngóh yāt piu.
I wish you vote me one vote
'I want you to vote for me.'

Idiom: with *hóuchíh* 'seem', *séung* denotes prediction and may take an inanimate subject:

Hóuchíh séung lohk-yúh gám.
seem want fall-rain so
'It looks like it's going to rain.'

Dī sāanggwó hóuchíh séung waaih gám.
CL fruit seem want bad so
'That fruit looks like it's going bad.'

---

hēimohng 'hope, wish' has a similar syntax to *séung*:

Ngóh hēimohng hah chi háau dāk hóu dī.
I hope next time exam ADV good a-bit
'I hope to do better in the exam next time.'

Ngóh hēimohng léih wúih yùhnleuhng ngóh.
I hope you will forgive me
'I hope you'll forgive me.'

háng means 'be willing', i.e. not objecting to doing something:

Léih	mahn	kéuih	háng-m̀h-háng	je	gihn	sāam	béi
you	ask	her	will-not-willing	lend	CL	shirt	for

léih	jeuk	lā.
you	wear	PRT

'Ask her if she'll lend you a shirt to wear.'

Kéuih	m̀h háng	je	chín	béi	ngóh.
s/he	not willing	lend	money	to	me

'She won't lend money to me.'

jai 'comply, agree' and *m̀h jai* 'not comply, not agree' is similar in meaning to *háng* and *m̀h háng* typically used in response to a proposal or a deal; unlike *háng, jai* cannot occur with a following verb but is itself a verb and can only be used intransitively:

Ngóh	séung	gitfān,	daahnhaih	ngóh	làahm-pàhngyáuh
I	wish	marry	but	my	boy-friend

m̀h	jai.
not	comply

'I'd like to get married but my boyfriend won't comply.'

jai can appear in A-not-A questions:

A:
Ngóhdeih	hàahng-louh	heui	chē	jaahm,	léihdeih
we	walk-road	go	bus	station	you-PL

jai-m̀h-jai	a?
agree-not-agree	PRT

'We are walking to the bus station, are you willing?'

B:
Ngóh	jai	kéuih	m̀h	jai.
I	agree	s/he	not	agree

'I am, he isn't.'

yuhnyi 'be willing' is a more formal term, suitable for solemn undertakings:

Léih	yuhn-m̀h-yuhnyi	jipsauh	nī	go	tīujin	a?
you	will-not-willing	accept	this	CL	challenge	PRT

'Are you willing to take on this challenge?'

gám 'dare' and the colloquial *gau dáam* 'have the guts' also function as auxiliaries:

Léih	gám-m̀h-gám	jeuk	sāam	dím	sīk	wihngyī	a?
you	dare-not-dare	wear	three	point	style	swim-clothing	PRT

'Would you dare wear a bikini?'

Ngóh m̀h gau dáam wán kéuih.
I not enough guts seek him
'I daren't approach him.'

12.1.6 PREFERENCE

lìhngyún 'rather' expresses a preference among two possibilities. It may be used, for example, to express the speaker's priorities:

Ngóh lìhngyún dō dī tùhng ngóh ūkkéi-yàhn
I rather more a-bit with my home-people

yātchàih, m̀h wáan gamdō.
together not play so much
'I'd rather be with my family more, and go out less.'

Kéuih lìhngyún séi, dōu m̀h wúih jouh faahnfaat
s/he rather die also not will do illegal

ge sih.
LP thing
'He'd rather die than break the law.'

Note the conjunctions *júngjī* 'as long as' and *jí yiu* 'if only', a prominent function of which is to introduce a clause following *lìhngyún*:

Ngóh **lìhngyún** jaahn síu dī, **júngjī** m̀h siht
I rather earn less some as-long-as not lose

jauh dāk ge lak.
then okay PRT PRT
'I'd rather make a bit less, as long as I don't make a loss.'

Kéuih **lìhngyún** jihgéi séi, **jí yiu** hóyíh gau fāan go
s/he rather self die if-only can save back CL

jái tìuh mehng.
son CL life
'She's prepared to die, as long as she can save her son's life.'

As these examples suggest, *lìhngyún* often implies a rather negative form of preference: the preferred option is not particularly attractive, but the alternative is worse (i.e. the preference is for the lesser of two evils): thus *Ngóh lìhngyún jihgéi heui* 'I'd rather go myself' implies that the speaker prefers not to trust someone else with an errand.

More positive preferences may be expressed by *jūngyi . . . dō dī* 'like . . . more' or *jeui jūngyi* 'most like':

Léih	jūngyi	heui	Faatgwok	dihng	heui	Yīnggwok
you	like	go	France	or	go	England

dō	dī	a?
more	a-bit	PRT

'Which do you prefer to go to, France or Britain?'

Léih	jeui	jūngyi	cheung	bīn	leuih	gō	a?
you	most	like	sing	which	kind	song	PRT

'Which kind of song do you prefer to sing?'

12.2 MODAL ADVERBS

Possibility and necessity may also be expressed by adverbs. Like sentence adverbs in general (10.3), these items immediately precede the verb. When used in conjunction with a modal auxiliary, they precede the modal rather than the main verb:

Ngóh	**dōsou**	wúih	chāamgā	kéuihdeih	ge	fānlái.
I	probably	will	attend	their	LP	wedding

'I'll probably attend their wedding.'

Note that the typical English order, with the adverb between auxiliary and verb, is not possible here. Colloquially, modal adverbs may come at the end of the sentence (10.3.1, 4.1.3):

A:	A-Wóng	hái	bīn	a?
	A-Wong	is	where	PRT

'Where's Wong?'

B:	Heui-jó	máaih	yéh,	dōsou.
	go-PFV	buy	things	most-likely

'Gone shopping, most likely.'

12.2.1 ADVERBS OF POSSIBILITY

hólàhng 'maybe' typically comes between the subject and verb:

Jingfú	hólàhng	wúih	gā	seui.
government	maybe	will	raise	tax

'The government might be going to raise taxes.'

waahkjé 'perhaps' may also begin the sentence:

Waahkjé	ngóh	hàahng-háh-gūngsī	sīn	fāan	ūkkéi.
perhaps	I	walk-DEL-store	first	return	home

'Perhaps I'll do some shopping before coming home.'

dōu mdihng is used as a tag after a sentence raising a possibility:

Waahkjé kéuih mgeidāk-jó, **dōu mdihng**.
perhaps s/he forget-PFV also not-sure
'It's quite possible he forgot.'

dōsou 'mostly' may be used as a modal adverb meaning 'probably':

Ngóh chēut-lín dōsou wúih heui Méihgwok
I next-year probably will go America

jouh sāangyi.
do business
'I'll probably go to the States on business next year.'

12.2.2 ADVERBS OF NECESSITY

saht, *yātdihng* and *hángdihng* all express certainty ('definitely'). They are
often used to reinforce the modal verbs, such as *wúih* and *yiu*:

Gó jek máh **saht wúih** yèhng ge.
that CL horse sure will win PRT
'That horse is bound to win.'

Léih hah chi **yātdihng yiu** síu-sām dī a.
you next time definitely need careful a-bit PRT
'You really must be more careful next time.'

These adverbs, together with *haih* 'be', also express the epistemic or
inferential sense of *must* ('x must be the case'):

Léih **yātdihng haih** Yihp Sāang laak.
you definitely are Yip Mr PRT
'You must be Mr Yip?'

Gó dī gāsī **hángdihng haih** yihsáu ge.
that CL furniture certainly is second-hand PRT
'That furniture must be second-hand.'

Like the modal verbs *hóyíh* and *yīnggōi*, this construction can also be used
retrospectively, meaning 'must have':

Nī go gwónggou **yātdihng haih** kéuih lám
this CL advertisement definitely is s/he think

chēut làih ge.
out come PRT
'This advertisement must have been his idea.'

Seuhng chi **hángdihng haih** léih ge cho.
last time certainly is your CL wrong
'It must have been your fault last time.'

A: A-Mūi   dōsou   mgeidāk-jó gāau seui.
   Ah-Mui   probably   forget-PFV pay   tax
   'Mui probably forgot to pay her taxes.'

B: **Saht haih** lā.
   sure   is   PRT
   'She must have done.'

jyuhtdeui 'definitely, absolutely' may modify a modal verb:

Ngóh jyuhtdeui   m̀h   wúih jūngyi nī   tíng   yàhn.
I   absolutely   not   will like   this kind   person
'There's no way I could like this kind of person.'

meih bīt is a negative counterpart of these adverbs, literally meaning 'no compulsion', i.e. 'not necessarily':

Gó   jek máh   **meih bīt**   **yèhng** ge   wo.
that CL horse not   necessarily   win   PRT   PRT
'That horse may not win, you know.' (expressing doubt)

It may combine with a modal verb:

Ngóh meih bīt   wúih sānchíng yìhmàhn.
I   not   necessarily   will apply   emigrate
'I won't necessarily apply to emigrate.'

Idiom: the phrases [verb] *gáng* or [verb] *ngaahng* 'bound to . . .' express the inevitable:

Gam dō   hóu   sīusīk, dī   gúpiu   **héi** **gáng**.
so   much good   news   CL   stocks rise   bound
'With so much good news, stocks are bound to go up.'

Gām chi   **séi** **ngaahng** la,   léih!
this time die   bound   PRT   you
'You've had it this time!'

ngaahng is an adjective meaning 'hard, firm' as in *kéih ngaahng* 'stand firm'.

12.3 SYNTACTIC CONSTRUCTIONS EXPRESSING MODALITY

In addition to the modal verbs and adverbs, modal notions such as possibility can be conveyed by various syntactic constructions. These are particularly common in their negative forms, indicating inability or impossibility.

12.3.1 VERB – *DĀK* EXPRESSING POTENTIAL

This use of *dāk* should be distinguished from *dāk* in adverbial constructions (10.1.1), although the same character is used for both. This construction is said to indicate potential, including both possibility and permission:

Jáu dāk ge lak.
leave can PRT PRT
'We can leave now.'

Yahp dāk làih meih a?
enter can come not-yet PRT
'Can I come in yet?'

Si-m̀h-si dāk a?   (used in clothing stores)
try-not-try can PRT
'Can I try this on?'

The construction is also widely used in negative and interrogative form:

Sahpbaat seui yíhhah yàhnsih **m̀h yahp dāk** heiyún
eighteen years under person not enter can cinema

tái sāam kāp pín.
watch three class film
'Those under eighteen are not allowed to enter a cinema to watch a category III film.'

A: Nī jek sáubīu hóu yáuh-yìhng wo!
   this CL watch very have-style PRT
   'That watch is pretty stylish!'

B: Léih **máaih-m̀h-máaih dāk** héi sìn?
   you buy-not-buy can up first
   'But can you afford it?'

The *dāk* construction may be modified by *hóu* or *géi*, indicating potential or ability:

Nī go léuihjái hóu dá dāk ga.
this CL girl very fight able PRT
'This girl really knows how to fight.'

Kéuih bún syū hóu maaih dāk wo.
s/he CL book very sell able PRT
'His book is very marketable.'

Idioms with dāk: [verb] *dāk gwo* implies that something is safe or can be trusted:

Ngóh   seun   dāk   gwo   léih.
I   believe   can   pass you
'I can trust you.'

Nī   dī   jīlíu   m̀h   seun   dāk   gwo.
this CL information   not   believe can   pass
'These figures are not worth believing.'

The negative counterpart with *m̀h* in place of *dāk* has a similar meaning:

Nī   dī   ūk   dōu   haih máaih m̀h   gwo, móuh
this CL house also   are buy   not   pass not-have

bóuyéuhng   gé.
maintenance   PRT
'It's not safe to buy these houses, there's no maintenance.'

In addition to its use with perception verbs (8.1.3), verb – *dāk chēut* can indicate ability with a negative connotation, meaning 'capable of doing':

Ngóh   tái   dāk   chēut léih   jūngyi   kéuih. (neutral)
I   see can   out   you   like   her
'I can see that you like her.'

Dī   hāk   séhwúi   mātyéh   dōu   jouh   dāk
CL   black society what   all   do   can

chēut ge.   (negative)
out   PRT
'Those triads are capable of anything.'

Gám   dōu   góng   dāk   chēut   gé!   (negative)
so   also say   can   out   PRT
'I didn't know you were capable of saying such things!'

Géi   sihk   dāk   wo,   léih!
quite eat   able PRT   you
'You certainly can eat a lot!'

dāk alone may be used as a predicate, meaning 'okay':

Léih   háau-síh   dāk-mdāk   a?
you   take-exam   okay-not-okay   PRT
'Was your exam okay?'

Léih gám yéung mdāk   ge.
you   so   way   not-okay PRT
'You can't behave like that.'

Dāk   meih   a?
okay not-yet PRT
'Is it ready yet?'

---

m̀h sé dāk is a complex idiom with several related meanings. With a noun as its object, it means 'cannot do without':

Léih m̀h   sé   dāk léih (go) léuih-pàhngyáuh àh?
you   not miss can your (CL) girl-friend   PRT
'Missing your girlfriend, are you?'

Followed by a verb phrase or clause, it means 'cannot face':

Ngóh m̀h   sé   dāk léih jáu.
I   not miss can you   leave
'I can't face your leaving.'

Kéuih dím   dōu m̀h   sé   dāk maaih-jó   kéuih
s/he   how   all not miss can sell-PFV   his

ga   páauchē.
CL   race-car
'He can't face selling his sports car at any cost.'

The positive form *sé dāk* means 'willing to part with':

Léih sé dāk yuhng gam dō   chín   làih máaih
you   willing use   so   much money come buy

leng jáu   àh?
fine wine PRT
'You can part with that much money to buy fine wine?'

Léih gam hāan,   dím   gáai   wúih   **gam sé dāk**
you   so   frugal how   come   would so   willing

máaih sāam   gé?
buy   clothes PRT
'How come you're so extravagant about buying clothes, when you're so frugal?'

12.3.2 *YÁUH/MÓUH DĀK* – VERB

Possibility or impossibility may also be expressed by the existential words *yáuh* and *móuh* respectively (see ch. 15) followed by *dāk* and a verb:

Jauhlàih yáuh   dāk   sihk   la.   (reporting that a meal is ready)
soon   have   can   eat   PRT
'We can eat soon.'

Gakèih móuh   dāk   dehng-tói.   (referring to restaurant)
holiday   not-have   can   reserve-table
'There's no way to reserve a table on holidays.'

Yáuh hóu   dō   gwaai   sih   faatsāng haih **móuh**
have very   many   strange   thing   happen   is   not-have

dāk gáai   ge.
can   explain   PRT
'Lots of strange things happen which cannot be explained.'

Idioms: *móuh dāk béi* 'there's no comparison' is used with the coverb *tùhng*:

Yīnggwok choi **tùhng** Faatgwok choi **móuh**   **dāk**
English   food   with   French   food   not-have   able

béi   ge.
compare   PRT
'There's no comparison between English and French cooking.'

The rhetorical version with *bīndouh yáuh* (see 17.3.4) in place of *móuh* is equivalent:

Bīndouh yáuh   dāk   béi   a?
where   have   can   compare   PRT
'How can you compare the two?'

móuh dāk díng or *móuh dāk tàahn* means 'there's no beating' or 'there's nothing like . . .':

Gūngfū-chàh   tùhng nī   dī   dím sām   jānhaih
skill-tea   with   these   CL   pastries   really

móuh dāk díng   ge.
cannot   substitute   PRT
'There's no beating kung-fu tea with these pastries.'

This construction is also used in question form, i.e. *yáuh-móuh dāk* [verb]? to ask about a possibility:

Gódouh yáuh-móuh   dāk yàuh-séui ga?
there   have-not-have   can swim   PRT
'Can you go swimming there?'

Gó júng behng yáuh-móuh   dāk yī   ga?
that CL disease have-not-have   can treat PRT
'Can that disease be treated?'

12.3.3 VERB – (*M̀H*) – VERBAL PARTICLE EXPRESSING INABILITY

The combination [verb] – *m̀h* – [particle] is the negative counterpart of [verb] – *dāk* – [particle], as seen in the following exchange:

A: Ngóh gēng **gáau**   **m̀h dihm**   a.
    I   fear manage not V-PRT PRT
    'I'm afraid I can't manage it.'

B: Gánghaih **gáau**   **dāk dihm**   lā!
    of-course manage can V-PRT PRT
    'Of course you can!'

The negative construction is very widely used to indicate inability; any of the verbal particles discussed in section 11.3 may be used in this way:

Dī hohksāang **yahp m̀h dóu**   daaihhohk jauh yiu
CL student   enter not V-PRT university then need

wán gūng jouh.
seek work do
'If students can't get into university they have to find work.'

Ngóhdeih **sihk m̀h saai** dī   sung.
we   eat not up CL food
'We can't finish (eating) the food.'

Léih yāt go yàhn **chau m̀h dihm** sāam go jái.
you one CL person care not manage three CL son
'You can't manage three sons by yourself.'

Ngóh **fān m̀h hōi** gó deui mā-sāang jímúi.
I   tell not apart that pair twin-born sisters
'I can't tell those twin sisters apart.'

As an alternative word order, an object pronoun or short noun phrase may come between the verb and the negative *m̀h*:

Ngóh **bōng** léih **m̀h** dóu.　(cf. Ngóh bōng m̀h dóu léih.)　(TV)
I　help　you　not　succeed
'I can't help you.'

Ngóh **giu** kéuih **m̀h séng**.　(cf. Ngóh giu m̀h séng kéuih.)
we　call　him　not　awake
'I can't wake him up.'

Ngóh wán-jó　léih hóu loih, dōu **wán** léih **m̀h dóu**.　(film)
I　seek-PFV you very long still　seek you not V-PRT
'I've been looking for you for ages and I still couldn't find you.'

Yáuh dī　　wūjīk sái-yī-gēi　　　dōu **gáau**　　kéuih
have some stain washing-machine also deal-with it

m̀h dihm.　(TV)
not manage
'There are some stains even the washing machine can't get rid of.'

Idiom: *yán m̀h jyuh* followed by a verb means 'cannot help':

Ngóh yán　m̀h jyuh　siu-jó　　cheut làih.
I　endure not V-PRT laugh-PFV out come
'I couldn't help bursting out with laughter.'

Ngóh yán　m̀h jyuh　góng béi léih tēng.
I　endure not V-PRT talk to you hear
'I just had to tell you.'

13 NEGATION

Cantonese has a rich range of negative words according to what is negated: the word (13.1), the adjective (13.2) or a verb (13.3). Cantonese also makes extensive use of double negation (13.5). The native Cantonese negative words are distinguished by beginning with the nasal consonant *m*- and low-register tones:

ṁh 'not'
mhaih 'no/not' (ṁh + the copular *haih* 'be')
móuh 'have not' (negative form of the existential verb *yáuh* 'have'; see 15.4)
meih 'not yet' (used to form questions: see 17.1.4)
mhóu, máih 'don't' (in imperative sentences: see 19.4)
mjí, ṁh dāan jí 'not only'

In addition to these, the following Mandarin negative words are used in formal or literary Cantonese and in fixed expressions:

bāt, the Cantonese reading for the Mandarin negative marker *bù*, is heard in some fixed expressions adopted from Mandarin, such as:

bāt	tìhng	gám	haam		bāt	hó	sī-yíh
not	stop	so	cry		not	can	think
'cry without stopping'					'unthinkable'		

bāt may also be substituted for *ṁh* to give a literary quality, for example in songs:

Ngóh	bāt	sé	dāk	léih.	(cf. ṁh sé dāk: 12.3.1)
I	not	lose	can	you	
'I miss you.'					

fēi is an archaic negative word meaning 'not be' in Mandarin. Like *bāt*, it is also used in Cantonese primarily in fixed expressions and compounds:

fēi-faat		góng	sih-fēi
not-legal		talk	right-wrong
'illegal'		'gossip'	

fēi	heui	bāt	hó	(note the double negation: 13.5)
not	go	not	possible	
'absolutely must go'				

13.1 LEXICAL NEGATION: NEGATIVE VERBS AND ADJECTIVES

An important distinction is to be made between **lexical negation**, which negates a single word, and **sentential negation** which negates a statement (13.2, 13.3). A large number of verbs and adjectives are inherently negative in form. For example:

mgin 'lose'   mhóuyisi 'embarrassed'
mgeidāk 'forget'   msyūfuhk 'uncomfortable' *or* 'unwell'

Such words are written here as prefixed with *m-*, as the falling tone of *m̀h* tends not to be clearly heard.[1] These prefixed negative forms are distinct from negation with *m̀h* in several respects:

(a) The meaning of negative verbs and adjectives is not simply that of the verb or adjective negated, but often more specific:

gin means 'see' but *mgin* means specifically 'lose';
tùhng means 'with' or 'same' but *mtùhng* can only mean 'different';
syūfuhk 'comfortable' but *msyūfuhk* 'uncomfortable' *or* 'unwell, sick'.

(b) Verbs and adjectives with the negative prefix may take the perfective aspect *jó*, which is incompatible with the negative particle *m̀h* (11.2.4, 13.3):

Léih **mgeidāk-jó** sīk dāng.
you forget-PFV turn-off light
'You forgot to turn off the light.'

Ngóh **mhōisām-jó** hóu loih.
I un-happy-PFV very long
'I've been unhappy for a long time.'

(c) The prefixed forms of stative verbs and adjectives may be preceded by modifiers such as *hóu* 'very' and *fēisèuhng (jī)* 'extremely':

Ngóh hóu mséung heui.
I very not-want go
'I very much don't want to go.'

Gám léih hóu mdākhàahn lā!
so you very not-free PRT
'You must be very busy, then!'

Léihdeih jouh dāk fēisèuhng jī mcho!
you-PL do ADV extremely most not-bad
'You didn't do badly at all!'

The difference is brought out where the adjective is qualified (see 13.2):

Mhaih hóu syūfuhk.
not-be very comfortable
'It's not very comfortable.'

Hóu msyūfuhk.
very un-comfortable
'It's very uncomfortable.'

(d) Only sentential negation with *m̀h* allows an indefinite interpretation of a question word (13.4):

Ngóh gāmyaht m̀h séung heui bīndouh.
I today not wish go where
'I don't want to go anywhere today.'

The same verb prefixed with *m-* does not allow this (it is not possible to modify the verb as in (c) and have an indefinite question word, as in **Ngóh hóu mséung heui bīndouh*).

While the distinction between sentential and prefixed negation is clear in principle in the above constructions, in some cases either form of negation will be possible, in particular with adjectives and stative verbs:

Nī tìuh sou m̀h ngāam.
this CL figure not correct
'This figure is not right.'

or

Nī tìuh sou m-ngāam.
this CL figure incorrect
'This figure is wrong.'

Ngóh gāmyaht m̀h séung jouh-yéh.
I today not wish do-work
'I don't feel like working today.'
or Ngóh gāmyaht m-séung jouh yéh.

In such cases the difference in meaning is minimal (with stative verbs, the two may be distinguished by criterion (d) above).

13.2 ADJECTIVAL NEGATION

To negate an adjective, the particle *m̀h* precedes the adjective:

Gihn sāam m̀h leng.
CL shirt not nice
'The shirt doesn't look nice.'

Where the adjective is modified, *mhaih*, the negative form of *haih* 'be' is used:

Gó gihn mhaih hóu leng jē.
that CL not-be very nice PRT
'That one's not very nice.'

Gám yéung mhaih géi gūngpìhng.
so way not-be quite fair
'It's not quite fair that way.'

Idioms with m̀h: *m̀h gwaai dāk (jī)* or *m̀h gwaai jī dāk* 'no wonder' is
used on realizing an explanation:

A: A-Mīng sīng-jó jīk wo.
   Ah-Ming rise-PFV grade PRT
   'Ming's been promoted, you know.'

B: M̀h gwaai dāk kéuih gam hōisām lā!
   no wonder ADV s/he so happy PRT
   'No wonder she's so pleased!'

Yùhnlòih bún syū haih léih ló-jó, m̀h gwaai
finally CL book is you take-PFV no wonder

dāk jī wán m̀h dóu.
ADV know find not V-PRT
'I see, you took the book, no wonder I couldn't find it.'

m̀h chēut kèih means 'not surprising':

A: A-Dāk kàhmmáahn yám-jeui-jó wóh.
   Ah-Dak last night drink-drunk-PFV PRT
   'Apparently Dak got drunk last night.'

B: M̀h chēut kèih ā.
   not surprising PRT
   'That's not surprising.'

It may also be used rhetorically, with the final particle *mē* (18.3.1) in
place of *m̀h*:

Hóu chēut kèih mē?
very surprising PRT
'That's hardly surprising?'

13.3 VERBAL NEGATION

In the case of verbs, the negative marker used depends on the time to
which the verb phrase refers. Where the verb refers to the present or
future, *m̀h* is used:

Gām-yaht ngóh m̀h gin haak.
today I not see client
'I'm not seeing any clients today.'

Tīngyaht ngóhdeih m̀h heui wáan.
tomorrow we not go play
'We're not going out tomorrow.'

Where the verb refers to the past, and the function of negation is to state that some event did not occur, the existential negative word *móuh* is used instead:

Ngóh kàhmyaht móuh chēut heui.
I yesterday have-not out go
'I didn't go out yesterday.'

Gām-yaht móuh lohk-yúh.
today not-have fall rain
'It hasn't rained today.'

In the case of verbal particles (11.3), the negative marker *m̀h* comes between the verb and the particle, with a meaning of inability (12.3.3):

Kéuih gaai yīn gaai m̀h sèhng.
s/he quit smoke quit not succeed
'He can't manage to stop smoking.'

Idiom: *juhng m̀h* 'still not' is used rhetorically to make a forceful suggestion:

Léih juhng m̀h jáu àh?
you still not leave PRT
'Why haven't you gone yet?'

Léih juhng m̀h faai dī heui sānchíng? (radio ad.)
you still not fast-ish go apply
'Why not hurry up and apply?'

---

móuh *versus* meih

Both *móuh* and *meih* correspond to Mandarin *méiyǒu* in negating verbs. They differ in meaning and grammatical function: *meih* expresses the more specific meaning 'not yet':

A: Chéng mahn Dahng Sāang hái-m̀h-háidouh?
request ask Tang Mr here-not-here
'Is Mr Tang there, please?'

B: Kéuih meih   fāan   làih   wo.
   he   not-yet return come PRT
   'He hasn't come back yet.'

meih fāan làih would imply that the person is expected to return, whereas *móuh fāan làih* would not have any such implication:

B: Kéuih gām-yaht móuh   fāan   làih   wo.
   s/he today   not-have return come PRT
   'He hasn't been in today.'

meih may be reinforced by the adverbs *juhng* 'still' and *dou yìhgā* 'up till now':

Ngóhdeih **juhng meih**   gāau jōu.
we   still not-yet   pay rent
'We haven't paid the rent yet.'

Ngóh **dou yìhgā juhng meih**   heui-gwo Hóiyèuhng Gūngyún.
I   until now   still not-yet   go-EXP   Ocean   Park
'Even now I still haven't been to Ocean Park.'

meih is also used to form questions, especially perfective and experiential (17.1.4):

A-Dūng fāan-jó   làih   **meih**?
Ah-Dung return-PFV come   not-yet
'Has Dung come back (yet)?'

No such question can be formed with *móuh*.

meih . . . jyuh in statements and *mhóu . . . jyuh* in imperatives also mean 'not yet':

Meih dāk jyuh.   Léih mhóu jáu   jyuh.
not okay yet   you don't leave yet
'It's not ready yet.'   'Don't go yet.'

This use of *jyuh* differs syntactically and semantically from aspectual *jyuh* (see 11.2.3). Note also the use of *meih* in *meih chìh* 'it's not too late' meaning that there is still time to act:

Léih juhng hóyíh sānchíng ga,   yìhgā dōu meih   chìh.
you still can   apply   PRT now   also not-yet late
'You can still apply, it's not too late.'

Léih tīngyaht gāau   gūngfo   dōu meih   chìh.
you tomorrow hand-in homework also not-yet late
'You can hand in your homework tomorrow, it'll still be in time.'

Note that none of the negative words *m̀h*, *móuh* or *meih* can occur preceding a verb with the perfective marker *jó*. *jó* asserts the existence of an event (normally in the past: cf. 11.2.4) and is incompatible with negation, which would entail that such an event did not take place. By contrast, the experiential marker *gwo* (11.2.5) occurs with both *móuh* and *meih*, indicating the lack of an experience or occurrence:

Ngóh   móuh   heui-gwo daaihluhk.
I   have-not go-EXP   mainland
'I haven't been to mainland China.'

Kéuih yìhmàhn-jó gam loih juhng meih   fāan-gwo
s/he   emigrate   so   long still   not-yet return-EXP

Hēunggóng.
Hongkong
'She hasn't been back to Hongkong since emigrating.'

Both *móuh* and *meih* may be reinforced by the adverb *chùhnglòih* to mean 'never' when referring to the past, typically with the experiential *gwo*:

Ngóh chùhnglòih móuh   lám-gwo   gitfān.
I   never   not-have think-EXP marry
'I never thought about getting married.'

Ngóh chùhnglòih meih   sihk-gwo sèh-gāng.
I   never   not-yet eat-EXP   snake-soup
'I've never eaten snake soup.'

As noted above, the choice of *meih* implies that the speaker may have the experience in the future, while *móuh* has no such implication. Referring to the present, *chùhnglòih* is used with the modal verb *m̀h wúih* (12.1.1):

Kéuih nī júng yàhn **chùhnglòih** **m̀h** **wúih** je   chín
s/he this kind person ever   not would lend money

béi yàhn   ge.
to   people PRT
'People like him would never lend money to anyone.'

chùhnglòih is not used to refer to the future: instead, *yíhhauh dōu* and *wíhngyúhn dōu* are used with *m̀h wúih*:

Ngóh yíhhauh   dōu m̀h wúih fāan   làih. (film)
I   afterwards also not will return come
'I'll never come back.'

Ngóh wíhngyúhn dōu m̀h wúih mgeidāk léih. (film)
I   forever   also not will forget   you
'I'll never forget you.'

m̀h joi 'no more' combines with *wíhngyúhn* to mean 'never again':

Ngóh	**wíhngyúhn**	**m̀h**	**joi**	tùhng	kéuih	jouh	sāangyi.
I	forever	not	again	with	him	do	business

'I'll never do business with him again.'

mjí *'not only'*

mjí 'not only' is used to combine two sentences:

Mjí	séung	leng,	yàhn	dōu	leng	dī.	(TV ad.)
not-only	photo	pretty	person	also	pretty	some	

'Not only do the pictures look good, the people in them look better too.'

mjí . . . juhng 'not only . . . but also' is completed by the verbal particle *màaih* (11.3.3) and/or the sentence particle *tìm* (18.3.5):

Kéuih	mjí	bōng	ngóh	gáan,	juhng	béi	màaih
s/he	not-only	help	me	choose	even	pay	V-PRT

chín	tìm.
money	too

'She not only helped me choose, she even paid for it.'

m̀h dāan jí or *bāt dáan jí* 'not just . . . ' is used in the same way:

Kéuihdeih	m̀h	dāan	jí	làuh	háidouh,	juhng	wah
they	not	just	only	stay	here	even	say

yiu	máaih	ūk	tìm.
want	buy	house	too

'They're not only staying here, they're even talking about buying a house.'

mjí . . . yìhché is more formal:

Nī	wái	síujé	mjí	yàhn	leng,	yìhché
this	CL	young-lady	not-only	person	beautiful	also

sēng	tìhm.
voice	sweet

'This young lady is not only beautiful, she has a lovely voice.'

mjí may be used alone as a response to a statement or question:

A:
Kéuih	go	yéung	hóuchíh	sāamsahp-géi	seui	gám.
s/he	CL	appearance	seem	thirty-some	years	so

'She looks about thirty-something.'

B:
Mjí	gwa!
not-only	PRT

'She must be more than that!'

bīndouh jí, with the rhetorical use of *bīndouh* (17.3.4), is equivalent to *mjí*
in this sense.

m̀h *versus* mhaih

mhaih meaning 'it is not the case' may be used to correct an error or false
impression:

> Ngóhdeih mhaih yáuh-sām jíng-gú léih ga.
> we not-be have-heart do-trick you PRT
> 'We didn't mean to trick you.'

> Mhaih tīngyaht, haih hauh-yaht.
> not-be tomorrow is after-day
> 'It's not tomorrow, it's the day after.'

Note that *mhaih*, unlike the other negative words, can be used with the
perfective *jó*:

> Ngóh mhaih dáng-jó hóu loih jē.
> I not-be wait-PFV very long PRT
> 'I haven't been waiting very long.'

mhaih is also the form of negation used with quantified phrases (14.1.1).

Idiom: mhaih wah 'it's not as if' is often used in a double negative
construction (13.5) and followed by a *bātgwo* clause:

> Ngóhdeih **mhaih wah móuh** chín, bātgwo hāan
> we not-be say not-have money but save

> dī sái hóu dī.
> some spend good a-bit
> 'It's not as if we have no money, but it's better to spend a bit
> frugally.'

> Ngóh **mhaih wah m̀h jūngyi** kéuih, bātgwo
> I not-be say not like him however

> ngóh yíhgīng yáuh-jó làahm-pàhngyáuh la.
> I already have-PFV boy-friend PRT
> 'It's not that I don't like him, but I already have a boyfriend.'

---

m̀hóu *and* máih

The words *mhóu* and *máih* serve to introduce negative commands: *mhóu* is
the usual word, while *máih* is relatively direct and more likely to be used
among close friends or peers. The subject pronoun is optional:

(Léih) mhóu wah béi yàhn   tēng wo.
(you) don't say to people hear PRT
'Don't (you) tell anyone.'

(Léih) máih gám góng yéh   lā!
(you) don't so   talk thing PRT
'Don't talk like that.'

See further 19.4 on negative imperatives.

móuh *versus* mòuh

móuh is the negative form of *yáuh* (15.4), and means 'have not' or 'there is/are not'. *mòuh* (note the low falling tone) is the Cantonese pronunciation of Mandarin *wú* 'without'; it overlaps with *móuh* and hence tends to replace it in formal and written Cantonese. *mòuh* is also used in a number of phrases and idioms:

mòuhleuhn 'no matter, whether' (16.2.4):

Mòuhleuhn chèuhng dihng dyún, léih dī   tàuhfaat
no-matter long   or   short your CL   hair

dōu haih gam leng ge.
also is   so   fine PRT
'Whether it's long or short, your hair still looks so good.'

mòuhwaih 'no need' or 'no use':

Ngóhdeih mòuhwaih gam hāan lā.
we   no-reason so   frugal PRT
'We have no need to be so frugal.'

Haam   dōu mòuhwaih la.
cry   also no-reason PRT
'It's no use crying (over spilt milk).'

mòuh-dyūn-dyūn 'for no reason':

Bìhbī yáuh jahn sìh   mòuh-dyūn-dyūn haam héi séuhng-làih.
baby have some time no-reason-reason cry up begin
'Babies sometimes start crying for no reason.'

13.4 INDEFINITE NEGATION: 'NOT . . . ANY'

Indefinite expressions meaning 'not . . . anyone/anything', etc., are formed with a question word (17.3) together with a negative word such as *m̀h*, *móuh*, *meih* or *mhóu*. There are two distinct forms, with slightly different shades of meaning:

(a) *m̀h*, *móuh* etc., followed by the question word:

Ngóh gām-yaht móuh   heui **bīndouh**.
I   today   not-have go   anywhere
'I haven't been anywhere today.'

(b) the question word followed by the quantifier *dōu* (see 14.1.1), both coming before the verb regardless of the grammatical function of the question word (see 8.2.3):

Ngóh gām-yaht **bīndouh** **dōu** móuh   heui.
I   today   anywhere   all   not-have go
'I haven't been anywhere today.'

The structure (a) is less emphatic than (b) which might be translated 'any . . . at all'. This difference in force is brought out by the following two contexts:

Ngóh gām-yaht **móuh**   **heui** **bīndouh**, jihnghaih hàahng
I   today   not-have   go   anywhere   merely   walk

háh   gūngyún je.
a-while   park   PRT
'I haven't been anywhere (much) today, I just went for a walk in the park.'

Ngóh gām-yaht **bīndouh** **dōu** móuh   heui, jihnghaih
I   today   anywhere   all   not-have go   merely

chóh hái ūkkéi je.
sit   at   home   PRT
'I haven't been anywhere (at all) today, I just sat around at home.'

Note that *bīndouh dōu móuh heui* is incompatible with *jihnghaih hàahng háh gūngyún je*.

A similar contrast obtains for other question words, such as *mātyéh* 'what' meaning 'anything' and *dím yéung* 'how':

(a) Ngóh móuh   góng **mātyéh** ak.
    I   not-have say   what   PRT
    'I didn't say anything (much).'

(b) Ngóh **māt(yéh)** **dōu** móuh   góng ak.
    I   what   all   not-have say   PRT
    'I didn't say anything (at all).'

(a) Kéuihdeih m̀h   wúih **dím** **yéung** chaapsáu ge.
    they   not will how   manner   interfere PRT
    'They won't interfere in any way.'

(b) Kéuihdeih **dím** **yéung** **dōu** m̀h   wúih chaapsáu   ge.
    they   how   manner   all   not will interfere PRT
    'There's no way they'll interfere.'

Note that if the indefinite phrase is the subject of the sentence, only the *dōu* construction (b) may be used:[2]

Gām-yaht bīngo dōu móuh   wán   léih.
today   who   all   not-have contact you
'Nobody has contacted you today.'

In the alternative structure, as in (a) above, *bīngo* would have to be understood as 'who?':

Gāmyaht bīngo móuh   wán   léih   a?
today   who   not-have contact   you   PRT
'Who didn't contact you today?'

m̀h/móuh . . . māt(yéh) with a noun means 'hardly any' or 'not much':

Ngóh bōng m̀h dóu   mātyéh   sáu,   daahnhaih
I   help   not   PRT   any   hand   but

hóyíh   si-háh.
can   try-DEL
'I can't be of much help, but I'll give it a try.'

Kéuihdeih dou   yìhgā dōu   móuh   wán   dóu
they   until now   also   not-have find   V-PRT

mātyéh   jinggeui.
what   evidence
'They still haven't found much in the way of evidence.'

Similarly, *móuh māt dím* is an adverbial phrase meaning 'hardly':

Léih móuh   māt   dím   bin   wo!
you   not-have what   how   change   PRT
'You've hardly changed at all!'

Idiom: *dím dōu m̀h . . .* uses *dím* 'how' in the structure (b) above to mean 'not . . . anyway' or 'no matter what':

Kéuih dím   dōu m̀h. háng   tēng   ngóh góng.
s/he   how   all   not   willing   listen   me   talk
'He won't listen to me, no matter what.'

13.5 DOUBLE NEGATIVES

A feature of negation in Chinese is the use of double negatives, typically to make a point in an indirect or subtle way. The meaning is not that of double negatives in non-standard English, as in Cockney English *I dunno nothing* meaning 'I don't know anything', but the logical meaning whereby the two negatives make a (qualified) positive statement:

Ngóh **mhaih mséung** heui.
I not-be not-want go
'It's not that I don't want to go.'

A: Go daahngōu léih sihk-m̀h-sihk dāk saai a?
CL cake you eat-not-eat able all PRT
'Can you eat the whole cake?'

B: **Mhaih móuh hólàhng** gé.
not-be not-have possible PRT
'I wouldn't say it's impossible.'

Similarly, the existential negative *móuh* followed by a negated verb gives the meaning 'all' or 'every':

Móuh fuhmóuh **m̀h sek** jihgéi ge jái-léui ge.
no parent not love self POSS children PRT
'All parents love their children.'

Móuh yàhn **m̀h séung** gá dō dī yàhngūng.
no one not want raise more a-bit salary
'Everyone wants a pay rise.'

Double negatives are widely used in modal constructions, for example to express obligation:

Ngóh m̀h heui m̀h dāk ge.
I not go not okay PRT
'I absolutely have to go.'

Léih m̀h hóyíh m̀h tēng kéuih góng ga.
you not can not listen him speak PRT
'You have to listen to him.'

14 QUANTIFICATION

Quantification concerns terms such as *all*, *everyone*, *anything* and *some-where*, which do not refer to specific objects but define classes of objects. Quantifiers in language generally have a syntax which is distinct from that of other parts of speech, and Cantonese is no exception here. The expression of quantification in Cantonese differs substantially from English. There are no words corresponding straightforwardly to 'everything' or 'something', for example, and each of these types of quantification calls for a different structure. To express universal quantification ('all/every/any') a quantifying expression is used in conjunction with *dōu* before the verb (14.1.1). There are distinct constructions corresponding approximately to the meanings 'all', 'each/every' and 'any':

Go-go hohksāang **dōu** séung jáu. (14.1.2)
CL-CL student all want leave
'**All** the students want to go.'

Múih yaht **dōu** haih gám. (14.1.4)
each day also is so
'It's like this **every** day.'

Bīngo hohksāang **dōu** sīk heui tòuhsyūgún. (14.1.5)
which student all know go library
'**Any** student knows the way to the library.'

To express existential quantification ('some, none'), the existential verb *yáuh* and its negative counterpart *móuh* are used (see also ch. 15):

Yáuh dī yéh gáaisīk m̀h dóu ge. (14.2)
have CL thing explain not V-PRT PRT
'Some things cannot be explained.'

Móuh yàhn bōng-ngóh-sáu. (14.3)
not-have person help-me-hand
'No one is helping me.'

Comparisons using quantifiers ('more' and 'less': 14.4) follow the same patterns as comparison of adjectives (9.3).

14.1 UNIVERSAL QUANTIFICATION: 'ALL', 'EVERY' AND 'EACH'

A variety of means are used to express universal quantification, corresponding to English *all*, *every* and *each*. Quantification in Chinese is discussed in Lee (1986), a theoretical study of Mandarin *dōu* which is largely applicable to Cantonese *dōu*. (Note that Cantonese *dōu*, however, may have the meaning 'also', corresponding to Mandarin *yě*: see 10.3.2.)

14.1.1 SYNTAX OF *DŌU*

The adverb *dōu*, appearing immediately before the verb, is used in nearly all forms of universal quantification, i.e. in expressing the meanings 'all', 'every' and 'each'. The various constructions with *dōu* have a similar syntax; in particular, quantified objects with *dōu* precede the verb (4.1, 8.2.3). While *dōu* immediately precedes the verb, the quantified phrase may come in either of two positions:

(a) between the subject and *dōu*:

Kéuih **go-go** **léuihjái** dōu jēui ge.
s/he CL-CL girl all pursue PRT
'He chases all the girls.'

(b) preceding the subject, as sentence topic:

Go-go **léuihjái** kéuih dōu jēui ge.
CL-CL girl s/he all pursue PRT
'He chases all the girls.'

Where both an auxiliary and a main verb are present, the quantified phrase and *dōu* typically precede the auxiliary:

Ngóh **mātyéh dōu** yiu jihgéi máaih.
I what all need self buy
'I have to buy everything myself.'

Kéuih **jek-jek** sáubīu dōu séung máaih.
s/he CL-CL watch all want buy
'He wants to buy all the watches.'

The negative word used in sentences with *dōu* is *mhaih*, which immediately precedes the quantified phrase:

Mhaih go-go dōu gam dākhàahn ga.
not-be CL-CL all so free PRT
'Not everyone has so much free time.'
(*not* *Go-go dōu mhaih gam dākhàahn)

Daaihhohk mhaih bīngo dōu sāu ga.
university not-be who all accept PRT
'The university doesn't just accept anyone.'

Similarly, questions involving quantifiers are formed with *haih-mhaih* (17.1.3) rather than a simple A-not-A question:

Haih-mhaih   go-go   dōu   séung   yāusīk   a?
be-not-be   CL-CL   all   wish   rest   PRT
'Does everyone want a break?'
(*not* *Go-go dōu séung-mséung yāusīk a?)

Haih-mhaih   douh-douh   dōu   yāt-yeuhng   ga?
be-not-be   there-there   all   one-same   PRT
'Is it the same everywhere?'

dōu is also used in the expression *léuhng* [CL] *dōu* 'both' and similarly with other numbers:

Léuhng   ga   dōu   leng.
two   CL   all   nice
'They're both nice.'

Kéuihdeih   sāam   go   dōu   heui.
they   three   CL   all   go
'All three of them are going.'

Idiom: *haih . . . dōu* may express the meaning 'every' or 'any' in colloquial speech:

Haih   yàhn   dōu   jī   ga   lā.
is   people   all   know   PRT   PRT
'Everyone knows that.'

Haih   yàhn   dōu   wúih   tùhng-chìhng   léih   ge.
is   people   all   will   sympathize   you   PRT
'Anyone would sympathize with you.'

---

sèhng 'the whole' is optionally accompanied by *dōu* and/or the quantifying verbal particle *saai* (11.3.3):

Sèhng   ga   gēi   (dōu)   báau   saai.
whole   CL   plane   (all)   full   V-PRT
'The whole plane is full.'

Note that the presence of *dōu* requires an object with *sèhng* to come before the verb, while *saai* alone does not:

Ngóhdeih   sèhng   gāan   ūk   dōu   chaak   saai.
we   whole   CL   house   all   demolish   V-PRT
'We're knocking the whole house down.'

Ngóhdeih	chaak	saai	sèhng	gāan	ūk.
we	demolish	V-PRT	whole	CL	house

'We're knocking the whole house down.'

Phrases with *sèhng* may be used adverbially:

Kéuih	**sèhng**	**go**	**hahjau**	jāuwàih	hàahng-gūngsī.
s/he	whole	CL	afternoon	around	walk-store

'She went around shopping all afternoon.'

Idiomatically, *sèhng* has the emphatic meaning 'all of':

Kéuih	sèhng	sāamsahp	seui	dōu	meih	git-fān.
s/he	whole	thirty	years	also	not-yet	marry

'She's all of thirty and still not married.'

Ngóh	go	léui	sèhng	luhk	dím	jūng	dōu	meih
my	CL	daughter	whole	six	o'clock		also	not-yet

fāan	ūkkéi.
return	home

'It was all of six o'clock and my daughter still wasn't home.'

sèhngyaht 'always' is an adverb which may optionally be reinforced by *dōu*:

Kéuih	sèhngyaht	(dōu)	chìh	dou	ge.
s/he	always	(all)	late	arrive	PRT

'He's always late.'

Note that *sèhngyaht* is often used hyperbolically, as in the above example, and should not be taken to mean literally 'every time'.

chyùhnbouh . . . *dōu* 'the whole lot' is a colloquial quantifier phrase used with *dōu* and/or the quantifying particle *saai* (11.3.3):

Idiom: hahm-baahng-laahng, usually reduced to *hahmba'laahng*, is used colloquially to mean 'all' or 'completely':

Hahmba'laahng	(dōu)	haih	léih	ge	cho.
completely	(all)	is	your	PRT	fault

'It's all your fault.'

Note that *dōu* can be omitted here, or replaced by the verbal particle *saai* (11.3.3):

Dī	yàhn	hahmba'laahng	jáu	saai.
CL	people	completely	leave	PRT

'They've all gone.'

Nī   dī   chyùhnbouh   (dōu)   haih   Yahtbún   fo   lèihga.
this   CL   whole-lot   (all)   is   Japan   goods   PRT
'All this stuff is Japanese.'

Ngóh   chyùhnbouh   (dōu)   yiu   saai.
I   whole-lot   (all)   want   all
'I want it all.'

Idiom: lìhn . . . dōu 'even' emphasizes a noun phrase or pronoun:

Lìhn   léih   **dōu**   m̀h   béi   mín   ngóh.
even   you   also   not   give   face   me
'Not even you respect me.'

Lìhn   jeui   lēk   gó   dī   hohksāang   **dōu**   m̀h
even   most   smart   that   CL   student   also   not

sīk   daap.
know   answer
'Even the brightest students didn't know the answer.'

Note that as for other sentence types with *dōu*, objects modified by *lìhn* must precede the verb:

Ngóh   guih   dou   **lìhn**   **faahn**   dōu   sihk   m̀h   lohk.
I   tired   until   even   food   also   eat   not   down
'I'm so tired I can't even eat.'

---

daaihgā 'everyone (here)' is used especially in public contexts, addressing or referring to everyone present:

Yùhgwó   daaihgā   tùhngyi   ge   wah,   ngóhdeih   jauh
if   everyone   agree   the   case   we   then

kyutdihng   gám   jouh.
decide   so   do
'If everyone agrees, we'll decide to do it this way.'

Dōjeh   daaihgā   sāu-tēng.   (radio announcement)
thank   everyone   receive-hear
'Thank you for listening.'

gok wái, using the polite classifier *wái* (6.2.4), is a formal term to address everyone present:

Fūnyìhng   gok wái.
welcome   every-one
'Ladies and gentlemen, welcome.'

14.1.2 REDUPLICATED QUANTIFIERS

A classifier (6.2) may be reduplicated to express quantification, with *dōu* coming before the verb as discussed in 14.1.1. The noun to which the classifier refers may be omitted where the context makes its identity clear:

Go-go   (yàhn)   dōu séung yiu   dō   dī   màhnjyú.
CL-CL   (person)   all   want need more some democracy
'Everyone wants a bit more democracy.'

Mhaih jek-jek (gúpiu) dōu sīng ga.
not-be CL-CL (share)   all   rise PRT
'Not all shares go up in price.'

Kéuih tou-tou (hei) dōu wah mhóu   tái gé. (film critic)
s/he   CL-CL (film) all   say not-good see PRT
'He says every film is not worth seeing.'

Haih-mhaih yeuhng-yeuhng dōu hóu   sihk ga? (at meal)
be-not-be   CL-CL   all   good eat   PRT
'Is everything good?'

Note especially *douh-douh dōu* 'everywhere' (*douh* being used as the classifier for nouns such as *deihfōng* 'place'):

Nī dī yàhn   douh-douh   dōu yáuh ge   lā.
this CL people there-there all   have PRT PRT
'You find these people everywhere.'

In addition to classifiers, certain common nouns have reduplicated forms, such as *yàhn-yàhn dōu* 'everyone':

Yàhn-yàhn   dōu yīnggōi bóuwuh   wàahngíng.
person-person all   should   protect   environment
'Everyone should protect the environment.'

Time words are reduplicated to form adverbs with habitual meaning:

Chi-chi   dōu haih gám ge.
time-time   all   is   so   PRT
'It's like this every time.'

Lìhn-lìhn (dōu) yáuh nī   go mahntàih.
year-year   (all)   have this CL problem
'This problem arises every year.'

Kéuih **yaht-yaht** heui yàuh-séui.
s/he   day-day   go   swim-water
'She goes swimming every day.'

In compound nouns such as *fānjūng* 'minute' and *míuhjūng* 'second', only the first syllable is reduplicated, giving *fān-fān-jūng* 'any moment' and *míuh-míuh-jūng* 'any second':

Fān-fān-jūng   dōu   hólàhng   béi   chāailóu   jūk   dóu.
minute-minute   all   can   by   cops   catch   V-PRT
'(You) could be caught by the cops at any moment.'

Fān-fān-jūng   sēui-yiu   léih.   (title of a song)
minute-minute   need   you
'I need you every moment of the day.'

14.1.3 *SÓ YÁUH (GE)*

This phrase literally means 'whatever . . . there are', and is used in relatively formal contexts as an emphatic 'all'. If the quantified phrase comes before the verb (as the subject or topicalized object), it must be accompanied by *dōu*:

Só   yáuh   (ge)   tùhngsih   **dōu**   tùhngyi.
whatever   have   (LP)   colleague   all   agree
'All our colleagues agree.'

Ngóh   só   yáuh   (ge)   jīlíu   **dōu**   daai   saai   làih.
I   whatever   have   (LP)   material   all   bring   all   come
'I'll bring all the materials with me.'

Só   yáuh   (ge)   jīlíu   **dōu**   yiu   daai   saai   làih.
whatever   have   (LP)   material   all   need   bring   all   come
'We need to bring all the materials with us.'

If the quantified phrase is the object of the sentence, it may remain in its usual position after the verb, which may take the quantifying particle *saai* (11.3.3):

Ngóhdeih tái-gwo   só   yáuh   (ge)   jinggeui.
we   see-EXP   whatever   have   (LP)   evidence
'We've seen all the evidence there is.'

Ngóh   **daai   saai**   só   yáuh   (ge)   jīlíu   làih.
I   bring   all   whatever   have   (LP)   material   come
'I'll bring all the materials with me.'

14.1.4 *MÚIH* 'EACH, EVERY'

The word *múih* 'each' functions like *bīn* 'which', being followed by the relevant classifier and accompanied by *dōu* before the verb:

Múih   go   hohksāang   dōu   yiu   gāau   hohkfai.
each   CL   student   all   need   pay   tuition
'Each student has to pay tuition fees.'

Léih   múih   jēung   dāan   dōu   yiu   chīm.
you   each   CL   form   all   need   sign
'You have to sign every form.'

múih combines with time expressions to form adverbs of frequency such as
múih yaht 'each/every day' (10.3.4).

múih chi 'every time' serves as a conjunction to mean 'whenever', often
together with the verbal particle *chān* (11.3.4):

Ngóhdeih   múih   chi   làih   (chān)   nī   gāan   jáulàuh
we   every time   come   (PRT)   this   CL   restaurant

dōu   hái   gódouh   chóh   ge.
all   at   there   sit   PRT
'We sit there whenever we come to this restaurant.'

14.1.5 'ANY'

The quantifier 'any' differs from 'each' and 'every' in implying an element
of choice: the sentence is true whichever you choose. This **free choice 'any'**
is closely related to the **negative polarity 'any'**, which occurs in negative
sentences (see 13.4), the two types being expressed by similar means in
both English and Cantonese. Cantonese expresses this concept using the
appropriate question word followed by *dōu*:

bīngo dōu	mātyéh dōu
who all	what all
'anyone'	'anything'

bīndouh dōu	géisìh dōu
where all	when all
'anywhere'	'any time'

bīn [CL] dōu	dím (yéung) dōu
which all	how (manner) all
'any'	'any way'

Like other *dōu*-phrases (14.1.1), these phrases must precede the verb,
whether they function as subjects or objects:

Ngóh   bīndouh   dōu   hóyíh   heui.
I   where   all   can   go
'I can go anywhere I like.'

or

Bīndouh   ngóh   dōu   hóyíh   heui.
anywhere   I   all   can   go
'I can go anywhere I like.'

bīngo and *mātyéh* are used similarly with nouns to mean 'any':

Léih **bīngo tùhngsih** dōu hóyíh chéng ga.
you which colleague all can invite PRT
'You can invite any of your colleagues.'

Ngóh **mātyéh yú** dōu sihk ge.
I what fish all eat PRT
'I eat any kind of fish.'

The question words may have the indefinite meaning 'any' in a number of contexts:

(a) followed by *dōu*, as above;

Kéuih mātyéh baatgwa yéh dōu yáuh-hingcheui ge.
s/he what gossip stuff all have-interest PRT
'He's interested in any kind of gossip.'

(b) in negative contexts (13.4);

Ngóh móuh góng mātyéh ak.
I not-have say what PRT
'I haven't said anything.'

(c) in conditional sentences (16.3):

Yùhgwó yáuh mātyéh mahntàih, léih jīkhāak wán ngóh wo.
if have any problem you at-once seek me PRT
'Let me know straight away if there's any problem.'

(d) in A-not-A questions (17.1.2):

Léih gāmyaht yáuh-móuh gin dóu
you today have-not-have see V-PRT

mātyéh sāang bóu-yàhn a?
what unfamiliar-person PRT
'Have you seen any strangers today?'

Léihdeih fong-ga wúih-m̀h-wúih heui bīndouh a?
you-PL take-leave will-not-will go where PRT
'Will you be going anywhere in your vacation?'

Several alternative terms meaning 'any' exist:

yahmhòh is a formal term for 'any'. As with other quantifiers, *dōu* is required when the *yahmhòh* phrase comes before the main verb:

Yahmhòh yāt go yàhn dōu hóyíh sānchíng.
any one CL person all can apply
'Anyone may apply.'

Yahmhòh lìhngéi dōu fūnyìhng.
any age all welcome
'Any age is welcome.'

The adverbs *sihdaahn* 'at random' and *chèuihbín* 'as you please' are colloquial alternatives to express the choice 'any'. As adverbs, they come before the verb:

Léih **sihdaahn** **ló** yāt go dōu móuh sówaih.
you at-random take one CL all not-have importance
'You can take any one, it makes no difference.'

Léih **chèuihbín** **gáan** yāt gihn. (referring to clothing)
you as-you-please choose one CL
'Choose any one you like.'

Similarly, *chèuihsìh* 'at any time':

Léih chèuihsìh jáu dōu dāk.
you any-time leave all okay
'You can leave any time you like.'

dím dōu 'anyway' typically expresses resignation or determination:

Ngóhdeih dím dōu yiu yìhmàhn.
we how all need emigrate
'We have to emigrate whatever happens.'

Kéuih dím dōu m̀h háng bōng ngóh.
s/he how all not willing help me
'She doesn't want to help me anyway.'

Léih béi kéuih jouh jyúgok, kéuih dím dōu jai.
you allow him do lead-star s/he how all accept
'If you give him the lead role he'll agree to anything.'

14.2 EXISTENTIAL QUANTIFICATION: 'SOME'

14.2.1 INDEFINITE 'SOME'

Indefinite or existential quantification ('some') is expressed by the existential word *yáuh* (see ch. 15):

Yáuh (dī) yàhn gokdāk nī tou héi hóu dái-tái.
have (CL) people feel this CL film very worth-see
'Some people feel this film is well worth seeing.'
(i.e. you get your money's worth)

Yáuh (dī) yéh mhaih géi tóh.
have (CL) thing not quite right
'Something's not quite right.'

yáuh combines with time and place words to produce indefinite adverbs:

yáuh (jahn) sìh 'sometimes'

Yáuh (jahn) sìh ngóhdeih léuhng gūngpó dōu wúih
have (CL) time we two couple still will

aaigāau ge.
argue PRT
'Sometimes we (as a couple) still argue.'

yáuh dī deihfōng or *yáuh géi douh (deihfōng)* 'some places':

Yáuh dī deihfōng m̀h béi yàhn sihk yīn ge.
have some place not let people eat smoke PRT
'In some places they don't let you smoke.'

An alternative form of indefinite quantification is a question word follow-ing an expression of possibility such as *hóuchíh*:[1]

Hóuchíh **hái bīndouh** gin-gwo léih.
seem at where see-EXP you
'I seem to have seen you somewhere before.'

m̀h jī bīndouh 'I don't know where' may also express an indefinite location:

Méihgwok **m̀h jī bīndouh** yáuh gáan gám
America not know where have CL such

ge hohkhaauh.
LP school
'Somewhere in America there's a school like that.'

Similarly, *m̀h jī géisìh* 'I don't know when' might be used to express 'sometime':

Nī tìuh tàihmuhk ngóhdeih **m̀h jī géisìh** góng-gwo.
this CL topic we not know when talk-EXP
'We've discussed this topic sometime before.'

14.2.2 NEGATIVE 'NONE, NO ONE, NOTHING'

Negative quantifiers are formed with the negative existential word *móuh* (15.4): *móuh yàhn* 'no one' and *móuh yéh* 'nothing':

Móuh yàhn mìhng(baahk) léih góng māt.
not-have person understand you say what
'No one understands what you're talking about.'

Ngóhdeih móuh   yéh   mùhn-jyuh   léih.
we   not-have thing hide-CONT   you
'We have nothing to hide from you.'

These expressions may be qualified by the addition of *māt*, *mātyéh* or *géi dō*, giving the meaning 'hardly any':

Gām-yaht móuh   māt yàhn   fāan   gūng.
today   not-have any person return work
'Hardly anyone is going to work today.'

Móuh   mātyéh syū   góng Gwóngdūng-wá ge yúhfaat.
not-have any   book talk   Cantonese   LP grammar
'There are hardly any books about Cantonese grammar.'

Móuh   géi dō   sìhgaan jihng   la.
not-have how much time   remain   PRT
'There isn't much time left.'

móuh with the numeral *yāt* 'one' represents a more emphatic denial:

Móuh yāt go   hóuchíh léih gam chéun   ge.
no   one CL   like   you   so   stupid   PRT
'There's no one as stupid as you.'

Yāt lāp sēng   dōu móuh.
one CL   sound also not-have
'There's not even a sound.'

Nī bouh gēi   **yāt dī yuhng** dōu **móuh**.
this CL   machine one bit use   also not-have
'This machine is no use at all.'

móuh is readily used in double negatives (13.5), meaning 'every':

Móuh   làahmyán m̀h   séung yáuh   go   leng   lóuhpòh.
not-have man   not   wish have   CL   pretty wife
'Every man wants to have a beautiful wife.'

14.3 RELATIVE QUANTITIES: MUCH/MANY, LITTLE/FEW

As there is no systematic distinction between count and mass nouns in Cantonese, *dō* may mean either 'many' or 'much' and *síu* 'few' or 'little':

dō yàhn 'many people'
dō yéh 'a lot of stuff'
síu yàhn 'few/not many people'
síu chín 'little/not much money'

These may be modified, for example: *hóu dō* 'a lot', *gam dō* 'so many/much', *géi dō* 'quite a lot', *hóu síu* 'very little', *gam síu* 'so little'. *dō* and *síu* also function as 'more' and 'less' respectively in comparative contexts (14.4).

Idiom: haih gam dō 'that's all' is used in shopping, dining and other service situations:

A: Juhng sái-msái   giu   yéh   a?
    still   need-not-need   order things PRT
    'Do you need to order anything else?'

B: Msái   la,   haih gam dō   ga   laak.
    no-need PRT is   so   much PRT PRT
    'No thanks, that'll be all.'

---

daaih bá 'plenty' is a colloquial quantifier:

Daaih bá   yàhn   yáuh-hingcheui   ge.   (conv.)
big   bunch people have-interest   PRT
'Plenty of people are interested.'

Ngóh yíhgīng daaih bá   yéh   jouh.
I   already big   bunch things do
'I already have plenty of work to do.'

msíu 'not little' is often used to mean 'quite a few' or 'quite a bit':

Jeui gahn   msíu   yàhn   sānchíng yahp   wúi.
most recent not-few people apply   enter society
'Quite a lot of people have applied to join the society recently.'

Làuhga   yíhgīng sīng-jó   msíu   ge   la.
flat-price already rise-PFV not-little PRT PRT
'The price of flats has gone up quite a bit.'

Idiom: mdō msíu, literally 'not a lot but not a little' often conveys modesty:

A: Léih sīk-m̀h-sīk   yāmngohk a?
    you   know-not-know   music   PRT
    'Do you know about music?'

B: Mdō   msíu   dōu sīk   dī   lā.
    not-much not-little all know some PRT
    'A little.'

dō-dō síu-síu has a similar meaning.

The quantifiers *dō* and *síu/msíu* may be used as predicates, like adjectives:

Góbihn   yàhn   juhng   dō.
that-way   people   even   more
'There are even more people over there.'

Hóuchíh   kéuih   gam   sīmàhn   ge   yàhn   yuht   làih
like   him   so   gentle   LP   people more   and

yuht   síu.
more   little
'People as genteel as him are getting fewer and fewer.'

Máaih   bóuhím   ge   yàhn   dōu   msíu   wo.
buy   insurance   LP   people   also not-few   PRT
'There are quite a few people buying insurance.'

When used predicatively in this way, *dō* and *síu* may take the perfective aspect *jó*:

Bún   Góng   yàhnháu   dō-jó   yāt   púih.
local HK   population   much-PFV   one   part
'The population of Hongkong has grown by 100 per cent.'

Dím   gáai   síu-jó   gam   dō   gé?
how   come   less-PFV   so   much   PRT
'Why is there so much less?'

dō-jó and *síu-jó* have the idiomatic meanings 'extra' and 'missing' respectively:

Gām   chi   dō-jó   (yāt)   go   yàhn.
this   time   more-PFV   (one)   CL   person
'There's one extra person this time.'

Gām   chi   síu-jó   (yāt)   go   yàhn.
this   time   less-PFV   (one)   CL   person
'There's one person missing this time.'

sēsíu or the reduplicated form *síu-síu* 'a little' are used adverbially with verbs or adjectives:

Kéuih   Gwóngdūng-wá   jeunbouh-jó   síu-síu.
s/he   Cantonese   improve-PFV   little-little
'His Cantonese has improved a little.'

Méih   gām   sīng-jó   sēsíu.
US   gold rise-PFV   little
'The US dollar has gone up a little.'

Léih fèih síu-síu   jauh leng   hóu dō.
you fat little-little then pretty very much
'You're much prettier when you're a bit fatter.'

The excessive constructions with *taai*, *gwotàuh* and *dāk jaih* (see 9.3.4) may occur with *dō* and *síu*:

Ngóh him léih **taai dō**   la!   (film)
I   owe you too much PRT
'I owe too much to you.'

Léih yám jáu yám dāk **dō**   **gwotàuh**.
you drink wine drink ADV much excess
'You drink a bit too much.'

Dī tìhmbán tòhng **dō** **dāk jaih**.
CL dessert sugar much a-bit
'The sugar in the dessert is a bit much.'

taai síu 'too little, too few' is often equivalent to 'not enough':

Léih sihk taai síu   yéh   la.
you eat too little stuff PRT
'You're not eating enough.'

Taai síu yàhn gwāansām kéuih.
too few people care   him/her
'Not enough people care for her.'

14.4 COMPARING QUANTITIES

14.4.1 'MORE' AND 'LESS'

The words *dō* 'much/many' and *síu* 'little/few' also mean 'more' and 'less' respectively when combined with comparative constructions such as those with *gwo* and *béi* (9.3):

Ngóh sihk dāk **dō**   **gwo** léih.
I   eat ADV more than you
'I eat more than you do.'

Ngóh jaahn dāk **síu** **gwo** ngóh lóuhpòh.
I   earn ADV less than my   wife
'I earn less than my wife does.'

Ngóh fan dāk **béi** yíhchìhn **dō**.
I   sleep ADV than before   more
'I sleep more than I used to.'

Where the object of comparison is omitted, *dī* is used (9.3). As with adjectives (9.3.1), such comparisons may be modified by *hóu dō* 'much, a lot', *dī* 'a little' and its reduplicated form *dī-dī* or *dīt-dīt* 'a wee bit':

Kéuihdeih séung yiu **dō** **dī** sìhgaan.
they want need more a-little time
'They'd like a little more time.'

Ngóh lìhngyún jaahn **síu** **dī** chín.
I rather earn less a-bit money
'I'd rather make less money.'

Yìhgā hái Hēunggóng ge daaihluhk yàhn béi
now in Hongkong that mainland people than

yíhchìhn **dō** **hóu** **dō.**
before more very much
'The mainland people in Hongkong are many more than they used to be.'

Kéuih nī pàaih sé yéh sé dāk **síu hóu dō.**
s/he these days write thing write ADV less very much
'He writes a lot less nowadays.'

dō and *síu* also take on their comparative meanings 'more' and 'less' when followed by a quantity expression:

Ngóhdeih lám-jyuh joi jyuh **dō** **sāam yaht.**
we think-CONT again live more three day
'We're thinking of staying three more days.'

Kéuih yìhgā fahn gūng jaahn **dō** **sāam púih.**
s/he now CL job earn more three time
'Her job pays three times as much now.'

Ngóh béi **síu** **sahp fān** gó go hohksāang.
I give less ten mark that CL student
'I gave ten marks less to that student.'

dō gwo and *síu gwo* may compare two clauses:

Ngóh jī léih jūngyi chín **dō** gwo jūngyi ngóh. (film)
I know you like money more than like me
'I know you love money more than you love me.'

chīu gwo 'more than' is used with figures, being more formal than *dō gwo*:

Jek gáu sātjūng **chīu** **gwo** sāam yaht.
CL dog missing more than three days
'The dog was missing for more than three days.'

Máaih sān chē yiu **chīu gwo** sahp maahn mān.
buy new car need more than ten ten-thousand dollar
'To buy a new car costs over \$100,000.'

Chīu gwo sahp gāan Jūnggwok gūngsī làih
more than ten CL Chinese company come

Hēunggóng séuhng-síh.
Hongkong go-up-market
'Over ten Chinese companies are to be listed on the Hongkong stock
exchange.'

yuht làih yuht 'more and more' may be used with *dō* and *síu*, as with
adjectives (9.3.1):

Gūngsī jaahn ge chín yuht làih yuht síu.
company earn that money more-come-more less
'The company is making less and less money.'

Yuht làih yuht dō hohksāang duhk daaihhohk.
more-come-more many student study university
'More and more students are going to university.'

14.4.2 MOST

daaih bouh fahn 'a large part' renders *most of* [noun]:

Kéuih sé dī yéh daaih bouh fahn haih jān ge.
s/he write CL stuff large CL part is true PRT
'Most of what he writes is true.'

Daaih bouh fahn yàhn dōu wúih làuh hái Hēunggóng.
large CL part people all will stay at Hongkong
'Most people are staying in Hongkong.'

Note also the related phrase *síu bouh fahn* 'a small portion' and *yāt bouh
fahn* 'part of, some of'.
dōsou 'most' or 'mostly' is used as an adjective or adverb, to quantify
people, things or events:

Dōsou yàhn syú-ga heui léuih-hàhng.
most people summer-holiday go travel
'Most people go travelling in the summer holidays.'

Yàhndeih **dōsou** yuhng nī jek pàaih-jí.
people mostly use this CL brand
'Most people use this brand.'

síusou is the opposite of *dōsou*, meaning 'few':

Jíyáuh   síusou   yàhn   jaansìhng gám yéung jouh.
only-have few   people approve   this way do
'Only a few people approve of this way of doing things.'

Yáuh síusou hohksāang heui sihwāi.
have few   student   go   demonstrate
'There are a few students who demonstrate.'

Note the idiomatic expression:

Síusou   fuhkchùhng dōsou.
few   obey   many
'Minority obeys majority.'

Unlike *dōsou*, however, *síusou* is not used as an adverb.

15 EXISTENTIAL SENTENCES

Existential sentences, introduced by the word *yáuh*, are important to idiomatic Cantonese. *yáuh* essentially means 'have' or 'there is/there are' but often does not correspond to anything in English. For example, in many cases *yáuh* is required to introduce an indefinite noun phrase as the subject of a sentence, due to the constraint that subjects should be definite (see 4.2.5, 15.5). The negative counterpart *móuh* 'there isn't/there aren't' behaves in a parallel fashion: essentially all those structures which occur with *yáuh* also occur with *móuh* (15.4). The corresponding A-not-A question form, *yáuh-móuh*, is used to form existential questions (17.1.5).

15.1 *YÁUH* + NOUN

yáuh translates either as 'have' or as 'there is/are'. There is no clear distinction between the 'possessive' and 'existential' functions of *yáuh*, and sentences such as the following have a similar structure:

Kéuihdeih yáuh sāam go jái. (possessive)
they   have three CL son
'They have three sons.'

Nī   go deihfōng yáuh mahntàih. (existential)
this CL place   have problem
'There's something wrong with this place.'

As a verb, *yáuh* can take the aspect markers *gwo* and *jó*, (but not *gán* or *jyuh*) and verbal particles such as *fāan* (11.3.1):

Ngóhdeih hohkhaauh chùhnglòih meih **yáuh-gwo** gam
our   school   never   not-yet have-EXP so

lēk   ge hohksāang.
smart LP student
'Our school has never had such a bright student.'

Kéuih **yáuh-jó** nī go behng hóu loih.
s/he   have-PFV this CL disease very long
'She's had this disease for a long time.'

Léih **yáuh fāan** seunsām jauh móuh   mahntàih ge   la.
you   have back confidence then not-have problem PRT PRT
'When you get your confidence back there'll be no problem.'

Idioms: *yáuh-jó* (*bìhbī*), with the perfective marker *jó*, colloquially means 'to be pregnant':

Mhóu góng béi yàhn(deih) tēng ngóh **yáuh-jó** wo.
don't speak to people hear I have-PFV PRT
'Don't tell anyone I'm pregnant, okay?'

yáuh fāan gam seuhng há idiomatically describes a recurrent or typical quality (note the change tone in *hah* to *há*):

Ló dóu jéung gó dī hei dōu haih **yáuh**
get V-PRT award those CL film all are have

fāan gam seuhng há ge.
V-PRT so up down PRT
'The films that get awards are all of a certain standard.'

Idiom: *yáuh sām*, literally 'to have a heart', means 'to have the intention' or 'to do something on purpose':

Kéuih yáuh sām jíng-gú ngóh ge.
s/he have heart trick me PRT
'He tricked me intentionally.'

Deui-mjyuh, ngóh mhaih yáuh sām ga.
sorry I not-be have heart PRT
'Sorry, I didn't do it on purpose.'

The negative form *móuh sām* has a similar meaning:

Ngóh móuh sām sēunghoih léih ga.
I not-have heart hurt you PRT
'I didn't mean to hurt you.'

yáuh sām may also refer to a well-wisher's concern:

A: Léih go jái behng hóu fāan meih a?
you CL son sick well back not-yet PRT
'Has your son recovered yet?'

B: Dōjeh, léih jānhaih yáuh sām lo!
Oh you really have heart PRT
'You're so nice to ask!'

15.2   *YÁUH/MÓUH* + VERB

yáuh and *móuh* are used before a verb primarily in questions and negative statements referring to the past (13.3, 17.1.5):

A: Yáuh-móuh   gin   dóu   A-Chán   a?   B: Yáuh.
   have-not-have   see   PRT   Ah-Chan   PRT   have
   'Did you see Chan?'   'Yes.'

Ngóh   gām-yaht   móuh   heui   gāai.
I   today   not-have   go   street
'I haven't been out today.'

These constructions correspond to [verb] – *jó* in affirmative sentences (11.2.4, 13.3).

In addition, the combination *yáuh/móuh* + verb can occur in declarative sentences in two ways:

(a) referring to the past; this usage is the counterpart of the negative and interrogative construction discussed above, but is highly emphatic:

A: Gó   chi   ngóhdeih   heui-jó   Chekchyúh   wáan.
   that   time   we   go-PFV   Stanley   visit
   'That time we went to Stanley.'

B: Haih   a,   ngóh   dōu   **yáuh   heui**.
   is   PRT   I   also   have   go
   'That's right, I went too!'

A: Léih   yáuh-móuh   sihk   saai   dī   yeuhk   a?
   you   have-not-have   eat   all   CL   medicine   PRT
   'Have you taken all the medicine?'

B: Gánghaih   **yáuh   sihk   saai**   lā.
   surely   have   eat   all   PRT
   'Of course I have.'

Ngóh   mgeidāk   **yáuh   je-gwo**   léih   bún   syū   wo.
I   not-remember   have   borrow-EXP   your   CL   book   PRT
'I don't remember borrowing your book.'

(b) referring to the present, with a habitual meaning:

Boují   yaht-yaht   dōu   **yáuh   góng**   gúsíh.
newspaper   day-day   all   have   talk   stock-market
'The paper talks about the stock market every day.'

The habitual interpretation (b) also occurs in *yáuh-móuh* questions:

Léih   juhng   **yáuh-móuh**   heui   yàuh-séui   a?
you   still   have-not-have   go   swimming   PRT
'Do you still go swimming?'

---

yáuh + *verb idioms*: this combination also occurs in some idiomatic expressions and proverbs:

Mgōi, gāai háu **yáuh lohk**. (used on minibuses etc.)
please street corner have descend
'Please let me off at the corner.'

Kéuihdeih léuhng go **yáuh góng yáuh siu**.
those two CL have talk have laugh
'Those two (people) get on well together.'

Dóu-chín gánghaih **yáuh yèhng yáuh syū** ge lā.
bet-money of course have win have lose PRT PRT
'In gambling, of course there are times to win and there are times to lose.'

15.3 *YÁUH* + ADJECTIVE

yáuh with a quantity expression such as *dī* or *síu-síu* may be used to modify an adjective:

Kéuih góng ge yéh hóuchíh **yáuh dī m-ngāam**.
s/he say LP things seem have bit not-right
'There seems to be something not quite right in what he says.'

Ngóh gokdāk yáuh síu-síu mtùhng.
I feel have little-little different
'I feel there's a slight difference.'

Ngóh **yáuh dī guih**, séung fāan ūkkéi sìn. (film)
I have some tired want return home first
'I'm a bit tired, I'd like to go home.'

yáuh is also used in comparison of adjectives (9.3.3) and adverbs (10.2), in the form *yáuh-móuh* for interrogative comparisons or alone in rhetorical questions:

Léih yáuh-móuh kéuih gam jīngsàhn a?
you have-not-have her so energetic PRT
'Are you as energetic as her?'

Ngóh bīn(douh) yáuh kéuih gam búnsih a?
I where have her so capable PRT
'I'm nothing like as capable as she is.'

Note the rhetorical use of *bīn(douh)*: see 17.3.4.

---

idioms in exclamatives: gam [adj] *dōu yáuh* is an expression of exclamation or surprise:

Wa!	Lohk	gam	daaih	yúh	dōu	yáuh	gé!
wow	fall	so	big	rain	also	exist	PRT

'Gosh, I never knew it could rain like this!'

Gam	yuhksyūn	dōu	yáuh	gé!
so	ugly	also	exist	PRT

'What could be so ugly?'

yáuh mātyéh [adj] is used to query the value of something:

Jūkkàuh	yáuh	mātyéh	hóu	tái	a?
football	have	what	good	watch	PRT

'What's so good about football?'

Yùhchi	yáuh	mātyéh	gam	dahkbiht	a?
shark-fin	have	what	so	special	PRT

'What's so special about shark fin (soup)?'

15.4 *MÓUH*

Móuh is the negative counterpart of *yáuh*, meaning 'there isn't/there aren't' (there is no combination **m̀h yáuh* in Hongkong Cantonese). It behaves in a parallel fashion to *yáuh*: those structures which occur with *yáuh* generally also occur with *móuh*, with a similar pattern of possessive or existential usage:

Possessive

Ngóh	móuh	saai	chín	la	wo.
I	not-have	all	money	PRT	PRT

'I'm out of money.'

Existential

Nīdouh	móuh	yéh	máaih.
here	not-have	things	buy

'There's nothing to buy here.'

The meaning may be emphasized in the expression *yāt dī . . . dōu móuh* meaning 'none at all':

Ngoihgwok-yàhn hái nī gāan gūngsī yāt dī deihwaih
foreign-people in this CL company one bit status

dōu móuh.
also not-have
'Foreigners have no status at all in this company.'

As a verb, *móuh* can take the perfective *-jó*; it then denotes a change from
having something to not having it:

Tēng góng kéuihdeih ngāam-ngāam **móuh-jó** go
hear say they just-just not-have-PFV CL

gūngyàhn, hóu mdihm wóh.
maid very not-manage PRT
'Apparently they've just lost their maid, and they can't cope.'

Yùhgwó **móuh-jó** ngóh fahn yàhngūng jauh
if not-have-PFV my CL salary then

cháam lo.
poor PRT
'If I didn't have my salary, I'd be in trouble.'

Similarly, *móuh* may take the verbal particles *saai* and *màaih* (11.3.3):

Gám ngóhdeih maih **móuh** **saai** mín!
so we then not-have all face
'We'll lose face completely, that way!'

Kéuih lìhn nī go gēiwuih dōu **móuh** **màaih**,
s/he even this CL chance also not-have V-PRT

jānhaih hósīk.
really pitiable
'She's lost even this chance, it's really a shame.'

móuh together with a question word expresses a qualified 'any' (14.2.2).
Thus *móuh mātyéh* or *móuh māt* means 'not much':

Ngóh gokdāk cháau-láu **móuh** **mātyéh** mhóu.
I feel deal-flats not-have any not-good
'I don't really see anything wrong with speculating on flats.'

Kéuih deui sāi yī **móuh** **māt**
s/he towards Western doctor not-have any

seunsām ge.
confidence PRT
'She doesn't have much confidence in Western doctors.'

Similarly, *móuh géi dō* means 'not many/much' and *móuh géi loih* (*chìhn*) 'not long ago':

Gām-lìhn **móuh** **géi** **dō** yàhn heui ngoihgwok.
this-year not-have how many people go abroad
'Not many people are going abroad this year.'

Kéuihdeih **móuh** **géi** **loih** **chìhn** git-jó-fān.
they not-have how long ago marry-PFV
'They got married not long ago.'

Note that the time phrase with *chìhn* (see 10.4) must come before the verb; without *chìhn*, the phrase *móuh géi loih* would follow the verb with a slight difference in meaning:

Kéuihdeih git-jó-fān móuh géi loih.
they marry-PFV not-have how long
'They haven't been married for long.'

Idioms: *móuh baahnfaat* 'no way' and *móuh hólàhng* 'no chance' are used adverbially:

Ngóhdeih **móuh** baahnfaat gáaisīk nī gihn sih.
we not-have way explain this CL matter
'There's no way we can explain this.'

Ngóhdeih **móuh** hólàhng gám yéung jouh lohk-heui.
we not-have chance this way do continue
'We can't possibly go on like this.'

móuh léihyàuh, literally 'no reason', is used to show the speaker's incomprehension or incredulity:

Kéuih móuh léihyàuh m̀h tēng ngóh dihnwá.
s/he no reason not listen my phone
'How come he's not answering my calls?'

Léih móuh léihyàuh bīk ngóhdeih sihk léih
you no reason force us inhale your

dī yih-sáu yīn ge! (film)
CL second-hand smoke PRT
'There's no need to force us to breathe your second-hand smoke.'

---

móuh is also used in negative comparisons (9.3.3, 10.2):

Ngóh tìuh mehng móuh léih sāang dāk gam hóu.
I CL fate not-have you born ADV so good
'My fate is not as good as yours.'

Idioms: móuh (ngóh/léih) fán 'I/you have no part to play' (note the tone change: *fahn* 'part, portion' → *fán*):

Gām-máahn yauh **móuh** **ngóh** **fán** la. (TV ad.)
tonight again not-have my part PRT
'There's no place for me here again tonight.'

Kéuih hauh-móuh **yáuh-móuh** **fán** fān
her step-mother have-not-have part divide

sāngā a?
property PRT
'Does her step-mother have a share in the family property?'

móuh sówaih '(I) don't mind' expresses indifference:

Heui Méihgwok waahkjé heui Yīnggwok dōu
go America or go Britain all

móuh sówaih.
not-have mind
'I don't mind whether we go to America or Britain.'

Kéuih sihk mātyéh dōu móuh sówaih ge.
s/he eat what all not-have mind PRT
'He doesn't mind what he eats.'

15.5 PRESENTATIVE SENTENCES

Because subjects/topics are normally definite (4.2.5), indefinite noun phrases must be introduced by *yáuh* in order to appear as subjects:

Yáuh dī yàhn m̀h séung jáu.
have some people not want leave
'Some people don't want to leave.'

Yáuh dī yéh m̀h góng dāk ge.
have some thing not can say PRT
'Some things cannot be mentioned.'

A locative phrase (7.1) may precede *yáuh*:

Léuihmihn yáuh hóu dō yàhn dáng-gán léih.
inside have very many people wait-PROG you
'Inside there are a lot of people waiting for you.'

Hēunggóng déi yáuh yàhn móuh ūk jyuh, yáuh
Hongkong land have people no house live have

ūk móuh yàhn jyuh.
house no person live
'In Hongkong there are people without a house to live in, and houses without anyone living in them.'

This construction is naturally used to begin a story or fairy-tale:

Chùhngchìhn yáuh go hóu daaih ge sāmlàhm . . .
from-before have CL very big LP forest
'Once upon a time, there was a big forest . . .'

Hóu loih jīchìhn, yáuh go hóu leng ge gūngjyú
very long before have CL very pretty LP princess

jyuh hái gúbóu douh . . .
live in castle there
'Long, long ago, there was a beautiful princess who lived in a castle . . .'

Other presentative sentences resemble existential sentences in structure and function, but lack the distinctive existential verb *yáuh*/*móuh*. Instead, another verb is used to introduce an indefinite noun phrase about which more is said in the following clause:

Ngóh gām-yaht gin dóu tou sāam géi leng ge.
I today see V-PRT CL clothes quite nice PRT
'I saw a suit which was quite nice today.'

Note that this type of sentence corresponds functionally to a non-restrictive relative clause in English.

16 COORDINATION AND SUBORDINATE CLAUSES

16.1 COORDINATION

Cantonese uses a variety of devices for coordination, according to the items to be conjoined. In many cases where English would use *and*, coordination is expressed by juxtaposition without any overt conjunction:

Hóu dōu yàhn làih nīdouh yám-chàh, sihk-faahn.
very many people come here drink-tea eat-food
'Lots of people come here for dim sum and meals.'

The serial verb construction (8.3) is a case of juxtaposition without any overt indication of coordination or subordination. Where conjunction is explicit, a variety of connecting words are used according to the items to be joined.

16.1.1 COORDINATION OF WORDS AND PHRASES

tùhng 'with' is used to coordinate noun phrases:

Ngóh tùhng kéuih heui-jó Wohngkok hàahng-gūngsī.
I with him go-PFV Mongkok walk-store
'He and I went shopping in Mongkok.'

There is no restriction on the order of the personal pronouns here: *kéuih tùhng ngóh* and *ngóh tùhng kéuih* are equally possible, the difference involving which person the sentence is felt to be about (the sentence **topic** is placed first).

yauh . . . yauh 'both . . . and' is an emphatic conjunction used to coordinate adjectives and verbs:

Dī tàuhfaat yauh yúhn yauh yáuh-daahnsing. (shampoo ad.)
CL hair both soft and have-bounce
'Your hair will be soft and bouncy.'

Yauh pèhng yauh leng. (idiom)
both cheap and nice
'(It's) cheap and cheerful.'

Gaau daaihhohk ge yàhn yīnggōi **yauh** gaau-syū
teach university LP people should both teach-book

yauh sé-syū.
and write-book
'University teachers should both teach and write.'

Ngóh yauh oi kéuih yauh hahn kéuih.
I both love him and hate him
'I both love and hate him.'

16.1.2 LISTS

Lists typically do not require a coordinating conjunction, but are expressed as a sequence of words or phrases separated by a slight pause:

Máaih ūk nē, héimáh yiu béi yanfā seui, leuhtsī
buy house PRT at-least need pay stamp duty lawyer

fai, gīnggéi yúng.
fee agent commission
'To buy a house, you have to pay stamp duty, legal fees and commission, to start with.'

The adverb *dōu* 'all' (14.1.1) is used to sum up a list of two or more topicalized items:

Yanfā seui, leuhtsī fai, gīnggéi yúng **dōu** yiu
stamp duty lawyer fee agent commission all need

béi ge.
pay PRT
'You have to pay stamp duty, legal fees and commission.'

tùhng or *tùhngmàaih* 'and also' may be used, like English *and*, to join the last item to a list:

Ngóh yiu máaih dauhfuh, choi tùhngmàaih láaih.
I need buy tofu vegetable and milk
'I need to buy tofu, vegetables and milk.'

It also allows an item to be added by way of afterthought:

Gódouh dī yéh leng dī . . . tùhngmàaih hóyíh
there CL stuff nice some . . . what's-more can

yahm léih gáan géiloih ge.
up-to you choose how-long PRT
'They have nicer things there . . . and you can choose as long as you like.'

A sentence particle such as *a* or *lā* may follow any item in a list, typically to fill a pause while the speaker comes up with the next item (see 18.2.1):

A: Léih dím gáai gam mòhng ga?
   you how come so busy PRT
   'How come you're so busy?'

B: Ngóh yiu gói gyún **lā**, sé seun **lā**,
   I need correct paper PRT write letter PRT

   juhng yiu jyú-màaih-faahn tìm.
   still need cook-also-food too
   'Well, I have to grade papers, write letters, and even do the cooking as well.'

16.1.3 COORDINATION OF CLAUSES

For connecting whole phrases or clauses, a number of adverbials or conjunctions are used:

juhngyáuh or *juhngyiu* 'also' adds an item which is felt to be important or to have been missed out:

A: Yiu chéng bíujé lā, fèihlóu lā . . .
   need invite cousin PRT fatty PRT
   'We should invite your cousin, fatty . . .'

B: Juhngyáuh kéuih léuih-pàhngyáuh wo.
   still-have his girl-friend PRT
   'And his girlfriend, too.'

Ngóh yiu jyú-faahn, juhngyiu sái màaih wún.
I need cook-food also-need wash also dish
'I have to do the cooking, and the washing-up too.'

gānjyuh 'next' and *yìhnhauh* 'afterwards' coordinate a sequence of events:

Ngóhdeih sīn sihk-faahn, gānjyuh heui tái hei.
we first eat-food following go see film
'We'll have dinner first, then go and see the film.'

jauh 'then, therefore' is a general-purpose conjunction which follows the subject of the second clause. It performs a variety of functions:

(a) temporal sequence:

Ngóhdeih háau yùhn síh **jauh** heui wáan.
we take finish exam then go play
'When we've finished exams we're going to have some fun.'

(b) consequence: *jauh* introducing the second of two clauses indicates that the content of the second clause follows from that of the first:

Ngóh **jauh** kyut-dihng m̀h tùhng kéuih hahpjok.
I therefore decide not with him collaborate
'So I decided not to collaborate with him.'

Léih wah dím, **jauh** dím lā. (see 6.4.3)
you say how then how PRT
'Whatever you say.'

(c) conditional, as in the consequent clause of conditional sentences (16.3).

sóyíh also introduces consequence clauses, meaning 'so' or 'therefore':

Dī chē hōi dāk hóu faai, sóyíh yiu síusām dī.
CL car drive ADV very fast therefore need careful bit
'The cars are going very fast, so you need to be careful.'

A: Kéuihdeih léuhng-gūngpó sèhngyaht m̀h hái
they two-couple always not at

ūkkéi ga.
home PRT
'Those two (that couple) are never at home.'

B: **Sóyíh** dī sailouhjái móuh yàhn léih lō.
so CL children not-have person care PRT
'That's why no one cares for their children.'

sóyíh is also used as a double conjunction with *yānwaih* 'because' (16.2.2).

daahnhaih and *bātgwo* introduce 'but' clauses, usually together with *sēuiyìhn* 'although' (16.2.4):

Ngóh mhaih mséung bōng-sáu, bātgwo, dōu haih
I not-be not-want help-hand but also is

léih jouh jeui hóu.
you do most good
'It's not that I don't want to help, but it's really best for you to do it.'

fáanyìh 'however, on the other hand' also conveys a contrast between two clauses, but occurs, like *jauh*, in the second position of the second clause, following the subject:

Sahpsāam nī go soumuhk-jih deui gwáilóu làih
thirteen this CL number to foreigner come

góng haih bāt chèuhng, Jūnggwok-yàhn **fáanyìh**
say is not lucky Chinese-person however

gokdāk haih hóu yitàuh.
feel is good luck
'Thirteen is an unlucky number for foreigners, to the Chinese, however, it's a lucky one.' (see 21.1.4)

gitgwó 'as a result' or 'as it turned out' is a connective used to join clauses:

Ngóh búnlòih lám-jyuh heui Yīnggwok, gitgwó
I originally think-CONT go England result

móuh heui dou.
not-have go arrive
'I was planning to go to England, but as it turned out I didn't get there.'

16.1.4 DISJUNCTION: 'EITHER' . . . 'OR'

Disjunction (coordination with *or*) is expressed by *waahkjé* or *yāthaih*, which are repeated to express the meaning 'either . . . or':

Ngóhdeih waahkjé yìhmàhn waahkjé làuh háisyu.
we perhaps emigrate perhaps stay here
'We may emigrate or stay here.'

Ngóhdeih yāthaih yìhmàhn yāthaih làuh háisyu.
we either emigrate or stay here
'We will either emigrate or stay here.'

The two sentences differ in that *waahkjé* is less certain and *yāthaih* more decisive. Consequently, *yāthaih* . . . *yāthaih* is appropriate in an ultimatum:

Léih yāthaih jīkhāak béi jōu yāthaih būn jáu.
you either at-once pay rent or move leave
'Either pay the rent right now or move out.'

Note that the words *waahkjé* and *yāthaih* are not used in alternative ('A or B?') questions, which are expressed by *dihng* and *yīkwaahk* (17.2).

To express the disjunction 'neither . . . nor', *yauh . . . yauh* (16.1.1) may be used with negated verbs or adjectives:

Kéuih yauh m̀h sái tàuh yauh m̀h chūnglèuhng.
s/he both not wash hair and not shower
'He won't wash his hair or take a shower.'

Dī sailouhjái yauh m̀h duhk-syū yauh m̀h jouh-yéh.
CL children both not study-book and not do-thing
'Those kids neither study nor work.'

16.2 SUBORDINATE CLAUSES

Subordinate clauses behave very differently in Cantonese from the way they do in European languages. In general, the differences involve the use of parataxis (juxtaposition of two clauses) rather than hypotaxis or subordination. That is, the two clauses are more symmetrical than main and subordinate clauses in English. The following characteristics are notable:

(a) Many subordinate clause constructions consist of two clauses each beginning with a conjunction. The following pairs or **double conjunctions** normally go together:

yāt . . . jauh 'as soon as . . . then' (16.2.1)
yānwaih . . . sóyíh 'because . . . therefore' (16.2.2)
sēuiyìhn . . . daahnhaih 'although . . . nevertheless' (16.2.4)
yùhgwó . . . jauh 'if . . . then' (16.3)

(b) Certain subordinate clauses have a conjunction at both the beginning and the end of the clause:

Chèuihjó nī yeuhng **jī-ngoih**, juhngyáuh mātyéh mahntàih a?
apart from this CL outside also-have what problem PRT
'Other than this, what problems are there?'

Dōng ngóhdeih jouh hohksāang **gójahnsí**, sáu-tàih dihnwá
while we do students that-time hand-carry phone

juhng meih làuhhàhng.
still not popular
'While we were students, mobile phones were not popular yet.'

(c) Subordinate clauses, like sentence adverbs (10.3), may follow the subject/topic:

Léih Táai yānwaih taai guih sóyíh móuh làih.
Lee Mrs because too tired so did-not come
'Mrs Lee didn't come because she was too tired.'

Subordinate clauses of purpose, reason and time all occur before the main verb they modify. Tai (1985) has observed that this ordering of clauses iconically reflects the temporal sequence of events and the logical sequence of cause and effect. In English, by comparison, this tendency is much weaker as the reverse order of clauses readily occurs.

(d) Several of the conjunctions can follow the clause as well as preceding it, especially as an 'afterthought':

Ngóh m̀h sihk-faahn la. Móuh sìhgaan a, yānwaih.
I not eat-food PRT no time PRT because
'I'm not eating. There's no time, that's why.'

Taai gwai la.   Hóu leng wo,   daahnhaih.
too dear PRT very nice PRT however
'It's too expensive. Very nice, though.'

Ngóh séung heui ngoihgwok duhk-syū.   Móuh chín
I   want go   abroad   study-book no   money

jē,   bātgwo.
PRT though
'I want to go abroad to study. But I don't have any money.'

(e) It is not possible to have a forward-referring pronoun within such a
clause. Instead, the name or noun phrase comes first as the sentence topic:

Léih Táai yānwaih m̀h séung taai guih, sóyíh
Lee Mrs because not want too tired so

yāt-jóu   fan-jó.
way-early sleep-PFV
'Because **she** didn't want to be too tired, Mrs Lee went to bed early.'

16.2.1 TIME CLAUSES

Time clauses are subordinate clauses which specify the time to which the
following main clause refers. The temporal conjunctions *gójahnsí* 'when',
jīchìhn 'before' and *jīhauh* 'after' come at the *end* of the time clause:

Ngóh jyuh Gáulùhng **gójahnsí**, Gáulùhng Sìhng Jaaih
I   live Kowloon that-time   Kowloon City village

juhng meih   chaak   ge.
still not-yet demolish PRT
'When I lived in Kowloon, the Walled City hadn't yet been demolished.'

gójahn or *góján* (with change of tone) is a short form of *gójahnsí*:

Ngóh tùhng léih yātchàih gójahn, dōu hóu
I   with you together that-time also very

hōisām gé. (film)
happy PRT
'I was happy while I was with you.'

An alternative is *ge sìhhauh*, based on the Mandarin construction *de
shíhòu*:

Ngóh sai go ge sìhhauh, sèhngyaht gám yéung wáan ge.
I   little CL that time always   this way play PRT
'When I was a little girl, I used to play like this.'

dáng 'until' may be used together with *gójahnsí* or *ge sìhhauh*, meaning 'by the time':

Dáng léih fāan dou làih **gójahnsí** dī sung
until you back V-PRT come that-time CL food

yíhgīng dung saai la.
already cold all PRT
'By the time you get back the food will all be cold.'

dōng 'when, while' is also matched by *gójahnsí* or *ge sìhhauh* at the end of the clause:

(Dōng) ngóh duhk daaih-hohk gójahnsí, juhng meih
while I study university that-time still not-yet

yáuh dihnlóuh ge.
have computer PRT
'When I was at university, we didn't have computers.'

(Dōng) yàhndeih kīng-gái ge sìhhauh, léih mhóu
while people chit-chat LP time you don't

tāu-tēng wo.
steal-listen PRT
'While people are chatting, don't eavesdrop.'

dōng is optional here, being used largely in writing and formal speech.
jīchìhn 'before' and *jīhauh* 'after' come at the end of the subordinate clause:

Léih gei-jyuh heui Méihgwok **jīchìhn** yiu ló
you remember go America before need take

dihng chīmjing.
ready visa
'Remember to get a visa in advance before going to America.'

Kéuih héi-sān **jīhauh** jauh tái boují.
s/he get-up after then read newspaper
'He reads the newspaper after getting up.'

With *jīchìhn* 'before', the negative *meih* may be used expletively in the subordinate clause:

Ngóh meih heui Méihgwok jīchìhn juhng lám-jyuh
I not-yet go America before still intend

jouh yīsāng ge.
work doctor PRT
'Before I went to America I was intending to be a doctor.'

The phrase *yùhn (jó) jīhauh* 'afterwards' serves as an adverbial phrase:

Ngóhdeih tēng **yùhn** yíngóng **jīhauh** heui sihk-faahn.
we listen finish talk after go eat-food
'After the talk we'll go and eat.'

gam loih 'so long' is used as a conjunction indicating a length of time, corresponding to *since*:

Ngóh gaau-jó gam loih syū, dōu meih gin-gwo
I teach-PFV so long book still not-yet see-EXP

gam láahn ge hohksāang.
so lazy LP student
'I've never seen such a lazy student since I've been teaching.'

Note that *gam loih* need not refer to a particularly long period of time as the gloss 'so long' implies. For example, after a few weeks in Hongkong a new arrival might be asked:

Léih làih-jó Hēunggóng gam loih, gwaan-mgwaan
you come-PFV Hongkong so long used-not-used

douh-douh dōu gam dō yàhn a?
to place-place all so many people PRT
'Have you got used to so many people everywhere since you came to Hongkong?'

jihchùhng 'since' is a formal conjunction, matched by *jīhauh* at the end of the clause:

Jihchùhng ngóh būn-jó làih nīdouh jīhauh, meih
since I move-PFV come here after not-yet

fāan-gwo heui gauh ūk.
return-EXP go old home
'Ever since I moved here, I've never been back to my old home.'

Note: the time relationships expressed by *before* and *after* in English are often expressed by serial verb constructions (8.3), without any subordinating conjunction. In such serial constructions, the sequence of events may be made explicit by an adverb such as *sīn (ji)* 'first' (10.3.3):

Ngóh yiu jouh màaih dī yéh sīn jáu dāk.
I need do V-PRT CL work first leave able
'I need to do some work before I can leave.'

Similarly, the verbal particle *yùhn* 'finish' (11.3.2) is often used in preference to the conjunction *jīhauh* 'after':

Dī tùhngsih gaau-yùhn-syū jauh heui yám-yéh.
CL colleague teach-finish-book then go drink-things
'My colleagues go for a drink after teaching.'

The combination *yāt* . . . *jauh* 'once . . . then' means 'as soon as' or 'whenever . . . ':

Ngóh yāt   yáuh sīusīk jauh tūngjī   léih.
I   once have news   then inform you
'As soon as I have any news, I'll inform you.'

Kéuih yāt   mhōisām jauh   m̀h   chēut-sēng.
s/he   once unhappy   then   not out-voice
'Whenever she's unhappy, she doesn't speak.'

Kéuih yāt   yám-jáu   jauh sèhng faai mihn hùhng saai.
s/he   once drink-wine then whole CL face red   all
'Whenever he drinks, his whole face goes red.'

The combination *nītàuh* . . . *gótàuh*, literally 'this end . . . that end', also juxtaposes two near-simultaneous events:

Kéuih nītàuh wah yiu   git-fān gótàuh yauh wah
s/he   here   say want marry   there   again say

yiu   lèih-fān.
want divorce
'No sooner has she said that she wants to get married than she says she wants a divorce.'

Ngóh nītàuh hōi-yùhn-wúi,   gótàuh yauh yiu   hōi   hah
I   here   open-finish-meet there   again need open next

go   wúi.
CL   meeting
'No sooner have I finished a meeting than I need to go to another meeting.'

yāt louh . . . *yāt louh* or *yāt bihn* . . . *yāt bihn* marks two simultaneous activities:

Yáuh dī   yàhn yāt louh jā-chē   yāt louh góng dihnwá.
have CL   people one time drive-car one time talk phone
'Some people drive while talking on the phone.'

Note that neither clause is subordinate to the other, unlike the English, where *while* begins a subordinate clause: the parallelism of the clauses matches the simultaneous actions.

16.2.2 REASON CLAUSES

In sentences expressing reason, the 'because' clause normally comes first, followed by the main clause containing *jauh* or *sóyíh* 'so'.

yānwaih 'because' is matched by *sóyíh* 'so, therefore' in the following clause:

Yānwaih gón sìhgaan, sóyíh ngóh wúih jeuhn faai
because rush time so I will most fast

góng yùhn.
speak finish
'Since time is short, I'll finish speaking as soon as possible.'

More rarely, the 'because' clause may follow the main clause, especially with an emphatic *haih* linking the two clauses:

Ngóh gam faai góng yùhn **haih** yānwaih gón sìhgaan.
I so fast speak finish is because rush time
'I finished speaking so quickly because time is short.'

Note that *yānwaih* is often used together with a noun denoting reason such as *yùhnyān*:

Ngóh kyutdihng yìhmàhn ge **yùhnyān** haih **yānwaih**
I decide emigrate LP reason is because

séung dī jái-léui duhk-syū duhk dāk hōisām dī.
wish CL son-daughter study-book study ADV happy bit
'The reason I decided to emigrate is that I want my children to be happier at school.'

geiyìhn 'since' is a formal conjunction:

Geiyìhn léihdeih yíhgīng kyutdihng-jó, ngóh mòuhwaih
since you-PL already decide-PFV I no-point

dō góng.
more say
'Since you've already decided, there's no point in my saying more.'

jauh may be used in a clause expressing a consequence or result, whether or not the first clause is explicitly causal. It comes second in the consequent clause:

Tīng jīu yáuh tòhng, ngóh jauh yiu
tomorrow morning have class I thus need

beih-fo.
prepare-lesson
'I have a class tomorrow morning, so I have to prepare.'

maih is an unstressed particle (often reduced to *mah*) with a similar function to *jauh*, meaning 'as a result' or 'then':

A: Ngóh hah go yuht jauh fong-ga la.
   I next CL month then take-leave PRT
   'I'll be on leave next month.'

B: Gám léih maih hōisām lō!
   so you then happy PRT
   'Well, good for you!'

maih has a special affinity with the particle *lō* (18.3.3), as in the above example.

16.2.3 PURPOSE CLAUSES

waihjó is used to introduce a purpose clause:

Yáuh yàhn waihjó jaahn chín mātyéh dōu
have people in-order earn money what all

háng jouh.
willing do
'Some people will do anything to earn money.'

Note that the purpose clause comes between the subject and the verb, rather than after the main verb as in English. This is consistent with the general pattern of cause before effect, the Chinese order reflecting this logical relationship. As with *yānwàih* (16.2.2), the order may be reversed with *haih* linking the two clauses:

Kéuih ga béi léih **haih** waihjó jyuh dāk
she marry to you is in-order live ADV

syūfuhk dī.
comfortable a-bit
'She married you in order to live more comfortably.'

làih is used as the complement to an object, typically following the verb *yuhng* in a serial construction (8.3):

Léih **yuhng** bá leih dī ge dōu **làih** **chit**
you use CL sharp a-bit LP knife come cut

daahn-gōu lā.
egg-cake PRT
'Use a sharper knife to cut the cake.'

yiu làih describes the purpose of something:

Nī dī haih **yiu** **làih** **jouh** **māt** ga?
this CL is want come do what PRT
'What are these for?'

16.2.4 CONCESSIVE CLAUSES: 'ALTHOUGH'

Concessive clauses are subordinate clauses with a meaning of 'although
. . . ' where the first clause admits or concedes a fact which the following
main clause counteracts or contradicts. In Cantonese, the subsequent main
clause must contain a balancing expression meaning 'still' or 'nevertheless'.
Thus *sēuiyìhn* 'although' in the subordinate clause is matched in the main
clause by either *daahnhaih* 'nevertheless' or *dōu* 'still':

Ngóh **sēuiyìhn** m̀h tùhngyi kéuih góng ge yéh,
I although not agree s/he speak LP things

daahnhaih juhng hóu jyūnjuhng kéuih.
however still much respect him
'Although I disagree with what he says, I still respect him.'

Sēuiyìhn mhaih hóu daaih gihn sih, léih **dōu** m̀h
although not-be very big CL matter you still not

yīnggōi mùhn-jyuh ngóh.
should hide-CONT me
'Although it's only a small matter, you still ought not to conceal it from
me.'

Note that *sēuiyìhn*, like *yānwaih*, may come after the subject of the clause.
    mòuhleuhn . . . '(no matter) whether . . . ' forms a concessive sentence
together with a question structure, which may be an A-not-A question
(17.1.2), an alternative question (17.2) or a wh-question (17.3):

Mòuhleuhn sān dihng gauh ge, ngóhdeih mātyéh
no-matter new or old PRT we what

sāam dōu yiu.
clothing all want
'We want all kinds of clothes, (whether) new or old.'

Mòuhleuhn bīngo dá làih, ngóh dōu m̀h tēng.
no-matter who call come I still not listen
'No matter who calls, I won't answer.'

The adverb *dōu* is again required to match *mòuhleuhn*.
    m̀h léih 'no matter' is an alternative to *mòuhleuhn*:

M̀h léih léih jūng-m̀h-jūngyi, dōu yiu gāau seui.
not care you like-not-like still need pay tax
'Whether you like it or not, you still have to pay tax.'

In addition, a wh-question word in the first clause followed by *dōu* in the
second produces a concessive sense. These 'whatever' constructions can be
formed with any question word (17.3) and the quantifier *dōu*:

Kéuih góng **mātyéh** dōu mgányiu ge. (film)
s/he say what all not-important PRT
'Whatever he says it doesn't matter.'

Léih **dím yéung** jouh dōu dāk.
you how(ever) do also OK
'However you do it is OK.'

Idioms: an implicitly concessive construction is *gam* [adjective] *dōu*
[verb]:

Gam gwai léih dōu máaih àh?
so dear you still buy PRT
'You're still buying it at that price?' (even though it's so expensive)

mìhng jī is a concessive phrase implying that someone who ought to
know better nevertheless persists in an ill-advised activity. This
persistence may be emphasized by *jiu* in the main clause:

Kéuih mìhng jī móuh yuhng dōu jiu góng.
s/he clear know no use still carry-on speak
'He goes on talking even though he knows it's no use.'

Dī yàhn mìhng jī yáuh sāyú juhng gau
CL people clear know have shark still enough

dáam heui yàuh-séui.
dare go swimming
'People still dare go swimming when they know there are sharks.'

16.3 CONDITIONAL SENTENCES

Like many sentence types, conditional statements may be expressed either
explicitly (using a conjunction such as *yùhgwó* 'if': 16.3.1) or implicitly, by
juxtaposition of clauses (16.3.2):

Yùhgwó yáuh sìhgaan jauh hóyíh heui tái-háh.
if have time than can go look-DEL
'If there's time we can go and take a look.'

Hēunggóng yáuh chín mātyéh dōu máaih dóu.
Hongkong have money what all buy V-PRT
'In Hongkong you can buy anything if you have money.'

It has often been noted that Chinese, lacking distinctions of tense, makes
no formal distinction between real, hypothetical and counterfactual conditionals. However, too much has been made of the alleged paucity of

Chinese in this regard.[1] Much as Chinese compensates for the lack of tense with aspect and adverbs (10.3.3, 11.1), there are ways of expressing all kinds of conditionals.

16.3.1 EXPLICIT CONDITIONALS

Like the conjunctions discussed in section 16.2, *yùhgwó* 'if' is generally matched by a second conjunction, in this case *jauh* 'then', in the consequent clause:

Yùhgwó léih   dākhàahn, ngóhdeih (jauh) yeuk màaih
if   you   free   we   (then) fix   together

dá-bō   ā.
hit-ball PRT
'If you're free we can arrange a game (of tennis, etc.).'

Yùhgwó léih yáuh hingcheui, ngóh jauh bōng léih sānchíng.
if   you   have   interest   I   then help you   apply
'I'll apply for you if you're interested.'

Note:

(a) The *if*-clause comes first, the reverse order being a common alternative in English but not usual in Cantonese, unless the *if*-clause is added as an afterthought. This word order preserves the logical sequence of cause and effect, as in the case of reason clauses (16.2.2).
(b) There is no systematic distinction between open, hypothetical and counterfactual conditionals as there is in European languages. Usually only the context makes this clear, although some of the conjunctions given below are explicitly hypothetical.

yùhgwó . . . ge wá: in formal speech (as in written Chinese) the phrase *ge wá* may be added at the end of the *if*-clause, making a double conjunction like those illustrated in 16.2 (a):

Yùhgwó léih yáuh loihsing **ge wá**, jauh hóyíh
if   you   have   patience   LP say   then can

dáng lohk-heui.
wait   continue
'If you have the patience, you can go on waiting.'

Yùhgwó ngóh m̀h   jīdou **ge wá**, jauh m̀h   gám
if   I   not-yet know   LP say   then not   dare

daaih-sēng góng lā.
big-voice   say   PRT
'If I hadn't known, I wouldn't have said it so loud.'

This phrase may be compared to English *say . . .* meaning 'suppose . . .'
although the Cantonese expression is more formal. The topic particle *lē*
(18.2.1) may follow the 'if'-clause:

Yùhgwó	léih	séung	tàuhjī	ge	wá	**lē,**	jeui	hóu	jauh
if	you	wish	invest	LP	say	PRT	most	good	then

haih	máaih	làahm-chàuh	gú.
is	buy	blue-chip	stock

'If you want to invest, the best way is to buy blue-chip stocks.'

gáyùh 'suppose . . . ' is an explicitly hypothetical conjunction used in
formal speech:

Gáyùh	léih	haih	ngóh,	léih	wúih	dím	jouh a?
suppose	you	are	me	you	would	how	do PRT

'Suppose you were in my position, what would you do?'

Gáyùh	yáuh	gám	ge	chìhngyìhng,	léih	yiu	jīkhāak
suppose	have	such	LP	situation	you	need	at-once

yahp	yīyún.
enter	hospital

'If such a situation should arise, you should go into hospital at once.'

jauhsyun 'even if . . .' is a stronger conjunction, forming conditionals with
a concessive sense. Like other concessive sentences (16.2.4), it is followed
in the consequent clause by *dōu* before the verb:

Jauhsyun	léih	béi	hóu	dō	chín,	kéuih	**dōu**
even	you	give	very	much	money	he	still

m̀h	wúih	jouh.
not	will	do

'Even if you pay him a lot of money he still won't do it.'

Jauhsyun	léih	sāamsahp	seui	meih	git-fān,	**dōu**
even	you	thirty	years	not-yet	marry	still

msái	gēng.
no-need	fear

'Even if you're not married at thirty, you don't have to worry.'

Aspect in conditionals

In the second (consequent) clause, the perfective aspect *jó* may be used to
indicate a hypothetical resultant state, corresponding to *would have* in an
English conditional:

Yùhgwó móuh   ngóh, léih yíhgīng séi-jó   hóu
if   not-have me   you   already die-PFV very

loih   la! (film)
long   PRT
'If it wasn't for me, you would have been dead long ago!'

Yùhgwó jóu   sahp lìhn   sīk   léih, ngóh jauh
if   early   ten   years know you   I   then

yāt jóu   chī-jó-sin.
long-ago   crazy-PFV
'If I'd known you ten years earlier, I would have gone mad long ago.'

Idioms: *yùhgwó béi ngóh* [verb] is a phrase used to introduce hypothetical conditionals, meaning 'if I were you/him', etc:

Yùhgwó béi   ngóh gáan,   ngóh wúih   gáan   chìh
if   give   me   choose I   would choose late

sahp lìhn   chēut-sai.
ten   years be-born
'Given the choice, I'd definitely choose to be born ten years later.'

Yùhgwó béi   ngóh jouh lóuhbáan, saht   m̀h   wúih
if   give   me   do   boss   sure   not   will

chéng kéuih.
invite him
'If I were the boss, I certainly wouldn't give him a job.'

Note also *yùhgwó haih gám* 'if that's the way it is':

Yùhgwó haih gám, ngóhdeih jauh yāt   dī   hēimohng
if   is   so   we   then one   bit   hope

dōu móuh   la.
also not-have PRT
'If that's the way it is, we don't have any chance at all.'

16.3.2 IMPLICIT CONDITIONALS

In implicitly conditional sentences, two juxtaposed clauses may be interpreted as a conditional sentence, without any overt indication of the
connection:

Léih yáuh líu, tūngjī ngóh. (film)
you have material inform me
'Let me know if you have any information.'

Jūk dóu dōu m̀h béi chín ge laak. (conv.)
catch V-PRT also not pay money PRT PRT
'Even if I'm caught I won't pay.'

Such implicit conditionals are readily formed where the first clause is negative:

Ngóh m̀h fēi gwo heui, ngóh go sām m̀h
I not fly over go my CL heart not

ōnlohk ge. (film)
at-ease PRT
'If I don't fly over there, I won't feel at ease.'

Léih m̀h séung làih dōu yiu làih ge la. (conv.)
you not want come also must come PRT PRT
'You have to come even if you don't want to.'

An implicit conditional may be of any kind: real, hypothetical or counter-factual. In implicit counterfactual conditionals, the past time reference may be established by adverbs such as *búnlòih* 'originally' together with a modal verb (12.1):

Kéuih **búnlòih hóyíh** jouh yīsāng ge.
s/he originally can work doctor PRT
'He could have been a doctor.'

Idiom: *jóu jī* 'if I had known' (literally 'early know') is a case of an implicit conditional with counterfactual meaning:

Jóu jī daai màaih léih heui lā. (conv.)
early know take along you go PRT
'If I'd known I'd have taken you along.'

---

peiyùh 'for example' may also introduce a hypothetical situation:

Peiyùh, léih móuh saai chín wúih dím lē?
example you not-have V-PRT money would how PRT
'Imagine, what would you do if you ran out of money?'

sīn, *sīnji* or *ji* 'only' (see also 10.3.3) are used in the consequent clause of an implicit conditional to give the specific meaning 'only if':

Ngóh   je   dóu   chín   sīnji hóyíh máaih láu.
I   borrow   V-PRT   money   only   can   buy   flat
'I can only buy a flat if I succeed in borrowing money.'

Léih daai ngóh heui jeui leng   gó   gāan
you take me   go   most beautiful   that CL

ngóh ji   tùhng léih heui!
I   only with you   go
'I'll only go with you if you take me to the nicest [restaurant].'

The conditional meaning here must be inferred from the context, since
clauses with *sīn/sīnji/ji* may also have a temporal, causal or other meaning
(10.3.3):

Kéuih fāan   làih   ngóh sīnji tùhng kéuih góng.
s/he   return come   I   only   with him   talk
'I won't talk to him until he comes back.'

Kéuih haih yānwaih mhóuyisi   sīnji móuh   làih.
s/he   is   because embarrassed only   not-have come
'He hasn't come just because he's embarrassed.'

16.3.3 NEGATIVE CONDITIONALS: 'IF NOT', 'UNLESS'

yùhgwó mhaih 'if not, otherwise' is used to elaborate on a previous
statement:

Léih yiu faai dī, yùhgwó mhaih, gón   m̀h dóu
you need fast-ish if   not   hurry not V-PRT

daap fóchē.
catch train
'You should hurry up, otherwise, you won't catch the train.'

In the second clause of a sentence, *mhaih* alone is sufficient:

Léih faai dī   jāp yéh,   mhaih jauh chìh dou
you fast a-bit pack things if-not then late arrive

ga   la.
PRT PRT
'Hurry up and pack, or you'll be late.'

Gánghaih sīk-jó   sān ge léuih-pàhngyáuh lā, **mhaih**
of-course know-PFV   new LP girlfriend   PRT if-not

dím wúih gam hōisām a?
how would so happy PRT
'He's obviously found a new girlfriend, otherwise why would he be so
happy?'

chèuihfēi 'unless' is typically matched by *yùhgwó mhaih* in the following clause:

Chèuihfēi yáuh mahntàih, yùhgwó mhaih jauh hóyíh jáu
unless have problem if not-be then can go

ga la.
PRT PRT
'Unless there's a problem, we can go.'

16.4 CLEFT SENTENCES AND EMPHASIS

The copula *haih* (8.1.1) is used to emphasize the following word, much like the English cleft construction with *it's . . . that . . .* :

Ngóh **haih** duhk Yīngmán **ge**.
I am study English PRT
'It's English I study.'

Nī dī fā **haih** ngóh máaih làih sung béi
these CL flower are I buy come give to

léih **ge**.
you PRT
'These are some flowers I bought for you.'

haih . . . sīn . . . ge further emphasizes the word by following it with the adverb *sīn* 'only':

Haih léih sīn wúih lám dóu ge jēk!
is you only would think up PRT PRT
'Only you would think of that!'

The cleft construction is commonly used for contrast:

Haih léih lám chēut làih ga, **mhaih ngóh**.
be you think out come PRT not-be me
'It was you that thought of it, not me.'

A formal equivalent of this construction is *sih . . . dīk*, with the Mandarin words *sih* for *haih* and *dīk* for *ge*:

Guhaak wíhngyúhn sih deui dīk.
customer forever is right PRT
'The customer is always right.'

16.5 INDIRECT SPEECH

The syntax of indirect speech is relatively straightforward, as is that of indirect questions (17.4) and indirect commands (19.5). There is no conjunction corresponding to English *that*, and a sentence of reported speech simply follows the reporting verb:

Síu   Yìuh   wah   m̀h   séung   làih   wóh.
little Yiu   say   not   want   come   PRT
'Yiu says she doesn't want to come.'

Note that a subject pronoun need not be used in the reported clause, as the subject of the main verb can function as its subject.

To introduce reported speech, serial verb constructions (8.3) are widely used. Typical formulae are *wah/góng béi . . . tēng* or *wah . . . jī* 'tell':

A-Lìhng   **góng béi ngóh teng**   jauhlàih   git-fān.
Ah Ling   say to me   hear   soon   marry
'Ah Ling told me she was getting married soon.'

Ngóh   **wah kéuih jī**   m̀h   séung   gám   yéung
I   say him   know   not   wish   so   way

jouh   lohk-heui.
work   continue
'I told him I didn't want to go on working like this.'

Idiom: *wah jī* [pronoun] means to ignore somebody or something or simply means 'couldn't care less':

Ngóh   **wah jī**   kéuih   lā,   m̀h   gwāan   ngóh   sih.
I   say know   him   PRT   not   relate me   matter
'I'm not taking any notice of him, it's nothing to do with me.'

Ngóh   **wah jī**   léih   dím   lám   dōu   hóu,
I   say know   you   how   think also good

ngóh   yātdihng   yiu   yìhmàhn.   (film)
I   certainly must   emigrate
'I couldn't care less what you think, I will certainly emigrate.'

Note that the third person pronoun *kéuih* in this expression can be pleonastic, i.e. not referring to any particular person or thing (see 5.1 for other uses of pleonastic pronouns). This phrase should be distinguished from *wah* (*léih/kéuih*) *jī* meaning 'tell'.

---

góng . . . wah 'talk . . . say' is a serial verb construction in which the second verb *wah* appears redundant:

Kéuih tùhng ngóh góng wah hóu sānfú wóh.
s/he with me talk say very difficult PRT
'He told me he was having a hard time.'

The sentence particle *wóh* (18.3.4) may be used in indirect statements and questions as an overt indicator of reported speech:

Kéuih wah msái joi dáng wóh.
s/he say no-need again wait PRT
'She said it wasn't necessary to wait any longer.'

Yáuh yàhn mahn ngóhdeih yiu-m̀h-yiu maaih ga chē wóh.
have people ask us want-not-want sell CL car PRT
'Someone's asking if we want to sell the car.'

See 17.4 for further features of indirect questions, and 19.5 for indirect commands.

17 QUESTIONS

Questions are indicated not by changes in word order as in English, but by a number of interrogative constructions and by sentence-final particles (see ch. 18). As will be seen from the examples in the following sections, a particle (typically *a*) is often used together with an interrogative construction.

A distinctive feature of Cantonese is the use of rhetorical questions to imply negation, as in English *Who knows what will happen?* and *Who cares?* In Cantonese, rhetorical questions are especially common with wh-questions (17.3) and in exclamatory questions (17.6).

17.1 YES/NO QUESTIONS

There are several distinct forms of yes/no question, which differ in their range of application and their function. Syntactically, certain constructions call for particular forms of questions, such as *haih-mhaih* (17.1.3) with quantified sentences. Functionally, the various question forms differ in their **presuppositions**: whether they expect a positive or negative answer, or are neutral with respect to the answer.

17.1.1 PARTICLE QUESTIONS

The simplest form of question is formed by simply adding a particle to a declarative sentence. Cantonese, however, has no general-purpose question particle counterpart to Mandarin *ma*. *ma* is used in the greeting *Léih hóu ma?* 'How are you?' but is relatively formal in Cantonese. The question particle *àh* indicating surprise or disapproval (18.3.1) may form a question:

Léih hah go láihbaai fong-ga àh?
you next CL week take-leave PRT
'You're going on leave next week?'

This form of question tends to presuppose a positive answer, being used to check the validity of an assumption.

mē is exclusively an interrogative particle, denoting surprise and used to check the truth of an unexpected state of affairs:

Māt léih m̀h jī ge mē?
what you not know PRT PRT
'You mean you don't know?'

Léih jouh-gwo gam dō chi dōu m̀h sīk ge mē?
you do-EXP so many times still not know PRT PRT
'You still don't know after doing it so many times?'

mē and *àh* are also commonly used in rhetorical questions:

Juhng sái léih góng mē?
still need you say PRT
'As if I need you to tell me.'

Ngóh sái kéuih léih ngóh àh?
I need s/he care me PRT
'As if I needed him to care about me.'

17.1.2 A-NOT-A QUESTIONS

The most neutral form of yes/no question is known as the **A-not-A** question. This form of question is like asking *Is* A *the case or not*? The construction involves repeating (**reduplicating**) the verb or adjective, with the negative marker *m̀h* between:

Léih **sīk-m̀h-sīk** ngóh sailóu a?
you know-not-know my brother PRT
'Do you know my brother?'

Gihn sāam **leng-m̀h-leng** a?
CL dress pretty-not-pretty PRT
'Does the dress look good?'

In the case of verbs of more than one syllable, only the first syllable is repeated:

Léih **jūng-m̀h-jūngyi** jyuh hái Hēunggóng a?
you like-not-like live at Hongkong PRT
'Do you like living in Hongkong?'

Nī go yàhn **chēut-m̀h-chēutméng** ga?
this CL person famous-not-famous PRT
'Is this person well known?'

The answer to an A-not-A question is the verb alone, or with the negative *m̀h* for a negative answer:

Jūngyi/m̀h jūngyi (a).
like/not like (PRT)
'Yes/No.'

Idiom: an A-not-A question followed by *dī* 'a bit' is an ironic or sarcastic form of question:

Chìh-m̀h-chìh dī   a?
late-not-late some PRT
'Don't you think it's a bit late?'

Yāt baak   mān   gwai-m̀h-gwai dī   a?
one hundred dollar dear-not-dear some PRT
'Isn't a hundred dollars a bit much?'

Daaih-m̀h-daaih sāai   dī   a?
big-not-big   waste a-bit PRT
'What a waste!'

17.1.3 COPULAR QUESTIONS: *HAIH-MHAIH*

Any A-not-A question may be expressed more explicitly by using the copular verb *haih* 'be' in A-not-A form, i.e. *haih-mhaih*, preceding the main verb:

Kéuih **haih-mhaih** séung chóh jihk-tūng-chē a?
s/he be-not-be   wish ride through-train PRT
'Does he want to take the through train?'

This form of question is neutral with respect to the expected answer; it may be compared to *Is it true that . . . ?* or French *Est-ce que . . . ?* It is also required in questions with a quantified phrase (see ch. 14) preceding the verb. *haih-mhaih* then comes immediately before the quantified phrase:

Haih-mhaih **yàhn-yàhn dōu** gám lám   ga?
be-not-be   everyone also so   think PRT
'Does everyone think that way?'

Léih haih-mhaih **jek-jek gáu dōu** jūngyi ga?
you be-not-be   CL-CL dog all like   PRT
'Do you like all the dogs?'

Haih-mhaih **douh-douh dōu** yáuh Jūnggwok choi sihk a?
be-not-be   everywhere also have Chinese food eat PRT
'Is there Chinese food to eat everywhere?'

Note that a simple A-not-A question, as illustrated in 17.1.2, would not be possible in these cases (e.g. one cannot ask * *Douh-douh dōu yáuh-móuh Jūnggwok choi sihk a?* meaning 'Is there Chinese food to eat everywhere?').

haih-mhaih typically occurs between subject and verb, as in the above examples, but may also occupy alternative positions:

(a) at the beginning of the sentence:

Haih-mhaih	léih	taaitáai	tùhng	léih	yātchàih	heui	a?
be-not-be	your	wife	with	you	together	go	PRT

'I suppose your wife is going with you?'

This form of question is used to seek confirmation.

(b) as a **question tag** (see 17.1.6):

Léih	yíhgīng	jīdou,	haih-mái?
you	already	know	is that right

'You knew already, didn't you?'

This usage clearly conveys the expectation of a positive answer.

Idiom: *haih-mhaih a?* is a sceptical response to a statement:

A:	Kéuih	sīk	géi-sahp	júng	yúhyìhn	ga.
	s/he	know	some-ten	CL	languages	PRT

'He knows dozens of languages.'

B:	Haih-mhaih	a?
	be-not-be	PRT

'Are you sure?'

The particle *a* may be drawn out to emphasize the speaker's disbelief.

---

hóu-mhóu, the A-not-A form of *hóu* 'good' is used to ask if a course of action is desirable or not (compare the use of *mhóu* 'don't' in negative imperatives: 19.4):

Ngóh	hóu-mhóu	tùhng	kéuih	heui	lē?	(talking to oneself)
I	good-not-good	with	him	go	PRT	

'Should I go with him?'

Léih	wah	hóu-mhóu	béi	go	jái	heui
you	say	good-not-good	let	CL	son	go

Méihgwok	duhk-syū	a?
America	study-book	PRT

'Do you think we should let our son go to study in America?'

If *hóu-mhóu* is used with a quantified phrase as the subject, *hóu-mhóu* must precede the subject (as for *haih-mhaih* above):

Hóu-mhóu   yàhn-yàhn   dōu heui a?
good-not-good person-person   all go   PRT
'Would it be a good idea for everyone to go?'

Hóu-mhóu   go-go   dōu gyūn   síu-síu   chín a?
good-not-good CL-CL all donate little-little money PRT
'How about everybody donating a little cash?'

hóu-mhóu is also used as a tag attached to requests or suggestions (17.1.6).

17.1.4 *MEIH* QUESTIONS

The negative word *meih* 'not yet' (13.3) added to a declarative sentence
forms a question asking whether something has occurred. In the most
typical case, the verb has the perfective aspect marker *jó* or the experiential *gwo*:

Léih sihk-jó-faahn   meih   a?
you eat-PFV-food   not-yet PRT
'Have you eaten yet?' (commonly used as a greeting: see 20.4)

Léih sihk-gwo gāi-jūk   meih   a?
you eat-EXP chicken-congee not-yet PRT
'Have you ever eaten chicken congee?'

Both types translate with the present perfect in English; the distinction
between them involves whether the question concerns the present situation
(*jó*) or past experience (*gwo*; see 11.2.5). Note that *meih* translates as 'yet'
in the case of a perfective and 'ever' in an experiential question: these
adverbs bring out the distinction in English. Similar questions may be
formed with a verbal particle indicating completion or accomplishment
(11.3) in place of *jó/gwo*:

Léih **jyú** **hóu**   faahn meih   a?
you cook V-PRT   food not-yet PRT
'Have you finished cooking?'

Gó bún syū léih **tái** **yùhn** meih   a?
that CL book you read finish not-yet PRT
'Have you finished that book yet?'

Léih **jouh** **saai** yéh   meih   a?
you do   all   work not-yet PRT
'Have you done all your work (yet)?'

meih questions may also be formed with *dāk* (12.3.1) to enquire whether
something can be done, and with modal verbs, referring to the present:

Hàahng dāk meih a?
walk can not-yet PRT
'Are we ready to go?'

Sihk dāk meih a?
eat can not-yet PRT
'Is dinner ready yet?'

Léih go jái sīk hàahng meih a?
your CL son know walk not-yet PRT
'Can your son walk yet?'

Léih hōichí wān-syū meih a?
you begin revise-book not-yet PRT
'Have you started revising yet?'

The positive response to questions of this type is to repeat the predicate, often with an affirmative sentence particle such as *la* added:

A: Lóuhbáan jáu-jó meih?
boss leave-PFV not-yet
'Has the boss left yet?'

B: Jáu-jó la.
leave-PFV PRT
'Yes, she's left.'

A: Léih jouh saai gūngfo meih?
you do all homework not-yet
'Have you finished your homework?'

B: Jouh saai ga la.
do all PRT PRT
'Yes, I have.'

For a negative answer, the reply is to repeat *meih*, which may be accompanied by an adverb or sentence particle:

A: Léih sé-jó seun meih?
you write-PFV letter not-yet
'Have you written the letter?'

B: (Juhng) meih a.
(still) not-yet PRT
'Not yet.'

17.1.5 EXISTENTIAL QUESTIONS: *YÁUH-MÓUH*

yáuh-móuh is basically the A-not-A form of the existential word *yáuh* (15.1), asking whether something exists or not:

Yáuh-móuh   mahntàih a?
have-not-have problem   PRT
'Are there any problems?'

Léih go waih   yáuh-móuh   sih   a?
your CL stomach have-not-have problem PRT
'Is anything wrong with your stomach?'

Note that when verb–object compounds are questioned in this sense, the order of verb and object is reversed:

Léih juhng yáuh-móuh **yéh** **jouh** a? (jouh-yéh 'work')
you still   have-not-have things do   PRT
'Do you have any more work to do?'

Yáuh-móuh   **faahn sihk** ga? (sihk-faahn 'eat')
have-not-have food eat PRT
'Is there anything to eat?'

An important use of *yáuh-móuh* is to question whether something has happened or not, as an alternative to the *meih* type of question (17.1.4):

Yáuh-móuh   gāau gūngfo   a?
have-not-have hand homework PRT
'Have you handed in your homework?'

Idiom: *Yáuh-móuh gáau cho?* is a very common expression of outrage or ridicule. Although literally 'Is there some mistake?', it has become generalized through overuse:

(Léih) yáuh-móuh   gáau cho a?
(you) have-not-have make wrong PRT
'Are you crazy?'

It is often used impersonally, with the subject omitted:

A: Ngóh nī   deui hàaih máaih-jó baat
    I   this pair shoes buy-PFV eight

    baak   māan.
    hundred dollar
    'I bought this pair of shoes for 800 dollars.'
B: Gam gwai, yáuh-móuh   gáau   cho?
    so expensive have-not-have make mistake
    'So expensive, are you out of your mind?'

B's reply could imply either that A is crazy to spend so much money, or that the price itself is outrageous.

Note that the perfective aspect marker *jó* does not occur in this construction as it is incompatible with the negative word *móuh* (see 11.2.4, 13.3). The experiential *gwo*, however, may occur with it:

Léih **yáuh-móuh** **duhk-gwo** mahtléihhohk a?
you have-not-have study-EXP physics PRT
'Have you (ever) studied physics?'

yáuh-móuh dāk [verb], the question form of *yáuh dāk* (12.3.2) is used to ask if something is possible:

Nǵh yuht **yáuh-móuh** **dāk** waaht-syut a?
five month have-not-have can slide-snow PRT
'Is it possible to go skiing in May?'

Léih gú kéuihdeih **yáuh-móuh** **dāk** chóh jihk-tūng-chē
you guess they have-not-have can ride through-train

ā làh?
PRT PRT
'Do you think they'll be able to take the through train?'

17.1.6 TAG QUESTIONS

Tag questions are used, as in English, to turn statements into questions. The usual tag is *haih-mhaih*:

Léih jouh yīsāng ge, haih-mhaih a?
you work doctor PRT right PRT
'You're a doctor, aren't you?'

Naturally, such questions tend to presuppose a positive answer. Note that the Cantonese tag is invariant in form, translating *aren't you?*, *isn't she?*, *don't they?*, etc.

hóu-mhóu (the A-not-A form of *hóu* 'good') is attached as a tag to requests or suggestions, meaning 'okay?':

Ngóhdeih jóu dī jáu, hóu-mhóu a?
we early-ish leave okay PRT?
'Let's leave early, shall we?'

Pronunciation note: these tags are often contracted, resulting in the loss of the second *h* sound:

haih-mhaih → haih-maih/haih-mái 'isn't that so?'
hóu-mhóu → hóu-móu 'okay?'

Note also the optional tone change in the question tag: *mhaih* → *mái*.

---

dāk-mdāk (12.3.1) is used as a tag to elicit consent or approval:

Ngóh tīngyaht wán léih kīng-háh, dāk-mdāk a?
I tomorrow seek you chat-a-while okay-not-okay PRT
'I'll come and talk to you tomorrow, okay?'

17.1.7 INTONATION AND ECHO QUESTIONS

As in English and many languages, a question may be indicated by rising intonation alone. Although the Cantonese tones leave relatively little room for intonation (1.4.3), the end of the sentence may be given a characteristic rising pattern indicating a question:

Léih jānhaih heui?
you really go
'You're really going?'

This intonation pattern primarily affects the last word of the sentence, modifying or exaggerating its basic tone; in the case of a mid level tone as in *heui*, the rise is more pronounced and ends higher than a typical high rising or changed tone.[1]

This type is used especially for **echo** questions, where the questioner is repeating a statement out of surprise or incredulity:

A: Ngóh mgin-jó tìuh sósìh a.
    I lose-PFV CL key PRT
    'I've lost the key.'

B: Mātyéh wá? Léih mgin-jó tìuh sósìh?
    what words you lose-PFV CL key
    'What? You've lost the key?'

A: Ngóh ngāam-ngāam heui-gwo Gānàhdaaih.
    I just-just go-EXP Canada
    'I've just been to Canada.'

B: Léih heui-jó Gānàhdaaih?
    you go-PFV Canada
    'You've been to CANADA?'

A second type of echo question, where the questioner wishes a particular word or phrase to be repeated, ends with the particle *wá* (18.3.1):

Léih ga chē paak hái bīndouh wá?
your CL car park at where PRT
'Where did you say your car was parked?'

A: Ngóh tùhng Wàh-jái tīng   jīu   gáu   dím   hái
   I   with   Wah   tomorrow morning nine   o'clock at

Tīn Sīng Máhtàuh dáng léih.
Star   Ferry   wait you
'Wah and I'll be waiting for you at the Star Ferry tomorrow morning at nine.'

B: Léih tùhng bīngo dáng ngóh **wá**? Hái bīndouh dáng **wá**?
   you   with   who   wait me   say   at   where   wait say
'You'll be waiting with who? Where did you say?'

17.1.8 RESPONSES TO YES/NO QUESTIONS

The normal reply to a yes/no question is to repeat the verb of the question, preceded in a negative answer by the appropriate negative marker (see ch. 13):

A: Heui-m̀h-heui máhtàuh   a?
   go-not-go   ferry-pier PRT
'Are you going to the ferry pier?'

B: Heui a /   M̀h heui la.
   go   PRT /   not go   PRT
'Yes/No.'

A: Yáuh-móuh   sái-wún   a?
   have-not-have wash dish PRT
'Have you washed the dishes?'

B: Yáuh a /   Móuh   a.
   have PRT / not-have PRT
'Yes / No.'

A: Léih gin-gwo   kéuih meih   a?
   you   meet-EXP   her   not-yet PRT
'Have you met her?'

B: Gin-gwo   la /   Meih   a.
   meet-EXP   PRT   not-yet PRT
'Yes / No.'

Note that a negative reply is often accompanied by a sentence particle: a 'no' answer without a particle to moderate it is likely to be perceived as abrupt or too direct. A positive answer may also be modified with an adverb and/or a sentence particle:

A: Go bìhbī chíh-m̀h-chíh lóuhdauh a?
   CL baby   like-not-like father   PRT
'Does the baby look like his father?'

B: Gánghaih chíh lā!
of-course like PRT
'Of course he does!'

In the case of copular questions (17.1.3), the copula alone is an appropriate response:

A: Léih haih-mhaih Méihgwok-yàhn a?
you are-not-are American PRT
'Are you American?'

B: Haih a / Mhaih a.
yes PRT / no PRT
'Yes/No.'

haih (*ak*) as a response may be contracted to *haahk*:

A: Léih guih làh?
you tired PRT
'Tired, are you?'

B: Haahk.
Yes
'Yes.'

Note that *haih* does not correspond straightforwardly to *yes*, however. It is **not** used in answer to an A-not-A question without the copula. Instead, the verb repeated in the question is the answer:

A: Heui-mh-heui hōi-wúi a?
go-not-go hold-meeting PRT
'Are you going to the meeting?'

B: Heui a. (*not* *haih)
go PRT
'Yes (I am).'

Similarly, if a modal verb is used in the question it alone forms the answer:

A: Léih wúih-mh-wúih bōng kéuih a?
you would-not-would help her PRT
'Would you help her?'

B: Wúih.
would
'Yes, I would.'

Note that the affirmative reply to *sái-msái* is its positive counterpart, *yiu* (12.1.3):

A: Sái-msái   ngóhdeih   chīm-méng a?
   need-not-need   we   sign-name   PRT
   'Do we have to sign?'

B: Yiu   a /   msái   la.
   need   PRT /   no need   PRT
   'Yes, we do / No, we don't.'

Idiomatic answers: *móuh cho* is an approving response to a query, typically one expecting a positive answer. It is a double negative (13.5) in which 'no wrong' in effect means 'right':

  A: Léih   haih-mhaih   Máh   Sīnsāang   a?
     you   be-not-be   Ma   Mr   PRT
     'You're Mr Ma, aren't you?'

  B: Móuh   cho,   ngóh   jauh   haih.
     no   wrong   I   then   am
     'Right, that's me!'

dōu mhaih is a qualified negative answer, similar in meaning to 'not really':

  A: Léih   ngāam-ngāam   làih   dou   Hēunggóng   haih-mhaih
     you   just-just   come   arrive   Hongkong   be-not-be

     hóu   mgwaan   a?
     very   not-used   PRT
     'Do you feel strange, having just arrived in Hongkong?'

  B: Dōu   mhaih   ak,   hóu   faai   jaahp-gwaan
     also   is-not   PRT   very   fast   get-used

     saai la.   (TV interview)
     all   PRT
     'Not really, you soon get used to it.'

17.1.9 REPLIES TO NEGATIVE QUESTIONS

If the question is in negative form, containing *m̀h*, *móuh* or *meih*, the appropriate response differs significantly from the English. To confirm the negative of the question, there are two kinds of possible reply:

(a) repeat the negated verb:

  A: Léih   m̀h   dáng   làh?
     you   not   wait   PRT
     'Aren't you going to wait any more?'

B: M̀h dáng la.
not wait PRT
'No, I'm not.'

(b) confirm the negative statement with *haih* or *haahk* (17.1.8):

A: Léih móuh daai chín àh?
you not-have bring money PRT
'Didn't you bring any money?'

B: Haih a.
yes PRT
'No, I didn't.'

A: Léih haih-mhaih meih heui-gwo Oujāu a?
you be-not-be not-yet go-EXP Australia PRT
'You haven't been to Australia yet, right?'

B: Haahk.
yes
'No, I haven't.'

Note that English uses *no* here. To clarify, both strategies may be used together, *haih* as an affirmative answer and the negated verb or adjective for confirmation:

A: Móuh sīusīk àh?
not-have news PRT
'There's no news?'

B: Haih a, móuh.
yes PRT have-not
'No, there isn't.'

To contradict a negative question, the verb of the question is repeated in positive form. Note that if *mhaih* is used, its force is to contradict the negative, rather than to confirm it as in English:

A: Léih m̀h dáng àh?
you not wait PRT
'Aren't you waiting?'

B: Dáng /Mhaih ak, ngóh wúih dáng lohk-heui ge.
wait / not-be PRT I will wait continue PRT
'Yes, I am. / Yes, I'll carry on waiting.'

17.2 ALTERNATIVE QUESTIONS

Questions of the form 'A or B?' which offer a choice between two alternatives are known as alternative or disjunctive questions. They are expressed by conjoining two phrases with the conjunction *dihnghaih*, often reduced to *dihng*:

Léih yiu   jūk   dihng(haih) faahn a?
you want congee or (be)   rice PRT
'Would you like congee or rice?'

Ngóhdeih heui máaih yéh   dihng fāan   ūkkéi a?
we   go   buy   things or   return home PRT
'Shall we go shopping or go home?'

An alternative conjunction is *yīkwaahk*:

Kéuihdeih   yìhmàhn yīkwaahk làuh háisyu a?
they   emigrate or   stay here   PRT
'Are they emigrating or staying here?'

The reply to such questions is to repeat the appropriate phrase, with or without the remainder of the sentence, e.g. *Jūk* 'Congee,' *Yiu jūk* 'Want congee' or *Ngóh yiu jūk* 'I want congee'; *Làuh háisyu* 'Stay' or *Kéuihdeih làuh háisyu* 'They stay'.

Note: the words *waahkjé* and *yāthaih*, which can also mean 'or', are not used in alternative questions, but in disjunctive 'either . . . or' statements (16.1.4).

17.3 WH-QUESTIONS

Wh-words do not come at the beginning of the sentence as in English, unless they belong there as sentence subjects. A question with the subject as the wh-word thus resembles an English question in word order; a wh-word representing an object, however, occurs after the verb like any direct object:

Subject question	*Object question*
Bīngo wán ngóh a?	Léih wán **bīngo** a?
who seek me PRT	you seek who PRT
'Who is looking for me?'	'Who are you looking for?'

The main question words are based on the words *bīn* 'which', *māt* 'what', *dím* 'how' and *géi* 'how much':

bīngo 'who' (17.3.1)   māt(yéh) 'what' (17.3.2)
bīn [CL] 'which' (17.3.3)   géisìh 'when' (17.3.5)
bīndouh, bīnsyu 'where' (17.3.4)   géiloih 'how long' (17.3.5)
dím gáai 'why' (17.3.6)   géi [adj] 'how' (17.3.7)
dím yéung 'how' (17.3.7)   géidō 'how many/much' (17.3.8)

These question words have a number of important uses other than in questions. In free relative clauses (6.4.3) and concessive sentences (16.2.4) they have the indefinite meanings 'whoever, whatever', etc. They may have the meaning 'any(one)', 'anything' etc. in negative contexts (13.4), in A-not-A questions and conditional sentences, and as quantifiers with *dōu* (14.1.5).

Like other forms of question, wh-questions typically have a question particle such as *a* or *nē/lē* (18.3.1). The adverb *gauging* 'really, exactly' may be used to emphasize such a question:

Léih gauging séung góng mātyéh a?
you actually want say what PRT
'What do you really want to say?'

Léih gauging dím lám ga?
You actually how think PRT
'What do you really think?'

17.3.1 'WHO' QUESTIONS

The usual word for 'who?' is *bīngo*, formed from *bīn* 'which?' with the classifier *go*:

Bīngo dá-dihnwá làih a?
who call-phone come PRT
'Who was it that called?'

Léih gáan bīngo jouh Hēunggóng síujé a?
you pick who do Hongkong Miss PRT
'Who are you choosing for Miss Hongkong?'

bīngo is much used rhetorically, as in *who says.. . .?*:

Bīngo wah ngóh ga-m̀h-chēut a?
who say I marry-not-out PRT
'Who says I can't get married [i.e. nobody wants me]?'

bīn wái 'which person' is a polite alternative to *bīngo*, often used on the telephone:

Chéng mahn wán bīn wái a?
request ask seek which person PRT
'May I ask who you're calling for?'

a-bīngo 'what's-his-name', with the personal prefix *a-* (2.1.1, 20.2) refers to someone whose name escapes the speaker:

A-bīngo wah yiu chéng ngóhdeih sihk máahnfaahn wóh.
a-who say want invite us eat evening-meal PRT
'What's-his-name says he wants to invite us to dinner.'

17.3.2 'WHAT' QUESTIONS

The word *mātyéh* is formed from *māt* 'what?' and *yéh* 'thing':

Kéuih góng-jó mātyéh gīk dou léih gam lāu a?
s/he say-PFV what annoy till you so angry PRT
'What did he say to make you so angry?'

Gimkìuh ge hohksāang yáuh mātyéh gam dahkbiht a?
Cambridge POSS students have what so special PRT
'What's so special about Cambridge students?'

mātyéh may also be used with a noun, like English *what*:

Yám **mātyéh chàh** a? (asked by waiter)
drink what tea PRT
'What kind of tea will you have?'

Kéuihdeih góng-gán **mātyéh wá** a?
they speak-PROG what language PRT
'What language are they speaking?'

Note: *mātyéh wá* also means 'I beg your pardon?' (20.1.3.)

Pronunciation note: *mātyéh* is often reduced to one syllable, becoming *m'yē*, especially in set expressions:

Sihk m'yē a?   Léih dáng m'yē?
eat what PRT   you wait what
'What shall we eat?'   'What are you waiting for?'

Note that the high tone of *māt* transfers to the vowel [e] in the contraction.

---

dī mātyéh is a colloquial combination typically used where the item being questioned is an uncountable commodity or plural (see *dī*: 6.2.2):

Sihk dī mātyéh hóu a?
eat CL what good PRT
'What shall we eat?'

Yáuh dī mātyéh hóyíh góng a?
have CL what can talk PRT
'What is there we can talk about?'

Idiom: *mātyéh* may be inserted into a bisyllabic verb or verb–object combination. The effect of this is to ridicule or play down a suggestion:

A: Ngóh séung sé   bún syū   a.
   I   want write CL book   PRT
   'I'd like to write a book.'

B: Sé   mātyéh syū   a?
   write   what   book   PRT
   'What? Write a book?'

A: Bātyùh ngóhdeih heui   tái   hei   ā.   (see 19.2)
   why-not we   go   watch film PRT
   'Let's go and see a film.'

B: Tái mātyéh hei a,   ngóhdeih gam   dō
   see what   film PRT   we   so   many

   yéh   jouh!
   things do
   'What do you mean, see a film? We have so much work to do!'

mātyéh may follow a monosyllabic word with similar effect:

A: Yiu   hàahng hóu   yúhn wo.
   need walk   very far   PRT
   'It's a long way to walk.'

B: Yúhn mātyéh jēk?
   far what   PRT
   'What do you mean, a long way?'

---

māt can also be used alone in informal speech (this occurs especially in indirect questions: see 17.4):

Léihdeih háidouh jouh māt   a?
you-PL   here   do   what PRT
'What are you (guys) up to?'

māt is also used in exclamatory fashion:

Māt   léih móuh   chín   ge   mē?
what you not-have money PRT   PRT
'What? You mean you haven't got any money?'

Māt   léih dōu làih-jó   àh?
what you also come-PFV   PRT
'What, you here too?'

> *Idiom*: *māt gwái* (*yéh*) is an expletive expression for 'what':
>
> Kéuih gauging góng-gán dī māt gwái yéh?
> s/he really say-PROG CL what *** stuff
> 'What on earth is he on about?'
>
> Gáau māt gwái a, léih?
> do what *** PRT you
> 'What on earth are you up to?'

17.3.3 'WHICH' QUESTIONS

In 'which' questions, *bīn* 'which' is followed by the classifier and noun:

Léih gokdāk **bīn** **jek** **gáu** jeui leng a?
you feel which CL dog most nice PRT
'Which dog do you think is the nicest?'

Gam dō júng fā léih jeui jūngyi **bīn** **júng** a?
so many CL flower you most like which CL PRT
'Which of these flowers do you like best?'

Bīn **sāam** **go** yàhn heui a?
which three CL person go PRT
'Which three are going?'

Note that *bīn* [classifier] *dōu* means 'any' (13.4, 14.1.5).

17.3.4 'WHERE' QUESTIONS

bīndouh is used for 'where to' questions:

Ngóhdeih heui bīndouh yám-chàh a?
we go where drink-tea PRT
'Where shall we go for dim sum?'

'Where' questions concerning location require *hái bīndouh*, literally 'at where':

Léih hái bīndouh séuhng tòhng a?
you at where attend class PRT
'Where is your class?'

bīnsyu is a more formal alternative.

As *mātyéh* is reduced to *māt*, *bīndouh* may be reduced to *bīn* in colloquial speech:

Léih gānjyuh heui bīn a?
you next go where PRT
'Where are you going next?'

Idiom: rhetorical *bīndouh*: *bīndouh* is used idiomatically to form rhetorical questions, with a meaning similar to *since when . . . ?* in English:

Léih pìhngsìh **bīndouh** yáuh sihk gam dō
you normally where have eat so much

tìhmbán a?
dessert PRT
'Since when have you eaten so much dessert?'

A: Léih go jái hóu lēk wo.
you CL son ADJ clever PRT
'Your son is really clever.'

B: **Bīndouh** haih lē?
where is PRT
'I hardly think so!'

A: Bātyùh léih jihgéi gáan ā.
rather you self choose PRT
'Why don't you choose yourself?'

B: Ngóh **bīn** sīk jēk?
I where know PRT
'But I don't know how to choose!'

17.3.5 'WHEN' AND TIME QUESTIONS

The word *géisìh* or *géisí* 'when?' comes between the subject and verb, like a time adverb:

Léih géisìh fāan làih a?
you when return come PRT
'When will you be back?'

The adverb *sīn* 'first' may be added in 'when' questions, often indicating impatience:

Léih géisìh sīn jī a? (tel.)
you when first know PRT
'When **will** you know?'

géiloih 'how long' follows the verb like an adverbial object (8.2.5):

Léih hái Hēunggóng jyuh-jó **géiloih** a?
you in Hongkong live-PFV how-long PRT
'How long have you lived in Hongkong?'

It is used with *móuh* to mean 'how long . . . since':

Léih **géiloih** **móuh** fāan Yīnggwok a?
you how-long have-not return England PRT
'How long has it been since you went back to England?'

Together with *yāt chi* 'once', *géiloih* means 'how often':

Kéuihdeih **géiloih** hōi **yāt** **chi** wúi a?
they how-long hold one time meeting PRT
'How often do they meet?'

Géi dō go jūngtàuh yiu sihk **yāt chi** yeuk a?
how many CL hour need eat one time medicine PRT
'How often do you have to take the medicine?'

17.3.6 'WHY' QUESTIONS: REASON AND PURPOSE

The most general expression for 'why?' is *dím gáai*, while *jouh mātyéh* tends to mean more specifically 'for what purpose?'

dím gáai 'how come?' is used for questions of cause or purpose. It may come either at the beginning of the sentence or between the subject and the verb:

Dím gáai wúih gám gé? (conv.)
how come would thus PRT
'Why is it like this?'

Léih dím gáai m̀h chēut-sēng a?
you how come not out-voice PRT
'Why don't you say something?'

dím gáai literally means 'how to explain?' and is also used metalinguistically to ask what a word or phrase means:

Ngóh m̀h mìhng nī go jih dím gáai.
I not understand this CL word how explain
'I don't understand what this word means.'

jouh māt(yéh), literally 'do what?', is used colloquially for 'why' questions. It is used specifically for questions of purpose, very much like English *what . . . for?* It may occur, like *dím gáai*, between subject and verb:

Léih jouh mātyéh gam gánjēung a?
you do what so nervous PRT
'What are you so nervous for?'

Alternatively it may come at the end of the sentence:

Léih gam mángjáng jouh mātyéh a?
you so frustrated do what PRT
'What are you so frustrated for?'

As these examples suggest, *jouh mātyéh* is restricted to colloquial register; in more formal contexts *dím gáai* is preferred for questions of purpose.

Note: idiomatically, *jouh mātyéh* can also mean 'what's the matter?' as in:

Léih gòhgō jouh mātyéh a, yāt lūk muhk gám
your brother do what PRT one piece wood so

kéi háidouh?
stand here
'What's the matter with your brother, standing there like a stiff board?'

Idiom: *sái māt* is a colloquial form of 'why' question meaning 'what's the use?' or 'what's the point?' *sái māt* is essentially a rhetorical question, using the positive form of the modal verb *msái* 'no need' (12.1.3):

Sái māt mahn kéuih jēk?
need what ask him PRT
'What's the point of asking him?'

Sái māt gam fàahn a? (TV ad.)
need what so complicated PRT
'Why make things so complicated?'

This is typically an impersonal construction, although a subject may be specified:

Léih sái māt gam gēng a?
you need what so fear PRT
'What are you so afraid of?'

17.3.7 'HOW' QUESTIONS: MANNER AND DEGREE

The usual word for 'how?' is *dím yéung*, in which *yéung* means 'manner':

Léih dím yéung jīng tìuh yú a?
you how way steam CL fish PRT
'How are you steaming the fish?'

Nī	go	jih	dím	yéung	fāanyihk	a?
this	CL	word	how	way	translate	PRT

'How can we translate this word?'

dím alone is also commonly used for manner questions:

Dím	heui	a?
how	go	PRT

'How do we get there?'

Léih	dím	wán	dóu	nī	fahn	gūng	ga?
you	how	find	V-PRT	this	CL	job	PRT

'How did you find this job?'

Rhetorical 'how' questions, in particular, typically use *dím* alone:

Ngóh	dím	gwái	jī	jēk?
I	how	devil	know	PRT

'How on earth should I know?'

Gam	chìh	dím	gón	dāk	chit	a?
so	late	how	rush	can	on-time	PRT

'How can we be on time when it's so late?'

Idiom: *dím tùhng* 'how same?' is a rhetorical idiom, implying that there is no comparison to be made:

Gām	chi	dím	tùhng	a?
this	time	how	same	PRT

'Of course it's different this time.'

Ngóhdeih	nī	go	lìhndoih	dím	tùhng	jēk?	(film)
our		this	CL	generation	how	same	PRT

'Of course it was different for our generation.'

Like many Cantonese rhetorical questions, this idiom cannot readily be translated with a question in English.

---

dím may be used without a main verb, meaning 'how is . . . ?' or 'what about . . . ?':

Léih	gòhgō	dím	a?		Dī	sāam	dím	a?
your	brother	how	PRT		CL	clothes	how	PRT

'How's your brother?'   'What about those clothes?'

A similar function following an auxiliary is the interrogative counterpart of *gám* (10.1.2):

Léih gaugíng séung dím jēk? (film)
you actually want how PRT
'What exactly do you want to do?'

Yàhn-yàhn dōu séung jī gáuchāt hauh ge Hēunggóng
person-person all wish know 97 after LP Hongkong

haih dím ge.
will how PRT
'Everyone is wondering what post-1997 Hongkong will be like.'

Questions of degree, meaning 'how [adjective]?' are expressed by *géi*:

Yīnggōi géi chèuhng ga? Juhng yáuh géi yúhn a?
should how long PRT still have how far PRT
'How long should it be?' 'How much further is it?'

Idiom: [verb/adjective] – *sìhng* – *dím?* (also pronounced *sèhng dím*) is
an idiomatic form of 'how' question. The word *sìhng* as a verb means
'accomplish', as in *sìhng-gūng* 'succeed'. As a verbal complement it
makes a 'how' question, focusing on how well or how successfully an
action is accomplished:

Sé sìhng dím a? (conv.)
write how PRT
'How's the writing going?'

It is especially common in indirect questions:

Tái-háh kéuih cheung sìhng dím. (conv.)
see-DEL s/he sing how
'Let's see how she sings.'

Ngóh séung tái-háh kéuih leng sìhng dím. (film)
I want see-DEL s/he pretty how
'I want to see how pretty she is.'

Note that the construction applies equally to verbs (*cheung*) and
adjectives (*leng*). The idiom [verb] *sìhng* also occurs in declarative
form with *gám* (10.1.2) in place of *dím*.

17.3.8 'HOW MANY'/'HOW MUCH'

géi dō means 'how many?' or 'how much?' It is used, for example, to ask
the price of an item or to ask a person's age:

Géi   dō   chín   a?
how   much money   PRT
'How much is it?'

Géi   dō   wái   a?
how   many people PRT
'How many are you?'

Léih géi   dō   seui a?
you   how   many year PRT
'How old are you?'

(used by a waiter when a party
            enters a restaurant)

With countable nouns, *géi* (*dō*) is followed by the appropriate classifier (6.2):

Léih ūkkéi yáuh **géi** **dō** **(go)** yàhn   a?
you   home   have how   many   (CL)   people PRT
'How many are there in your family?'

Yiu   yuhng **géi** **dō** **jēung** jí   a?
need use   how   many   CL   paper PRT
'How many sheets of paper do you need?'

With uncountable (mass) nouns, no classifier is required:

Bōu   tōng yuhng **géi** **dō** **séui** a?
boil soup use   how   much   water   PRT
'How much water do you use to make the soup?'

Juhng yáuh **géi** **dō** **sìhgaan** jihng   a?
still have   how   much   time   remain PRT
'How much time do we have left?'

17.4 INDIRECT QUESTIONS

Because questions are formed without inversion as in English, there is little difference between a direct question and an indirect (embedded) question. A-not-A, *meih*, existential and wh-questions may all be used to report questions in indirect speech:

(a) *Direct question*

Léih séung-m̀h-séung tái   ūk   a?
you   want-not-want look house PRT
'Do you want to see the house?'

(b) *Indirect question*

Kéuih mahn ngóh séung-m̀h-séung tái   ūk.
s/he   ask   me   want-not-want look house
'She asked me if I wanted to see the house.'

(a) Léih yáuh-móuh   lám-gwo   a?
you   have-not-have think-EXP PRT
'Have you ever thought about it?'

(b) Ngóh séung jīdou léih yáuh-móuh   lám-gwo.
    I   want know you have-not-have think EXP
    'I wonder if you've ever thought about it.'

(a) Léih jyuh hái bīndouh a?
    you live at where PRT
    'Where do you live?'

(b) Yàhndeih mahn ngóh jyuh hái bīndouh.
    people ask me live at where
    'People ask me where I live.'

Note, however, that the question particle, if any, may be omitted from the indirect version. A particle often used in indirect questions is *wóh*, as used in reported speech (16.5, 18.3.4):

A-Kèuhng mahn ngóhdeih yáuh-móuh   jitmuhk **wóh**.
Ah Keung ask us   have-not-have plan PRT
'Ah Keung is asking if we have any plans.'

Another feature of indirect questions is the frequent reduction of bisyllabic question words: in informal speech especially, *mātyéh* tends to be reduced to *māt*, *bīndouh* to *bīn* and *dím yéung* to *dím*:

Direct question
Kéuih jouh mātyéh a?
s/he do what
'What is he up to?'

Léih heui bīndouh a?
you go where PRT
'Where are you going?'

Kéuih dím yéung lám yéh ga?
s/he how manner think thing PRT
'How does his mind work?'

Indirect question
Ngóh mjī   kéuih jouh **māt** bo.
I   not-know s/he do what PRT
'I don't know what he's up to.'

Ngóh mjī   léih heui **bīn** a.
I   not-know you go where PRT
'I don't know where you're going.'

Ngóh mjī   kéuih **dím** lám yéh ga.
I   not-know s/he how think thing PRT
'I don't know how his mind works.'

Note that because *dím* means 'how', *dím gáai* 'why' cannot be reduced in this way.

An indirect question can serve as the subject of a sentence:

Léih seun-m̀h-seun   **ngóh** dōu m̀h gányiu.   (film)
you believe-not-believe   me   also   not   important
'Whether you believe me or not doesn't matter.'

Bīngo ngāam bīngo cho   dōu m̀h gwāan   ngóh   sih.
who right who wrong   also   not   involve   me   thing
'Who's right and who's wrong has nothing to do with me.'

The indirect question may also be topicalized to come before the verb:

Gaugíng **jēunglòih haih dím**, móuh yàhn jī   gé.   (radio int.)
exactly future   is   how   no   one   know   PRT
'What the future will be like, no one knows.'

hóu-mhóu (17.1.3, 17.1.6) is used in indirect questions with the meaning 'whether to':

Kéuih yíhgīng lám-jó   hóu   loih   **hóu-mhóu**   **chìh-jīk**.
s/he already think-PFV very   long   good-not-good   resign
'He's been wondering whether to resign for ages.'

Ngóh mjī   **hóu-mhóu**   **jēung** dī   chín
I   not-know   good-not-good   make   CL   money

jyun   jouh   Méih   gām.
switch   do   US   dollar
'I don't know whether to put that money into US dollars.'

haih-mhaih in an indirect question, by contrast, means 'whether' in asking whether something is the case or not:

Ngóh mjī   kéuih haih-mhaih góng-siu   ge.
I   not-know   s/he   be-not-be   talk-joke   PRT
'I don't know whether he's joking or not.'

17.5 MULTIPLE QUESTIONS

Questions may contain two or more question words at once:

Ngóhdeih géisìh hái bīndouh gin-mihn a?
we   when   at   where   see-face   PRT
'Where and when are we going to meet?'

Léih sung mātyéh láihmaht béi bīngo?
you send what   presents   to   who
'What presents are you giving to whom?'

Multiple questions are particularly common in indirect questions:

Léih	gei-mgeidāk	hái	bīndouh	máaih-jó	mātyéh	a?
you	remember-or-not	at	where	buy-PFV	what	PRT

'Do you remember where you bought what?'

17.6 EXCLAMATORY QUESTIONS

As in English, several forms of question are used as exclamations. These resemble rhetorical questions in that they do not expect an answer.

mjī géi is an expression corresponding to 'how [adjective]!', literally 'I don't know how':

Ngóhdeih	gám	yéung	hāan	**mjī**	**géi**	**dō**	chín.
we	this	way	save	not-know	how	much	money

'We save an enormous amount of money this way.'

Kéuih	tēng	dóu	**mjī**	**géi**	**hōisām**.
s/he	hear	V-PRT	not-know	how	happy

'She was so happy when she heard about it.'

dím jī is an exclamation of surprise, similar to 'what d'you know':

Seuhng chi	móuh	mahntàih,	**dím**	**jī**	gām chi
last	time	not-have	problem	how	know	this	time

wúih	mdāk	ge.
would	not-okay	PRT

'There was no problem last time, and what d'you know, it's not working again.'

dím syun 'what now?' is a despairing form of rhetorical question, often accompanied by the exclamation *āiya!* (18.4.2):

Dím syun a? 'What can we do?'
Āiya! Ngóh mjī dím syun lo! 'I don't know what to do!'

mtūng also introduces rhetorical questions, of two distinct kinds:

(a) expressing scepticism or sarcasm. It is typically used with the question particles *a/àh* and *mē*:

Mtūng	ngóh	wúih	seun	léih	àh?
as-if	I	would	believe	you	PRT

'As if I'd believe you!'

Mtūng	léih	séung	séi	mē?
as-if	you	want	die	PRT

'Are you crazy?'

The nearest translation is probably *as if* . . . , although this is not a question construction in English.

(b) to speculate on possible causes, meaning 'I wonder if . . . ?' as in:

Dím gáai juhng m̀h gin kéuih gé? Mtūng
how come still not see her PRT as-if

kéuih behng-jó?
s/he ill-PFV
'Why hasn't she shown up yet? I wonder if she's fallen ill?'

Kéuih nī pàaih sèhngyaht jok-áu, mtūng
she these days always throw-up as-if

kéuih yáuh-jó? (see 15.1)
she have-PFV
'She's been vomiting a lot recently, I wonder if she's pregnant?'

18 SENTENCE PARTICLES AND INTERJECTIONS

18.1 ROLE OF THE SENTENCE PARTICLE

The sentence-final particles are an important feature of Cantonese speech, serving various communicative (**pragmatic**) functions such as:

(a) indicating speech-act types such as questions (18.3.1), assertions (18.3.2) and requests (18.3.3);
(b) evidentiality (indicating the source of knowledge:18.3.4);
(c) affective and emotional colouring (18.3.5).

In casual conversation, many sentences seem incomplete without one or more final particles; in broadcasting, by contrast, they are reduced to a minimum, whether to save time or to preserve a higher degree of formality.

They are not easily translated into English, where many of their functions are often conveyed by intonation patterns. While they sometimes correspond functionally to English question 'tags', they differ in that there is no pause between the main sentence and the particle. They are particularly difficult for the foreign learner to use idiomatically, and their use also varies considerably between individuals, between the sexes and age groups.

The term **utterance particle** is preferred by some authors (Yau 1965; Gibbons 1980; Luke 1990), who distinguish between a *sentence* as an abstract entity and an *utterance* as an instance of use of the sentence in a particular context. Given that it is difficult or even impossible to define the function of particles without reference to the speech context, it is arguably more accurate to treat them as associated with individual utterances rather than sentences. Moreover, particles may be used with phrases and fragments which do not form complete sentences.

Cantonese is especially rich in particles, having some thirty basic forms compared to seven in Mandarin,[1] and they are one of the few areas of Cantonese grammar to have been extensively studied. The functions of the particles remain elusive, however, and rather different conclusions are drawn according to whether the approach taken focuses on semantics (Kwok 1984), pragmatics and speech acts (Gibbons 1980) or conversational analysis (Luke 1990). While the function of a particle may be clear in individual utterances, it is extremely difficult to identify a common denominator.

The particles do not correspond straightforwardly to those in Mandarin, although their functions are broadly similar. Moreover, combinations of two or more particles occur readily in Cantonese (18.2.3), whereas in Mandarin only *le* combines with other particles.

18.1.1 PRONUNCIATION: TONE AND INTONATION

Particles vary in their pronunciation, including vowel quality, duration and intonation, to a greater extent than other Cantonese words. For example, the particle *gé* is conventionally written with a high rising tone, but the rise of tone is typically more pronounced than that in an ordinary word with this tone such as the verb *sé* 'write'. Moreover, some particles such as *sìn* and *tìm* occur with a high falling tone which does not occur regularly with other words (see 1.4).

The vowel of a sentence particle may be pronounced short or prolonged for up to a second or so. This typical drawing out of the particles is a characteristic of Cantonese which distinguishes it from other Chinese dialects, notably Mandarin. It also allows nuances of intonation to be superimposed, thereby colouring the tone of the sentence. In several cases there are related particles with the same consonants and vowels but different tone patterns. Table 18.1 shows the main variants, which are liable to be confused (particles with a fixed form such as *gwa*, *hó*, etc. are omitted).

These related forms involve the following factors:

(a) contraction of a basic particle with *a/ā/àh*, *ak* amd *āma* (see 18.2.3);
(b) tonal variants: these forms differ systematically in function. Typically, the high-tone variants are more tentative, the low-tone ones assertive and the mid-tone ones neutral.[2]
(c) closure with [-k]: the forms *ak*, *jēk*, *lak* and *lok* are related to *a*, *je*, *la* and *lō/lòh*, ending with an unreleased [-k] (often heard simply as a glottal stop).

18.2 SYNTAX OF PARTICLES

Particles normally occur in the sentence-final position, as in most of the examples given in section 18.3. However, they may also occur after the sentence topic and at other natural breaks in the sentence. This possibility is, in fact, one reflection of the division of the Chinese sentence into topic and comment (4.2).

Table 18.1   Related particles

ā	lively statement, question or request
a	softening statement or question
àh	disapproving, surprised or suspicious
áh	seeking confirmation
ak	abrupt (dis)agreement
ge	affirmative: 'this is the case'
gé	tentative or uncertain affirmation
ga	(ge + a)
gá	(ge + ā)
gak/gaak	(ge + ak)
gàh	(ge + àh)
jē	playing down a fact: 'that's all'
je	'just, only'
jēk	cheeky, intimate
ja	(je + a)
já	(je + ā)
jàh	(je + àh)
lā	requesting, seeking common ground
la	current relevance; advice
làh	(la + àh)
lak/laak	current relevance + finality
lō	seeking agreement, settlement, etc.
lo	emphasizing current situation, seeking sympathy, etc.
lòh	impatient: 'of course'
lok	definitive: 'that's the way it is'
bo/be	exclamatory, appreciative
wo	informative (noteworthiness)
wòh	discovery
wóh	evidential (hearsay, reported speech)
āma	indicating obvious reason, excuse, etc.
amáh	as above, negative or impatient
gāma	(ge + āma)
jāma/jīma	(je + āma)

18.2.1 TOPIC PARTICLES

Certain sentence particles, notably *a/àh* and *nē/lē*, may occur after the sentence topic. The topic and particle are typically followed by a slight pause (intonation break):

Hái Yīnggwok **àh**,   móuh yàhn sihk nī   dī yéh   ga.
in England PRT no   one eats this CL thing PRT
'In England, no one eats this kind of thing.'

Nī go **nē**, msái   joi   yuhng lak, hóyih
this CL PRT no-need again use   PRT   can

ló fāan heui.
take back go
'This we don't need any more, we can take it back.'

Juhngyáuh **wo**, léih gei-jyuh   daai sósìh a.
still-have   PRT you remember-CONT bring key PRT
'And also, remember to bring the keys.'

àh and *nē/lē* serve here to draw attention to the topic which they follow, while *wo* is used to draw attention to the following message. *a/àh* and *lā* often function purely to fill a pause, for example in lists:

Yīnggwok **a**,   Fāatgwok **a**,   douh-douh dōu yáuh
England   PRT France   PRT there-there all have

leng fūnggíng.
nice scenery
'England, France, there's nice scenery everywhere.'

A: Gūng-gwāan   yiu jouh dī mātyéh ga?
   public-relations need do CL what   PRT
   'What does public relations involve?'

B: Móuh māt dahkbiht ge,   tùhng yàhn   dá-háh-jīufū **lā**,
   nothing special PRT with people greet-DEL   PRT

   kīng-háh-gái **lā**,   sihk-háh-yéh   **lā**.   (film)
   chat-DEL   PRT eat-DEL-stuff PRT
   'Nothing special, just greeting people, chatting to them, eating.'

Note also that such a topic particle does not prevent a different particle from occurring in the sentence-final position:

Léih **àh**, mhóu joi   dáng **la**! Kéuih m̀h wúih fāan
you PRT don't again wait PRT s/he not will back

lèih ge   la.
come PRT PRT
'You know, you really shouldn't wait any longer. He's not coming back.'

18.2.2 CLAUSE-FINAL PARTICLES

A particle can also appear at other natural breaks in a sentence, notably at the end of a clause:

Léih gei-jyuh **wo**, nī gihn sih mhóu wah béi
you remember PRT this CL matter don't say to

yàhn tēng.
people hear
'Now remember, don't tell anyone about this.'

Similarly, the reported-speech particle *wóh* (18.3.4) may be used after a verb of reporting, before the clause reporting the statement (see indirect speech: 16.5):

Kéuih wah **wóh**, gām chi móuh yàhn jung
s/he say PRT this time not-have person win

tàuh jéung.
first prize
'You know what she said? Nobody won the first prize this time.'

18.2.3 PARTICLE COMBINATIONS

Many of the particles can occur together at the end of a sentence, leading to some expressive combinations. Although a very large number of permutations are logically possible,[3] the combinations actually found and the order of particles are relatively restricted. The columns in Table 18.2 indicate the possible choices of two to four particles. The particles *tìm, sìn, ge* and *lèihga* must come first in a combination, with two alternative orders: *sìn/tìm – ge/lèihga*, or *ge – tìm*. Following these, one or two particles may occur: one from column 3 and one from column 4. As an alternative to particles from columns 3 and 4, one of those in the row below columns 3 and 4 may occur. Note that the question and exclamation particles in column 4 and the particles ending with -*k* may only come last in a series. Combinations are also limited by (a) pronounceability and (b) semantic coherence of the combination. For example, *la lē* is avoided due to the clash of similar sounds, while *lèihge gwa* does not occur as the assertiveness of *lèihge* conflicts with the uncertainty expressed by *gwa*.

The particle *a/ā/àh* combines with other particles to produce contracted forms:[4]

ge + ā → gá   je + ā → já
ge + a → ga   je + a → ja
ge + àh → gàh   je + àh → jàh   la + àh → làh
ge + ak → gak/gaak
ge + āma → gāma   jē + āma → jāma   la + āma → lāma

Table 18.2 Particle combinations

1 Adverbial particle	2 Assertion	3 Evaluation/ modification	4 Question/ exclamation
sìn	ge	je/ja, jē	a, ā, àh
			bo
tìm	lèih(ge/ga)	la, lā	gwa
			há, hó
			nē/lē
			ma, āma
			mē
			wo, wòh, wóh
ge	tìm		ak
			jēk
			lak/laak
			lo, lō
			lok
			léh

Note that the mid tone of *ge* and *je* combines with the high tone of *ā* to produce a high rising tone in *gá* and *já*. The function of these forms is a combination of those of the two particles: *a* adds its function of questioning or mollifying a statement to the function of the first particle. Thus, the assertive particle *ge* combined with *a* has the effect of seeking confirmation of a statement:

Haih-mhaih jān   ga?
is-not-is   true   PRT
'Is that true?'

Similarly, *gak* (also *gaak*) is formed from *ge* and *ak*:

Juhng yáuh gak.
still   have   PRT
'There are some more.' (Why didn't you bring them all?)

ge here marks an assertion, with *ak* implying reproach.

làh combines *la* indicating current relevance with *àh* indicating surprise or disapproval:

Léih gam faai séung sāu-gūng   làh?
you so   fast   want   finish-work   PRT
'You want to finish work so soon, do you?'

The force of the combinations is a function of that of each of the two particles as used in isolation. The following are some typical examples of combinations, by no means exhaustive; note that the order of the particles follows Table 18.2.

ge la (assertion + relevance)

> Sihk dāk ge la.
> eat can PRT PRT
> 'Dinner's ready.'

> Ngóh yiu Vincent deui ngóh hóu jauh dāk
> I want Vincent to me good then okay
>
> **ge la**. (film)
> PRT PRT
> 'All I want is for Vincent to be good to me.'

ge wo (assertion + noteworthiness)

> Léih yāt-yuht heui dūng on, hóu dung **ge wo**!
> you first-month go east coast very cold PRT PRT
> 'If you're going to the East Coast in January, it's going to be very cold!'

jē ma (playing down + 'of course')

> Lóuhgūng: Léih mhóu joi máaih yéh la.
> (husband) you don't again buy things PRT
> 'Don't you go buying more stuff.'

> Lóuhpòh: Ngóh tái-háh **jē ma**.
> (wife) I look-DEL PRT PRT
> 'I'm just going to take a look.'

la wo (current relevance + noteworthiness)

> Yihp Síujé fāan-jó ūkkéi **la wo**.
> Yip Miss return-PFV home PRT PRT
> 'Miss Yip has just gone home!'

leihge wo (explanation + discovery)

> Mhaih póutūng muhk, haih hùhng-muhk **leihge wo**.
> not-be ordinary wood be red-wood PRT PRT
> 'Oh, I see it's not ordinary wood but rosewood.'

Combinations of three consecutive particles are common, for example:

> Léih sīk heui ge l'āma? (spoken by passenger in car)
> you know go PRT PRT PRT
> 'You do know the way, don't you?'

ge here is assertive, *la* marks current relevance and *āma* seeks confirmation (*la* and *āma* contract to *l'āma*: compare the statement *Ngóh sīk heui ge la* 'I know the way').

Làahmjái	tek-bō	tùhngmàaih	léuihjái	tek-bō	móuh
boy	kick-ball	and	girl	kick-ball	not-have

māt	fānbiht	**ge**	**je**	**bo!**
any	difference	PRT	PRT	PRT

'Boys play football and girls play football – what's the difference?'

Here *ge* asserts the fact, *je* plays it down as something unremarkable, and *bo* invites agreement.

Four consecutive particles occur in the following example:

Kéuih	ló-jó	daih	yāt	mìhng	tìm	ge	la	wo.
s/he	take-PFV	number	one	place	too	PRT	PRT	PRT

'And she got first place too, you know.'

Here *tìm* is evaluative, *ge* assertive, *la* adds currency and *wo* newsworthiness. Note that the order and selection of particles follows that shown in Table 18.2. More than four particles are rare, though not impossible (Leung Chung-Sum reports the occurrence of some seven particles as an extreme case).

18.3 FUNCTIONS OF THE PARTICLES

The particles may usefully be divided according to their functions in terms of speech acts such as questions and assertions. However, this classification is not exclusive: for example, *a* is by no means restricted to questions. Within each section, particles are listed alphabetically for ease of reference.

18.3.1 QUESTION PARTICLES

These particles are typically or exclusively used in questions. Of this group, some (e.g. *a*) may be added to all types of questions, while others such as *àh* and *mē* only occur in yes-no questions, their addition turning a statement into a question.

a is one of the most frequent particles, appearing especially commonly in questions. *a* is not sufficient to mark a question by itself, but accompanies interrogative constructions such as A-not-A and copular questions:

Léih	jūng-m̀h-jūngyi	Hēunggóng	a?
you	like-not-like	Hongkong	PRT

'Do you like Hongkong?'

Kéuih haih-mhaih teui-jó-yāu a?
s/he be-not-be retire-PFV PRT
'Has he retired?'

a is so used in most types of question if there is no other question particle present, as seen in the examples of A-not-A (17.1.2), alternative (17.2) and wh-questions (17.3). *a* is also used to soften the force of statements or confirmations:

A: Māt yiu béi chín gàh?   B: Haih a.
   what need pay money PRT   yes PRT
   'You mean you have to pay?'   'Yes (I'm afraid so).'

ā may serve as a more tentative form of *a*, typically used in questions and requests:

Go-go dōu wah mdākhàahn gám léih bōng-m̀h-bōng
CL-CL all say not free so you help-not-help

ngóh ā?
me PRT
'Everybody says they are busy, so will you help me?'

ā is also used to invite attention and arouse interest:

Ngóh góng go beimaht béi léih tēng ā . . .
I tell CL secret for you listen PRT
'Let me tell you a secret . . .'

àh has a stronger force than *a*, and is sufficient to turn a statement into a question (17.1.1). It may suggest surprise, scepticism or disapproval:

Léih juhng geidāk ngóh àh?
you still remember me PRT
'You still remember me?'

Léih gú gam yùhngyih àh?
you guess so easy PRT
'You think it's that easy, do you?'

Léih lám-jyuh msái jouh yéh àh?
you think-CONT no-need do thing PRT
'I suppose you're thinking you don't need to do any work?'

áh is used to check the addressee's meaning or intention:

Léih jūngyi nī jek gáu dō dī áh?
you like this CL dog more bit PRT
'You like this dog more, is that it?'

Léih wah séung sihk Chìuhjāu   choi   **áh**?   Móuh   mahntàih.
you say wish eat Chiuchow food PRT no   problem
'You said you wanted to eat Chiuchow food, right? No problem.'

há and *hó* invite and expect confirmation of a statement or suggestion.
Like question tags (17.1.6), these particles may be separated from the
sentence by a slight pause. Like tag questions in English, they serve to
indicate the presuppositions behind a statement. *há* presupposes the
addressee's agreement, expecting compliance:

Léih gwāai   ngóh jauh góng gú-jái béi léih tēng
you   behave I   then tell story   for you   listen

há?   (to children)
PRT
'If you're good, I'll tell you a story, okay?'

Yātyū   haih gám wah lā   há?
definitely is   so   say PRT PRT
'Let's do as we agreed, okay?'

hó expects the addressee's confirmation:

A: Géi leng a,   hó?   B: Haih a.
   quite nice PRT PRT   is   PRT
   'Pretty nice, huh?'   'Yes, it is.'

Jouh yīsāng dōu géi   mòhng ge   hó?
be   doctor also quite busy   PRT PRT
'I guess it must be quite a busy life as a doctor?'

léh is used to invite agreement or appreciation:

Hóu sihk léh! (TV ad.)   Hóu dākyi léh!
good eat PRT   very cute PRT
'Tasty, huh?'   'You see how cute it is?'

Tāu yéh   sihk léh! (TV ad: mother to child reaching for a cookie)
steal thing eat PRT
'Pinching things to eat, are you?'

Ngóh cheung dāk   hóu ah   léh? (film)
I   sing   ADV   very nice PRT
'Don't I sing well?'

mē marks questions with negative presuppositions, i.e. expressing
surprise:

Sīnsāang wah   m̀h dāk   ge   mē?
teacher say   not okay PRT PRT
'What, did the teacher say it wasn't okay?'

It is especially common in rhetorical questions (17.1.1):

Ngóh   kīng-háh-gái   dōu   mbéi   mē?
I   have-DEL-chat   also   not-allow   PRT
'Aren't I even allowed to have a chat?'

Kéuih   hóu   lēk   mē?
s/he   very clever PRT
'As if he was so clever!'

nē or *lē* follows a noun phrase, with the meaning 'what about?':

Ngóh   hah-lín   yiu   jyun   gūng. **Léih nē?**
I   next-year want   change   job   you PRT
'I'm going to switch jobs next year. How about you?'

A: Dī gāsī   maaih saai béi yàhn   la.
    CL furniture   sell   all   to   people   PRT
    'The furniture has all been sold.'

B: Ga chē **lē?**
    CL car PRT
    'What about the car?'

This usage resembles that of Mandarin *ne* (Li and Thompson 1981).
   wá is used in echo questions (17.1.7), to elicit repetition of a piece of information:

Léih **géisìh** fāan   làih   **wá?**
you   when   return come   PRT
'When did you say you were coming back?'

Léih séung **dím yéung** jíng tìuh yú   **wá?**
you   wish   how   manner   cook CL   fish PRT
'How did you say you wanted to cook the fish?'

18.3.2 ASSERTIVE PARTICLES

ak in assertions conveys a sense of finality. It has two typical uses, which might seem to be mutually contradictory but share the same assertiveness:

(a) to contradict a statement:

A: Léih m̀h jouh yéh   àh?
    you   not do   thing PRT
    'Aren't you working?'

B: **Mhaih ak**,   ngóh duhk-gán-syū.
    not-be PRT   I   study-PROG-book
    'Yes I am, I'm studying.'

Such a response represents a forceful denial (contrast the response *mhaih a* which softens the force of the denial).

(b) to accept a suggestion, with the implication that the matter is settled:

A: Tīngyaht   gáu   dím   gin   wo.   B: **Hóu   ak.**
   tomorrow   nine o'clock see   PRT   good   PRT
   'See you at nine tomorrow.'   'Okay, right.'

ge is used for assertions of facts, often marking focus or emphasis:

Nī   bouh   gēi   hóu   hókaau   ge.
this   CL   machine   ADJ   reliable PRT
'This machine's very reliable.'

Together with the copula *haih*, *ge* forms an emphatic construction (8.1.1, 16.4):[5]

Ngóh   haih   gaau   yāmngohk   ge,   mhaih   gaau   màhnhohk.
I   be   teach music   PRT   not-be   teach literature
'It's music I teach, not literature.'

Note that *ge* precedes all other particles except *tìm* and *sìn* which may precede it (18.2.3).

gé, the same particle with rising intonation, is a more tentative version of *ge*. It combines the assertion of *ge* with a sense of uncertainty or reservation, giving two distinct functions:

(a) to express puzzlement about a fact:

Yīnggōi   háidouh   gé.
should   be-here   PRT
'It should be here.' (I don't understand why it's not here.)

Dím   gáai   wúih   gám   gé?
how   come   would   so   PRT
'Why is it like this?'

Gám   dung   gé!
so   cold   PRT
'It's so cold!' (Why?)

(b) expressing assertion and reservation at once:

Kéuih   go   yàhn   **géi**   **lēk**   **gé**,   sēuiyìhn   móuh
s/he   CL   person   quite   smart   PRT   although   not-have

duhk-gwo   daaihhohk.
study-EXP   university
'She's quite a smart person, although she didn't go to university.'

Léih tìuh kíu **yīnggōi dāk** **gé**, bātgwo mhóu taai
your CL idea ought okay PRT but don't too

sām-gāp wo.
hasty PRT
'Your idea should be okay, but don't be too hasty.'

lak or *laak* has a similar force to the 'current relevance' meaning of *la*, with a greater sense of finality:

Sānfú-jó gam loih, jūngyū sé yùhn bún syū lak.
difficult-PFV so long finally write finish CL book PRT
'After so much effort, I've finally finished the book.'

A: Ngóh yiu kàhnlihk dī duhk-syū.
   I need diligent a-bit study-book
   'I need to study harder.'

B: Gám jauh ngāam lak.
   so then right PRT
   'That's right, you do.'

Nīdouh jauh haih Tòhngyàhn Gāai lak. (used by tour guide)
here then is Chinese Street PRT
'This is Chinatown.'

Hóu yéh! Béi ngóh wán dóu léih lak.
good stuff by me find V-PRT you PRT
'Great! I've found you!'

lèihga marks an explanation, like the English tags *you see* or *you know*:

Nī go ngóh tùhngsìh lèihga.
this CL my colleague PRT
'This is my colleague, you know.'

lèihga is also used in questions, typically to request an explanation:

Tàuhsīn gó go yàhn haih bīngo lèihga?
just-now that CL person is who PRT
'Who was that person just now?'

Although most comonly used in the form *lèihga*, *lèih* may also combine with other particles, such as *jē*:

Ngóhdeih póutūng pàhngyáuh **lèih** **jē**. (film)
we ordinary friends PRT PRT
'We're just ordinary friends.'

In this context *lèih* serves to explain the situation and *jē* plays down the fact, denying a romantic attachment.

18.3.3 IMPERATIVE AND PERSUASIVE PARTICLES

These particles are typically used in giving directions, including not only straightforward commands, but also suggestions, requests and advice. The examples of imperative sentences in chapter 19 contain further illustrations of these particles.

lā often accompanies an invitation or polite request:

Chèuihbín   chóh   lā!
as-you-please sit   PRT
'Please take a seat.'

Léih béi dō   dī   sìhgaan ngóh lā!
you give more some time   me   PRT
'Give me a bit longer, won't you?'

la, with a mid level tone, has two rather different functions:

(a) in giving advice, like *lā* above:

Léih mhóu joi   tēng kéuih góng **la**, dōu
you don't again listen him   speak PRT   all

móuh   yuhng gé.
not-have use   PRT
'Don't take any more notice of him, it's no use anyway.'

(b) to emphasize a point of current relevance:

Taai chòuh **la**,   ngóh fan   m̀h   dóu.
too noisy PRT   I   sleep not   V-PRT
'I can't sleep, it's too noisy.'

Ga bāsí jáu-jó   la   wo.
CL bus leave-PFV PRT   PRT
'The bus has left, you know.'

lō invites agreement, cooperation or sympathy. Luke (1990) shows how this particle serves to negotiate endings to conversations and discussions. It may be used, for example, to negotiate a settlement:

Gám jauh dāk lō.
so   then okay PRT
'That'll be all right, won't it?'

Ngóh gokdāk kéuih m-ngāam lō.
I   feel   s/he not-right PRT
'I feel he's being unreasonable.'

Idiomatically, *lō* combines with *maih* 'then' (16.2.2):

Gám léih maih faat-daaht   lō!
so   you then make-money PRT
'That way you'll be rich!'

lo, like *la*, refers to a current situation. It may express resignation or a plea for sympathy:

Ngóh mjī   dím syun lo!
I   not-know how act PRT
'I really don't know what to do.'

lok is related to *lo* as *lak* is to *la*, being more definitive. It suggests the irrevocability of a situation (Kwok 1984):

Léih dōu kyutdihng-jó **lok**, juhng mahn ngóh jouh māt?
you also decide-PFV   PRT still ask me   what for
'You've made your decision, why ask my opinion?'

Léih yíhgīng sihk-jó-faahn   **lok**, juhng yáuh
you already eat-PFV-food   PRT still have

waih-háu sihk-yéh   àh?
appetite eat-things   PRT
'You've already eaten, and you still want to eat more?'

Léih gú   jihnghaih léih mòhng àh, ngóh gau
you guess only   you busy PRT I   enough

haih **lok**.
am   PRT
'Do you think you're the only one who's busy? I am too.'

18.3.4 EPISTEMIC PARTICLES

Epistemic particles indicate the source and nature of knowledge expressed in the sentence. Such particles are common in Southeast Asian languages, though not found in Mandarin, with the exception of *ba* in its 'speculative' sense which resembles that of Cantonese *gwa*.

āma or *āmáh* provides an explanation that the speaker should already know, or readily understand:

A: Bīngo lèihga?
   who   PRT
   'Who's that?'

B: Ngóhdeih sān   lóuhbáan āma.
   our   new   boss   PRT
   'Our new boss, of course.'

Exploiting the suggestion of obviousness, *āmáh* is often used to make an excuse:

A: Dím gáai gam chìh gé?
    how come so   late PRT
    'How come you're so late?'

B: Yiu jouh saai dī yéh   sīn āmáh.
    need do   all   CL things first PRT
    'I have to do my own work first, don't I?'

In questions, it is used to check an assumption, typically one which the speaker regards as obvious:

Léih sīk   yuhng dihnlóuh āmáh?
you know use   computer PRT
'You know how to use the computer, don't you?'

amáh may have a slight derogatory connotation, as seen in some phrases:

Léih mhaih amáh   lìhn kéuih haih bīngo dōu mh jī?
you not-be PRT   even s/he is   who   also not know
'How could you possibly not know who she is?'

gwa indicates the speaker's uncertainty about the information in the sentence, like 'I suppose' in British or 'I guess' in American English. *gwa* resembles the 'speculative' meaning of *ba* in Mandarin. It is most typically used in reply to a question or proposition:

A: Léih gánjēung àh?   B: Haih gwa.
    you nervous PRT   yes PRT
    'Are you nervous?'   'I suppose so.'

A: Dīksí yauh gā   ga   la.
    taxi again raise price PRT
    'Taxi fares are going up again.'

B: Mhaih gwa! Móuh   léihyàuh ge!
    no   PRT not-have reason   PRT
    'They're not, are they?'

wo serves to emphasize a noteworthy or 'newsworthy' piece of information.[6] It has a number of discourse functions relating to this notion. For example, it may indicate a surprising piece of news or discovery:

Méih-gām sīng-jó   wo!
US dollar rise-PFV PRT
'Look, the US dollar has gone up!'

wo is also used in reminders; note that it may appear either after the reporting verb or at the end of the sentence:

Léih gei-jyuh **wo**, mhóu chìh dou.
you remember PRT don't late arrive
'Remember, don't be late, okay?'

Léih síu-sām jā-chē **wo**.
you careful drive-car PRT
'Drive carefully!'

Chèuihbín tái wo! (used by shop assistants)
as-you-please look PRT
'Please take a look.'

wòh, a variant of *wo*, specifically indicates discovery:

Yùhnlòih kéuih haih ngóh yíhchìhn ge tùhnghohk lèihge wòh.
after-all s/he is my before POSS schoolmate PRT PRT
'It turned out she was my former classmate.'

Note the combination of *wo* with falling intonation to indicate the unexpected, as in the case of *àh* (18.3.1).

wóh is used to indicate reported information, as in reported speech (16.5) and indirect questions (17.4):

Tēngmàhn-wah léih lóuhbáan yiu chìhjīk wóh.
hear-say your boss want resign PRT
'I hear your boss is going to resign.'

Tīnhei bougou wah gāmyaht wúih lohk-yúh wóh.
weather report say today will fall-rain PRT
'According to the weather report, it's going to rain today.'

18.3.5 EXCLAMATORY AND AFFECTIVE PARTICLES

These particles add emotional or affective colouring to a statement or exclamation.

bo expressess appreciation, as in exclamations of approval:

Hóu yéh bo!   Mcho bo!
good stuff PRT   not-bad PRT
'Well done!'   'Not bad!'

Jeng yéh bo!   Haih bo!
great stuff PRT   yes PRT
'Great stuff!'   'Yes, that's right!'

jē serves to play down an idea, typically a quantity or amount, meaning 'only' or 'just':

Jihnghaih yāt chi gam dō jē.
only one time so many PRT
'It's only just this once.'

Hóu pèhng jē! Máaih béi ngóh lā.
very cheap PRT buy for me PRT
'It's a bargain! Why don't you buy it for me?'

A: Yí, gam leng-léui gé, léih léuih-pàhngyáuh lèihgàh?
Hey so good-looking PRT your girl-friend PRT
'Hey, is that good-looking girl your girl-friend?'

B: Mhaih ak, póutūng pàhngyáuh lèihge je.
not-be PRT ordinary friend PRT PRT
'No, just a friend.'

jēk has a highly affective value, and is characteristic of children's and younger women's speech; it suggests a degree of intimacy, and is only used between close acquaintances:

Gwāan léih mātyéh sih jēk? (rhetorical)
concern you what matter PRT
'It's none of your business.'

Ngóh gāmyaht leng-m̀h-leng jēk? (wife to husband)
I today pretty-not-pretty PRT
'Do you think I look good today?'

Léih tàuhsīn heui bīn jēk?
you just-now go where PRT
'So where did you go just now?'

sìn is related to the adverb *sīn* 'first' (10.3.3). When used as a sentence particle, it has a high falling tone:

Dáng (yāt) jahn sìn, ngóh yiu heui sái-sáu-gāan.
wait (a) moment PRT I need go wash-hand-room
'Hang on a moment. I need to go to the washroom.'

It is also used idiomatically with the aspect marker *háh* (11.2.6) as in *tái háh* 'let's see':

Dáng ngóh tái-háh sìn.
let me look-DEL PRT
'Let me look for a moment.'

Tái-háh léih jyú dāk hóu-mhóu sihk sìn.
see-DEL you cook ADV good-not-good eat PRT
'Let's see how good your cooking is!'

In questions, it may express reservations about a possible course of action:

Léih sīk-m̀h-sīk jouh sìn?
you know-not-know do PRT
'Do you know how to, though?'

Ngóh yáuh mātyéh jeuhksou sìn? (responding to a
I have what advantage PRT suggestion)
'What's in it for me?'

tìm is an emphatic particle meaning 'too' or 'even'. *tìm* often accompanies the verbal particle *màaih* (11.3.3) and/or the adverb *juhng* 'still':

Kéuih hóuchíh hóu jūngyi ngóh, **juhng** sung **màaih**
s/he seem much like me also send PRT

fā **tìm**.
flower too
'He seems to like me, he even sent flowers.'

Juhng hóyíh yàuhséui **tìm**. (radio ad.)
still can swim too
'And you can go swimming, too.'

It is also used ironically on discovering that one has been mistaken, with the verb *yíhwàih* denoting erroneous belief:

Haih mē? Ngóh **yíhwàih** haih léih sung ge **tìm**!
is PRT I think is you give that too
'Really? And I thought it was you that gave it to me!'

Note: *tìm* has a clear high falling tone, like *sìn* used as a particle.

18.4 INTERJECTIONS

Interjections typically occur preceding a sentence or clause. Like the sentence-final particles, these may be pronounced with the vowel short or prolonged, and with exaggerated intonation patterns.

18.4.1 PLACE-FILLERS

The adverbial *gám* (10.1.2) may serve to fill a pause or transition, often together with a particle (18.2.1):

Gám àh . . . dáng ngóh lám-háh sìn.
So PRT let me think-DEL first
'Well . . . let me think about it.'

Dī yuhk yip-jó, gám lē, jauh hóu-sihk dī.
CL meat marinate-PFV so PRT then good-eat a-bit
'If you marinate the meat, you see, it tastes better.'

The interjection *nàh/làh* serves to seek the addressee's attention:

Nàh, ngóhdeih sīn heui máaih sung, gānjyuh fāan ūkkéi.
PRT we first go buy food next return home
'Right, first we go and buy some food, then we go home.'

Làh, léih tái-háh!
PRT you see-DEL
'You see, just look at that!'

léih wah, literally 'you say', is used like 'you see?' to make a point. It takes an indirect question:

Léih wah haih-mhaih hóu fōngbihn a?
you say is-not-is very convenient PRT
'You see how convenient it is?'

Léih wah kéuih haih-mhaih jeunbouh-jó lē?
you say s/he is-not-is improve-PFV PRT
'Don't you think she's improved?'

jīkhaih functions as a conversational place-filler like *err . . .* , *um . . .* , etc. It literally means 'That is, . . .' or 'I mean, . . .'

Ngóh lám . . . jīkhaih . . . ngóh ge yisī haih . . .
I think . . . that is . . . my LP meaning is . . .
'I think . . . er . . . what I mean is . . .'

jīkhaih is often contracted to *jé'eh*.

18.4.2 EXCLAMATIONS

āiya! is a negatively charged exclamation, expressing shock or disapproval. Like several sentence particles, it has various alternative forms such as *āiya*, *āiyáh* and *āiyak*:[7]

Āiya! Yauh mgeidāk daai sósìh la!
oh again forget bring key PRT
'Oh no, I've forgotten my keys again!'

Āiyáh, m̀h dihm la! (despairing)
oh not okay PRT
'Oh no, I can't deal with this!'

Āiyak, tung séi ngóh la! (sudden pain)
ouch hurt die me PRT
'Ouch, that really hurts.'

séi la (also *baih la*) expresses panic or despair in an emergency:

Séi la, gām chi saht chìh dou.
die PRT this time sure late arrive
'Oh no, we're bound to be late this time.'

Baih la, móuh saai yáu.
uh-oh PRT not-have all gas
'Uh-oh, we're out of gas!'

wa expresses surprise or wonder, often together with the adverb *gam* 'so':

Wa! Léih gāmyaht gam leng gé!
wow you today so beautiful PRT
'Wow, you look great today!'

Wa! Gām-máahn gam hóu sung gé!
wow tonight so good food PRT
'Wow! Such good food tonight!'

yí? is an exclamation of surprise:

Yí? Mātyéh lèihga? Yí? Léih dōu háidouh àh?
huh what PRT huh you also here PRT
'Hey, what's this?' 'Hey, what are you doing here?'

Chē! is a disparaging particle of onomatopoeic origin, like *tut-tut* in English:

Chē! Sái māt léih góng jēk!
PRT need what you say PRT
'Huh! You don't have to tell me!'

Chē! Gam síu chín gé!
PRT so little money PRT
'Huh! Is that all (the money)?'

hóu yéh! is an exclamation of approval:

A: Gām-máahn ngóh chéng sihk-faahn. B: Hóu yéh!
tonight I invite eat-food good stuff
'I'm treating you to dinner tonight.' 'Great!'

It is also used ironically:

Léih hóu yéh! Gām chi jauh dong léih yèhng lā.
you good stuff this time then count you win PRT
'Good for you! Let's say you've won this time . . .' (implying 'watch out')

19 IMPERATIVE SENTENCES: COMMANDS AND REQUESTS

Imperative sentences are used to give commands and directions. In Cantonese, they are also much used to make requests, in a manner which may seem direct to a Western ear. For example, where English would use a modal verb as in '*Would you . . .?*' an imperative sentence may be used in Cantonese:

> Léih ló fahn boují làih ā.
> you bring CL newspaper come PRT
> 'Bring the paper over, will you?'

> Jām būi chàh béi ngóh ā.
> pour cup tea for me PRT
> 'Pour me a cup of tea, will you?'

Note, however, that the particle *ā* (18.3.1) softens the force of the request, with a similar effect to the English tag. As with questions, imperatives without a particle tend to be abrupt and may be perceived as impolite; the sentence particles thus play an important role in moderating commands and requests. The particle *lā* is also characteristically used in requests and instructions, and hence appears in many of the following examples:

> Léih mhóu tēng kéuih góng lā!
> you don't listen him talk PRT
> 'Don't take any notice of him, okay?'

> Héi-sān lā!
> rise-body PRT
> 'Get up!'

19.1 SECOND PERSON IMPERATIVES

In an imperative sentence, the subject pronoun *léih* 'you' may be present or left understood, unlike in English where it is normally dropped:

> (Léih) faai dī jāp yéh jáu!
> (you) fast-ish pack things leave
> 'Hurry up and get ready to leave.'

> (Léih) dākhàahn béi dihnwá ngóh ā.
> (you) at-leisure give telephone me PRT
> 'Give me a call when you have time.'

To turn these commands into more polite requests, *mgōi* 'please' may be added (20.1.1).

Idioms: *sīn (ji) dāk* after an imperative serves to reinforce the message:

Léih dáng màaih   ngóh **sīn**   **dāk**   gá!
you wait V-PRT me   only okay   PRT
'You'd better wait for me, you know!'

Léih jouh yéh   **mhóu** gam maahn **sīn**   **dāk**   gá!
you do   work don't so   slow   only okay PRT
'Don't work so slowly, okay?'

The coverb *tùhng (ngóh)* is also used to reinforce imperatives:

Léih faai dī   **tùhng   ngóh** ché!
you fast-ish for   me   leave
'Do me a favour and get out of here!'

Léih **tùhng ngóh** tēng-jyuh!
you with   me   listen-CONT
'Listen to me, will you?'

tùhng ngóh here does not mean 'with me', but suggests 'for me' or 'on my orders'. Like the ironic use of *Do me a favour* in English, it is by no means polite.

In imperatives, the reduplicated adjective (see 10.1.3) serves as an adverb in preference to the adverbial construction with *dāk* (see 10.1.1):

Léih lóuh-lóuh-saht-saht tùhng ngóh góng a   há! (film)
you honest-honest   with me   say PRT PRT
'Tell me honestly, will you?'

Another adverb construction used in imperative sentences is [adjective] *dī* before the verb:

Léih hóu   lóuh-saht dī   tùhng ngóh góng la   wo.
you better honest a-bit with me   say PRT PRT
'You'd better tell me honestly.'

Léih faai dī   làih   lā!
you fast-ish come PRT
'Hurry up and come.'

Jóu dī   fan   wo!
early-ish sleep PRT
'Go to bed early, won't you?'

Note that the meaning of *dī* here is not explicitly comparative. By contrast, [adjective] *di* after the *dāk* construction (10.1.1) has comparative meaning (cf. 9.3):

Mgōi   léih   jāp   dāk   jeng   dī   lā!
please you   dress ADV   smart   more PRT
'Couldn't you dress a bit smarter?'

19.2   FIRST PERSON IMPERATIVES

'We' imperatives (as expressed in English by *let's* . . .) may retain or omit the subject pronoun *ngóhdeih*:

Ngóhdeih   heui   góbihn   tái-háh   ā.
we   go   that-side   look-DEL   PRT
'Let's go and take a look over there.'

Ngóhdeih   heui   máaih   sāam   lo.
we   go   buy   clothes   PRT
'Let's go and shop for some clothes.'

Note that a sentence particle such as *ā*, *lā* or *lo*, seeking cooperation or compliance, often accompanies such an imperative.

The adverb *bātyùh* 'rather' is used in a first or second person imperative to make a suggestion. As an adverb, it may come between subject and verb or before the subject:

Bātyùh ngóhdeih   heui   mahn   yàhn   lo.
rather we   go   ask   people   PRT
'Why don't we go and ask someone?'

Léih   bātyùh   chóh   háidouh   sìn.
you   rather   sit   here   PRT
'Why don't you sit here for a moment?'

First person singular imperatives are formed with *dáng* 'let':

Dáng   ngóh   bōng   léih   ā.   (offering to help with a task)
let   me   help   you   PRT
'Let me help you.'

Dáng   ngóh   tēng   lā.   (offering to answer phone)
let   me   listen PRT
'Let me answer the phone.'

Note: 'let' in the sense of allowing something to happen is expressed by *béi*, while *dáng* expresses a proposal.

19.3 THIRD PERSON IMPERATIVES

Imperative sentences in the third person may be expressed by *dáng* 'let':

Dáng kéuih jihgéi kyutdihng lā!
let him self decide PRT
'Let him think for himself!'

Dáng go bìhbī jihgéi séng, mhóu chòuh séng kéuih a.
let CL baby self awake don't disturb awake him PRT
'Let the baby wake up himself, don't wake him.'

Note that *dáng* as a main verb means 'wait', and this meaning is retained to some extent in the imperative usage.

yáu/yáuh dāk (pronoun) is an alternative and the high rising tone form *yáu* is often used for emphasis:

Yáu dāk kéuih fan lā!
let can him sleep PRT
'Let him sleep.'

Idiom: *yáu dāk kéuih* may also mean 'let it be' or 'don't worry':

A: Léih sailóu jouh mātyéh a?
your brother do what PRT
'What's the matter with your brother?'

B: Yáu dāk kéuih lā!
let okay him PRT
'Don't worry about him!'

Note that *kéuih*, here as in many idioms, may refer to things as well as to people (5.1):

A: Géisìh sái-wún a?
when wash-dish PRT
'When shall we do the washing-up?'
B: Yáu dāk kéuih sìn.
let okay it first
'Leave it for the moment.'

A related idiom is *yáuh . . . yáuh*, used to contrast pronouns with the implication 'each to his own':

Léih yáuh léih cheung-gō, ngóh yáuh ngóh duhk-syū.
you let you sing-song I let me study-book
'You keep on singing, and I'll keep on studying.'

Yáu dāk kéuihdeih siu lā!
let okay them laugh PRT
'Let them laugh all they like.'

Yáu dāk kéuih heui bīndouh dōu hóu lā.
let okay him go where also good PRT
'He can go anywhere he likes.'

Yáu dāk kéuih dím lám dōu móuh mahntàih.
let okay him how think also no problem
'He can think what he likes, it doesn't matter.'

19.4 NEGATIVE IMPERATIVES

The words *mhóu* and *máih* serve to introduce negative commands: *mhóu* is the usual word, while *máih* is relatively direct and more likely to be used among close friends or peers. With *mhóu*, the subject pronoun is optional as for positive imperatives:

(Léih) mhóu wah béi yàhn tēng ngóh yáuh-jó wo!
(you) don't say to people hear I pregnant-PFV PRT
'Don't tell anyone I'm pregnant, okay?'

With *máih*, the pronoun is typically omitted:

Máih gám góng yéh lā!
don't so talk thing PRT
'Don't talk like that.'

To make a request more polite, *mgōi* 'please' may precede *mhóu*:

Mgōi léih mhóu chìh dou wo.
please you don't late arrive PRT
'Please don't be late.'

Mgōi léih góng yéh mhóu gam daaih sēng lā.
please you say things don't so big voice PRT
'Please don't talk so loud.'

mhóu is also used in first person plural imperatives (19.2):

Ngóhdeih mhóu béi kéuih leihyuhng a!
we let's-not by him exploit PRT
'Let's not allow ourselves to be exploited by him!'

> *Pronunciation note*: *mhóu* may be contracted in rapid speech to a single syllable *móuh*:
>
> Móuh chòuh a!
> don't noisy PRT
> 'Be quiet.'
>
> This contraction is liable to be confused with the existential *móuh* (15.4).

máih is an alternative to *mhóu*, used for short and direct commands, and usually without the subject *léih*:

Máih gam baatgwa lā!
don't so gossipy PRT
'Don't talk so much gossip, okay?'

Máih yūk a!
don't move PRT
'Don't move!'

Máih jyuh!
don't yet
'Hang on a moment!'

(Note the use of the particle *jyuh* (11.2.3) in lieu of a verb.) *máih* is less polite and more abrupt than *mhóu*, as seen in the contrast:

Mhóu sihk lā, gam làahnsihk.
don't eat PRT so bad-eat
'Don't eat it, it tastes so bad.'

Máih sihk lā!
don't eat PRT
'Don't eat that!' (I told you not to.)

Note that both *mhóu* and *máih* can be used in **indirect** commands, especially after the verb *giu* 'tell, instruct' (19.5):

Ngóh giu léih mhóu chìh dou ge.
I tell you don't late arrive PRT
'I told you not to be late.'

Léih giu kéuih máih jáu jyuh.
you tell him don't leave yet
'Tell him not to leave yet.' *or* 'You told him not to leave yet.'

Idioms: *mhóu yiu*, literally 'don't want it', is an instruction to reject or dispose of something:

Mhóu yiu dī gaakyeh sung la!
don't want CL leftover food PRT
'Get rid of that leftover food.'

Mhóu yiu kéuih la! (note the idiomatic use of *kéuih*: 5.1)
don't want it PRT
'Get rid of it!'

chīnkèih mhóu is a stronger form of prohibition, similar in force to *Whatever you do, don't . . .* :

Chīnkèih mhóu cho gwo nī go gēiwuih! (radio ad.)
by-all-means don't miss pass this CL opportunity
'Make sure you don't miss this opportunity!'

Léih chīnkèih mhóu yuhng gó dī wūjōu ge būi.
you by-all-means don't use those CL dirty LP glasses
'Don't use those dirty glasses, whatever you do!'

19.5 INDIRECT COMMANDS

Indirect or reported commands work like indirect speech in general (16.5). Verbs of commanding such as *giu* 'tell' are followed straightforwardly by a clause containing the reported command:

Ngóh giu-jó kéuih sāam dím jūng háidouh
I tell-PFV him three o'clock be-here

dáng ngóhdeih.
wait us
'I told him to be waiting for us at three o'clock.'

In reporting negative commands, *mhóu* or *máih* is retained:

Ngóh giu-jó léih **mhóu** gam gāp ge lā.
I tell-PFV you don't so hasty PRT PRT
'I told you not to be in such a hurry.'

Ngóh giu-jó léihdeih **máih** chòuh ge lā.
I tell-PFV you-PL don't noisy PRT PRT
'I told you not to make a noise.'

The serial verb construction *wah* (*béi*) [pronoun] *tēng/jī* 'tell (to) him listen/know' used to introduce indirect speech (16.5) may also introduce indirect commands:

Léih wah béi kéuih tēng **mhóu** joi dá-dihnwá làih.
you say to him listen don't again call-phone come
'Tell him not call again, okay?'

Wah ngóh jī léih jūngyi bīngo.
tell me know you like who
'Tell me who you like.'

Note that if *béi* is left out, only a pronoun can occur between *wah* 'say' and *tēng/jī* 'listen/know'.

(*ngóh*) *dōu wah* is used to remind someone of a command, often ironically:

A: A-Hùhng yauh háidouh chòuh wo.
   A-Hung again be-here noisy PRT
   'Ah Hung is making trouble again.'

B: Ngóh **dōu wah**(**-jó**) mhóu tēng kéuih góng ge lā.
   I also say (-PFV) don't listen him talk PRT PRT
   'I told you not to take any notice of him.'

20 CANTONESE SPEECH CONVENTIONS: POLITENESS AND TERMS OF ADDRESS

The conventions governing the use of speech in context vary substantially across cultures and languages. These differences are important in that they may lead one culture to find another impolite, whereas in reality each has its own form of politeness. Several such differences exist between English and Cantonese.

An important aspect of Chinese politeness is the concept of **face** (*mihn-jí* or *mín* with change of tone), from which we derive expressions such as *to lose face* and *face-saving*. The Cantonese expressions are:

béi mín, séung mín 'give face'
móuh (saai) mín 'lose (all one's) face'
lohk (ngóh) mín 'make (me) lose face'
dīu (ngóh) gá 'make (me) lose face'

Face is similar to the Western concept of (self-)esteem, but its social significance is greater, especially for those in higher social positions. Politeness in speech involves concern for one's own face on the one hand, and for that of the addressee on the other. Reference to face is also made in various polite formulae:

Dōjeh	séung	mín.	(used at formal dinners etc.)
thank-you	give	face	

'Thank you for coming.'

haakhei 'be polite' is found in a number of formulae:

msái	haakhei		mhóu	haakhei
need-not	polite		don't	polite

'make yourself at home'   'don't be polite, you're welcome'

Léih	taai	haakhei	la!		Sái	māt	gam	haakhei	a?
you	too	polite	PRT		need	what	so	polite	PRT

'you're too kind'   'Why so polite!'

láihmaauh refers to polite behaviour; *yáuh láihmaauh* is to be polite, *móuh láihmaauh* to be impolite.

20.1 POLITENESS CONVENTIONS

The English speaker used to a straightforward distinction between 'please' and 'thank you' faces difficulty with the corresponding Cantonese expressions. The ubiquitous *mgōi* is used to mean both 'please' and 'thank you' (20.1.1), while 'thank you' is expressed sometimes by *mgōi* and sometimes by *dōjeh* (20.1.2).

20.1.1 REQUESTS

mgōi or *mgōi léih* 'please' is used before or after a request:

> Mgōi   béi   būi   séui   ngóh.
> please   give   cup   water   me
> 'May I have a glass of water, please?'

> Mgōi   léih   bōng   ngóh   ló   go   gīp   ā.
> please   you   help   me   carry CL   case   PRT
> 'Would you help me carry the suitcase, please?'

> Ngóh   yiu   būi   gafē,   **mgōi**.
> I   want   cup   coffee please
> 'A cup of coffee, please.'

> Léih   faai   dī   jouh   yùhn   lā,   **mgōi**   **léih**.
> you   fast   rather do   finish PRT   please   you
> 'Hurry up and finish, will you?'

mgōi is also used to accept an offer:

> A: Yám-m̀h-yám   bējáu   a?
>   drink-not-drink beer   PRT
>   'Would you like some beer?'

> B: Hóu   a,   mgōi   léih.
>   good   PRT   thank you
>   'Yes, please.'

Note that if speaker A is going to pay for the beer, *dōjeh* 'thank you' (see below) is called for; otherwise *mgōi* is appropriate, for example when a waiter asks whether you want a beer.

hóu sām léih is a stronger form of request followed by a critical suggestion:

> Hóu   sām   léih,   mhóu   gam   láahn   lā!
> good   heart you   don't so   lazy   PRT
> 'Don't be so lazy, please!'

> Hóu   sām   léih,   gáam-háh-fèih   lā!
> good   heart you   lose-DEL-weight   PRT
> 'Lose some weight, please!'

Requests which are invitations may be preceded by *chéng*, which as a verb means 'invite', or *chèuihbín* 'as you like':

Chéng yahp làih lā.
invite enter come PRT
'Come in, please.'

Chèuihbín chóh wo.
as-you-like sit PRT
'Please take a seat.'

Chèuihbín tái wo, màaih geng ping-háh lā.
as-you-please look PRT approach mirror try-DEL PRT
'You're welcome to look and try it on at the mirror.'
(used by salespersons)

Note the use of the sentence particle lā (18.3.3) in invitations.

20.1.2 THANKS

mgōi is used for small favours, such as serving drinks or dishes. A polite
form suitable for more extensive services is mgōi saai, 'thank you very
much' (adding the quantifying particle saai 'all': see 11.3.3). mgōi (saai) is
also used in saying 'no thank you':

A: Juhng yiu-mh-yiu chàh a?
   still want-not-want tea PRT
   'Would you like more tea?'

B: Mh yiu la, mgōi.
   not want PRT thanks
   'No thanks.'

A: Sái-msái ngóh bōng-sáu a?
   need-not-need I help-hand PRT
   'Do you need me to help?'

B: Msái la, mgōi saai.
   no-need PRT thank-you
   'No, thank you.'

dōjeh is used to thank people for gifts and major services:

A: Nī jek bīu sung béi léih ge.
   this CL watch send give you PRT
   'This watch is (a gift) for you.'

B: Wa! Hóu leng a. Dōjeh saai.
   Wow so pretty PRT thank-you
   'Wow, it's so pretty. Thank you very much.'

This includes metaphorical gifts such as compliments (although these are
typically played down: see 20.1.4):

A: Leih gāmyaht hóu leng wo!   B: Dōjeh!
   you today very pretty PRT   thank-you
   'You're looking great today!'   'Oh, thanks.'

Similarly, a meal provided or paid for by a host is regarded as a gift rather than a service, and calls for *dōjeh*. When buying goods, the buyer uses *mgōi* on receiving the goods, while the seller replies with *dōjeh* on receiving payment. *dōjeh saai* means 'thanks for everything' or serves as a reinforced thank-you. To reply to an expression of thanks, *msái (dōjeh/ mgōi)* 'no need (for thanks)' or *msái haakhei* 'no need to be so polite' may be used:

A: Dōjeh léih chāan faahn wo.   B: Msái   dōjeh.
   thank you CL   rice   PRT   no-need thanks
   'Thank you for treating us to this meal.'   'It's a pleasure.'

A: Dōjeh léih bōng-sáu.   B: Msái   haakhei.
   thank you help-out   no-need polite
   'Thank you for your help.'   'You're welcome.'

20.1.3 APOLOGIES

deui-mjyuh is a general apology:

Deui-mjyuh, ngóh mhaih yáuh sām ge.
sorry   I   not-be have heart PRT
'I'm sorry, I didn't mean it.'   (do it on purpose)

To reply to an apology, the following formulae are used:

Mgányiu.   Móuh   sih   ge.
unimportant.   not-have matter PRT
'Never mind'   'It's alright.'

deui-mjyuh is also used to apologize for an intrusion, for example in asking directions:

Deui-mjyuh, chéng   mahn Hóiyuht Jáudim hái
sorry   request ask   Hyatt   Hotel at

bīndouh a?
where   PRT
'Excuse me, could you tell me where the Hyatt Hotel is?'

deui-mjyuh is *not* used like English *sorry?* to elicit a repetition. 'I beg your pardon?' is expressed colloquially by *Há? Mātyéh wá?* (note that *mātyéh* is often reduced to *mē* in casual speech) 'What's that?', 'What did you say?' or more politely by the phrase:

Mgōi (léih) joi   góng yāt chi.
please (you) again say one time
'I beg your pardon?'

mhóuyisi is an alternative apology, literally meaning 'I'm embarrassed' but widely used to admit fault:

Mhóuyisi, ngóhdeih baau   saai   la.   (used in restaurants)
sorry   we   explode all   PRT
'Sorry, our tables are all full.'

The phrase *màhfàahn léih* 'trouble you' is a polite expression used to apologize in advance for an intrusion or disturbance:

Màhfàahn   léih   bōng   ngóh   wán   bún   syū.
trouble   you   help   me   find   CL   book
'Excuse me, could you find a book for me?'

mgōi je gwo or *mgōi je-je* (literally 'please borrow past') means 'excuse me' i.e. 'would you let me past?' used when making one's way through a crowd.

20.1.4 COMPLIMENTS

Compliments are often made, as in other languages, for the sake of politeness. Traditional Chinese modesty demands that such compliments be rebuffed or played down. There are various strategies for playing down compliments. One is to deny the compliment, for example with a rhetorical question:

A: Léih   jānhaih   yáuh   tīnchòih   ge   wo!
    you   really   have   talent   PRT   PRT
    'You're really talented!'

B: Bīndouh   haih   lē?
    where   is   PRT
    'I don't think so!'

Alternatively, one can treat the compliment as an exaggeration:

A: Léih   Gwóngdūng-wá   góng   dāk   hóu-hóu   wo!
    you   Cantonese   speak   ADV   good-good   PRT
    'You speak very good Cantonese.'

B: Taai   gwojéung   la!
    too   over-compliment   PRT
    'You're too kind!'

One may also thank a speaker for a compliment (with *dōjeh*) before playing it down. For example, when invited to dinner it is customary to compliment the host lavishly:

A: Léih   Táai,   ngóh   làih-jó   Hēunggóng   gam   loih   dōu
    Lee   Mrs   I   come-PFV   Hongkong   so   long   still

    meih   sihk-gwo   gam   hóu   sihk   ge   sung!
    not-yet   eat-EXP   so   good   eat   LP   food
    'Mrs Lee, I've never eaten such good food since I've been in Hongkong!'

B: Dōjeh,   léih taai haakhei la!
thank-you   you too polite   PRT
'Thank you, but you're too kind.'

The phrase (*léih*) *taai haakhei* or *gam haakhei* 'so polite' is also used on receiving gifts.

20.1.5 INTRODUCTIONS

An introduction typically takes the following forms:

Dáng ngóh làih   gaaisiuh.   (see 19.3 for *dáng* 'let')
let   me   come introduce
'May I introduce you?'

(Dáng) ngóh làih   tùhng néihdeih gaaisiuh.
let   I   come   for   you   introduce
'Let me introduce you to each other.'

Nī wái   haih Fōgeih   Daaihhohk ge
this person is   technology university POSS

Chàhn gaausauh.
Chan   professor
'This is Professor Chan from the University of Science and Technology.'

Note that the affiliation precedes the name, with the title last. The parties greet each other with *Léih hóu!* 'How do you do?' or more formally, *Hahng wuih* 'Pleased to meet you'.

  gaaisiuh may also appear in a serial construction with *sīk* 'know':

Ngóh gaaisiuh   kéuih béi léih sīk.
I   introduce   him   to   you know
'I'll introduce him to you.'

The formula *gwai sing* is used to ask a person's surname:

A: Chéng mahn léih **gwai**   **sing** a?
request ask   your honourable name PRT
'May I ask what your name is?'

B: Ngóh sing   Yihp ge.
I   surname Yip PRT
'My surname is Yip.'

A person may be addressed by his or her name:

Yihp Sāang jouh bīn   hòhng   a?   (more formally:
Yip Mr   do   which profession PRT   jouh sihng hòhng?)
'What do you do for a living, Mr Yip?'

20.2 TERMS OF ADDRESS

Terms of address are particularly important in view of their use as greetings. For example, children are taught to address (*giu*) relatives and family friends appropriately. Family members are typically addressed with the appropriate kinship term, often preceded by the prefix *a-* (20.3). For more formal acquaintances where the surname is used, appropriate forms of address are:

Jeh léuihsih 'Ms Tse'   Chàhn Sāang 'Mr Chan'
Wòhng táai 'Mrs Wong'   Tàahm yīsāng 'Dr Tam (physician)'
Làuh síujé 'Miss Lau'   Làhm boksih 'Dr Lam (PhD)'
Máh gūlèuhng 'Madam Ma' (nurse)

Where first names are used, they are typically prefixed with *a-*: *a-Wàh*, *a-Mìhng*. This also applies to English names: *a-Robert*, *a-Cindy*, etc. Surnames may also be prefixed with *a-*; most Cantonese surnames have the low-registered tones and undergo the tone change. Even English names undergo the same process:

Wòhng → a-Wóng   Léih → a-Léi-jái (Lee-boy)
Chàhn → a-Chán   Sihn → a Sín
Winnie → a-Winníe   Ronnie → Ronníe

The tone change also occurs with the epithet *lóuh* 'old':

Yihp → lóuh-Yíp 'old Mr Yip'

Note that the word *lóuh* 'old' in these and other terms of address is not offensive, but expresses familiarity and seniority. It is generally used between long-time friends. It also appears in several terms used to address superiors:

lóuhbáan, lóuhsai 'boss' (could be male or female)
lóuhbáanlèuhng 'wife of boss'

For people whose names are not known, common forms of address include:

sīnsāang 'sir' (also *a-sèuh*, from *Sir*)

Note that *a-sèuh* is commonly used for addressing male teachers (especially those in primary and secondary schools) and also policemen.

síujé 'miss' (also *mītsìh*, from *Miss*)
sīfú ('master': used for craftsmen such as decorators, piano tuners, etc., as well as martial-arts teachers)

Certain kinship terms are also used generically as terms of address:

a-sám 'uncle's wife' (used for older women doing odd jobs such as
janitors, hawkers)
a-yī 'auntie' (used for women such as a friend's mother or one's parents'
friends; *baak-móuh* is more formal)
a-baak 'uncle' (used for older men)
a-sūk 'uncle' (used for middle-aged men)
a-gūng 'grandfather' (used for elderly men)
a-pòh 'grandmother' (used for elderly women)

Alternatively: (*lóuh*) *pòh-pó* '(old) elderly women' which should not be
confused with *lóuh-pòh* 'wife'.

lóuh-gū-pòh 'old maid'
daaih gājē 'big sister' (i.e. a big shot, leading entertainer, etc.)
daaih-lóu 'big brother' (i.e. boss, ringleader, etc.)

In Hongkong, mainland Chinese are colloquially referred to as 'cousins',
e.g. *bíu-múi* for young Chinese girls who often appear in beauty pageants
(*bíu-jé* for older ones), *bíu-gō* or *bíu-sūk* for mainland men. The generic
name *A-Chaan* referring to mainland men has also become popular. In
return, mainlanders call Hongkongers *Góng-Chaan*.

The deferential classifier *wái* (6.2.4) is used with a quantifier or numeral
as a polite form of address. For example, when addressing a formal
gathering, *gok wái* or *gam dō wái* is used to denote 'everyone':

Gok   wái,   fūnyìhng léihdeih.
each   person   welcome   you
'Ladies and gentlemen, welcome.'

Gok   wái sīnsāang,   gok   wái léuihsih
each CL   gentleman   each CL   madam
'Gentlemen and ladies (Chinese style)'

Gam   dō   wái,   yám   būi!
so   many   people   drink glass
'Have a drink, everyone!'

Chéng mahn léuhng wái   yám   mātyéh chàh a?
invite ask two   person   drink what   tea   PRT
'What tea would (the two of) you like to drink, please?'
(used by waiters)

20.3 KINSHIP TERMS

Chinese traditionally has a very complex system of kinship terms, distinguishing finely between elder and younger, paternal and maternal relatives. A further distinction is made between terms which are used to refer

to relatives (**designatives**) and those used to address them (**vocatives**), although in many cases the terms are the same or are interchangeable. With social change and the gradual demise of large extended families, this system tends to become simplified in Hongkong Cantonese, with many speakers making fewer than the full range of distinctions. Pan (1993) discusses the simplification of kinship terms currently happening in China. The same applies to Hongkong, where most families now have only one to two children. There is no need for terms addressing one's aunts or uncles let alone cousins if one family has only one child. The principles of the simplification process are characterized by the retention of paternal terms and the gradual dropping out of terms for distant relatives. Some terms such as *a-sám* 'uncle's wife' and *a-yī* 'mother's sister' have acquired generic reference (see 20.2); as a result of the semantic extension, these terms are used more frequently. On the other hand, some terms referring to very distant relatives which are not used at all are predicted to drop out of the system eventually. Moreover, in modern families, in-laws, for example, may be addressed and referred to by name rather than by the numerous kinship terms.

chānchīk is a general term for 'relatives':

Ngóhdeih hái Wāngōwàh gódouh yáuh hóu dō
we   at   Vancouver there   have very many

chānchīk ge.
relatives PRT
'We have a lot of relatives in Vancouver.'

20.3.1 PARENTS AND GRANDPARENTS

Like other terms of address, kinship terms are commonly prefixed with *a-*, especially those for elder relatives:

a-mā 'mother' (also *màhmā, māmìh*; colloquially *lóuhmóu* 'Mum')
a-bàh 'father' (also *bàhbā, dēdìh*; colloquially *lóuhdauh* 'Dad')

fuhmóuh refers collectively to 'parents' (*fuh* and *móuh* are formal terms for 'father' and 'mother', used in compound expressions such as *Móuh-chān-jit* 'Mother's Day' and *Fuh-chān-jit* 'Father's Day'). *gājéung* is the formal term used in school settings to refer to students' parents or guardians.

Step-parents are given the prefix *gai-* (formal) or *hauh-* (neutral) 'step-':

gai/hauh-fuh 'step-father'   gai/hauh-móuh 'step-mother'

But there are no special terms equivalent to the English *step-son*, *step-daughter*, etc.

Table 20.1 Terms for older relatives

	Paternal	Maternal
grandfather	a-yèh	a-gūng
grandmother	a-màh	a-pòh
uncle: old	a-baak	(daaih)-kaufú
uncle's wife	baak-lèuhng	kau-móuh
uncle: young	a-sūk	(sai)-kaufú
uncle's wife	a-sám	kau-móuh
aunt: old	gū-mā	yìh-mā
aunt's husband	gū-jéung	yìh-jéung
aunt: young	gū-jē	a-yī
aunt's husband	gū-jéung	yìh-jéung

Honorary parents (similar to Godparents, established by a formal ceremony called *séuhng-kai*) are known by the prefix *kai-*:

kai-yèh 'Godfather' kai-jái 'Godson'
kai-mā 'Godmother' kai-léui 'Goddaughter'

āiyā-lóuhdauh and *āiyā-a-mā* refer to those who treat one like one's own parents but without any formal ceremony.

Terms for older relatives distinguish between paternal and maternal lines (see Table 20.1).

20.3.2 BROTHERS, SISTERS AND COUSINS

Cantonese distinguishes between elder and younger siblings and cousins (see Table 20.2). There is no way to refer to a brother or sister without making this distinction, although the words *hīngdaih* 'brothers' and *jímíu/muih* 'sisters' are used collectively to include both elder and younger siblings:

Table 20.2 Terms for siblings and cousins

	Brother	Sister	Paternal cousin (uncle's children only)	Maternal cousin (also paternal aunt's children)
elder	gòh-gō	gā-jē, jèh-jē	tòhng-a-gō(m.) tòhng-gājē (f.)	bíu-gō (m.) bíu-jé (f.)
younger	sai-lóu	mùih-múi, sai-múi	tòhng-dái (m.) or tòhng-sailóu tòhng-múi (f.)	bíu-dái (m.) bíu-múi (f.)

Léih yáuh géi dō (go) hīngdaih jímuih a?
you have how many (CL) brother sister PRT
'How many brothers and sisters do you have?'

Ngóhdeih ūkkéi lìhn ngóh yáuh sāam jímuih.
we home include me have three sister
'There are three sisters in our family.'

These terms are also used metaphorically to denote close friendship, as in the following:

Ngóhdeih yāt sai yàhn léuhng hīngdaih.
we one life people two brother
'We are just like brothers.'

Jouh jímúi ge, jeui gányiu ge haih léih bōng
be sisters PRT most important LP is you help

ngóh, ngóh bōng léih.
me I help I help you
'To be sisters [i.e. close friends], the most important thing is to help each other.'

The words for cousins are based on the terms for 'brother' and 'sister' with the prefix *tòhng-* for paternal uncles' children and *bíu-* for maternal cousins and also paternal aunts' children (see Table 20.2). Note the changed tones: *muih-muih* → *mùihmúi*, *bíu + muih* → *bíumúi*, etc.

In large families, the brothers and sisters may be numbered, or distinguished by the epithets *daaih* 'big' and *sai* 'small':

yih gō 'second brother', i.e. the second eldest of one's elder brothers;
sāam múi 'third sister', i.e. the third eldest of one's younger sisters.
daaih gō 'big elder brother', i.e. the eldest of one's elder brothers;
daaih gājē 'big elder sister', i.e. the eldest of one's elder sisters;
sai jèhjē 'little sister', i.e. the younger of one's elder sisters.

20.3.3 RELATIONS BY MARRIAGE

There are several terms for spouses, belonging to different registers:

	Formal	*Neutral*	*Colloquial*
husband	jeuhngfū	sīnsāang	lóuh-gūng
wife	chāijí	taaitáai	lóuh-pòh

Traditionally, *lóuh-gūng* and *lóuh-pòh* were used only between couples, but these terms are now also used colloquially to refer to others' spouses.

Two different verbs of marriage *ga* and *chéui* are used, depending on whether the object of the verb is a (potential) husband or wife:

Léih faai   dī   **chéui**   fāan   go   **lóuh-pòh**   lā.
you quick bit marry V-PRT CL   wife   PRT
'Get yourself a wife quickly.'

A-Yīng   **ga**-jó   go   yáuh-chín   **lóuh-gūng**.
Ah-Ying marry-PFV   CL   have-money   husband
'Ying has married a rich husband.'

A-Lìhng   m̀h   háng   ga   (béi)   ngóh.
Ah-Ling   not   willing   marry   (to)   me
'Ling is not willing to marry me.'

While *ga* and *chéui* share certain properties, for example both can take the particle *dóu* as in *ga dóu go hóu lóuhgūng* 'manage to marry a good husband' and *chéui dóu go hóu lóuhpòh* 'manage to marry a good wife', they each have special properties which are not shared with each other, e.g. while *chéui* can also be used with the object *sānpóuh* 'daughter-in-law', *ga* cannot be used in this way with *léuihsai* 'son-in-law':

Wòhng Táai   tīngyaht   chéui   sānpóuh/sāmpóuh.
Wong   Mrs   tomorrow   acquire   daughter-in-law
'Mrs Wong is getting a daughter-in-law tomorrow.'

However, *ga* can take the object *léui* 'daughter' with the subject being the parent(s) of *léui* while *chéui* cannot be used in this way taking an object *jái* 'son':

Máh   Sāang   hah   go   yuht   ga   léui.
Ma   Mr   next   CL   month   marry   daughter
'Mr Ma is going to marry off his daughter next month.'

ga but not *chéui* can take directional particles such as *yahp* 'into' and *chēut* 'out':

Kéuih   m̀h   jī   géi   hahn   ga   yahp   hòuh   mùhn.
she   not   know   how   desire   marry   into   rich   family
'She wants very much to marry into a rich family.'

Ngóh   go   daaih   léui   jūngyū   ga   dāk   chēut
My   CL   eldest daughter   finally   marry   able   out

heui   la.
go   PRT
'My eldest daughter finally got married off.'

The terms for 'brother-in-law' and 'sister-in-law' take account of the distinctions between elder and younger siblings, giving a number of terms corresponding to the two in English:

elder sister's husband: jéfū   elder brother's wife: a-sóu
younger sister's husband: muihfū   younger brother's wife: daihfúh

A further set of terms refers to a spouse's siblings:

husband's older brother: daaih baak
wife's older brother: daaih káuh
husband's younger brother: sūk jái
wife's younger brother: káuhjái
husband's older sister: gū lāai
wife's older sister: daaih-yìh
husband's younger sister: gū jái
wife's younger sister: yī-jái

Terms for parents-in-law reflect the traditional practice of the wife living with the husband's family. Hence, the terms with which a woman refers to her parents-in-law have the prefix *gā-* 'home', while those used by the husband have the prefix *ngohk* or *ngoih*:

	Formal	Neutral
husband's father	gā-gūng	lóuh-yèh
husband's mother	gā-pó	làaih-láai
wife's father	ngohk-fú	ngoih-fú
wife's mother	ngohk-móu	ngoih-móu

While the formal terms are not used for direct address but for referring to the individuals (i.e. designatives: see 20.3), the neutral terms can serve both purposes (designatives and vocatives). A common practice in modern families is to use the same address terms as one's spouse does, simply *māmìh* for wife's mother or husband's mother.

Ex-spouses are denoted by the prefix *chìhn* (*yahm*):

chìhn-yahm-jeuhngfū, chìhn-fū 'ex-husband'
chìhn-yahm-taaitáai, chìhn-chāi 'ex-wife'

Similarly: *chìhn douh làahmyáuh/léuihyáuh* 'ex-boyfriend/girlfriend'.

20.3.4 CHILDREN AND GRANDCHILDREN

One's children are known collectively as *jái-léui* ('son-daughter'). Elder and younger sons and daughters may be distinguished by *daaih* 'big' and *sai* 'small':

ngóh	go	daaih	jái		kéuih	go	sai	léui
my	CL	big	son		her	CL	small	daughter
'my elder son'					'her younger daughter'			

The youngest child is known colloquially as *lāai-jái* (lit. 'last son') 'youngest son' or *lāai-léui* (lit. 'last daughter') 'youngest daughter'.

Following the patrilinear system, grandchildren are treated differently according to whether they are one's son's or one's daughter's children. The prefix *ngoih* 'outside' indicates that a daughter's children do not belong to one's own family, as in the terms used for one's wife's parents:

	Son's child	Daughter's child
grandson	syūn	ngoih-syūn
granddaughter	syūnléui	ngoih-syūnléui

A similar distinction is made in the case of nephews and nieces:

	Brother's child	Sister's child
nephew	ját or jaht-jái	yìh-sāng(-jái)
niece	jaht-léui	yìh-sāngléui

20.4 GREETINGS

The traditional greeting *Léih hóu (ma)?* 'How are you?' (corresponding to Mandarin *nǐ hǎo (ma)*) is now relatively formal, used between strangers, for example, at the first encounter and acquaintances rather than friends or family. Closer acquaintances are greeted by the following:

jeuigahn	dím	a?	Mātyéh	wàahngíng	a? (slangy)
recently	how	PRT	what	circumstances	PRT
'How've you been?'			'What's up?'		

Acquaintances may also be greeted by their name alone, often preceded by *A*, e.g. *A-Wóng!* Similarly, family members are greeted with their kinship term: *A-Bàh*, *A-Mā*, etc.

Greetings appropriate for specific occasions and times of day include:

jóu	sàhn	fūn-yìhng
early	morning	happy-receive
'good morning'		'welcome'

joi	gin	(formal; many speakers use *bāai-baai*)
again	see	
'goodbye'		

joi	wuih	(until next time; used in broadcasting)
again	meet	
'goodbye'		

jóu	táu	máahn	ōn	(formal)
early	rest	evening	peace	
'good night'		'good night'		

Many conventional greetings seem uninformative and puzzlingly redundant to the English speaker. A well-known example is the greeting:

Sihk-jó   faahn   meih   a?
eat-PFV   rice   not-yet   PRT
'How are you?' (lit. 'Have you eaten yet?')

The appropriate answer is *Sihk-jó la, mgōi* 'Yes, thank you'. This greeting is thus comparable to the British English *Lovely day, isn't it?*, with eating replacing the British obsession with weather as the 'dummy' topic of conversation.

The verb for sending regards is *mahn-hauh*; to convey regards via an intermediary the following can be used:

Léih gei-jyuh   bōng ngóh mahn-hauh léih   gòhgō   wo.
you remember   help me   ask-greet your brother PRT
'Remember to give my regards to your [elder] brother.'

Hóu dō   yàhn   mahn-hauh léih   wo.
very many people ask-greet you   PRT
'A lot of people sent their regards to you.'

gūnghéi or *gūnghéi léih* (*-deih*) 'congratulations' is suitable for occasions such as weddings, births, promotions and graduations. Greetings for special occasions include:

Birthday:

Sāangyaht faailohk!
birthday   happiness
'Happy Birthday!'

Jūk léih lìhn-lìhn yáuh gāmyaht seui-seui yáuh
bless you year-year have today   age-age   have

gām jīu!
this morning
'Many happy returns!' (formal)

Wedding:

Sān fān   faailohk!
newly-wed happiness
'Congratulations!'

Jūk léihdeih baahk tàuh dou lóuh!
bless you-PL white hair till old
'May you always be happy together.'

This should be replied to with *dōjeh* 'thank you'.

New Year:

Sān lìhn faailohk! 'Happy New Year!'
(applicable to Western or Chinese New Year)

Chinese New Year:

Gūnghéi   faat   chòih!
congratulations make wealth
'Have a prosperous year!'

This may be replied to with:

Daaihgā   gám   wah.
everyone so   say
'The same to you, too.'

Gūnghéi faat chòih! may also be followed by a request for a red packet of lucky money (*laih-sih*, traditionally given by married people only) from children, employees or close acquaintances:

Laih-sih   dauh   lòih!
lucky-money   elicit come
'Lucky-money time!'

Other New Year's greetings are tailored to the addressee:

Sāangyi   hīnglùhng! (addressed to businessmen)
business   prosperous
'May your business prosper.'

Hohkyihp   jeunbouh! (addressed to students)
study-career improve
'All the best with your studies.'

Sāntái gihnhōng! (addressed to elderly people)
body   healthy
'Wishing you good health.'

Acquaintances leaving on a journey may be wished:

Yāt louh seuhn fūng!
one road follow wind
'Have a smooth journey.'

20.5 TELEPHONE EXPRESSIONS

Wái is used to initiate contact on the telephone:

Wái? Haih-maih Chàhn Sāang a? 'Hello? Is that Mr Chan?'

chéng mahn 'may I ask' is a polite way to initiate a request:

Chéng   mahn   Làuh yīsāng   hái-m̀h-háidouha?
request ask   Lau doctor   here-not-here PRT
'Is Dr Lau there, please?'

Chéng   mahn   bīngo wán   kéuih   a?
request ask   who   call   her   PRT
'May I ask who's calling?'

Replies and excuses include:

Kéuih   hàahng   hōi-jó   wo.
s/he   walk   away-PFV   PRT
'He just stepped out.'

Kéuih   hōi-gán-wúi   wo.
s/he   hold-PROG-meeting   PRT
'She's in a meeting.'

Kéuih   góng-gán   dihnwá   wo.
s/he   talk-PROG   telephone   PRT
'He's on the phone.'

Other common replies include:

Hó-m̀h-hóyíh   làuhdāi   dihnwá   a?
can-not-can   leave   telephone   PRT
'Could you leave your number?'

Ngóh   jyun-tàuh   fūk   fāan   léih   ā.
I   turn-head   reply   back   you   PRT
'I'll call you back in a moment.'

Kéuih   m̀h   háidouh   wo.   Yáuh-móuh   gányiu   sih
s/he   not   here   PRT   have-not-have   important   matter

wán   kéuih a?
find   him   PRT
'She is not here. Do you have anything important for her?'

Hó-m̀h-hóyíh   góng-dāi   wán   kéuih   mātyéh sih   a?
can-not-can   leave-down   find   him/her what   matter PRT
'Could you leave a message?'

If there is a call-waiting service, a call comes in in the middle of a telephone conversation:

Deui-mjyuh,   yáuh   dihn-wá   yahp   làih,   mgōi
sorry   have   phone   enter   come   please

léih   dáng-dáng.
you   wait-wait
'Sorry, a call is coming in. Hold on a moment, please.'

Deui-mjyuh, ngóh yìhgā góng-gán, yāt ján dá
sorry I now speak-PROG one moment call

fāan béi léih ā.
back to you PRT
'Sorry, I'm on the phone. I'll call you right back.'

To respond to a person who has dialled the wrong number:

Chéng mahn léih dá géi houh dihn-wá a?
please ask you dial what number phone PRT
'May I ask what number you dialled?'

Or simply:

Deui-mjyuh, dá cho wo.
sorry dial wrong PRT
'Sorry, (you got the) wrong number.'

21 NUMERALS AND TIMES

21.1 NUMERALS

Table 21.1 Numerals

1 yāt	11 sahpyāt	100 yāt baak
2 yih, léuhng	12 sahpyih	1,000 yāt chīn
3 sāam	13 sahpsāam	10,000 yāt maahn
4 sei	14 sahpsei	1,000,000 yāt baak maahn
5 nǵh/m̀h[1]	15 sahpnǵh	100,000,000 yāt yīk
6 luhk	16 sahpluhk	1,000,000,000 yāt baak yīk
7 chāt	17 sahpchāt	
8 baat	18 sahpbaat	
9 gáu	19 sahpgáu	
10 sahp	20 yihsahp	

Compound numbers are formed in the same order as in English:

36	sāamsahp-luhk			
	thirty-six			
124	yāt	baak	yihsahp-sei	
	one	hundred	twenty-four	
3,652	sāam chīn	luhk baak	nǵhsahp-yih	
	three thousand	six hundred	fifty-two	

Note that where a zero appears before a final digit from 1 to 9 the zero must be pronounced:

104	yāt	baak	lìhng	sei
	one	hundred	zero	four
6,008	luhk	chīn	lìhng	baat
	six	thousand	zero	eight

Above 10,000 (*yāt maahn*), Cantonese speakers count in tens of thousands (*maahn*) rather than thousands (*chīn*):

15,000	yāt maahn nǵh chīn
130,000	sahpsāam maahn

There is no word for a million (expressed by *yāt baak maahn*). *yāt yīk* is one hundred million (100,000,000), a number much used in financial reports. One billion (1,000,000,000) is thus *sahp yīk*.

Idiom: maahn yāt, literally an expression of the odds 10,000:1, is
used to mean 'just in case':

Maahn yāt	léih	wán	m̀h	dóu	yéh	jouh,	hóyíh
10,000:1	you	find	not	succeed	work	do	can

yuhng	jyuh	ngóh	dī	chín	sìn.
use	CONT	my	CL	money	first

'Just in case you can't find any work, you can use my money for the
time being.'

Decimals

The decimal point is read as *dím* or *go*:

0.2	lìhng	dím	yih		3.2	sāam	dím	yih
	zero	point	two			three	point	two

$3.2	sāam	go	yih (note the use of *go* referring to money)
	three	CL	two
	'three dollars twenty'		

or	sāam	mān	lìhng	léuhng	hòuh-jí
	three	dollars	and	two	ten-cents
	'three dollars twenty cents'				

22.5	yah-yih	dím	ńgh
	twenty-two	point	five

$22.5	yah-yih	go	bun
	twenty-two	CL	half
	'twenty-two and a half'		

or	yah-yih	mān	(lìhng)	ńgh	hòuh-jí
	twenty-two	dollars	(and)	five	ten-cents

0.3	lìhng dím sāam 'zero point three'
1.3	yāt dím sāam 'one point three'

In the case of one dollar something, *yāt* is always left out:

$1.30	go	sāam
	CL	three
	'one dollar and thirty cents'	

1.5 hours   (yāt) go   bun   jūng(tàuh)   (here *yāt* is often left out)
            one CL   half   hour
            'one and a half hours' *or* 'an hour and a half'

1.5 months (yāt) go   bun   yuht
            one CL   half   month
            'one and a half months' *or* 'a month and a half'

1.5 years   yāt   lìhn   bun   (*not* *yāt go bun lìhn)
            one year half
            'one and a half years' *or* 'a year and a half'

In colloquial Cantonese, money is often referred to as *séui* 'water', as in:

yāt   gauh   séui
one   CL   water
'one hundred dollars'

yāt   pùhn   séui
one   basin water
'ten thousand dollars'

(Note that ten thousand dollars, i.e. *yāt maahn* is referred to as *yāt lāp* and one million, i.e. *yāt baak maahn* as *yāt baak lāp* where *lāp* is the classifier for small rounded objects as in *yāt lāp tàihjí* 'a grape'.)

Bōng ngóh **dohk**   **séui**.   (slang)
help   me   acquire water
'Help me get money.'   (usually by means of borrowing)

Faai dī **bohng** **séui**.   (slang)
quick bit pay   water
'Pay me quickly.'

Kéuih hóu **daahp-séui** ga.
s/he very heap water PRT
'She's got lots of money.'

Abbreviations

The compound numbers are readily abbreviated in informal speech, especially in quoting prices. *yihsahp* + *numeral* 'twenty + something' are often contracted to *yah/yeh*-numeral:

22   yihsahp-yih → yah/yeh-yih
24   yihsahp-sei → yah/yeh-sei

Similarly, in numbers from 30 onwards, the word *sahp* 'ten' is reduced to *ah*:

34   sāamsahp-sei → sà'ah-sei
41   seisahp-yāt → sei'ah-yāt
56   nǵhsahp-luhk → nǵh'ah-luhk
72   chātsahp-yih → chà'ah-yih

For numbers over one hundred which end in *sahp* 'tens', *sahp* can be left out:

120   (yāt) baak-yih(sahp) → baak yih
180   (yāt) baak-baat(sahp) → baak baat
240   yih baak-sei(sahp) → yih baak sei
650   luhk baak-nǵh(sahp) → luhk baak nǵh

For numbers over one thousand which end in *baak* 'hundreds', *baak* can be left out:

1,300   (yāt) chīn-sāam (baak) → chīn sāam
4,800   sei chīn-baat (baak) → sei chīn baat

For numbers over ten thousand which end in *chīn* 'thousands', *chīn* can be left out:

17,000   (yat) maahn-chāt (chīn) → maahn chāt
86,000   baat maahn-luhk (chīn) → baat maahn-luhk

Approximations

There are several ways to express approximate numbers, some of which are difficult to express in English:

sahp**géi** douh 'ten-and-a-few degrees', i.e. 13–19
baak-**géi** go yàhn 'hundred-something people', i.e. 130–99
chīn-**lèhng** mān 'thousand-odd dollars', i.e. 1,300–999
géisahp mān 'a few tens of dollars', i.e. 30–90
géibaak go yàhn 'a few hundred people'

These forms are also used to express ages approximately:

yah-**lèhng** seui 'twenty-odd'
sà'ah-**géi** seui 'thirty-something (years old)'
géi-sahp seui 'a few tens of years old' (usually middle age and over)

In colloquial usage, thirty years of age or above can be referred to as *sāam jēung* 'thirty', *sāam jēung géi* (*yéh*) 'thirty something' and forty years old as *sei jēung*, etc., where *jēung* is a classifier as in *yāt jēung jí* 'a piece of paper':

Lóuh	Wóng	gām	lìhn	luhk	jēung	ge	la.
Old	Wong	this	year	six	CL	PRT	PRT

'Mr Wong is sixty years old this year.'

daaihkoi 'approximately', *jóyáu*, *dóu* and *gam seuhng há* all meaning 'thereabouts' are also used to estimate an approximate figure:

daaihkoi	yihsahp	go	haakyàhn	**jóyáu**
approximately	twenty	CL	guests	left-right

'about twenty guests'

seisahp	seui	**dóu**
forty	years	about

'about forty, forty-ish'

yāt	chīn	mān	**gam**	**seuhng**	**há**
one	thousand	dollar	so	above	below

'a thousand dollars, give or take a bit'

sāam	chīn	mān	**dóu**
three	thousand	dollars	about

'around $3,000'

héimáh 'at least' sets a lower boundary:

héimáh luhksahp go yàhn 'at least sixty people'

Yàuh . . . jidou/ji/dou . . . or simply *X ji Y* or *X dou Y* without *yàuh* 'from' is used to give a range of figures 'from . . . to . . .':

(yàuh) sahp jidou sahpńgh seui 'from ten to fifteen years old'
(yàuh) sei dím ji luhk dím 'from four to six o'clock'
(yàuh) nī douh dou gó douh 'from here to there'

Juxtaposition of two adjacent numbers is also used to 'hedge':

yáuh	**sāam**	**sei**	go	yàhn	yáuh	hingcheui
have	three	four	CL	people	have	interest

'three or four people are interested'

luhk	**chāt**	chīn	mān	dóu
six	seven	thousand	dollar	there

'around six to seven thousand dollars'

Ngóh	tái-jó	**yāt**	**léuhng**	bún	syū	je.
I	read-PFV	one	two	CL	book	PRT

'I've only read one or two books.'

21.1.1 CARDINAL NUMBERS

The numeral appears before countable nouns, as in English, usually followed by the classifier:

```
sāam   go   yuht        luhk jek  gáu
three  CL   month       six  CL   dog
```

Note the following expressions which are similar in form but have very different meanings:

yāt yuht 'January'   sahpyih yuht 'December'
yāt go yuht 'one month'   sahpyih go yuht 'twelve months'

An alternative order is numeral + classifier phrase following the noun. This form is used especially in contexts of buying and selling, and in recipes:

Ngóh máaih-jó yuhtbéng **léuhng hahp**.
I   but-PFV mooncake two   box
'I bought two boxes of mooncake.'

Mgōi, yiu gaailáan **yāt gān**, dauhfuh **léuhng gauh**.
please want gailan one catty tofu two cake
'I'll have a catty of gailan and two cakes of tofu, please.'

Gā sihyàuh yāt gāng. (recipe)
add soy-sauce one spoon
'Add a spoonful of soy sauce.'

yih vs. *léuhng*: of the two distinct words for 'two', *yih* is used in counting and in compound numbers such as *yihsahp* 'twenty' and *yihbaak* 'two hundred', etc.:

yāt, yih, sāam . . .
'one, two, three . . .'

gā yih, gáam yih, sìhng yih, chèuih yih
add two minus two times two divide two
'add two, minus two, times two, divided by two'

daih   yih   (*not* *daih léuhng)
number two
'second'

léuhng is used to quantify nouns:

léuhng go yàhn
two   CL person
'two people'

léuhng dím jūng 'two o'clock'

ngóhdeih léuhng go
we   two   CL
'the two of us'

léuhng júng máih 'two kinds of rice'

An exception here is the literary phrase *yih yàhn saigaai* 'two people's world' referring to a happy couple. Similarly, *yih yàhn tou chāan* on a menu indicates a dinner for two.

In counting money, *yih* is called for in some contexts and *léuhng* in others and sometimes either one can be used. *léuhng* is used for units of money such as *mān* 'dollar' and *hòuhjí* 'cents':

2 dollars = léuhng mān   (*not* *yih mān)
20 cents = léuhng hòuhjí   (*not* *yih hòuhjí)
20 dollars = yihsahp mān   (*not* *léuhngsahp mān)

However, for 200, 2,000 and 20,000 dollars both *léuhng* and *yih* are acceptable:

200 dollars = léuhng/yihbaak mān
2,000 dollars = léuhng/yih chīn mān
20,000 dollars = léuhng/yih maahn mān
22,222 dollars = yih maahn yih chīn yihbaak yihsahp-yih mān

The word *mā* is often used to enumerate things that are doubled or come in a pair, e.g. twins are called *mā tōi*, the expression *dá-mā làih* means 'come in pair':

Kéuihdeih haih mā-sāang   hīngdaih/jímúi.
they   are   twin-birth   brothers/sisters
'They are twin brothers/sisters.'

Kéuih yáuh deui mā-jái/léui.
s/he has   CL   twin-son/daughter
'She has a pair of twin sons/daughters.'

Ngóh tùhng léih mā-pōu.
I   with   you   twin-bed
'I share a bed with you.'

Dīmgáai gām go yuht ge yuht-git dāan dá-mā
why   this   CL   month   LP   month-end   statement   pair

lèih gé?
come PRT
'How come this month's monthly statement comes in duplicate?'

mā is also used to refer to two identical digits, for example double zeroes are read as *mā lìhng* and double threes as *mā sāam*; similarly, 228899 = *mā yih mā baat mā gáu*.

21.1.2 ORDINAL NUMBERS

Numbers such as 'first', 'seventh', etc. are formed regularly by preceding the number word with *daih* 'number':

daih	yāt	daih	yih
number	one	number	two
'first'		'second'	

daih	mēi	daih	luhk	lìhng-gám
the	last	number	six	sense
'last'		'sixth sense'		

Idioms: *daih yāt*, *daih yih*: the phrase *daih yāt* 'number one' is also used idiomatically to mean 'the best' or 'the leading':

Chyùhn	góng	daih	yāt	ge	ngàhnhòhng
whole	harbour	number	one	PRT	bank

'Hongkong's leading bank'

The phrase *daih yih* 'number two' is also used to mean 'another':

Kéuihdeih	yìhgā	yiu	wán	daih	yih	go	yīsāng.
they	now	must	find	number	two	CL	doctor

'Now they have to look for another doctor.'

(Compare the adverb *daih yih sìh* 'another time, in the future': 10.3.3.)

---

daih may be questioned with *géi* 'how (many)?' (17.3.8):

Nī	go	haih	léih	**daih**	**géi**	go	jái	a?
this	CL	is	your	number	what	CL	son	PRT

'Which son of yours is this?'

Léih	**daih**	**géi**	**chi**	tái	nī	go	yīsāng	a?
you	number	what	time	see	this	CL	doctor	PRT

'How many times before have you seen this doctor?'

Note that these questions are difficult to translate due to the lack of an expression meaning 'which number?' in English. The translation 'how many times before?' for *daih géi chi* is thus not strictly accurate because the Cantonese question would include the current visit to the doctor in the expected answer.

21.1.3 FRACTIONS AND PERCENTAGES

Fractions of the form X/Y are expressed using *Y fahn X* or *Y fahn jī X*, as follows (note that the order of the numerals is the reverse of the English):

⅓	sāam	fahn	(jī)	yāt
	three	part	(of)	one
	'one-third'			

²/₃ sāam fahn (jī) yih
   three part (of) two
   'two-thirds'

¼ sei fahn (jī) yāt
   four part (of) one
   'a quarter'

¾ sei fahn (jī) sāam
   four part (of) three
   'three-quarters'

These expressions follow the noun which they quantify:

Gó bāt chín mgin-jó **sei fahn sāam**.
that CL money lose-PFV four part three
'Three-quarters of that money went missing.'

Fractions may also be used in the possessive construction with *ge* (6.3):

Ngóh jaahn ge yàhngūng haih kéuih ge **sāam fahn yāt**.
I earn that salary Is s/he LP three part one
'The salary I earn is a third of what he does.'

yāt bun 'half' is used similarly:

Yāt bun hohksāang móuh séuhng-tòhng.
one half student not-have up-class
'Half of the students did not attend class.'

Percentages are expressed in the same form as fractions, with the phrase *baak fahn jī* 'per cent' followed by the numeral:

Sēungdeui sāpdouh baak-fahn-jī baatsahp-luhk.
relative humidity hundred-part eighty-six
'The relative humidity is 86 per cent.'

Yīnggwok làuhga diht-jó baak-fahn-jī yihsahp.
Britain house-price fall-PFV hundred-part twenty
'The price of flats in Britain has fallen by 20 per cent.'

Dī hohksāang baak-fahn-jī nǵhsahp dōu m̀h sīk
CL student hundred-part fifty also not know

daap ge.
answer PRT
'Fifty per cent of the students don't know the answer.'

An alternative way to express percentages is in tenths, using *sìhng*:

20%   léuhng   sìhng   *or*
         two   tenth
         '20 per cent'

         baak   fahn jī   yihsahp
         hundred part of   twenty

65%   luhk sìhng bun   *or*
         six   tenth half
         '65 per cent'

         baak   fahn jī   luhksahp nǵh
         hundred part of   sixty   five

90%   gáu sìhng   *or*
         nine tenth
         '90 per cent'

         baak   fahn jī   gáusahp
         hundred part of   ninety

These expressions are used as in the following:

Jeuigahn làuh-ga   diht-jó   yāt sìhng.
recently   house-price fall-PFV one tenth
'House prices have recently fallen by 10 per cent.'

This construction is also used to express probabilities:

Nī   júng behng jí   dāk saam sìhng gēiwuih hóu fāan.
this CL   illness only just three tenths chance good return
'This disease has only a 30 per cent chance of recovery.'

Note: discounts are also expressed in tenths, but in terms of the fraction to be paid rather than the fraction discounted as in English:

Ngóh béi baat jit   léih.   (used by retailers to
I   give eight discount you   regular customers)
'I'll give you 20 per cent off.'

Nī gāan gūngsī gāmyaht yáuh chāt-nǵh jit.
this CL   store   today   have seven-five discount
'This store is offering 25 per cent off today.'

> *Idioms*: *gáu sìhng gáu* '99 per cent likely' expresses a near certainty:
>
> Ngóhdeih gáu sìhng gáu syū ge laak.
> we nine tenth nine lose PRT PRT
> 'We're bound to lose anyway.'
>
> *sahp chi yáuh gáu chi* 'nine times out of ten' functions as an adverbial phrase, much as in English:
>
> Kéuih sahp chi yáuh gáu chi dōu m̀h háidouh.
> s/he ten times have nine times also not here
> 'Nine times out of ten he's not there.'

In written Cantonese, the term *bāsīn* is the transliteration for English *per cent*. However, it is very rarely used in spoken Cantonese. Instead, the loan-word *pehsēn* is often used typically with the classifier *go*:

Gām go yuht tūngjeung gā-jó yāt go pehsēn.
this CL month inflation increase-PFV one CL per-cent
'This month's inflation (rate) has increased by 1 per cent.'

21.1.4 LUCKY AND TABOO NUMBERS

Numbers are endowed with both positive and negative connotations. The number *sei* 'four' is avoided because it sounds like *séi* 'die' (to the extent that some buildings lack a fourth floor between the third and fifth, or call the fourth floor *3A*). *sahpsei* 'fourteen' is worse still, because of its phonetic resemblance to *saht séi* 'certainly die'.

By contrast, *baat* 'eight' is favoured because it rhymes with *faat* 'produce', as in *faat daaht* or *faat chòih* 'make money'. *yih* 'two' resembles *yih* 'easy'. Similarly, *sāam* 'three' is lucky because it resembles *sāang* 'alive' and *sāangyi* 'business'. *gáu* 'nine' is associated with *chèuhng-gáu* 'long-lasting'. *Luhk* 'six' is associated with *louh* 'road', and *yāt* 'one' is associated with *yaht* 'day'. Vehicle licence plates often display these preferences:

328 sāam yih baat = sāangyi (yih) faat
business (easy) make-money

168 yāt luhk baat = yāt louh faat
one way make-money
'make money all the way'

118 yāt yāt baat = yaht yaht faat
day day make-money
'make money every day'

9888 gáu baat baat baat = gáu faat faat faat
                              long prosper-prosper-prosper

Partly for the same reason, prices often end in 0.88 or 0.99.
Speakers often use numbers creatively to make puns, e.g.:

709,394   chāt lìhng gáu sāam gáu sei
       = chēut làih   gáau sāam gáau sei
          out   come   do   three do   four

(usually referring to a man having an affair).

21.2 DAYS AND MONTHS

The days of the week from Monday to Saturday are expressed by *sīngkèih*
or *láihbaai* 'week' suffixed with the numbers one to six:

sīngkèih-yāt/láihbaai-yāt 'Monday'
sīngkèih-yih/láihbaai-yih 'Tuesday', etc.

Note that *yāt go sīngkèih/láihbaai* refers to 'one week'.

The exception is *sīngkèih-yaht/láihbaai-yaht* 'Sunday' (note that only a
difference of tone distinguishes *sīngkèih-yāt* 'Monday' from *sīngkèih-yaht*
'Sunday').

The months are also known by numbers, but the numeral precedes the
word *yuht* 'month': *yāt yuht* 'January', *yih yuht* 'February' and so on quite
regularly to *sahpyih yuht* 'December'. Stages within months may be
expressed by *tàuh* 'head' / *chō* 'beginning', *jūng* 'middle' and *méih* 'tail' /
dái 'bottom' both referring to 'end':

sei-yuht   tàuh
four-month   head
'(at) the beginning of April' (cf. the adverb *hōitàuh* 'at first')

luhk-yuht   chō
six-month   beginning
'(at) the beginning of June' (cf. *héichō* 'at first')

baat-yuht   méih
eight-month   tail
'(at) the end of August' (cf. *jeui méih* 'the very end')

or baat-yuht   dái
      eight-month bottom
      'the end of August'

luhk yuht   jūng
six   month   middle
'(in) mid-June'

The words for 'today', 'tomorrow', etc., treat the future as behind (*hauh*) and the past as in front (*chìhn*):

gāmyaht 'today'
gāmmáahn 'tonight'
kàhmyaht *or* chàhmyaht 'yesterday '
kàhmmáahn *or* chàhmmáahn 'last night'
tīngyaht 'tomorrow'
tīngmáahn 'tomorrow night'
chìhnyaht 'the day before yesterday'
chìhmáahn 'the night before last night'
hauhyaht 'the day after tomorrow'
hauhmáahn 'the night after tomorrow night'

These five terms may be extended by one day in either direction by adding *daaih*:

daaih chìhnyaht 'the day before the day before yesterday'
daaih chìhnmáahn 'the night before the night before last night'
daaih hauhyaht 'the day after the day after tomorrow'
daaih hauhmáahn 'the night after the night after tomorrow night'

Any of these expressions may combine with times of day, for example:

kàhmyaht jīujóu 'yesterday morning'
tīngyaht hahjau 'tomorrow afternoon'

Certain common combinations have a short form:

gām jīu 'this morning'
tīng jīu 'tomorrow morning'

Note that *kàhmjīu* 'yesterday morning' does not exist.

21.2.1 DATES

The order in dates is the reverse of the English, beginning with the year and ending with the day:

Yāt gáu gáu chāt lìhn luhk yuht sāamsahp houh.
one nine nine seven year six month thirty day
'The thirtieth of June, 1997.'

This may be compared to the form of addresses, in which the place name comes before the street address: in both cases, the general term precedes the more specific ones.

Decades are denoted by *lìhndoih*:

luhksahp lìhndoih
sixty decade
'the 1960s'

Centuries are denoted by *saigéi*:

> yihsahp-yāt   saigéi
> twenty-first   century
> 'the twenty-first century'

21.3 TIMES OF DAY

To count the number of hours, the classifier *go* is used and in colloquial Cantonese *lāp*, the classifier for small round objects, as in *yāt lāp yeuhkyún* 'a pill', is used:

> léuhng   go   jūng   sāam   lāp   jūng
> two   CL   hour   three   CL   hour
> 'two hours'   'three hours' (colloquial)

To specify the hours of day *dím* (*jūng*) is used:

> 4:00   sei dím (jūng)

To ask the time, *géi dím* is used:

> Yìhgā géi   dím   a?
> now   how   hour   PRT
> 'What time is it now?'

> Géi   dím   (jūng)   hōi-wúi   a?
> how   time   (hour)   hold meeting   PRT
> 'What time is the meeting?'

The half-hour is expressed by *bun* 'half' following the hour:

> 9:30   gáu dím bun

Between half-hours, Cantonese speakers tell the time in terms of five-minute intervals, called *jih* (referring to the marks on the clock-face), counted from the preceding hour:

> 7:20   chāt dím sei go jih   9:40   gáu dím baat go jih

The words *go jih* are often omitted:

> 8:15   baat dím   sāam
>   eight o'clock   three

A fifteen-minute interval, i.e. *quarter* in English, is called *yāt go gwāt* in Cantonese:

> 8:15   baat dím yāt go gwāt   8:45   baat dím sāam go gwāt

Note that *léuhng dím ńgh* 'two hours five' therefore means '2:25', *not* '2:05' (*léuhng dím yāt*). Similarly, stages in the hour are expressed by *daahp* and the number of *jih* past the hour:

daahp sāam 'at quarter past'   daahp sahpyih 'on the hour'

Where precision is required, the minutes (*fānjūng* or simply *fān*) can be spelled out:

10:56   sahp dím ńghsahp-luhk fān

Twelve o'clock is usually called simply *sahpyih dím*, although a word *bunyeh* or *bunyé* 'midnight' exists. There are many different ways to express 0:01 a.m. to 0:59 a.m.:

0.10 a.m. lìhng sìh/sàhn   sahp fān
           zero   o'clock/morning ten   minutes

           sām   yeh   sahpyih   dím   sahp fān
           deep   night twelve   o'clock ten   minutes

Note that *lìhng sàhn* 'zero morning = midnight' can be used for any time at midnight.

Times which might be understood as morning or evening may be preceded by *jīujóu* 'morning' or *yehmáahn* 'evening':

jīujóu   luhk   dím   bun
morning   six   o'clock   half
'six-thirty in the morning'

yehmáahn   sahp   dím   jūng
evening   ten   o'clock
'ten o'clock at night'

When a time of day is combined with a day of the week or month, the order follows that of dates, with the more general term coming first:

sīngkèih-yaht   sei   dím
Sunday   four   o'clock
'four o'clock on Sunday'

As adverbial expressions, all these expressions of time usually come between the subject and the verb:

Ngóhdeih   **tīngyaht**   **luhk dím**   gin.
we   tomorrow   six o'clock see
'We'll meet at six o'clock tomorrow.'

Alternatively:

Tīngyaht   luhk dím   ngóhdeih hái Daaih-Wuih-Tòhng gin.
tomorrow   six o'clock we   at   City Hall   meet
'We'll meet at the City Hall at six o'clock tomorrow.'

APPENDIX: ROMANIZATION SYSTEMS

INITIAL CONSONANTS

Yale	IPA	LSHK
b	p	b
p	p^h	p
m	m	m
f	f	f
d	t	d
t	t^h	t
n	n	n
l	l	l
g	k	g
k	k^h	k
ng	ŋ	ng
h	h	h
j	ts	z
ch	ts^h	c
s	s	s
y	j	j
gw	kw	gw
kw	kw^h	kw
w	w	w

FINAL CONSONANTS

Yale	IPA	LSHK
m	m	m
n	n	n
ng	ŋ	ng
p	p	p
t	t	t
k	k	k

VOWELS

Yale	IPA	LSHK
i	iː	i
i (before ng, k)	e	i
yu	yː	yu
u	uː	u
u (before ng, k)	o	u
e	ɛː	e
o	ɔː	o
eu	œː	oe
eu (before n, t)	ɵ	eo
a (with final consonant)	ɐ	a
a (no final consonant)	aː	aa
aa	aː	aa
iu	iw	iu
eui	ɵy	eoi
ui	uy	ui
ei	ej	ei
oi	ɔj	oi
ou	ow	ou
ai	ɐj	ai
au	ɐw	au
aai	aːj	aai
aau	aːw	aau

TONES (ILLUSTRATED WITH THE SYLLABLE U)

Yale	IPA	LSHK	
ū	55	u1	high level
ù	53	u1	high fall
ú	35/25	u2	high rise
u	33	u3	mid level
ùh	21/11	u4	low fall
úh	23/13	u5	low rise
uh	22	u6	low even

Notes: Yale refers to the Yale romanization system, the system adopted in this book, with the exception that the high falling tone is not used, the words concerned being shown with a high level tone. LSHK stands for the romanization scheme proposed and adopted by the Linguistic Society of Hongkong in 1993. The IPA symbols represent broad transcriptions. The descriptions in parentheses explain the condition under which the sound is used. For example, in the table for vowels, the romanized form *i* is generally pronounced as IPA [iː]; however, it is pronounced as IPA [e] before *ng* and *k*.

NOTES

INTRODUCTION

1 In fact very few grammars of Cantonese have been written in Chinese in the past twenty years. This may have to do with the prevalent attitude that Cantonese is just a Chinese dialect and does not enjoy the same privileged status as Putonghua/Mandarin, which is the official language of China and Taiwan. Thus most of the attention has been devoted to the study and description of Mandarin.

2 The priority of speech in descriptive linguistics is based on three main considerations:

   (i)   many of the world's languages lack any written form;
   (ii)   historically, all languages were spoken before they came to be written;
   (iii)   children learn to speak a language before they can read or write: moreover, the written language must be consciously taught, whereas children do not need to be taught to speak their first language.

3 Dialects belonging to other groups are spoken in parts of Guangdong province, such as Chiuchow (southern Min) in the east and Hakka dialects in the north.

4 Luke and Nancarrow (1991) describe the language of Hongkong newspapers as containing a whole range of registers, from classical Chinese to the colloquial style which comes very close to being a representation of spoken Cantonese.

5 By contrast, there are 'correct' and 'incorrect' pronunciations for certain words: *meihlihk* is preferred to *muihlihk* 'charm', and *sìhgāan* to *sìhgaan* 'time'. The 'correct' pronunciations (based on etymological considerations) are generally used in broadcasting and promoted by language purists, with sporadic effects on general usage.

6 Standard written Chinese refers to the written form of Mandarin (Putonghua) which is taught in schools and used in academic contexts. It is based on the northern variety of Mandarin spoken in Beijing.

7 In view of the lack of a unified romanization system for Cantonese, the Linguistic Society of Hongkong has developed a system intended to serve all purposes of romanization (see appendix).

8 The use of numbers to represent tones is not entirely arbitrary. For example, 1, 2 and 3 by convention refer to high register tones and 4, 5 and 6 low register tones, etc. following traditional classification of tones (see Chao 1947).

9 This type of error is discussed in Yip and Matthews (1992), where the Chinese and English constructions with adjectives such as *easy* and *difficult* are compared.

1 PHONOLOGY: THE CANTONESE SOUND SYSTEM

1 The Yale symbols in the book appear in italics whereas the IPA symbols are given in square brackets.

2 According to experiments conducted by Dr Eric Zee, the alveolar consonants before *eu/eui* retain their place of articulation, although the simultaneous palatal contact may give the consonants a palatal quality. Full palatalization, as in *séung* [ʃeung], is characteristic of non-native speakers such as Mandarin and

English speakers. By contrast, before *yu* these consonants are fully palatalized in Cantonese. Moreover, it has been observed that young female speakers are more likely to produce these palatalized sounds. Further research is necessary to ascertain the relationship between the sociolinguistic factors and the palatalization phenomenon.

3 In certain mainland varieties of Cantonese *-k* and *-t* are merged, both being pronounced as unreleased *-t*. Moreover, the merger of *-p*, *-t* and *-k* is very common in other Chinese dialects, such as the Shanghai dialect.

4 The 'correct' forms may be traced etymologically: for example, the Mandarin cognate of *ōn* 'peace' is *ān*, without a nasal consonant, whereas the cognate of *ngàuh* 'cow' is *niú*, with initial *n* corresponding to Cantonese *ng*.

5 The romanization being developed by the Linguistic Society of Hongkong proposes to make this distinction, writing *aa* in open syllables as in *fāa* 'flower'.

6 Adjacent consonants do occur in compound expressions. For example, the negative prefix *m* as in *msái* 'no need' is an independent syllable. Clusters also occur in onomatopoeic words, such as *blīng-blàhng* 'tumbling' and the sound *klīk-klāk*, and are sometimes retained in certain loan-words from English, although the clusters are normally simplified in the course of borrowing.

7 Some linguists (e.g. Y-S. Cheung 1969) have reported distinctions between words with high level and high falling tones. In Guangzhou and other varieties of Cantonese spoken in Guangdong province, the tone at issue is often pronounced as high falling; however, the high level and high falling variants are not claimed to be distinctive in recent studies. A consequence of this variation is that Cantonese speakers have difficulty distinguishing the high level and falling tones in Mandarin (Wong 1982).

8 While the conventional scale involves five pitch levels, only four are strictly necessary to differentiate the tones, as pointed out by K-H. Cheung (1986). In a four-level system, the high level tone would be 44, high rising 24.

9 Acoustic experiments by Dr Eric Zee of the Chinese University of Hongkong have confirmed this observation. See also Wu (1989: 173)

10 As a result, the low rising tone (23) is sometimes confused or conflated with the mid level tone (33). In Malayan Cantonese, for example, the two tones are merged into one (Killingley 1982b, 1985).

11 On the spectrogram the pitch contour of the words in the replies, i.e. *sek*, *dāk* and *wúih*, shows a sharp rise followed by a sharp fall. The vowel is also lengthened considerably.

12 Chen and Wang (1975) is a classic study demonstrating the gradual progression of sound change through the vocabulary, which the authors term **lexical diffusion**. The evidence is from Chinese dialectology, supported by observations from Swedish and English.

2 WORD STRUCTURE: MORPHOLOGY AND WORD FORMATION

1 Note that *douh* 'degree' can also occur with *géi* (*dō*) 'how many' as in questioning the measurements of vision and temperature:

Léih	géi	dō	douh	gahnsih	a?
you	how	many	degrees	shortsighted	PRT

'How short-sighted are you?'

Gāmyaht	heiwān	géi	dō	douh	a?
today	temperature	how	many	degrees	PRT

'What's today's temperature?'

2 An idiomatic use of *séui-sing* occurs in the following context:

Kéuih hóu suhk séui-sing.
s/he very familiar water-nature
'She's in her element in water.'

3 Mandarin *zhèi-tou/nèi-tou* refers to the end or tip of an object or place, unlike Cantonese *nī-tàuh/gó-tàuh*, whose meaning not only covers that of the Mandarin counterpart but can also be extended to refer to this/that area or deictic here/ there. (For another interpretation related to concurrent events in time, i.e. 'as soon as' see 16.2.1.) Moreover, in Mandarin, *yī* is often inserted between the demonstrative *zhè/nà* and *-tou* possibly to avoid confusion arising from treating *tou* as a classifier as in *zhèi tou niú* 'this cow'. In Cantonese, *yāt* is often left out in *nī-(yāt)-tàuh/gó-(yāt)-tàuh*.

4 It has been observed that attaching *-sing* to nouns to form adjectives is a result of English influence especially when translating from English to Chinese. In many cases *-sing* can be left out without affecting the meaning:

lihksí(-sing) sìhhāk
history moment
'historic moment'

gwokjai(-sing) wuihyíh
international conference
'international conference'

chùhn-kàuh(-sing) jōilaahn
whole-globe disaster
'global disaster'

5 All the *-fa* suffixed compounds with disyllabic stems prefer to have the objects preposed in the *jēung* construction; i.e. the preferred order is *jēung* – NP – verb – *fa*. However, some compounds with monosyllabic stems such as *fó-fa* 'incinerate' are often used with a preposed object while others like *méi-fa gā-gēui* 'beautify the home' and *luhk-fa wàahn-gíng* 'make the environment green' can have the objects following the *-fa* compound. *-fa* suffixation is another example of English influence on Chinese.

6 *jyuh* is an apparent exception, as it may be used as a particle following the object or complement of a verb:

Léih mhóu sihk faahn **jyuh**.
you don't eat rice yet
'Don't eat just yet.'

Ngóh m̀h wúih góng béi yàhn tēng **jyuh**.
I not will say to people hear yet
'I won't tell anyone for the time being.'

However, while related semantically to the continuous aspect, this is a distinct usage of *jyuh*, meaning specifically 'for the time being' or in negative sentences 'not . . . yet' (see 11.2.3, 13.3). A similar argument applies in the case of *gwo*. which has distinct functions as an aspect marker and verbal particle (11.2.5, 11.3.1).

3   SYNTACTIC CATEGORIES: PARTS OF SPEECH IN CANTONESE

1 Some syntacticians, such as McCawley (1988), treat words such as *after*, *before* and *since* as prepositions which take either a noun phrase or a clause as their complement. Under this analysis, they belong to only one syntactic category even though they may also *function* as conjunctions.

2 McCawley (1992) suggests that so-called auxiliaries in Mandarin are simply verbs which are subcategorized for a clause.

4 SENTENCE STRUCTURE: WORD ORDER AND TOPICALIZATION

1 This should not be taken to imply that the notion of subject is inapplicable or unimportant in Chinese grammar, as is sometimes suggested. The possibility of omitting the subject is subject to constraints (see 5.1.1) and omitted subjects are treated in many analyses as null (zero) subjects, i.e. as playing the role in the structure of the sentence even though they are not overtly present.

2 An alternative analysis might be that this is a possessive construction, with *Hēunggóng* the possessor of the noun phrase *làuhga* (6.3). This is perhaps grammatically plausible in this case, as a possessive noun phrase *Hēunggóng (ge) làuhga* is possible, but not for all cases of 'double subject' constructions. Compare:

Hēunggóng go-go   dōu sīk   kéuih ge.
Hongkong   CL-CL   all know   her   PRT
'Everyone in Hongkong knows her.'

3 The treatment of generic noun phrases as definite is not unusual. Compare the usage of the definite article in French (*Les chats aiment le poisson* 'Cats like fish') and the generic usage of the English definite article as in *The koala is an endangered species*.

4 Topic chains were first discussed by Tsao (1979); their structure is examined in Shi (1989).

5 PRONOUNS

1 Both *yàhn* and *yàhndeih* can by used interchangeably when the reference intended is generic 'people':

Kéuih jūngyi hohk   yàhn(deih) cheung-gō.
s/he   like   imitate people   sing-song
'She likes to imitate people singing.'

Ngóh m̀h   séung béi yàhn(deih) jīdou.
I   not   want   let people   know
'I don't want people to know.'

2 Note that while *Mary* is the direct object in English, in the Cantonese *Màhleih* also serves as the subject of *fāan* within the serial verb construction. The example is thus consistent with the subject-orientation of *jihgéi*.

6 THE NOUN PHRASE

1 An exception is the numeral construction in which numeral + classifier follows the noun (21.1.1). This construction is used especially for commodities, and emphasizes the number, for example in advertising:

Tàuh jéung sung   gēipiu   léuhng jēung. (radio ad.)
head prize send   air-ticket two   CL
'The first prize is two free air tickets.'

2 The exact number depends on (a) variation between dialects and individuals, and (b) whether classifiers used in written Chinese are included. As these are dealt with in works on Mandarin, they are omitted here, as are some classifiers used in Malayan Cantonese (Killingley 1982b, 1983).

3 This distinction is made in Killingley (1983), a thorough study of the syntax and semantics of classifiers in Malayan Cantonese, using componential analysis for the semantics. Her discussion reveals substantial differences from Hongkong Cantonese in the usage of individual classifiers; for example, *jek* is applied to fruits such as *pìhnggwó* 'apple' which would take *go* in Hongkong Cantonese. Killingley (1982b), a glossary of classifiers, reveals numerous such differences.

4 While the distinction between these mensural and sortal classifiers is relatively clear, it does not divide the classifiers themselves into two discrete groups. Strictly speaking, the distinction is between mensural and sortal *uses* of classifiers, as the same classifier may serve both functions at different times. For example, *gauh* is the classifier for *sehk* 'stone, rock' but also used as a measure as in *yāt gauh fāangáan* 'a lump of soap'; *yāt faai* denotes 'a slice' as in *yāt faai yùhsāang* 'a slice of sashimi' but is also used as the type classifier for vertical thin surfaces such as *yāt faai bou* 'a cloth'.

5 Strictly speaking, the functional parallel here is misleading in that *one* is a pronoun, genuinely substituting for the noun phrase, while in Cantonese the head noun may be deleted leaving the classifier behind. As a result of this difference, one cannot say *this one picture* but one may say either *nī fūk* 'this one' or *nī fūk wá* 'this picture'.

6 A different use of *chāan* is in *yāt chāan* 'one dose' which appears as a verbal complement as in:

Kéuih béi yàhn dá-jó **yāt chāan**.
s/he by someone beat-PFV one dose
'He was badly beaten up (by someone).'

Ngóhdeih jouh **(yāt) chāan séi** dōu haih dāk go gāt.
we work (one) full death still be gain CL nothing
'We've worked ourselves to death but gained nothing.'

7 This idiom can function as a resultative complement as in:

Léih gáau dou ngóh **yāt wohk póuh**.
you make till I one wok bubble
'You make me end up in a lot of trouble.'

Also it can appear in the predicative complement position:

Gām chi ngóh jānhaih **yāt wohk póuh** la.
this time I really one wok bubble PRT
'This time I'm really in a lot of trouble.'

8 This idiom often functions as a predicative complement as in:

Ngóh tàuhjī sātbaaih, gām chi jānhaih **yāt hok**
I invest fail this time really one bowl

ngáahnleuih la.
tear PRT
'My investment has failed, this time I'm really in trouble.'

9 Note that the distal demonstrative *gó*, *not* the proximal demonstrative *nī* is used in Cantonese relatives unless a clear deictic function is intended as in:

Ngóh kàhmyaht máaih nī bún syū hóu gwai.
I yesterday buy this CL book very expensive
'This book that I bought yesterday was very expensive.'

10 Unlike Cantonese, Mandarin allows a demonstrative together with *de*, as in *wǒ rènshí de nèige yīnyuèjiā* 'that musician I know.'

8 THE VERB PHRASE

1 This word order alternation is a stylistic phenomenon comparable to Heavy Noun Phrase Shift in English: for example, the order (b) below is used to avoid the clumsiness of (c):

  (a) I put the articles on the table.
  (b) I put on the table all the articles I could find on Cantonese grammar.
  (c) I put all the articles I could find on Cantonese grammar on the table.

2 *béi* in this function might be treated as a preposition, as suggested by S-W. Tang (1992). As for the coverbs (3.1.3), it is difficult to show this to be the case, since constructions such as *sung . . . béi . . .* could equally well be serial verb constructions.
3 Y-H.A. Li (1990) attributes this repetition to the notion of structural Case: every noun phrase must be assigned Case by an adjacent verb, hence the verb must appear twice to assign Case to both the direct and the adverbial object.
4 *jēung* 'put' cannot be used independently as a main verb unlike coverbs such as *yuhng* 'use', *wán* 'look for', etc. Like Mandarin *bǎ*, *jēung* functions as a case marker or preposition rather than as a main verb.
5 *héi* 'up' is sometimes considered a directional verb, but does not participate in the patterns with *heui* and *làih* like the others in 8.3.2, with the exception of a few literary phrases such as *héi làih* 'pull up one's spirits'. *héi làih* as a verbal complement gives the meaning 'whenever' as in:

  Kéuih siu   héi làih   go   yéung   hóu   tìhm.
  s/he   smile   up-come   CL   appearance   very   sweet
  'She looks sweet when she smiles.'

héi is used as a verbal particle, as in *gwa héi* 'hang up' (11.3.1) and as a transitive verb, as in *héi láu/ūk* 'build flats/houses', *héi-sān* 'rise-body = get up'.
6 The indirect passive is found in a number of Southeast Asian languages, including Vietnamese and Thai; see Siewierska (1984).
7 Huang (1982) analyses the underlying structure of the Mandarin sentences with retained objects as [V-NP] NP where [V-NP] is a complex predicate taking the second post-verbal NP as semantic object.

9 ADJECTIVAL CONSTRUCTIONS: DESCRIPTION AND COMPARISON

1 Although stative verbs such as *jūngyi* 'like' may also be modified by *hóu*, the meaning differs in that *hóu* before a verb intensifies the meaning of the verb, while with a predicative adjective it is largely without meaning.
2 These constructions and the learning problems to which they give rise are analysed in Yip and Matthews (1992) and Yip (1995).
3 C-R Huang (1991) provides arguments that these apparent counterparts of English Tough Movement as in *hard to please* are lexical rather than syntactic in nature.

11 ASPECT AND VERBAL PARTICLES

1 Note that this construction requires either an aspect marker or a resultative particle to be present, hence *gán* cannot be omitted here. These so-called **pseudo-passive** constructions lead to characteristic errors in Chinese learners' English, such as *The books have ordered already.* As discussed by Yip (1995)

these appear to be failed attempts at forming English passives, but in fact involve transfer of the Chinese topicalization construction.

2 The term **delimitative** is also used for a similar aspectual meaning in Russian and other Slavonic languages.

3 These notions are sometimes known by the German term *Aktionsart*. The Chinese particles are also known as 'resultative verbal complements', as in Li and Thompson (1981).

4 *gwo*, *jyuh* and *hōi* do occur in these constructions, but only as verbal particles, with meanings which are clearly distinct from their aspectual functions:

> seun dāk gwo 'trustworthy'   (see 12.3.1)
> kaau dāk jyuh 'reliable'
> tái dāk hōi 'optimistic'

5 This criterion is due to H-N. S. Cheung (1972). The habitual *gwaan*, for example (11.2.7), is a particle under this criterion as it may be combined with an aspect marker as in *jyuh gwaan-jó* 'has got used to living'.

6 *saai* corresponds to Mandarin *guāng* in some contexts, e.g. *sihk saai/chī guāng* 'eat up', but *saai* is much more extensively used.

12   MODALITY: POSSIBILITY AND PROBABILITY

1 *sīk* 'know' can be used as a verb:

> Ngóh sīk-jó   kéuih sahp lìhn.
> I   know-PFV   her   ten   years
> 'I've known her for ten years.'

sēuiyiu 'need' and *yiu* 'want' are used as verbs in the following:

> Kéuih hóu   sēuiyiu yāt fahn gūng.
> s/he   very need   one CL   job
> 'He needs a job very much.'

> Ngóh yiu   būi   gafē.
> I   want cup   coffee
> 'I want a cup of coffee.'

ngoi, the word for 'love' can also mean 'want' and is often used in places where *yiu* occurs:

> Nī   bún syū   ngóh m̀h   ngoi/yiu ge   la,   hóyíh
> this CL   book I   not   want   PRT PRT   can

> dám-jó   kéuih.
> dump-PFV   it
> 'I don't want this book any more; it can be disposed of.'

> Gó   go fóng ngoi/yiu lèih jouh māt   ga?
> that CL room want   come do   what PRT
> 'What is that room for?'

msái 'don't need' is used as a verb in the following:

> Tái   nī   bún syū   msái   hóu dō   sìhgaan jē.
> read this CL   book doesn't-need very much time   PRT
> 'Reading this book doesn't take a lot of time.'

13 NEGATION

1 These words are typically written in the Yale system with * m̀* as in *m̀jūngyi* 'not like', which should indicate a high falling tone and is thus potentially misleading. The use of *m-* here is intended to show not that the negative prefix has a distinct mid level tone, but that the low falling tone of *m̀h* tends to be obscured in these forms in continuous speech, much as the vowel of *not* is lost through contraction in *didn't*.

2 Similarly, in English *anyone* may not be the subject of a negative sentence (cf. * *Anyone doesn't live here* and e.e. cummings' deviant line *Anyone lived in a pretty how town*). This prohibition may be attributed to the fact that the words *anyone* and *bīngo* in subject position are not within the scope of the negation.

14 QUANTIFICATION

1 The class of words or **operators** which license the indefinite usage of question words is complex. See Y-H.A. Li (1992) for Mandarin.

16 COORDINATION AND SUBORDINATE CLAUSES

1 Bloom (1981) noted the lack of distinctions between types of conditional in Chinese and postulated corresponding cognitive differences between Chinese and English speakers. These findings are disputed by Au (1983) and in much subsequent research.

17 QUESTIONS

1 The pitch contours of intonation questions, compared with the corresponding statements, are shown in spectrograms in Wu (1989: 174ff.). The rising intonation is carried on the final syllable, whatever its inherent tone: the rising tones are intensified, while in the case of the low falling tone, the rise begins after the fall. Wu also notes that the overall pitch level of an intonation question is raised slightly relative to the corresponding statement.

18 SENTENCE PARTICLES AND INTERJECTIONS

1 The precise number depends on the treatment of related particles such as *a/àh/ak*. If all related forms differing in tone are treated as distinct particles, there are around thirty as given in Kwok (1984). Counting all variants, Yau (1965) identified some 206 forms.

2 Some writers treat these intonation patterns as tonal particles, having no phonetic form apart from tone, which combine with other particles to produce the tonal variants. Law and Neidle (1992) propose such an analysis, based on Chao's (1968: 812) analysis of sentence-final intonation patterns in Mandarin as tonal particles. Law and Neidle posit three such tonal particles:

 (a) the high tone as in *ā*, *lā* and *lō*: a tonal 'weakener' indicating hesitancy;
 (b) the low falling tone as in *àh* and *wòh*: a tonal 'strengthener' indicating disapproval or abruptness;
 (c) the high rising tone, which does not affect particles but appears in forming echo questions (see 1.4.3, 17.1.7).

3 Kwok (1984) gives seventy-four possible combinations of two or three particles, of which sixty-eight actually occur in her corpus. Note that this is a small figure

compared to the theoretically possible number of permutations given the thirty basic particles recognized by Kwok (p. 8).

4 Both formal and functional arguments support the assumption made in Kwok (1984) and elsewhere that these forms are contractions. On the one hand, combinations such as *ge a* and *je àh* do not occur, a fact which is unexpected in terms of their functions but follows given the assumption that *ga* and *jàh* are contracted realizations of these combinations. Functionally, the contracted forms have the combined characteristics of the individual particles; for example, *ga* replaces *ge* in questions which would typically end with *a*:

Haih	jān	ge. (statement)	→	Haih-mhaih	jān	ga? (question)
is	true	PRT		is-not-is	true	PRT
'It's true.'				'Is it true?'		

Similar arguments follow for other combinations such as *ge + āma → gāma*.

5 Law and Neidle (1992) suggest that all uses of *ge* as particle involve the *haih . . . ge* construction, with the copula *haih* being optionally deleted. This is plausible in so far as *haih* can be omitted in various other constructions (see 8.1.1), such as:

Nī	go	(haih)	ngóh	sailóu	lèihga.
this	CL	(is)	my	brother	PRT
'This is my (younger) brother.'					

6 This characterization is due to Luke (1990).

7 This observation is due to Chui (1988). Note that the alternation *āiya/āiyā/āiyak/āiyáh* supports the analysis of *a/ā/ak/àh* as variants of a single particle. If these particles were unrelated, we would not expect a parallel set of variants of the exclamation *āiya*.

21 NUMERALS AND TIMES

1 The form *ḿh* is commonly heard as a result of the change from syllabic *ng* to *m*, being used especially by speakers who do not use initial *ng* (1.5).

GLOSSARY OF GRAMMATICAL TERMS

This grammar uses a mimimum of technical terms, most of which are established in the study of European languages. These are supplemented where necessary by terms drawn from Chinese linguistics, especially from studies of Mandarin Chinese, and occasionally from general linguistics and language typology. Terms which are not explained where they occur in the main text are glossed here.

Adjectives are words describing qualities or characteristics of nouns, like *good*, *red* and *poor*. The grammatical status of adjectives is less clear in Cantonese than in European languages, as they resemble verbs in most respects (see 3.1.1). Adjectives are distinguished, however, by taking comparative forms (9.3) and undergoing particular types of reduplication (9.2).

Adverbs are words which qualify verbs, describing either the manner of an action (**predicate adverbs**, like *quickly* or *well*) or its circumstances (**sentence adverbs**, like *today* or *probably*).

Adverbial constructions and phrases are those which perform the function of an adverb, describing the manner of an action, without specifically containing an adverb. This applies to many prepositional phrases in English (e.g. *for a change*) and to several Cantonese constructions (see 10.4).

An **antecedent** is a word or phrase to which a pronoun refers back, as in *John is proud of himself* where *John* is the antecedent of the reflexive pronoun *himself*.

A phrase **in apposition** is appended to another phrase to provide additional information about it, like *my best friend* in *John, my best friend, has left*.

Aspect is a grammatical category involving different ways of viewing and describing events, states or processes. Aspect distinguishes the time relations expressed by verbs, but in a different way from **tenses**, which relate the time of the events described to the time of speech. Aspects describe an event as ongoing or complete, rather than past, present or future. The distinction between the English progressive and simple forms as in *I was talking to her this morning* vs. *I talked to her this morning* is considered to be one of aspect rather than of tense, since both sentences clearly refer to the same time in the past (see **tense** below and 11.1).

Aspiration is an important phonetic characteristic (**distinctive feature**; see below) of Cantonese consonants, consisting of an emission of air immediately after oral release as the consonant is formed. This feature is normally present in English consonants such as *p*, *t* and *k*, but it is not a distinctive feature, as it is the lack of voicing which distinguishes these sounds from *b*, *d* and *g*. In Cantonese, the aspiration is the relevant distinctive feature (see 1.1).

Attributive adjectives are those used within a noun phrase to identify or describe the noun, as in *the blue book*.

Auxiliaries are verbs which are only used together with another verb, and carry a grammatical meaning or function, like *have* in *we have finished*. The main auxiliaries in Cantonese are modals, like *might* in *might be late*.

Baby-talk is the variety of language used to converse with small children, characterized by diminutives such as *doggie* and reduplicated expressions such as *choo-choo* in English.

Causative constructions are those which express causation of an event or state of affairs. In English and Cantonese, they involve auxiliary verbs such as *make* in English *make them wait* (see 8.5).

Classifiers are an important class of word which 'classify' nouns by features such as shape, size and function. They are used in counting, like *four pairs of shoes* and *forty head of cattle*, but are used much more extensively than their English counterparts and are required in many contexts (see 6.2).

A **clause** is part of a complex sentence, containing a subject and a verb. See also **subordinate clause**.

Comparative constructions are those which compare two noun phrases with respect to a quality, as in *Diana is taller than Charles*.

Complementation refers to the syntactic pattern appropriate to follow a particular word, as the English verb *promise* takes an infinitive in *promise to improve*.

Complements of verbs (8.5) and adjectives (9.4) are the types of clause appropriate to follow those particular items.

Compounding is the combination of two or more words, each of which exists independently, to form a new word, as in *wine-bar*.

Concessive clauses and constructions are those which concede or admit a point, usually counteracting that point in a following clause. Typically, they are introduced by a concessive conjunction such as *although* . . . In both English and Cantonese, however, many constructions without *although* are concessive in meaning, for example the phrase *no matter whether* . . . (see 16.2.4).

Conditional clauses, normally introduced by *if* in English, state a condition under which the following clause holds. Full conditional sentences contain both an antecedent (*if*) clause and a consequent (*then*) clause (see 16.3), as in *If we have time, (then) I'll show you the way*.

Continuous refers to the **aspect** expressed by *jyuh* in Cantonese. Although this term is also used for the English progressive (*-ing*) form, the continuous aspect as expressed by *jyuh* differs from the **progressive** expressed by *gán*, the continuous describing static situations and the progressive dynamic ones (see 11.1 and 11.2.3).

Contraction is a form of abbreviation whereby a word or phrase is shortened by loss of a vowel, consonant or syllable; for example, *did not* is reduced to *didn't*.

Coordination is the joining of words, phrases or clauses, whether by **conjunctions** like *and* or by juxtaposition as in many Cantonese constructions (see 16.1).

Copular verbs are those like English *to be* whose primary function is to link two noun phrases (see 8.1.1).

Counterfactual clauses are those expressing propositions which are known to be untrue. The most typical case is in a **conditional** sentence of the kind *If I had known, I would have come* in which it is implied that the speaker did not know and did not come.

Coverbs in Chinese are a subclass of verbs, so called because they are typically used together with another verb, often corresponding to prepositions in English (3.1.3).

Declination is the gradual decline in pitch as a sentence is spoken. In tonal languages, it has the consequence that a given tone, such as the mid level tone, will be pronounced at a progressively lower pitch over the course of the sentence.

Definiteness is the semantic notion expressed by *the* in English. A noun phrase is definite when it is clear what particular entity it refers to (see 6.1, 6.2).

Delimitative is the aspect expressed by *háh* in Cantonese (11.2.6), meaning to do something 'for a while'. The closest equivalent in English is the use of a verb as a noun as in *have a chat*.

Demonstratives are words used to pick out entities in time and space, including the adjectives *this* and *that* and adverbs such as *here* and *then*.

Designative terms are the kinship terms used to refer to one's relatives, but not necessarily to address them; see **vocatives**.

Directional verbs (8.3.2) and particles (11.3.1) are words denoting direction of movement. While the two categories overlap to some extent, some words function only as directional verbs, others only as directional particles following a verb (see 11.3.1).

Dislocation refers to the placing of an element outside the sentence, separated from it by a pause. **Left-dislocation** is a form of topicalization, as in *My aunt, everyone likes her*, where the object *my aunt* is made the topic and replaced as the object by the pronoun *her*. In **right-dislocation** an element is added at the end of a sentence (see below).

Distinctive features are an important concept in **phonology**, referring to those aspects of pronunciation which distinguish one sound from another. In English, the distinctive feature difference between *pat* and *bat* is that the [b] sound is voiced, while [p] is not.

Echo questions are those which elicit repetition of an item from a previous sentence spoken by another speaker. They have distinctive forms, such as *You did WHAT?* in which the word *what* is strongly stressed and is not moved to the beginning of the sentence as in an ordinary question. Echo questions are expressed in Cantonese by intonation and by particles (17.1.7).

Epistemic expressions concern the source of the information contained in a sentence, e.g. the particle *wóh* indicating hearsay information (18.3.4).

Epistemic modality is the meaning expressed by modal verbs such as *must* in *You must be Mr Brown*, where *must* indicates that the identity of the addressee is being inferred (see 12.1.3, 12.2.2).

Ergative verbs are a class of intransitive verbs denoting a change of state or location, which the subject undergoes, rather than an action which the subject performs. Examples in English are *The window broke* (compare *I broke the window* where *the window* is the object) and *The sign fell down*, where the fall is not initiated by *the sign*.

Excessives are forms or constructions with the meaning 'too' as in *too fast* (see 9.3.4).

Existential constructions denote the existence of something. In many languages, existential expressions are closely related to possessive ones, the same word (*yáuh* in Cantonese) meaning both 'have' and 'there is' (see ch. 15). **Existential quantifiers** are expressions like *something* and *sometimes*.

Experiential aspect (11.2.5) expresses an action which has been experienced at least once before. It corresponds to one of the meanings of the present perfect in English, as in *Have you seen this film?*, but contrasts with the **perfective** expressed by *jó*.

Expletives are 'empty' words without content. The term is used for (i) swear words such as *the hell* and Cantonese *gwái* (2.1.3, 9.1.3) which serve to give emphasis; (ii) meaningless pronouns such as *it* in *It's raining*, which serves simply to fill the subject position; such pronouns do not exist in Cantonese.

Finals are the endings of syllables, such as *-ān* in *sān* 'new' and *-āai* in *gāai* 'street', which may occur with various **initials** (1.3).

Generic terms are those which denote a class of items rather than a specific individual, such as *gardeners* in *Gardeners are hard to come by*.

Habitual aspect refers to a regular, repeated activity. In English the form *used to* as in *I used to go to the cinema on Saturdays* expresses habitual aspect, but is restricted to the past, whereas habitual forms of the verb in Cantonese may equally apply to the present (see 11.2.7).

Homonyms are words which have the same form, but different (and unrelated) meanings, like *trip* 'journey' and *trip* 'fall over'. **Homophonous** words sound alike, but are spelled differently, as in the case of *ate* and *eight*.

Hyperbole is a figure of speech involving exaggeration, as in *I've told you a thousand times*.

Hypercorrection is a type of error induced by misplaced notions of correctness. For example, English speakers who do not pronounce *h* in casual speech may take care to pronounce it in formal environments, leading to overuse of *h* in words where it does not belong, such as *apple*.

Imperative sentences express commands and requests, as in *Hurry up!* or *Please tell me the answer*.

Impersonal constructions are those which lack a specific subject, as in *There's no need to exaggerate*.

Inalienable possession refers to a possessive construction where the item possessed belongs intrinsically or permanently to the possessor, typical cases being body parts and kinship terms. These items may be marked differently from alienable items in possessive constructions (see 6.3).

Incorporation is a form of compounding in which a noun or other item becomes part of the verb. In verb–object compounds, the object is incorporated, losing part of its original meaning in the process (2.3.3, 8.2.4).

Indirect speech is speech which is reported or quoted by another speaker. **Indirect questions** are questions relayed by one speaker to another, as in *She asked me how much money I needed* which reports the question *How much money do you need?* **Indirect commands** are the reported counterpart of imperative sentences, e.g. *I told you to be quiet* reports the command *Be quiet!*

Infixes are words or inflections inserted within a word rather than at the beginning or end. In Cantonese and English, the main examples involve **expletive** words, as in *abso-blooming-lutely!* (see 2.1.3, 9.1.3, 17.3.2).

Intonation refers to the variation in pitch during the course of a sentence. It should be distinguished from **tone** which, in tonal languages like Chinese, is the inherent pitch pattern of words or syllables.

Inversion is when two words or phrases exchange their position, as in *Will he come?*, an inversion of *He will come*.

Lexical borrowing is the adoption of words from a foreign language. The term is something of a misnomer in that 'borrowed' words are rarely returned to the 'lending' language. The **lexicon** is the vocabulary of a language, as opposed to its grammar.

Localizers are a class of word used to specify location in space or time, such as *chìhnmihn* 'in front (of)' (see 3.1.4, 7.1.1).

Locative expressions denote location in space.

Modality is the linguistic expression of notions such as possibility, necessity and probability, all to some extent hypothetical rather than factual. **Modals** are verbs or auxiliaries which express modality, like *must* and *may* in English.

Morphemes are the smallest meaningful units in a language. **Morphology** is the study of the formation of words, including affixation and compounding.

Nasal sounds are those in which air is emitted through the nose, causing the nasal cavity to resonate. The nasal consonants in English and Cantonese are *m*, *n* and *ng*.

Negative polarity contexts are notionally negative environments in which **negative polarity items** such as *ever* and *anywhere* in English occur. Such contexts are as follows:

(a) following a negative predicate, as in *I don't think he'll ever succeed*;

(b) in a question, as in *Will he ever succeed?*;

(c) in the *if* clause of a conditional sentence, as in *If he ever succeeds* . . .

In Cantonese, question words used in negative polarity contexts may have an indefinite sense: for example, *bīndouh* 'where' has the meaning 'anywhere' in these contexts (see 13.4).

The **noun phrase** is the noun and any modifiers, such as demonstratives and **classifiers**, which accompany it. Technically, the subject or object of a sentence is a noun phrase, even if it consists of only a single noun or pronoun, as in *John saw me* where both *John* and *me* constitute noun phrases.

The **object** is the noun phrase immediately following the verb. A **direct object** is typically affected by the action denoted by the verb; there are also **directional objects** like *home* in *go home* in Cantonese (8.2.1). An **indirect object** (8.2.2) is a second object, being indirectly affected by the action, such as *her* in *Give her a break*.

Particles (3.1.7) are miscellaneous classes of words with grammatical function. **Verbal particles** (11.3) resemble those of phrasal verbs in English, such as *away* in *throw away*. **Sentence** or **utterance particles** are an important class of particles in Cantonese which have no direct counterpart in English (see ch. 18).

Passive constructions are those in which the subject undergoes some action, corresponding to the object of a simple (active) sentence. Thus the passive sentence *John was sacked by the company* corresponds to *The company sacked John*, the verb taking a special passive form (8.4). **Indirect passives** are those when the subject of the passive does not correspond to the direct object, as in *I had a tooth extracted* (8.4.1).

Perfective aspect, encoded in Cantonese by the particle *jó* (11.2.4) expresses the notion of a complete event. It should not be confused with either past tense or perfect as instantiated in English, although its range of use overlaps with both.

A **phoneme** is the smallest segment of sound that can be distinguished by their contrast within words, e.g. [p] in *pit* and [b] in *bit* are phonemes which can differentiate the two words.

Phonology is the study of the sounds of a language. It differs from **phonetics** in considering classes of sounds and their behaviour in various environments rather than focusing on individual sounds in isolation. As an example of the difference, **aspiration** is a purely phonetic feature in English, but a **phonological** one in Cantonese.

Pleonastic use of a word (from the Greek 'filling out') is the reinforcement of one expression by another with similar meaning, for example, *háidouh* reinforcing the progressive *gán* (11.2.2) and *gám* 'so' with *hóuchíh* 'seem' (10.1.2).

Predicative adjectives are used to assert that something has a certain quality or characteristic, as in *The house is dirty*. Contrast **attributive**.

Prefixes are items which do not exist independently, but only occur attached at the beginning of another word, like *un-* in *undo*. Cantonese has few prefixes (2.1.1).

Prepositions are a class of words which indicate the spatial, temporal or other relationships between noun phrases. In Cantonese, the role of prepositions is played largely by verbs and **coverbs** (3.1.3). **Postpositions** are the equivalent of prepositions, but follow the noun; the use of **localizers** following nouns resembles that of postpositions (3.1.4).

Presuppositions are the assumptions behind a statement or question, as *yet* in *Have you seen the queen yet?* implies that the addressee will see the queen at some point.

Productive processes and constructions are those by which new words and sentences may be created: for example, *under-* is a productive prefix as we may coin new words such as *under-described* meaning 'insufficiently described'.

Progressive aspect, as expressed by *gán*, resembles the English progressive form *-ing* as in *she's reading*, describing an ongoing action. The Cantonese progressive is much more restricted in usage, however (11.2.2).

Quantifiers are terms which refer not to individual entities, but to classes or quantities of them. *All*, *most*, *some* and *none* are typical quantifiers; see chapter 14.

Reciprocal constructions express the meaning 'each other'. Cantonese lacks reciprocal pronouns, expressing this meaning through adverbs and special constructions (5.3).

Reduplication is a feature of **morphology** whereby a word or syllable is doubled, sometimes with slight modifications. It often serves to intensify or modify the meaning of adjectives, as in English *teeny-weeny*. In Cantonese, however, it also has numerous grammatical functions (2.2), such as in forming adverbs (10.1.3), quantifiers (14.1.2) and questions (17.1.2).

Reflexive pronouns are those which must refer back to a noun phrase earlier in the sentence, like *herself*, *myself*, etc. (5.2).

Relative clauses are a form of subordinate clause serving to modify a noun phrase, as in *the story that you liked*. **Free relatives** lack a noun as their head, as in *(I'll do) whatever you say*, leaving the denotation of the clause 'free'.

Resultative constructions express the state which results from an action, typically as **complements** to a verb, as in *to squash the grass flat* or to an adjective as in *bored to death*. In Cantonese, resultative particles following verbs (11.3.2) have a similar function.

Rhetorical questions take the form of a question but do not expect an answer, typically serving to make a point. *How should I know?* and *Who cares?* are examples; Cantonese makes extensive use of rhetorical questions (see ch. 17).

Right-dislocation refers to the appearance of an item at the end of a sentence, i.e. to the right of where it would normally belong. It is a feature of casual speech, as in *She's pretty smart, that girl* or *They've gone, probably*.

Serial verb constructions (8.3) are a distinctive pattern in Chinese syntax, in which two or more verbs are juxtaposed without any conjunction. They resemble constructions like *Come say hello* in American English, or *Go and have a drink* in British English.

Stative verbs (8.1.2) are verbs such as *know* and *live* which refer to states of affairs rather than to actions or events. In Cantonese, it is difficult to distinguish between stative verbs and adjectives (3.1.1).

Subject is a grammatical role performed by a noun phrase with respect to a predicate. The subject of a sentence is normally a noun phrase, combining with a predicate to form a sentence. In both English and Cantonese, the subject precedes the verb. Other properties of subjects depend on the language concerned: in English, it is the subject which determines the form of agreement on the verb, while in Cantonese, the antecedent of a reflexive pronoun must normally be a subject (5.2).

Subject orientation refers to the behaviour of items such as the reflexive pronoun *jihgéi* which obligatorily or preferentially refer back to the subject of the sentence.

Subordinate clauses are clauses containing a sentence and a conjunction, which are subordinate to (dependent on) the main clause (16.2). A subordinate clause, such as *because there's no time*, cannot be used alone as an independent sentence.

Suffixes are items (usually single syllables) which do not occur independently, but are attached at the ends of words, like *-ist* in *typist*; Cantonese has relatively few suffixes (2.1.2).

Superlatives are forms of adjectives or adverbs expressing the meaning 'most', such as *the fastest* and *the most expensive*.

Syllable structure refers to the way in which sounds are combined to form syllables. For example, English allows consecutive consonants such as *st* as in *stop* and *fl* as in *flat*, whereas Cantonese does not (see 1.3).

Syntax is the way words are put together to form sentences: the rules of sentence structure.

Tags are attached to statements to form questions, like *isn't it* in *It's a shame, isn't it?* (17.1.6) and suggestions, as in *Let's go, shall we?*

Tense is the grammatical expression of location in time. Cantonese lacks tense in this sense, as time is expressed by adverbs (10.3.3) and by **aspect** (11.1).

Tone is the pitch assigned to each syllable of a word (1.4). Tone in Cantonese is a **distinctive feature**, making the distinction between words as in *yāt* 'one' with a high tone versus *yaht* 'day' with a low level tone. It should not be confused with **tone of voice** (see also intonation).

Tone change is the phenomenon whereby the original tone changes in certain contexts, typically to a high rising tone, e.g. *mùhn* 'door' becomes *mún* in *hauh-mún* 'back door'.

Topic refers to a prominent phrase, typically a noun phrase, at the beginning of the sentence. Related to the the notion 'topic of a conversation', the sentence topic establishes what the sentence is about, or sets the background against which the rest of the sentence is to be understood. It is distinct from the **subject** as topics may have grammatical roles other than that of subject (4.2).

Topicalization is the promotion of some element of the sentence to the topic position, as in *John, I really can't stand* in which the object *John* is topicalized (4.2.1, 4.2.2).

Transitive verbs are those which take or require a direct object. In Cantonese, many verbs are transitive whose counterparts in English are intransitive; in particular, verbs of motion such as *heui* 'go' may take objects (see 8.2.1).

Typology is the study of language types, in which languages are compared in terms of their structural similarities, regardless of their historical relationships. The classification of Cantonese as an **isolating** language (ch. 2) and as a **topic-prominent** language (4.2) are typological concepts.

Unreleased consonants are formed as if to pronounce a stop, but without the release of air which accompanies a stop. In Cantonese *p*, *t* and *k* are unreleased when they come at the end of a syllable.

Verb–object compounds (2.3.3, 8.2.4) are set combinations of a verb and an object in which the object loses some of its original meaning, e.g. *duhk-syū* 'to study' where the object *syū* 'book' lacks any direct reference to books.

The **verb phrase** contains the verb, its objects (*eat rice, lend him money*) and any adverbs modifying it (as in *walk fast*).

Vocatives are terms used to address people, such as *Sir* or *darling*. In some cases Cantonese has distinct terms used to address people (vocatives) and to refer to them (**designatives**; see 20.3).

Voicing is a phonetic feature of consonants, *b* being voiced in *bit* and *p* voiceless in *pit*. It is a **distinctive feature** in English, but not in Cantonese (see **aspiration** and 1.1).

REFERENCES

Au, T.K. (1983) 'Chinese and English counterfactuals: the Sapir–Whorf Hypothesis revisited', *Cognition* 15:155–87.

Bauer, R.S. (1982) 'Cantonese sociolinguistic patterns: correlating social characteristics of speakers with phonological variables in Hongkong Cantonese', unpublished PhD dissertation, University of California at Berkeley.

—— (1983) 'Cantonese sound change across subgroups of the Hongkong speech community', *Journal of Chinese Linguistics* 11: 301–54.

—— (1985) 'The expanding syllabary of Hongkong Cantonese', *Cahiers de Linguistique Asie Orientale* 14, 1: 99–111.

—— (1986) 'The microhistory of a sound change in progress in Hongkong Cantonese', *Journal of Chinese Linguistics* 14: 1–42.

—— (1988) 'Written Cantonese of Hongkong', *Cahiers de Linguistique Asie Orientale* 17, 2: 245–93.

Binstead, N. (1978) *Getting Around in Cantonese*. Hongkong: Heinemann Asia.

Bloom, A. (1981) *The Linguistic Shaping of Thought: a Study of the Impact of Language on Thinking in China and the West*. Hillsdale, NJ: Lawrence Erlbaum.

Bolton, K. and Kwok, H. (eds) (1992) *Sociolinguistics Today: International Perspectives*. London: Routledge.

Bourgerie, D. (1990) 'A quantitative study of sociolinguistic variation in Cantonese', unpublished PhD dissertation, Ohio State University.

Boyle, E.L. (1970) *Cantonese Basic Course* (vols 1 and 2). Washington: Foreign Service Institute.

Browning, L.K. (1974) 'The Cantonese dialect with special reference to contrasts with Mandarin as an approach to determining dialect relatedness', unpublished PhD dissertation, Georgetown University.

Chafe, W. L. (1976) 'Givenness, contrastiveness, definiteness, subjects, topics, and point of view', in C. Li (ed.): *Subject and Topic*. New York: Academic Press.

Chan, B. (1992) 'Code-mixing in Hongkong Cantonese–English bilinguals: constraints and processes', unpublished MA thesis, Chinese University of Hongkong.

Chan, M. and Kwok, H. (1984) *A Study of Lexical Borrowing from English in Hongkong Chinese*. University of Hongkong: Centre for Asian Studies.

—— (1990) *Fossils from a Rural Past: a Study of Extant Cantonese Children's Songs*. Hongkong: Hongkong University Press.

Chao, Y-R (1947) *A Cantonese Primer*. Cambridge, MA: Harvard University Press.

—— (1968) *A Grammar of Spoken Chinese*. Berkeley: University of California Press.

Chappell, H. (1986) 'Formal and colloquial adversity passives in standard Chinese', *Linguistics* 24: 1025–52.

Chen, M.Y. and Wang, W.S-Y. (1975) 'Sound change: actuation and implementation', *Language* 51, 2: 255–81.

Cheung, H-N.S. (1972) [in Chinese] *Cantonese as Spoken in Hongkong*. Hongkong: Chinese University of Hongkong.

—— (1987) 'Terms of address in Cantonese', *Journal of Chinese Linguistics* 18, 1: 1–43.

—— (1992) 'The pretransitive in Cantonese'. *Zhongguo Jingnei Ji Yuyanxue* 1: 241–303.

Cheung, K-H. (1986) 'The phonology of present-day Cantonese', unpublished PhD thesis, University of London (to appear: Linguistic Society of Hongkong).

Cheung, L-Y. (1983) [in Chinese] 'A total count of Cantonese syllables with no character representations', *Yuwen Zazhi* 10: 28–35.

Cheung, Y-S. (1969) [in Chinese] 'Xianggang Yueyu yinping-diao ji biandiao wenti (A study on the upper even tone and tone sandhi in the Cantonese dialect as spoken in Hongkong)', *Journal of the Institute of Chinese Studies of the Chinese University of Hongkong*. 2, 2: 81–105.

Chik, H-M. and Ng-Lam, S-Y. (1989) *Chinese English Dictionary: Cantonese in Yale Romanization, Mandarin in Pinyin*. New Asia–Yale-in-China Chinese Language Centre, Chinese University of Hongkong.

Chiu, B. H-C. (1993) 'The inflectional structure of Mandarin Chinese', unpublished PhD dissertation, University of California at Los Angeles.

Chui, C.K-W. (1988) 'Topics in Hongkong Cantonese syntax', unpublished MA thesis, Fu Jen Catholic University, Taiwan.

Cowles, R.T. (1949) *Cantonese Speaker's Dictionary*. Hongkong: Hongkong University Press.

de Francis, N. (1984) *The Chinese Language: Fact and Fantasy*. University of Hawaii Press.

Fok, C.Y-Y. (1974) *A Perceptual Study of Tones in Cantonese*. Centre of Asian Studies, University of Hongkong.

Gao, H-N. (1980) [in Chinese] *Gwongjau Fongyihn Yihngau* ('Research on the Guangjau Dialects'). Hongkong: Commercial Press.

Gibbons, J. (1979) 'U-gay-wa: a linguistic study of the campus language of students at the University of Hongkong', in R. Lord (ed.) *Hongkong Language Papers*. Hongkong: Hongkong University Press, 3–43.

—— (1980) 'A tentative framework for speech act description of the utterance particle in conversational Cantonese'. *Linguistics* 18: 763–75.

—— (1987) *Code-mixing and Code Choice: a Hongkong Case Study*. Multilingual Matters.

Hashimoto, A-Y. (1972) *Studies in Yue Dialects*, vol. 1: *The Phonology of Cantonese*. Cambridge: Cambridge University Press.

Huang, C-T. J. (1982) 'Logical relations and the theory of grammar', unpublished PhD dissertation, Massachusetts Institute of Technology.

Huang, C-R. (1991) 'Mandarin Chinese and the lexical mapping theory: a study of the interaction of morphology and argument changing', unpublished ms., Academica Sinica, Taiwan.

Huang, P. (1970) *Cantonese Dictionary*. Newhaven: Yale University Press.

Huang, P. and Kok, G. (1970) *Speak Cantonese*, vols 1–3. Newhaven: Yale University Press.

Jurafsky, D. (1988) 'On the semantics of Cantonese changed tone', *Proceedings of the Berkeley Linguistic Society*, University of California at Berkeley.

Kam, T.H. (1977) 'Derivation by tone change in Cantonese: a preliminary survey', *Journal of Chinese Linguistics* 5: 186–210.

Kao, D. (1971) *The Structure of the Syllable in Cantonese*. The Hague: Mouton.

Killingley, S-Y. (1979) *Internal Structure of the Cantonese Word and General Problems of Word Analysis in Chinese*. Kuala Lumpur: Penerbit Universiti Malaya.

—— (1982a) *The Grammatical Hierarchy of Malayan Cantonese*. Published by the author, Newcastle-upon-Tyne.

—— (1982b) *A Short Glossary of Cantonese Classifiers*. Newcastle-upon-Tyne: Grevatt and Grevatt.

— (1983) *Cantonese Classifiers: Syntax and Semantics*. Newcastle-upon-Tyne: Grevatt and Grevatt.

— (1985) *A New Look at Cantonese Tones: Five or Six?* Newcastle-upon-Tyne: Grevatt & Grevatt.

Kwan, C-W. (ed.) (1989) *The Right Word in Cantonese: Gwongjauwa Jinaahm*. Hongkong: The Commercial Press.

Kwan, C-W. *et al.* (eds) (1991) *English–Cantonese Dictionary: Cantonese in Yale Romanization*. New Asia–Yale-in-China Chinese Language Centre, Chinese University of Hongkong.

Kwok, H. (1972) *A Linguistic Study of the Cantonese Verb*. Centre of Asian Studies, University of Hongkong.

— (1984) *Sentence Particles in Cantonese*. Centre of Asian Studies, University of Hongkong.

Kwok, H. and Chan, M. (1985) *A Study of Lexical Borrowing from Chinese in English, with special reference to English in Hongkong*. University of Hongkong: Centre of Asian Studies.

Kwok, H. and Luke, K-K. (1986) [in Chinese] 'Cantonese intonation: form and function', *Yuwen Zazhi* 13: 32–40.

Lau, S. (1968) *Intermediate Cantonese*, vols. 1 and 2. Hongkong Government Publications.

— (1975) *Advanced Cantonese*, vols. 1 and 2. Hongkong Government Publications.

— (1977) *A Practical Cantonese–English Dictionary*. Hongkong Government Publications.

Law, S-P. (1990) 'The syntax and phonology of sentence particles in Cantonese', unpublished PhD dissertation, Boston University.

Law, S-P. and Neidle, C. (1992) 'A syntactic analysis of Cantonese sentence-final particles', unpublished ms., Johns Hopkins University and Boston University.

Lee, T. H-T. (1983) 'The vowel system in two varieties of Cantonese', *UCLA Working Papers in Phonetics* 55: 97–114.

— (1986) 'Studies on quantification in Chinese', unpublished PhD dissertation, University of California at Los Angeles.

— (1987) [in Chinese] 'Yuhtyuh "saai" dik lohchap dahkdim' (The logical properties of Cantonese 'saai'), paper presented at the first International Conference on Cantonese.

Li, C. and Thompson, S. (1976) 'Subject and topic: a new typology of language', in C. Li (ed.): *Subject and Topic*. New York: Academic Press.

— (1981) *A Functional Reference Grammar of Mandarin Chinese*. Berkeley: University of California Press.

Li, Y-H.A. (1990) *Order and Constituency in Mandarin Chinese*. Dordrecht: Kluwer.

— (1992) 'Indefinite *Wh* in Mandarin Chinese', *Journal of East Asian Linguistics* 1, 2: 125–56.

Luke, K-K. (1990) *Utterance Particles in Cantonese Conversation*. Amsterdam: John Benjamins.

Luke, K-K. and Nancarrow, O.T. (1991) 'On being literate in Hongkong', *Institute of Language in Education Journal* 8: 84–92.

McCawley, J. (1988) *The Syntactic Phenomena of English*, 2 vols. Chicago: Chicago University Press.

— (1992) 'Justifying part of speech assignments in Mandarin Chinese', *Journal of Chinese Linguistics* 20: 211–45.

Morris, P.T. (1992) *Cantonese Love Songs: an English translation of Jiu Ji-Yung's Cantonese Songs of the Early Nineteenth Century*. Hongkong: Hongkong University Press.

Pan, P. (1993) [in Chinese] 'The trend of simplification of kinship terms', *Chinese Language Review* 40: 56–61.

Sapir, E. (1921) *Language: an Introduction to the Study of Speech*. New York: Harcourt Brace Jovanovich.

Shi, D. (1989) 'Topic chain as a syntactic category in Chinese', *Journal of Chinese Linguistics* 17, 2: 223–61.

Siewierska, A. (1984) *The Passive: a Comparative Linguistic Analysis*. London: Croom Helm.

Tai, J. (1985) 'Temporal sequence and Chinese word order', in J. Haiman (ed.) *Iconicity in Syntax*. Amsterdam: John Benjamins.

Tang, C-C.J. (1989) 'Chinese reflexives', *Natural Language and Linguistic Theory* 7: 93–121.

Tang, S-W. (1992) 'Classification of verbs and dative constructions in Cantonese', Paper presented at the Linguistic Society of Hongkong Annual Research Forum, Chinese University of Hongkong, 1992.

Tong, K. and James, G. (1994) *Colloquial Cantonese*. London: Routledge.

Tsao, F-F. (1979) *A Functional Study of Topic in Chinese: the First Step Towards Discourse Analysis*. Taipei: Student Book Co.

Whitaker, K. P. (1956) 'A study on the modified tones in spoken Cantonese', *Asia Major*, series 2.5, Parts I and II.

Wong, M. (1982) 'Tone change in Cantonese', unpublished PhD dissertation, University of Illinois at Urbana-Champaign.

Wong, M-Y. (1990) 'Referential choice in spoken Cantonese discourse', unpublished PhD dissertation, Georgetown University.

Wong, S-L. (1941) *Yuht Yam Wahn Wuih* ('A Chinese Syllabary according to the Dialect of Canton'). Hongkong: Chung Hwa.

Wu, K-Y. (1989) 'A linguistic study of interrogation in Cantonese', unpublished MPhil. thesis, University of Hongkong.

Yau, S-C. (1965) 'A study of the functions and presentations of Cantonese sentence particles', unpublished MA thesis, University of Hongkong.

Yeung, S-W.H. (1980) 'Some aspects of phonological variation in the Cantonese spoken in Hongkong', unpublished MA thesis, University of Hongkong.

Yip, M. (1990) *The Total Phonology of Chinese*. New York: Garland Publishing Inc.

Yip, V. (1995) *Interlanguage and Learnability: From Chinese to English*. Amsterdam: John Benjamins.

Yip, V. and Matthews, S. (1992) 'Tough movement in Chinese/English interlanguage: contrastive analysis and learnability', in T. Lee (ed.): *Research on Chinese Linguistics in Hongkong*. Hongkong: Linguistic Society of Hongkong.

Zhan, B-H. (1993) 'Putonghua "south-bound" and Cantonese "north-bound",' *Chinese Language Review* 39: 51–7.

INDEX

This index includes: (a) grammatical terms which are used in the grammar or commonly used in reference grammars or descriptions of Chinese (see the Glossary for explanations of these terms); (b) English grammatical words such as *all*; (c) Cantonese words which have a grammatical function or whose syntactic properties are described in the grammar. Idioms are not listed individually, but will be found under the grammatical words they contain.

Note: for ease of reference, the alphabetical ordering of Cantonese forms ignores the *h* marking low tones; consequently, for example, *m̀h* precedes *meih*. Words differing only in tone are given in the conventional order: high level, high rising, mid level, low rising, low falling, low level.